Schneier on Security

Bruce Schneier

WILEY

Wiley Publishing, Inc.

Schneier on Security

Published by
Wiley Publishing, Inc.
10475 Crosspoint Boulevard
Indianapolis, IN 46256
www.wiley.com

Copyright © 2008 by Bruce Schneier

Published by Wiley Publishing, Inc., Indianapolis, Indiana

Published simultaneously in Canada

ISBN: 978-0-470-39535-6

Manufactured in the United States of America

10 9 8 7 6 5 4 3 2 1

To Beth

Credits

Executive Editor
Carol Long

Senior Development Editor
Tom Dinse

Production Editor
Elizabeth Ginns Britten

Copy Editor
Kim Cofer

Editorial Manager
Mary Beth Wakefield

Production Manager
Tim Tate

**Vice President and
Executive Group Publisher**
Richard Swadley

**Vice President and
Executive Publisher**
Joseph B. Wikert

Project Coordinator, Cover
Lynsey Stanford

Compositor
Maureen Forys,
Happenstance Type-O-Rama

Proofreader
C.M. Jones

Indexer
Jack Lewis

Cover Designer
Michael Trent

Cover Photo
© Steve Woit

Contents

Introduction vii

1 Terrorism and Security 1

2 National Security Policy 25

3 Airline Travel 49

4 Privacy and Surveillance 61

5 ID Cards and Security 97

6 Election Security 111

7 Security and Disasters 131

8 Economics of Security 145

9 Psychology of Security 169

10 Business of Security 189

11 Cybercrime and Cyberwar 205

12 Computer and Information Security 227

A References 267

Index 315

Introduction

This book is a collection of essays on security: on security technology, on security policy, on how security works in the real world. Some are about specific technologies, like voting machines or national ID cards. Some are about specific targets, like airplanes or the Olympics. And some are about general trends, like increasing complexity or human behavior.

All have been published before—between June 2002 and June 2008—in newspapers, magazines, websites, and my own monthly e-mail newsletter *Crypto-Gram*.

Although I have grouped them by topic and have arranged them within those topics, they all stand alone and can be read in any order. (There is some overlap of material because it appeared in different locations for different audiences.) You don't even have to read this introduction first. Actually, it might be better if you read a few essays first, then returned once you started wondering who in the world I am and what authority I have to write this broadly about security.

I'm a security technologist. I've worked for many companies, small and large, both as an employee and as a consultant. Over the years, my career has been a series of generalizations: from cryptography and mathematical security to computer and network security, and from there to more general security technology. More recently, I've been researching and writing about the interaction between security technology and people: the economics of security and, most recently, the psychology of security.

It turns out that these human issues are the most important of all. Security is often about technology, but it's always about people. People are the reason security exists in the first place, and people are at the core of any security breach. Technology helps—both the attacker and defender, actually, although in different ways—but security is fundamentally about people.

There are four points I want to make in this introduction, points you should keep in mind as you read the essays in this book and whenever you encounter anything security-related:

1. **Security is a trade-off.** There's no such thing as absolute security. Life entails risk, and all security involves trade-offs. We get security by

giving something up: money, time, convenience, capabilities, liberties, etc. Sometimes we make these trade-offs consciously, and sometimes we make them unconsciously.

2. **You are a security consumer.** You get to make these trade-offs, whether they be personal, corporate, national, or whatever. "Is this security measure effective?" is not a good question. It's much better to ask: "Is this a good trade-off?" These trade-offs are subjective. There's not always one answer, because not all costs are objective. Costs like inconvenience, time, and a feeling of security are subjective. Just as different consumers choose different cleaning products, different television shows, and different vacation destinations, different people will make different security trade-offs.

3. **Security is a system.** People often think of security in terms of specific attacks and defenses. But it's not that simple. Security is always part of a system, and that system is always more complex than the individual components. Identification systems are much more than the ID card. Bank vault security is more than the metal box. Whatever the system is, security should always be analyzed in the context of the broader system.

4. **Technology causes security imbalances.** The thing about technology is that it changes trade-offs. It makes something cheaper, or more expensive; faster, or more time-consuming. Technological advances can make some attacks easier, or it can make some defenses easier. In today's rapidly changing technological world, it is important to watch for new security imbalances.

Much of this book consists of common-sense, although often uncommon, application of these four principles.

If you're done and want to read more, I have two recommendations. The first is my previous book, *Beyond Fear: Thinking Sensibly About Security in an Uncertain World,* first published in 2003. The second is to subscribe to my free monthly e-mail newsletter, *Crypto-Gram.* You can also visit my blog and wander through my pages of essays. The newsletter, the blog, and information about my books are all at http://www.schneier.com/.

1 Terrorism and Security

What the Terrorists Want

Originally published in Wired, *24 August 2006*

On August 16, two men were escorted off a plane headed for Manchester, England, because some passengers thought they looked either Asian or Middle Eastern, might have been talking Arabic, wore leather jackets, and looked at their watches—and the passengers refused to fly with them on board. The men were questioned for several hours and then released.

On August 15, an entire airport terminal was evacuated because someone's cosmetics triggered a false positive for explosives. The same day, a Muslim man was removed from an airplane in Denver for reciting prayers. The Transportation Security Administration decided that the flight crew overreacted, but he still had to spend the night in Denver before flying home the next day. The next day, a Port of Seattle terminal was evacuated because a couple of dogs gave a false alarm for explosives.

On August 19, a plane made an emergency landing in Tampa, Florida, after the crew became suspicious because two of the lavatory doors were locked. The plane was searched, but nothing was found. Meanwhile, a man who tampered with a bathroom smoke detector on a flight to San Antonio was cleared of terrorism, but only after having his house searched.

On August 16, a woman suffered a panic attack and became violent on a flight from London to Washington, so the plane was escorted to Boston's Logan Airport by fighter jets. "The woman was carrying hand cream and matches but was not a terrorist threat," said the TSA spokesman after the incident.

And on August 18, a plane flying from London to Egypt made an emergency landing in Italy when someone found a bomb threat scrawled on an air sickness bag. Nothing was found on the plane, and no one knows how long the note was on board.

I'd like everyone to take a deep breath and listen for a minute.

The point of terrorism is to cause terror—sometimes to further a political goal, and sometimes out of sheer hatred. The people terrorists kill are not the targets; they are collateral damage. And blowing up planes, trains, markets, or buses is not the goal; those are just tactics. The real targets of terrorism are the rest of us: the billions of us who are not killed but are terrorized because of the killing. The real point of terrorism is not the act itself, but our reaction to the act.

And we're doing exactly what the terrorists want.

We're all a little jumpy after the recent arrest of 23 terror suspects in Great Britain. The men were reportedly plotting a liquid-explosive attack on airplanes, and both the press and politicians have been trumpeting the story ever since.

In truth, it's doubtful that their plan would have succeeded; chemists have been debunking the idea since it became public. Certainly the suspects were a long way off from trying: None had bought airline tickets, and some didn't even have passports.

Regardless of the threat, from the would-be bombers' perspective, the explosives and planes were merely tactics. Their goal was to cause terror, and in that they've succeeded.

Imagine for a moment what would have happened if they had blown up ten planes. There would be canceled flights, chaos at airports, bans on carry-on luggage, world leaders talking tough new security measures, political posturing and all sorts of false alarms as jittery people panicked. To a lesser degree, that's basically what's happening right now.

Our politicians help the terrorists every time they use fear as a campaign tactic. The press helps every time it writes scare stories about the plot and the threat. And if we're terrified, and we share that fear, we help. All of these actions intensify and repeat the terrorists' actions, and increase the effects of their terror.

(I am not saying that the politicians and press are terrorists, or that they share any of the blame for terrorist attacks. I'm not that stupid. But the subject of terrorism is more complex than it appears, and understanding its various causes and effects are vital for understanding how to best deal with it.)

The implausible plots and false alarms actually hurt us in two ways. Not only do they increase the level of fear, but they also waste time and resources that could be better spent fighting the real threats and increasing actual security. I'll bet the terrorists are laughing at us.

Another thought experiment: Imagine for a moment that the British government had arrested the 23 suspects without fanfare. Imagine that the TSA and its European counterparts didn't engage in pointless airline security measures like banning liquids. And imagine that the press didn't write about it endlessly, and that the politicians didn't use the event to remind us all how scared we should be. If we'd reacted that way, then the terrorists would have truly failed.

It's time we calm down and fight terror with anti-terror. This does not mean that we simply roll over and accept terrorism. There are things our government can and should do to fight terrorism, most of them involving intelligence and investigation—and not focusing on specific plots.

But our job is to remain steadfast in the face of terror, to refuse to be terrorized. Our job is to not panic every time two Muslims stand together checking their watches. There are approximately 1 billion Muslims in the world, a large percentage of them not Arab, and about 320 million Arabs in the Middle East, the overwhelming majority of them not terrorists. Our job is to think critically and rationally, and to ignore the cacophony of other interests trying to use terrorism to advance political careers or increase a television show's viewership.

The surest defense against terrorism is to refuse to be terrorized. Our job is to recognize that terrorism is just one of the risks we face, and not a particularly common one at that. And our job is to fight those politicians who use fear as an excuse to take away our liberties and promote security theater that wastes money and doesn't make us any safer.

Movie-Plot Threats

Originally published in Wired, *8 September 2005*

Sometimes it seems like the people in charge of homeland security spend too much time watching action movies. They defend against specific movie plots instead of against the broad threats of terrorism.

We all do it. Our imaginations run wild with detailed and specific threats. We imagine anthrax spread from crop dusters. Or a contaminated milk supply. Or terrorist scuba divers armed with almanacs. Before long, we're envisioning an entire movie plot—without Bruce Willis to save the day. And we're scared.

Psychologically, this all makes sense. Humans have good imaginations. Box cutters and shoe bombs conjure vivid mental images. "We must protect the Super Bowl" packs more emotional punch than the vague "we should defend ourselves against terrorism."

The 9/11 terrorists used small pointy things to take over airplanes, so we ban small pointy things from airplanes. Richard Reid tried to hide a bomb in his shoes, so now we all have to take off our shoes. Recently, the Department of Homeland Security said that it might relax airplane security rules. It's not that there's a lessened risk of shoes, or that small pointy things are suddenly less dangerous. It's that those movie plots no longer capture the imagination like they did in the months after 9/11, and everyone is beginning to see how silly (or pointless) they always were.

Commuter terrorism is the new movie plot. The London bombers carried bombs into the subway, so now we search people entering the subways. They used cell phones, so we're talking about ways to shut down the cell-phone network.

It's too early to tell if hurricanes are the next movie-plot threat that captures the imagination.

The problem with movie-plot security is that it only works if we guess right. If we spend billions defending our subways, and the terrorists bomb a bus, we've wasted our money. To be sure, defending the subways makes commuting safer. But focusing on subways also has the effect of shifting attacks toward less-defended targets, and the result is that we're no safer overall.

Terrorists don't care if they blow up subways, buses, stadiums, theaters, restaurants, nightclubs, schools, churches, crowded markets or busy intersections. Reasonable arguments can be made that some targets are more attractive than others: airplanes because a small bomb can result in the death of everyone aboard, monuments because of their national significance, national events because of television coverage, and transportation because most people commute daily. But the United States is a big country; we can't defend everything.

One problem is that our nation's leaders are giving us what we want. Party affiliation notwithstanding, appearing tough on terrorism is important. Voting for missile defense makes for better campaigning than increasing intelligence funding. Elected officials want to do something visible, even if it turns out to be ineffective.

The other problem is that many security decisions are made at too low a level. The decision to turn off cell phones in some tunnels was made by those in charge of the tunnels. Even if terrorists then bomb a different tunnel else-where in the country, that person did his job.

And anyone in charge of security knows that he'll be judged in hindsight. If the next terrorist attack targets a chemical plant, we'll demand to know why more wasn't done to protect chemical plants. If it targets schoolchildren, we'll demand to know why that threat was ignored. We won't accept "we didn't know the target" as an answer. Defending particular targets protects reputa-tions and careers.

We need to defend against the broad threat of terrorism, not against spe-cific movie plots. Security is most effective when it doesn't make arbitrary assumptions about the next terrorist act. We need to spend more money on intelligence and investigation: identifying the terrorists themselves, cutting off their funding, and stopping them regardless of what their plans are. We need to spend more money on emergency response: lessening the impact of a terrorist attack, regardless of what it is. And we need to face the geopolitical consequences of our foreign policy and how it helps or hinders terrorism.

These vague things are less visible, and don't make for good political grandstanding. But they will make us safer. Throwing money at this year's movie plot threat won't.

Fixing Intelligence Failures

Originally published in Crypto-Gram, *15 June 2002*

Could the intelligence community have connected the dots? Why didn't any-one connect the dots? How can we make sure we connect the dots next time? Dot connecting is the metaphor of the moment in Washington, as the various politicians scramble to make sure that 1) their pet ideas for improving domes-tic security are adopted, and 2) they don't get blamed for any dot connection failures that could have prevented 9/11.

Unfortunately, it's the wrong metaphor. We all know how to connect the dots. They're right there on the page, and they're all numbered. All you have to do is move your crayon from one dot to another, and when you're done you've drawn a lion. It's so easy a three-year-old could do it; what's wrong with the FBI and the CIA?

The problem is that the dots can only be numbered after the fact. With the benefit of hindsight, it's easy to draw lines from people in flight school here, to secret meetings in foreign countries there, over to interesting tips from foreign governments, and then to INS records. Before 9/11, it's not so easy. Rather than thinking of intelligence as a simple connect-the-dots picture, think of it as a million unnumbered pictures superimposed on top of each other. Or a random-dot stereogram. Is it a lion, a tree, a cast iron stove, or just an unintelligible mess of dots? You try and figure it out.

This isn't to say that the United States didn't have some spectacular failures in analysis leading up to 9/11. Way back in the 30 September 2001 issue of *Crypto-Gram*, I wrote: "In what I am sure is the mother of all investigations, the CIA, NSA, and FBI have uncovered all sorts of data from their files, data that clearly indicates that an attack was being planned. Maybe it even clearly indicates the nature of the attack, or the date. I'm sure lots of information is there, in files, intercepts, computer memory." I was guessing there. It seems that there was more than I thought.

Given the bits of information that have been discussed in the press, I would have liked to think that we could have prevented this one, that there was a single Middle Eastern Terrorism desk somewhere inside the intelligence community whose job it was to stay on top of all of this. It seems that we couldn't, and that there wasn't. A budget issue, most likely.

Still, I think the "whose fault is it?" witch hunt is a bit much. Not that I mind seeing George Bush on the defensive. I've gotten sick of his "we're at war, and if you criticize me you're being unpatriotic" nonsense, and I think the enormous damage John Ashcroft has done to our nation's freedoms and liberties will take a generation and another Warren Court to fix. But all this finger-pointing between the CIA and FBI is childish, and I'm embarrassed by the Democrats who are pushing through their own poorly thought out security proposals so they're not viewed in the polls as being soft on terrorism.

My preference is for less politics and more intelligent discussion. And I'd rather see the discussion center on how to improve things for next time, rather than on who gets the blame for this time. So, in the spirit of bipartisanship (there are plenty of nitwits in both parties), here are some points for discussion:

- It's not about data collection; it's about data *analysis*. Again from the 30 September 2001 issue of *Crypto-Gram*: "Demands for even more surveillance miss the point. The problem is not obtaining data, it's deciding which data is worth analyzing and then interpreting it. Everyone already leaves a wide audit trail as we go through life, and law enforcement can already access those records with search warrants [and subpoenas]. The FBI quickly pieced together the terrorists' identities and the last few months of their lives, once they knew where to look. If they had thrown up their hands and said that they couldn't figure out who did it or how, they might have a case for needing more surveillance data. But they didn't, and they don't.

- Security decisions need to be made as close to the source as possible. This has all sorts of implications: airport X-ray machines should be right next to the departure gates, like they are in some European airports; bomb target decisions should be made by the generals on the ground in the war zone, not by some bureaucrat in Washington; and investigation approvals should be granted the FBI office that's closest to the investigation. This mode of operation has more opportunities for abuse, so oversight is vital. But it is also more robust, and the best way to make things work. (The U.S. Marine Corps understands this principle; it's the heart of their chain of command rules.)

- Data correlation needs to happen as far away from the sources as possible. Good intelligence involves finding meaning amongst enormous reams of irrelevant data, and then organizing all those disparate pieces of information into coherent predictions about what will happen next. It requires smart people who can see connections, and access to information from many different branches of government. It can't be by the various individual pieces of bureaucracy, whether it be the CIA, FBI, NSA, INS, Coast Guard, etc. The whole picture is larger than any of them, and each one only has access to a small piece.

- Intelligence and law enforcement have fundamentally different missions. The FBI's model of operation—investigation of past crimes— does not lend itself to an intelligence paradigm: prediction of future events. On the other hand, the CIA is prohibited by law from spying on citizens. Expecting the FBI to become a domestic CIA is a terrible idea; the missions are just too different and that's too much power to consolidate under one roof. Turning the CIA into a domestic intelligence agency is an equally terrible idea; the tactics that they regularly use abroad are unconstitutional here.

- Don't forget old-fashioned intelligence gathering. Enough with the Echelon-like NSA programs where everything and anything gets sucked into an enormous electronic maw, never to be looked at again. Lots of Americans managed to become part of al-Qaeda (a 20-year-old Californian did it, for crying out loud); why weren't any of them feeding intelligence to the CIA? Get out in the field and do your jobs.

- Organizations with investigative powers require constant oversight. If we want to formalize a domestic intelligence agency, we are going to need to be very careful about how we do it. Many of the checks and balances that Ashcroft is discarding were put in place to prevent abuse. And abuse is rampant—at the federal, state, and local levels. Just because everyone is feeling good about the police today doesn't mean that things won't change in the future. They always do.

- Fundamental changes in how the United States copes with domestic terrorism requires, um, fundamental changes. Much as the Bush administration would like to ignore the constitutional issues surrounding some of their proposals, those issues are real. Much of what the Israeli government does to combat terrorism in its country, even some of what the British government does, is unconstitutional in the United States. Security is never absolute; it always involved trade-offs. If we're going to institute domestic passports, arrest people in secret and deny them any rights, place people with Arab last names under continuous harassment, or methodically track everyone's financial dealings, we're going to have to rewrite the Constitution. At the very least, we need to have a frank and candid debate about what we're getting for what we're giving up. People might want to live in a police state, but let them at least decide willingly to live in a police state. My opinion has been that it is largely unnecessary to trade civil liberties for security, and that the best security measures—reinforcing the airplane cockpit door, putting barricades and guards around important buildings, improving authentication for telephone and Internet banking—have no effect on civil liberties. Broad surveillance is a mark of bad security.

All in all, I'm not sure how the Department of Homeland Security is going to help with any of this. Taking a bunch of ineffectual little bureaucracies and lumping them together into a single galumptious bureaucracy doesn't seem like a step in the right direction. Leaving the FBI and CIA out of the mix— the largest sources of both valuable information and turf-based problems— doesn't help, either. And if the individual organizations squabble and refuse to share information, reshuffling the chain of command isn't really going to make any difference—it'll just add needless layers of management. And don't forget the $37 billion this is all supposed to cost, assuming there aren't the usual massive cost overruns. Couldn't we better spend that money teaching Arabic to case officers, hiring investigators, and doing various things that actually will make a difference?

The problems are about politics and policy, and not about form and structure. Fix the former, and fixing the latter becomes easy. Change the latter without fixing the former, and nothing will change.

I'm not denying the need for some domestic intelligence capability. We need something to respond to future domestic threats. I'm not happy with this conclusion, but I think it may be the best of a bunch of bad choices. Given this, the thing to do is make sure we approach that choice correctly, paying attention to constitutional protections, respecting privacy and civil liberty, and minimizing the inevitable abuses of power.

Data Mining for Terrorists

Originally published in Wired, *9 March 2006*

In the post-9/11 world, there's much focus on connecting the dots. Many believe that data mining is the crystal ball that will enable us to uncover future terrorist plots. But even in the most wildly optimistic projections, data mining isn't tenable for that purpose. We're not trading privacy for security; we're giving up privacy and getting no security in return.

Most people first learned about data mining in November 2002, when news broke about a massive government data mining program called Total Information Awareness. The basic idea was as audacious as it was repellent: Suck up as much data as possible about everyone, sift through it with massive computers, and investigate patterns that might indicate terrorist plots. Americans across the political spectrum denounced the program, and in September 2003, Congress eliminated its funding and closed its offices.

But TIA didn't die. According to *The National Journal*, it just changed its name and moved inside the Defense Department.

This shouldn't be a surprise. In May 2004, the General Accounting Office published a report that listed 122 different federal government data mining programs that used people's personal information. This list didn't include classified programs, like the NSA's eavesdropping effort, or state-run programs like MATRIX.

The promise of data mining is compelling, and convinces many. But it's wrong. We're not going to find terrorist plots through systems like this, and we're going to waste valuable resources chasing down false alarms. To understand why, we have to look at the economics of the system.

Security is always a trade-off, and for a system to be worthwhile, the advantages have to be greater than the disadvantages. A national security data mining program is going to find some percentage of real attacks, and some percentage of false alarms. If the benefits of finding and stopping those attacks outweigh the cost—in money, liberties, etc.—then the system is a good one. If not, then you'd be better off spending that cost elsewhere.

Data mining works best when there's a well-defined profile you're searching for, a reasonable number of attacks per year, and a low cost of false alarms. Credit card fraud is one of data mining's success stories: all credit card companies data mine their transaction databases, looking for spending patterns that indicate a stolen card. Many credit card thieves share a pattern—purchase expensive luxury goods, purchase things that can be easily fenced, etc.—and data mining systems can minimize the losses in many cases by shutting down the card. In addition, the cost of false alarms is only a phone call to the cardholder asking him to verify a couple of purchases. The cardholders don't even resent these phone calls—as long as they're infrequent—so the cost is just a few minutes of operator time.

Terrorist plots are different. There is no well-defined profile, and attacks are very rare. Taken together, these facts mean that data mining systems won't uncover any terrorist plots until they are very accurate, and that even very accurate systems will be so flooded with false alarms that they will be useless.

All data mining systems fail in two different ways: false positives and false negatives. A false positive is when the system identifies a terrorist plot that really isn't one. A false negative is when the system misses an actual terrorist plot. Depending on how you "tune" your detection algorithms, you can err on one side or the other: you can increase the number of false positives to ensure that you are less likely to miss an actual terrorist plot, or you can reduce the number of false positives at the expense of missing terrorist plots.

To reduce both those numbers, you need a well-defined profile. And that's a problem when it comes to terrorism. In hindsight, it was really easy to connect the 9/11 dots and point to the warning signs, but it's much harder before the fact. Certainly, there are common warning signs that many terrorist plots share, but each is unique, as well. The better you can define what you're looking for, the better your results will be. Data mining for terrorist plots is going to be sloppy, and it's going to be hard to find anything useful.

Data mining is like searching for a needle in a haystack. There are 900 million credit cards in circulation in the United States. According to the FTC September 2003 Identity Theft Survey Report, about 1% (10 million) cards are stolen and fraudulently used each year. Terrorism is different. There are trillions of connections between people and events—things that the data mining system will have to "look at"—and very few plots. This rarity makes even accurate identification systems useless.

Let's look at some numbers. We'll be optimistic. We'll assume the system has a 1 in 100 false positive rate (99% accurate), and a 1 in 1,000 false negative rate (99.9% accurate).

Assume one trillion possible indicators to sift through: that's about ten events—e-mails, phone calls, purchases, web surfings, whatever—per person in the U.S. per day. Also assume that 10 of them are actually terrorists plotting.

This unrealistically accurate system will generate one billion false alarms for every real terrorist plot it uncovers. Every day of every year, the police will have to investigate 27 million potential plots in order to find the one real terrorist plot per month. Raise that false-positive accuracy to an absurd 99.9999% and you're still chasing 2,750 false alarms per day—but that will inevitably raise your false negatives, and you're going to miss some of those ten real plots.

This isn't anything new. In statistics, it's called the "base rate fallacy," and it applies in other domains as well. For example, even highly accurate medical tests are useless as diagnostic tools if the incidence of the disease is rare in the general population. Terrorist attacks are also rare, so any "test" is going to result in an endless stream of false alarms.

This is exactly the sort of thing we saw with the NSA's eavesdropping program: *The New York Times* reported that the computers spat out thousands of tips per month. Every one of them turned out to be a false alarm.

And the cost was enormous: not just the cost of the FBI agents running around chasing dead-end leads instead of doing things that might actually make us safer, but also the cost in civil liberties. The fundamental freedoms that make our country the envy of the world are valuable, and not something that we should throw away lightly.

Data mining can work. It helps Visa keep the costs of fraud down, just as it helps Amazon.com show me books that I might want to buy, and Google show me advertising I'm more likely to be interested in. But these are all instances where the cost of false positives is low—a phone call from a Visa operator, or an uninteresting ad—and in systems that have value even if there is a large number of false negatives.

Finding terrorism plots is not a problem that lends itself to data mining. It's a needle-in-a-haystack problem, and throwing more hay on the pile doesn't make that problem any easier. We'd be far better off putting people in charge of investigating potential plots and letting them direct the computers, instead of putting the computers in charge and letting them decide who should be investigated.

The Architecture of Security

Originally published in Wired, *19 October 2006*

You've seen them: those large concrete blocks in front of skyscrapers, monuments, and government buildings, designed to protect against car and truck bombs. They sprang up like weeds in the months after 9/11, but the idea is much older. The prettier ones doubled as planters; the uglier ones just stood there.

Form follows function. From medieval castles to modern airports, security concerns have always influenced architecture. Castles appeared during the reign of King Stephen of England because they were the best way to defend the land and there wasn't a strong king to put any limits on castle-building. But castle design changed over the centuries in response to both innovations in warfare and politics, from motte-and-bailey to concentric design in the late medieval period to entirely decorative castles in the 19th century.

These changes were expensive. The problem is that architecture tends toward permanence, while security threats change much faster. Something that seemed a good idea when a building was designed might make little sense a century—or even a decade—later. But by then it's hard to undo those architectural decisions.

When Syracuse University built a new campus in the mid-1970s, the student protests of the late 1960s were fresh on everybody's mind. So the architects designed a college without the open greens of traditional college campuses. It's now 30 years later, but Syracuse University is stuck defending itself against an obsolete threat.

Similarly, hotel entries in Montreal were elevated above street level in the 1970s, in response to security worries about Quebecois separatists. Today the threat is gone, but those older hotels continue to be maddeningly difficult to navigate.

Also in the 1970s, the Israeli consulate in New York built a unique security system: a two-door vestibule that allowed guards to identify visitors and control building access. Now this kind of entryway is widespread, and buildings with it will remain unwelcoming long after the threat is gone.

The same thing can be seen in cyberspace as well. In his book, *Code and Other Laws of Cyberspace*, Lawrence Lessig describes how decisions about technological infrastructure—the architecture of the Internet–become embedded and then impracticable to change. Whether it's technologies to prevent file copying, limit anonymity, record our digital habits for later investigation or reduce interoperability and strengthen monopoly positions, once technologies based on these security concerns become standard it will take decades to undo them.

It's dangerously shortsighted to make architectural decisions based on the threat of the moment without regard to the long-term consequences of those decisions.

Concrete building barriers are an exception: They're removable. They started appearing in Washington, DC, in 1983, after the truck bombing of the Marines barracks in Beirut. After 9/11, they were a sort of bizarre status symbol: They proved your building was important enough to deserve protection. In New York City alone, more than 50 buildings were protected in this fashion.

Today, they're slowly coming down. Studies have found they impede traffic flow, turn into giant ashtrays, and can pose a security risk by becoming flying shrapnel if exploded.

We should be thankful they can be removed, and did not end up as permanent aspects of our cities' architecture. We won't be so lucky with some of the design decisions we're seeing about Internet architecture.

The War on the Unexpected

Originally published in Wired, *1 November 2007*

We've opened up a new front on the war on terror. It's an attack on the unique, the unorthodox, the unexpected; it's a war on different. If you act different, you might find yourself investigated, questioned, and even arrested—even if you did nothing wrong, and had no intention of doing anything wrong. The problem is a combination of citizen informants and a CYA attitude among police that results in a knee-jerk escalation of reported threats.

This isn't the way counterterrorism is supposed to work, but it's happening everywhere. It's a result of our relentless campaign to convince ordinary citizens that they're the front line of terrorism defense. "If you see something, say something" is how the ads read in the New York City subways. "If you suspect something, report it" urges another ad campaign in Manchester, England. The Michigan State Police have a seven-minute video. Administration officials from then-attorney general John Ashcroft to DHS Secretary Michael Chertoff to President Bush have asked us all to report any suspicious activity.

The problem is that ordinary citizens don't know what a real terrorist threat looks like. They can't tell the difference between a bomb and a tape dispenser, electronic name badge, CD player, bat detector, or trash sculpture; or the difference between terrorist plotters and imams, musicians, or architects. All they know is that something makes them uneasy, usually based on fear, media hype, or just something being different.

Even worse: After someone reports a "terrorist threat," the whole system is biased towards escalation and CYA instead of a more realistic threat assessment.

Watch how it happens. Someone sees something, so he says something. The person he says it to—a policeman, a security guard, a flight attendant— now faces a choice: ignore or escalate. Even though he may believe that it's a false alarm, it's not in his best interests to dismiss the threat. If he's wrong, it'll cost him his career. But if he escalates, he'll be praised for "doing his job" and the cost will be borne by others. So he escalates. And the person he escalates to also escalates, in a series of CYA decisions. And before we're done, innocent people have been arrested, airports have been evacuated, and hundreds of police hours have been wasted.

This story has been repeated endlessly, both in the U.S. and in other countries. Someone—these are all real—notices a funny smell, or some white powder, or two people passing an envelope, or a dark-skinned man leaving boxes at the curb, or a cell phone in an airplane seat; the police cordon off the area, make arrests, and/or evacuate airplanes; and in the end the cause of the alarm is revealed as a pot of Thai chili sauce, or flour, or a utility bill, or an English professor recycling, or a cell phone in an airplane seat.

Of course, by then it's too late for the authorities to admit that they made a mistake and overreacted, that a sane voice of reason at some level should have prevailed. What follows is the parade of police and elected officials praising each other for doing a great job, and prosecuting the poor victim—the person who was different in the first place—for having the temerity to try to trick them.

For some reason, governments are encouraging this kind of behavior. It's not just the publicity campaigns asking people to come forward and snitch on their neighbors; they're asking certain professions to pay particular attention: truckers to watch the highways, students to watch campuses, and scuba instructors to watch their students. The U.S. wanted meter readers and telephone repairmen to snoop around houses. There's even a new law protecting people who turn in their travel mates based on some undefined "objectively reasonable suspicion," whatever that is.

If you ask amateurs to act as front-line security personnel, you shouldn't be surprised when you get amateur security.

We need to do two things. The first is to stop urging people to report their fears. People have always come forward to tell the police when they see something genuinely suspicious, and should continue to do so. But encouraging people to raise an alarm every time they're spooked only squanders our security resources and makes no one safer.

We don't want people to never report anything. A store clerk's tip led to the unraveling of a plot to attack Fort Dix last May, and in March an alert Southern California woman foiled a kidnapping by calling the police about a suspicious man carting around a person-sized crate. But these incidents only reinforce the need to realistically assess, not automatically escalate, citizen tips. In criminal matters, law enforcement is experienced in separating legitimate tips from unsubstantiated fears, and allocating resources accordingly; we should expect no less from them when it comes to terrorism.

Equally important, politicians need to stop praising and promoting the officers who get it wrong. And everyone needs to stop castigating, and prosecuting, the victims just because they embarrassed the police by their innocence.

Causing a city-wide panic over blinking signs, a guy with a pellet gun, or stray backpacks, is not evidence of doing a good job: It's evidence of squandering police resources. Even worse, it causes its own form of terror, and encourages people to be even more alarmist in the future. We need to spend our resources on things that actually make us safer, not on chasing down and trumpeting every paranoid threat anyone can come up with.

Portrait of the Modern Terrorist as an Idiot

Originally published in Wired, *14 June 2007*

The recently publicized terrorist plot to blow up New York's John F. Kennedy International Airport, like so many of the terrorist plots over the past few years, is a study in alarmism and incompetence: on the part of the terrorists, our government and the press.

Terrorism is a real threat, and one that needs to be addressed by appropriate means. But allowing ourselves to be terrorized by wannabe terrorists and unrealistic plots—and worse, allowing our essential freedoms to be lost by using them as an excuse—is wrong.

The alleged plan, to blow up JFK's fuel tanks and a small segment of the 40-mile petroleum pipeline that supplies the airport, was ridiculous. The fuel tanks are thick-walled, making them hard to damage. The airport tanks are separated from the pipelines by cutoff valves, so even if a fire broke out at the tanks, it would not back up into the pipelines. And the pipeline couldn't blow up in any case, since there's no oxygen to aid combustion. Not that the terrorists ever got to the stage—or demonstrated that they could get there—where they actually obtained explosives. Or even a current map of the airport's infrastructure.

But read what Russell Defreitas, the lead terrorist, had to say: "Anytime you hit Kennedy, it is the most hurtful thing to the United States. To hit John F. Kennedy, wow.... They love JFK—he's like the man. If you hit that, the whole country will be in mourning. It's like you can kill the man twice."

If these are the terrorists we're fighting, we've got a pretty incompetent enemy.

You couldn't tell that from the press reports, though. "The devastation that would be caused had this plot succeeded is just unthinkable," U.S. Attorney Roslynn R. Mauskopf said at a news conference, calling it "one of the most chilling plots imaginable." Sen. Arlen Specter (R-Pennsylvania) added, "It had the potential to be another 9/11."

These people are just as deluded as Defreitas.

The only voice of reason out there seemed to be New York's Mayor Michael Bloomberg, who said: "There are lots of threats to you in the world. There's the threat of a heart attack for genetic reasons. You can't sit there and worry about everything. Get a life.... You have a much greater danger of being hit by lightning than being struck by a terrorist."

And he was widely excoriated for it.

This isn't the first time a bunch of incompetent terrorists with an infeasible plot have been painted by the media as being poised to do all sorts of damage to America. In May, we learned about a six-man plan to stage an attack on Fort Dix by getting in disguised as pizza deliverymen and shooting as many soldiers and Humvees as they could, then retreating without losses to fight again another day. Their plan, such as it was, went awry when they took a videotape of themselves at weapons practice to a store for duplication and transfer to DVD. The store clerk contacted the police, who in turn contacted the FBI. (Thank you to the video store clerk for not overreacting, and to the FBI agent for infiltrating the group.)

The "Miami 7," caught last year for plotting—among other things—to blow up the Sears Tower in Chicago, were another incompetent group: no weapons, no bombs, no expertise, no money and no operational skill. And don't forget Iyman Faris, the Ohio trucker who was convicted in 2003 for the laughable plot to take out the Brooklyn Bridge with a blowtorch. At least he eventually decided that the plan was unlikely to succeed.

I don't think these nut jobs, with their movie-plot threats, even deserve the moniker "terrorist." But in this country, while you have to be competent to pull off a terrorist attack, you don't have to be competent to cause terror. All you need to do is start plotting an attack and—regardless of whether or not you have a viable plan, weapons or even the faintest clue—the media will aid you in terrorizing the entire population.

The most ridiculous JFK Airport-related story goes to the *New York Daily News*, with its interview with a waitress who served Defreitas salmon; the front-page headline blared: "Evil Ate at Table Eight."

Following one of these abortive terror misadventures, the administration invariably jumps on the news to trumpet whatever ineffective "security" measure they're trying to push, whether it be national ID cards, wholesale National Security Agency eavesdropping (NSA), or massive data mining. Never mind that in all these cases, what caught the bad guys was old-fashioned police work—the kind of thing you'd see in decades-old spy movies.

The administration repeatedly credited the apprehension of Faris to the NSA's warrantless eavesdropping programs, even though it's just not true. The 9/11 terrorists were no different; they succeeded partly because the FBI and CIA didn't follow the leads before the attacks.

Even the London liquid bombers were caught through traditional investigation and intelligence, but this doesn't stop Secretary of Homeland Security Michael Chertoff from using them to justify access to airline passenger data.

Of course, even incompetent terrorists can cause damage. This has been repeatedly proven in Israel, and if shoe-bomber Richard Reid had been just a little less stupid and ignited his shoes in the lavatory, he might have taken out an airplane.

So these people should be locked up ... assuming they are actually guilty, that is. Despite the initial press frenzies, the actual details of the cases frequently turn out to be far less damning. Too often it's unclear whether the defendants are actually guilty, or if the police created a crime where none existed before.

The JFK Airport plotters seem to have been egged on by an informant, a twice-convicted drug dealer. An FBI informant almost certainly pushed the Fort Dix plotters to do things they wouldn't have ordinarily done. The Miami gang's Sears Tower plot was suggested by an FBI undercover agent who infiltrated the group. And in 2003, it took an elaborate sting operation involving three countries to arrest an arms dealer for selling a surface-to-air missile to an ostensible Muslim extremist. Entrapment is a very real possibility in all of these cases.

The rest of them stink of exaggeration. Jose Padilla was not actually prepared to detonate a dirty bomb in the United States, despite histrionic administration claims to the contrary. Now that the trial is proceeding, the best the government can charge him with is conspiracy to murder, kidnap, and maim, and it seems unlikely that the charges will stick. An alleged ringleader of the U.K. liquid bombers, Rashid Rauf, had charges of terrorism dropped for lack of evidence (of the 25 arrested, only 16 were charged). And now it seems the JFK mastermind was more talk than action, too.

Remember the "Lackawanna Six," those terrorists from upstate New York who pleaded guilty in 2003 to "providing support or resources to a foreign terrorist organization"? They entered their plea because they were threatened with being removed from the legal system altogether. We have no idea if they were actually guilty, or of what.

Even under the best of circumstances, these are difficult prosecutions. Arresting people before they've carried out their plans means trying to prove intent, which rapidly slips into the province of thoughtcrime. Regularly the prosecution uses obtuse religious literature in the defendants' homes to prove what they believe, and this can result in courtroom debates on Islamic theology. And then there's the issue of demonstrating a connection between a book on a shelf and an idea in the defendant's head, as if your reading of this article—or purchasing of my book—proves that you agree with everything I say. (*The Atlantic* recently published a fascinating article on this.)

I'll be the first to admit that I don't have all the facts in any of these cases. None of us does. So let's have some healthy skepticism. Skepticism when we read about these terrorist masterminds who were poised to kill thousands of people and do incalculable damage. Skepticism when we're told that their arrest proves that we need to give away our own freedoms and liberties. And skepticism that those arrested are even guilty in the first place.

There is a real threat of terrorism. And while I'm all in favor of the terrorists' continuing incompetence, I know that some will prove more capable. We need real security that doesn't require us to guess the tactic or the target: intelligence and investigation—the very things that caught all these terrorist wannabes—and emergency response. But the "war on terror" rhetoric is more politics than rationality. We shouldn't let the politics of fear make us less safe.

Correspondent Inference Theory and Terrorism

Originally published in Wired, *12 July 2007*

Two people are sitting in a room together: an experimenter and a subject. The experimenter gets up and closes the door, and the room becomes quieter. The subject is likely to believe that the experimenter's purpose in closing the door was to make the room quieter.

This is an example of correspondent inference theory. People tend to infer the motives—and also the disposition—of someone who performs an action based on the effects of his actions, and not on external or situational factors. If you see someone violently hitting someone else, you assume it's because he wanted to— and is a violent person—and not because he's play-acting. If you read about someone getting into a car accident, you assume it's because he's a bad driver and not because he was simply unlucky. And—more importantly for this column— if you read about a terrorist, you assume that terrorism is his ultimate goal.

It's not always this easy, of course. If someone chooses to move to Seattle instead of New York, is it because of the climate, the culture, or his career? Edward Jones and Keith Davis, who advanced this theory in the 1960s and 1970s, proposed a theory of "correspondence" to describe the extent to which this effect predominates. When an action has a high correspondence, people tend to infer the motives of the person directly from the action: e.g., hitting someone violently. When the action has a low correspondence, people tend not to make the assumption: e.g., moving to Seattle.

Like most cognitive biases, correspondent inference theory makes evolutionary sense. In a world of simple actions and base motivations, it's a good rule of thumb that allows a creature to rapidly infer the motivations of another creature. (He's attacking me because he wants to kill me.) Even in sentient and social creatures like humans, it makes a lot of sense most of the time. If you see someone violently hitting someone else, it's reasonable to assume that he's a violent person. Cognitive biases aren't bad; they're sensible rules of thumb.

But like all cognitive biases, correspondent inference theory fails sometimes. And one place it fails pretty spectacularly is in our response to terrorism. Because terrorism often results in the horrific deaths of innocents, we mistakenly infer that the horrific deaths of innocents is the primary motivation of the terrorist, and not the means to a different end.

I found this interesting analysis in a paper by Max Abrahms in *International Security*. "Why Terrorism Does Not Work" analyzes the political motivations of 28 terrorist groups: the complete list of "foreign terrorist organizations" designated by the U.S. Department of State since 2001. He lists 42 policy objectives of those groups, and found that they only achieved them 7% of the time.

According to the data, terrorism is more likely to work if 1) the terrorists attack military targets more often than civilian ones, and 2) if they have minimalist goals like evicting a foreign power from their country or winning control of a piece of territory, rather than maximalist objectives like establishing a new political system in the country or annihilating another nation. But even so, terrorism is a pretty ineffective means of influencing policy.

There's a lot to quibble about in Abrahms' methodology, but he seems to be erring on the side of crediting terrorist groups with success. (Hezbollah's objectives of expelling both peacekeepers and Israel out of Lebanon counts as a success, but so does the "limited success" by the Tamil Tigers of establishing a Tamil state.) Still, he provides good data to support what was until recently common knowledge: Terrorism doesn't work.

This is all interesting stuff, and I recommend that you read the paper for yourself. But to me, the most insightful part is when Abrahms uses correspondent inference theory to explain why terrorist groups that primarily attack civilians do not achieve their policy goals, even if they are minimalist. Abrahms writes:

"The theory posited here is that terrorist groups that target civilians are unable to coerce policy change because terrorism has an extremely high correspondence. Countries believe that their civilian populations are attacked not because the terrorist group is protesting unfavorable external conditions such as territorial occupation or poverty. Rather, target countries infer the short-term consequences of terrorism—the deaths of innocent civilians, mass fear, loss of confidence in the government to offer protection, economic contraction, and the inevitable erosion of civil liberties—(are) the objects of the terrorist groups. In short, target countries view the negative consequences of terrorist attacks on their societies and political systems as evidence that the terrorists want them destroyed. Target countries are understandably skeptical that making concessions will placate terrorist groups believed to be motivated by these maximalist objectives."

In other words, terrorism doesn't work, because it makes people less likely to acquiesce to the terrorists' demands, no matter how limited they might be. The reaction to terrorism has an effect completely opposite to what the terrorists want; people simply don't believe those limited demands are the actual demands.

This theory explains, with a clarity I have never seen before, why so many people make the bizarre claim that al-Qaeda terrorism—or Islamic terrorism in general—is "different": that while other terrorist groups might have policy objectives, al-Qaeda's primary motivation is to kill us all. This is something we have heard from President Bush again and again—Abrahms has a page of examples in the paper—and is a rhetorical staple in the debate.

In fact, Bin Laden's policy objectives have been surprisingly consistent. Abrahms lists four; here are six from former CIA analyst Michael Scheuer's book *Imperial Hubris*:

- End U.S. support of Israel
- Force American troops out of the Middle East, particularly Saudi Arabia
- End the U.S. occupation of Afghanistan and (subsequently) Iraq
- End U.S. support of other countries' anti-Muslim policies
- End U.S. pressure on Arab oil companies to keep prices low
- End U.S. support for "illegitimate" (i.e., moderate) Arab governments like Pakistan

Although Bin Laden has complained that Americans have completely misunderstood the reason behind the 9/11 attacks, correspondent inference theory postulates that he's not going to convince people. Terrorism, and 9/11 in particular, has such a high correspondence that people use the effects of the attacks to infer the terrorists' motives. In other words, since Bin Laden caused the death of a couple of thousand people in the 9/11 attacks, people assume that must have been his actual goal, and he's just giving lip service to what he *claims* are his goals. Even Bin Laden's actual objectives are ignored as people focus on the deaths, the destruction and the economic impact.

Perversely, Bush's misinterpretation of terrorists' motives actually helps prevent them from achieving their goals.

None of this is meant to either excuse or justify terrorism. In fact, it does the exact opposite, by demonstrating why terrorism doesn't work as a tool of persuasion and policy change. But we're more effective at fighting terrorism if we understand that it is a means to an end and not an end in itself; it requires us to understand the true motivations of the terrorists and not just their particular tactics. And the more our own cognitive biases cloud that understanding, the more we mischaracterize the threat and make bad security trade-offs.

The Risks of Cyberterrorism

Originally published in Crypto-Gram, *15 June 2003*

The threat of cyberterrorism is causing much alarm these days. We have been told to expect attacks since 9/11; that cyberterrorists would try to cripple our power system, disable air traffic control and emergency services, open dams, or disrupt banking and communications. But so far, nothing's happened. Even during the war in Iraq, which was supposed to increase the risk dramatically, nothing happened. The impending cyberwar was a big dud. Don't congratulate our vigilant security, though; the alarm was caused by a misunderstanding of both the attackers and the attacks.

These attacks are very difficult to execute. The software systems controlling our nation's infrastructure are filled with vulnerabilities, but they're generally not the kinds of vulnerabilities that cause catastrophic disruptions. The systems are designed to limit the damage that occurs from errors and accidents. They have manual overrides. These systems have been proven to work; they've experienced disruptions caused by accident and natural disaster. We've been through blackouts, telephone switch failures, and disruptions of air traffic control computers. In 1999, a software bug knocked out a nationwide paging system for a day. The results might be annoying, and engineers might spend days or weeks scrambling, but the effect on the general population has been minimal.

The worry is that a terrorist would cause a problem more serious than a natural disaster, but this kind of thing is surprisingly hard to do. Worms and viruses have caused all sorts of network disruptions, but it happened by accident. In January 2003, the SQL Slammer worm disrupted 13,000 ATMs on the

Bank of America's network. But before it happened, you couldn't have found a security expert who understood that those systems were vulnerable to that particular attack. We simply don't understand the interactions well enough to predict which kinds of attacks could cause catastrophic results, and terrorist organizations don't have that sort of knowledge either—even if they tried to hire experts.

The closest example we have of this kind of thing comes from Australia in 2000. Vitek Boden broke into the computer network of a sewage treatment plant along Australia's Sunshine Coast. Over the course of two months, he leaked hundreds of thousands of gallons of putrid sludge into nearby rivers and parks. Among the results were black creek water, dead marine life, and a stench so unbearable that residents complained. This is the only known case of someone hacking a digital control system with the intent of causing environmental harm.

Despite our predilection for calling anything "terrorism," these attacks are not. We know what terrorism is. It's someone blowing himself up in a crowded restaurant, or flying an airplane into a skyscraper. It's not infecting computers with viruses, forcing air traffic controllers to route planes manually, or shutting down a pager network for a day. That causes annoyance and irritation, not terror.

This is a difficult message for some, because these days anyone who causes widespread damage is being given the label "terrorist." But imagine for a minute the leadership of al-Qaeda sitting in a cave somewhere, plotting the next move in their jihad against the United States. One of the leaders jumps up and exclaims: "I have an idea! We'll disable their e-mail...." Conventional terrorism—driving a truckful of explosives into a nuclear power plant, for example—is still easier and much more effective.

There are lots of hackers in the world—kids, mostly—who like to play at politics and dress their own antics in the trappings of terrorism. They hack computers belonging to some other country (generally not government computers) and display a political message. We've often seen this kind of thing when two countries squabble: China vs. Taiwan, India vs. Pakistan, England vs. Ireland, U.S. vs. China (during the 2001 crisis over the U.S. spy plane that crashed in Chinese territory), the U.S. and Israel vs. various Arab countries. It's the equivalent of soccer hooligans taking out national frustrations on another country's fans at a game. It's base and despicable, and it causes real damage, but it's cyberhooliganism, not cyberterrorism.

There are several organizations that track attacks over the Internet. Over the last six months, less than 1% of all attacks originated from countries on the U.S. government's Cyber Terrorist Watch List, while 35% originated from inside the United States. Computer security is still important. People overplay the risks of cyberterrorism, but they underplay the risks of cybercrime. Fraud and espionage are serious problems. Luckily, the same countermeasures aimed at cyberterrorists will also prevent hackers and criminals. If organizations secure their computer networks for the wrong reasons, it will still be the right thing to do.

2 National Security Policy

The Security Threat of Unchecked Presidential Power

Originally published in Minneapolis Star Tribune,
21 December 2005

Last Thursday [15 December 2005], *The New York Times* exposed the most significant violation of federal surveillance law in the post-Watergate era. President Bush secretly authorized the NSA to engage in domestic spying, wiretapping thousands of Americans and bypassing the legal procedures regulating this activity.

This isn't about the spying, although that's a major issue in itself. This is about the Fourth Amendment protections against illegal search. This is about circumventing a teeny tiny check by the judicial branch, placed there by the legislative branch 27 years ago—on the last occasion that the executive branch abused its power so broadly.

In defending this secret spying on Americans, Bush said that he relied on his constitutional powers (Article 2) and the joint resolution passed by Congress after 9/11 that led to the war in Iraq. This rationale was spelled out in a memo written by John Yoo, a White House attorney, less than two weeks after the attacks of 9/11. It's a dense read and a terrifying piece of legal contortionism, but it basically says that the president has unlimited powers to fight terrorism. He can spy on anyone, arrest anyone, and kidnap anyone and ship him to another country ... merely on the suspicion that he *might* be a terrorist. And according to the memo, this power lasts until there is no more terrorism in the world.

Yoo starts by arguing that the Constitution gives the president total power during wartime. He also notes that Congress has recently been quiescent when the president takes some military action on his own, citing President Clinton's 1998 strike against Sudan and Afghanistan.

Yoo then says: "The terrorist incidents of September 11, 2001, were surely far graver a threat to the national security of the United States than the 1998 attacks. ... The President's power to respond militarily to the later attacks must be correspondingly broader."

This is novel reasoning. It's as if the police would have greater powers when investigating a murder than a burglary.

More to the point, the congressional resolution of 14 September 2001, specifically refused the White House's initial attempt to seek authority to pre-empt any future acts of terrorism, and narrowly gave Bush permission to go after those responsible for the attacks on the Pentagon and World Trade Center.

Yoo's memo ignored this. Written 11 days after Congress refused to grant the president wide-ranging powers, it admitted that "the Joint Resolution is somewhat narrower than the President's constitutional authority," but argued "the President's broad constitutional power to use military force ... would allow the President to ... [take] whatever actions he deems appropriate ... to pre-empt or respond to terrorist threats from new quarters."

Even if Congress specifically says no.

The result is that the president's wartime powers, with its armies, battles, victories, and congressional declarations, now extend to the rhetorical "War on Terror": a war with no fronts, no boundaries, no opposing army, and— most ominously—no knowable "victory." Investigations, arrests, and trials are not tools of war. But according to the Yoo memo, the president can define war however he chooses, and remain "at war" for as long as he chooses.

This is indefinite dictatorial power. And I don't use that term lightly; the very definition of a dictatorship is a system that puts a ruler above the law. In the weeks after 9/11, while America and the world were grieving, Bush built a legal rationale for a dictatorship. Then he immediately started using it to avoid the law.

This is, fundamentally, why this issue crossed political lines in Congress. If the president can ignore laws regulating surveillance and wiretapping, why is Congress bothering to debate reauthorizing certain provisions of the USA PATRIOT Act? Any debate over laws is predicated on the belief that the executive branch will follow the law.

This is not a partisan issue between Democrats and Republicans; it's a president unilaterally overriding the Fourth Amendment, Congress and the Supreme Court. Unchecked presidential power has nothing to do with how much you either love or hate George W. Bush. You have to imagine this power in the hands of the person you most don't want to see as president, whether it be Dick Cheney or Hillary Rodham Clinton, Michael Moore or Ann Coulter.

Laws are what give us security against the actions of the majority and the powerful. If we discard our constitutional protections against tyranny in an attempt to protect us from terrorism, we're all less safe as a result.

Surveillance and Oversight

Originally published in Minneapolis Star Tribune, *November 2005*

Christmas 2003, Las Vegas. Intelligence hinted at a terrorist attack on New Year's Eve. In the absence of any real evidence, the FBI tried to compile a real-time database of everyone who was visiting the city. It collected customer data from airlines, hotels, casinos, rental car companies, even storage locker rental companies. All this information went into a massive database—probably close to a million people overall—that the FBI's computers analyzed, looking for links to known terrorists. Of course, no terrorist attack occurred and no plot was discovered: The intelligence was wrong.

A typical American citizen spending the holidays in Vegas might be surprised to learn that the FBI collected his personal data, but this kind of thing is increasingly common. Since 9/11, the FBI has been collecting all sorts of personal information on ordinary Americans, and it shows no signs of letting up.

The FBI has two basic tools for gathering information on large groups of Americans. Both were created in the 1970s to gather information solely on foreign terrorists and spies. Both were greatly expanded by the USA PATRIOT Act and other laws, and are now routinely used against ordinary, law-abiding Americans who have no connection to terrorism. Together, they represent an enormous increase in police power in the United States.

The first are FISA warrants (sometimes called Section 215 warrants, after the section of the USA PATRIOT Act that expanded their scope). These are issued in secret, by a secret court. The second are national security letters, less well-known but much more powerful, and which FBI field supervisors can issue all by themselves. The exact numbers are secret, but a recent *Washington Post* article estimated that 30,000 letters each year demand telephone records, banking data, customer data, library records, and so on.

In both cases, the recipients of these orders are prohibited by law from disclosing the fact that they received them. And two years ago, Attorney General John Ashcroft rescinded a 1995 guideline that this information be destroyed if it is not relevant to whatever investigation it was collected for. Now, it can be saved indefinitely, and disseminated freely.

September 2005, Rotterdam. The police had already identified some of the 250 suspects in a soccer riot from the previous April, but most were unidentified but captured on video. In an effort to help, they sent text messages to 17,000 phones known to be in the vicinity of the riots, asking that anyone with information contact the police. The result was more evidence, and more arrests.

The differences between the Rotterdam and Las Vegas incidents are instructive. The Rotterdam police needed specific data for a specific purpose. Its members worked with federal justice officials to ensure that they complied with the country's strict privacy laws. They obtained the phone numbers without any names attached, and deleted them immediately after sending the single text message. And their actions were public, widely reported in the press.

On the other hand, the FBI has no judicial oversight. With only a vague hinting that a Las Vegas attack might occur, the bureau vacuumed up an enormous amount of information. First its members tried asking for the data; then they turned to national security letters and, in some cases, subpoenas. There was no requirement to delete the data, and there is every reason to believe that the FBI still has it all. And the bureau worked in secret; the only reason we know this happened is the operation leaked.

These differences illustrate four principles that should guide our use of personal information by the police. The first is oversight: In order to obtain personal information, the police should be required to show probable cause, and convince a judge to issue a warrant for the specific information needed. Second, minimization: The police should get only the specific information they need, and not any more. Nor should they be allowed to collect large blocks of information in order to go on "fishing expeditions," looking for suspicious behavior. The third is transparency: The public should know, if not immediately then eventually, what information the police are getting and how it is being used. And fourth, destruction. Any data the police obtains should be destroyed immediately after its court-authorized purpose is achieved. The police should not be able to hold on to it, just in case it might become useful at some future date.

This isn't about our ability to combat terrorism; it's about police power. Traditional law already gives police enormous power to peer into the personal lives of people, to use new crime-fighting technologies, and to correlate that information. But unfettered police power quickly resembles a police state, and checks on that power make us all safer.

As more of our lives become digital, we leave an ever-widening audit trail in our wake. This information has enormous social value—not just for national security and law enforcement, but for purposes as mundane as using cell-phone data to track road congestion, and as important as using medical data to track the spread of diseases. Our challenge is not only to make this information available when and where it needs to be, but also to protect the principles of privacy and liberty our country is built on.

NSA and Bush's Illegal Eavesdropping

Originally published in Salon, *20 December 2005*
(Note: I wrote this essay in the days after the scandal broke.)

When President Bush directed the NSA to secretly eavesdrop on American citizens, he transferred an authority previously under the purview of the Justice Department to the Defense Department and bypassed the very laws put in place to protect Americans against widespread government eavesdropping. The reason may have been to tap the NSA's capability for data-mining and widespread surveillance.

Illegal wiretapping of Americans is nothing new. In the 1950s and 1960s, in a program called "Project Shamrock," the NSA intercepted every single telegram coming into or going out of the United States. It conducted eavesdropping without a warrant on behalf of the CIA and other agencies. Much of this became public during the 1975 Church Committee hearings and resulted in the now famous Foreign Intelligence Surveillance Act (FISA) of 1978.

The purpose of this law was to protect the American people by regulating government eavesdropping. Like many laws limiting the power of government, it relies on checks and balances: one branch of the government watching the other. The law established a secret court, the Foreign Intelligence

Surveillance Court (FISC), and empowered it to approve national-security-related eavesdropping warrants. The Justice Department can request FISA warrants to monitor foreign communications as well as communications by American citizens, provided that they meet certain minimal criteria.

The FISC issued about 500 FISA warrants per year from 1979 through 1995, and has slowly increased subsequently—1,758 were issued in 2004. The process is designed for speed and even has provisions where the Justice Department can wiretap first and ask for permission later. In all that time, only four warrant requests were ever rejected: all in 2003. (We don't know any details, of course, as the court proceedings are secret.)

FISA warrants are carried out by the FBI, but in the days immediately after the terrorist attacks, there was a widespread perception in Washington that the FBI wasn't up to dealing with these new threats—they couldn't uncover plots in a timely manner. So instead the Bush administration turned to the NSA. They had the tools, the expertise, the experience, and so they were given the mission.

The NSA's ability to eavesdrop on communications is exemplified by a technological capability called Echelon. Echelon is the world's largest information "vacuum cleaner," sucking up a staggering amount of voice, fax, and data communications—satellite, microwave, fiber-optic, cellular and everything else—from all over the world: an estimated 3 billion communications per day. These communications are then processed through sophisticated data-mining technologies, which look for simple phrases like "assassinate the president" as well as more complicated communications patterns.

Supposedly Echelon only covers communications outside of the United States. Although there is no evidence that the Bush administration has employed Echelon to monitor communications to and from the U.S., this surveillance capability is probably exactly what the president wanted and may explain why the administration sought to bypass the FISA process of acquiring a warrant for searches.

Perhaps the NSA just didn't have any experience submitting FISA warrants, so Bush unilaterally waived that requirement. And perhaps Bush thought FISA was a hindrance—in 2002 there was a widespread but false belief that the FISC got in the way of the investigation of Zacarias Moussaoui (the presumed "20th hijacker")—and bypassed the court for that reason.

Most likely, Bush wanted a whole new surveillance paradigm. You can think of the FBI's capabilities as "retail surveillance": It eavesdrops on a particular person or phone. The NSA, on the other hand, conducts "wholesale surveillance." It, or more exactly its computers, listens to everything. An example might be to feed the computers every voice, fax, and e-mail communication looking for the name "Ayman al-Zawahiri." This type of surveillance is more along the lines of Project Shamrock, and not legal under FISA. As Senator Jay Rockefeller wrote in a secret memo after being briefed on the program, it raises "profound oversight issues."

It is also unclear whether Echelon-style eavesdropping would prevent terrorist attacks. In the months before 9/11, Echelon noticed considerable "chatter": bits of conversation suggesting some sort of imminent attack. But because much of the planning for 9/11 occurred face-to-face, analysts were unable to learn details.

The fundamental issue here is security, but it's not the security most people think of. James Madison famously said: "If men were angels, no government would be necessary. If angels were to govern men, neither external nor internal controls on government would be necessary." Terrorism is a serious risk to our nation, but an even greater threat is the centralization of American political power in the hands of any single branch of the government.

Over 200 years ago, the framers of the U.S. Constitution established an ingenious security device against tyrannical government: they divided government power among three different bodies. A carefully thought-out system of checks and balances in the executive branch, the legislative branch, and the judicial branch, ensured that no single branch became too powerful.

After watching tyrannies rise and fall throughout Europe, this seemed like a prudent way to form a government. Courts monitor the actions of police. Congress passes laws that even the president must follow. Since 9/11, the United States has seen an enormous power grab by the executive branch. It's time we brought back the security system that's protected us from government for over 200 years.

Private Police Forces

Originally published in Minneapolis Star Tribune,
27 February 2007

In Raleigh, North Carolina, employees of Capitol Special Police patrol apartment buildings, a bowling alley, and nightclubs, stopping suspicious people, searching their cars and making arrests.

Sounds like a good thing, but Capitol Special Police isn't a police force at all—it's a for-profit security company hired by private property owners.

This isn't unique. Private security guards outnumber real police more than 5 to 1, and increasingly act like them.

They wear uniforms, carry weapons, and drive lighted patrol cars on private properties like banks and apartment complexes and in public areas like bus stations and national monuments. Sometimes they operate as ordinary citizens and can only make citizen's arrests, but in more and more states they're being granted official police powers.

This trend should greatly concern citizens. Law enforcement should be a government function, and privatizing it puts us all at risk.

Most obviously, there's the problem of agenda. Public police forces are charged with protecting the citizens of the cities and towns over which they have jurisdiction. Of course, there are instances of policemen overstepping their bounds, but these are exceptions, and the police officers and departments are ultimately responsible to the public.

Private police officers are different. They don't work for us; they work for corporations. They're focused on the priorities of their employers or the companies that hire them. They're less concerned with due process, public safety and civil rights.

Also, many of the laws that protect us from police abuse do not apply to the private sector. Constitutional safeguards that regulate police conduct, interrogation and evidence collection do not apply to private individuals. Information that is illegal for the government to collect about you can be collected by commercial data brokers, then purchased by the police.

We've all seen policemen "reading people their rights" on television cop shows. If you're detained by a private security guard, you don't have nearly as many rights.

For example, a federal law known as Section 1983 allows you to sue for civil rights violations by the police but not by private citizens. The Freedom of Information Act allows us to learn what government law enforcement is doing, but the law doesn't apply to private individuals and companies. In fact, most of your civil rights protections apply only to real police.

Training and regulation is another problem. Private security guards often receive minimal training, if any. They don't graduate from police academies. And while some states regulate these guard companies, others have no regulations at all: Anyone can put on a uniform and play policeman. Abuses of power, brutality, and illegal behavior are much more common among private security guards than real police.

A horrific example of this happened in South Carolina in 1995. Ricky Coleman, an unlicensed and untrained Best Buy security guard with a violent criminal record, choked a fraud suspect to death while another security guard held him down.

This trend is larger than police. More and more of our nation's prisons are being run by for-profit corporations. The IRS has started outsourcing some back-tax collection to debt-collection companies that will take a percentage of the money recovered as their fee. And there are about 20,000 private police and military personnel in Iraq, working for the Defense Department.

Throughout most of history, specific people were charged by those in power to keep the peace, collect taxes, and wage wars. Corruption and incompetence were the norm, and justice was scarce. It is for this very reason that, since the 1600s, European governments have been built around a professional civil service to both enforce the laws and protect rights.

Private security guards turn this bedrock principle of modern government on its head. Whether it's FedEx policemen in Tennessee who can request search warrants and make arrests; a privately funded surveillance helicopter in Jackson, Mississippi, that can bypass constitutional restrictions on aerial spying; or employees of Capitol Special Police in North Carolina who are lobbying to expand their jurisdiction beyond the specific properties they protect—privately funded policemen are not protecting us or working in our best interests.

Recognizing "Hinky" vs. Citizen Informants

Originally published in Crypto-Gram, *15 May 2007*

On the subject of people noticing and reporting suspicious actions, I have been espousing two views that some find contradictory. One, we are all safer if police, guards, security screeners, and the like ignore traditional profiling and instead pay attention to people acting hinky: not right. And two, if we encourage people to contact the authorities every time they see something suspicious, we're going to waste our time chasing false alarms: foreigners whose customs are different, people who are disliked by someone, and so on.

The key difference is expertise. People trained to be alert for something hinky will do much better than any profiler, but people who have no idea what to look for will do no better than random.

Here's a story that illustrates this: Last week, a student at the Rochester Institute of Technology was arrested with two illegal assault weapons and 320 rounds of ammunition in his dorm room and car:

"The discovery of the weapons was made only by chance. A conference center worker who served in the military was walking past Hackenburg's dorm room. The door was shut, but the worker heard the all-too-familiar racking sound of a weapon, said the center's director Bill Gunther."

Notice how expertise made the difference. The "conference center worker" had the right knowledge to recognize the sound and to understand that it was out of place in the environment he heard it. He wasn't primed to be on the lookout for suspicious people and things; his trained awareness kicked in automatically. He recognized hinky, and he acted on that recognition. A random person simply can't do that; he won't recognize hinky when he sees it. He'll report imams for praying, a neighbor he's pissed at, or people at random. He'll see an English professor recycling paper, and report a Middle-Eastern-looking man leaving a box on sidewalk.

We all have some experience with this. Each of us has some expertise in some topic, and will occasionally recognize that something is wrong even though we can't fully explain what or why. An architect might feel that way about a particular structure; an artist might feel that way about a particular painting. I might look at a cryptographic system and intuitively know something is wrong with it, well before I figure out exactly what. Those are all examples of a subliminal recognition that something is hinky—in our particular domain of expertise.

Good security people have the knowledge, skill, and experience to do that in security situations. It's the difference between a good security person and an amateur.

This is why behavioral assessment profiling is a good idea, while the Terrorist Information and Prevention System (TIPS) isn't. This is why training truckers to look out for suspicious things on the highways is a good idea, while a vague list of things to watch out for isn't. It's why an Israeli driver recognized a passenger as a suicide bomber, while an American driver probably wouldn't.

This kind of thing isn't easy to train. (Much has been written about it, though; Malcolm Gladwell's *Blink* discusses this in detail.) You can't learn it from watching a seven-minute video. But the more we focus on this—the more we stop wasting our airport security resources on screeners who confiscate rocks and snow globes, and instead focus them on well-trained screeners walking through the airport looking for hinky—the more secure we will be.

Dual-Use Technologies and the Equities Issue

Originally published in Wired, *1 May 2008*

On April 27, 2007, Estonia was attacked in cyberspace. Following a diplomatic incident with Russia about the relocation of a Soviet World War II memorial, the networks of many Estonian organizations, including the Estonian parliament, banks, ministries, newspapers, and broadcasters, were attacked and—in many cases—shut down. Estonia was quick to blame Russia, which was equally quick to deny any involvement.

It was hyped as the first cyberwar: Russia attacking Estonia in cyberspace. But nearly a year later, evidence that the Russian government was involved in the denial-of-service attacks still hasn't emerged. Though Russian hackers were indisputably the major instigators of the attack, the only individuals positively identified have been young ethnic Russians living inside Estonia, who were pissed off over the statue incident.

You know you've got a problem when you can't tell a hostile attack by another nation from bored kids with an axe to grind.

Separating cyberwar, cyberterrorism, and cybercrime isn't easy; these days you need a scorecard to tell the difference. It's not just that it's hard to trace people in cyberspace, it's that military and civilian attacks—and defenses—look the same.

The traditional term for technology the military shares with civilians is "dual use." Unlike hand grenades and tanks and missile targeting systems, dual-use technologies have both military and civilian applications. Dual-use technologies used to be exceptions; even things you'd expect to be dual use, like radar systems and toilets, were designed differently for the military. But today, almost all information technology is dual use. We both use the same operating systems, the same networking protocols, the same applications, and even the same security software.

And attack technologies are the same. The recent spurt of targeted hacks against U.S. military networks, commonly attributed to China, exploit the same vulnerabilities and use the same techniques as criminal attacks against corporate networks. Internet worms make the jump to classified military networks in less than 24 hours, even if those networks are physically separate. The Navy Cyber Defense Operations Command uses the same tools against the same threats as any large corporation.

Because attackers and defenders use the same IT technology, there is a fundamental tension between cyberattack and cyberdefense. The NSA has referred to this as the "equities issue," and it can be summarized as follows: when a military discovers a vulnerability in a dual-use technology, they can do one of two things. They can alert the manufacturer and fix the vulnerability, thereby protecting both the good guys and the bad guys. Or they can keep quiet about the vulnerability and not tell anyone, thereby leaving the good guys insecure but also leaving the bad guys insecure.

The equities issue has long been hotly debated inside the NSA. Basically, the NSA has two roles: eavesdrop on their stuff, and protect our stuff. When both sides use the same stuff, the agency has to decide whether to exploit vulnerabilities to eavesdrop on their stuff or close the same vulnerabilities to protect our stuff.

In the 1980s and before, the tendency of the NSA was to keep vulnerabilities to themselves. In the 1990s, the tide shifted, and the NSA was starting to open up and help us all improve our security defense. But after the attacks of 9/11, the NSA shifted back to the attack: vulnerabilities were to be hoarded in secret. Slowly, things in the U.S. are shifting back again.

So now we're seeing the NSA help secure Windows Vista and releasing their own version of Linux. The DHS, meanwhile, is funding a project to secure popular open source software packages, and across the Atlantic the U.K.'s GCHQ is finding bugs in PGPDisk and reporting them back to the company. (NSA is rumored to be doing the same thing with BitLocker.)

I'm in favor of this trend, because my security improves for free. Whenever the NSA finds a security problem and gets the vendor to fix it, our security gets better. It's a side-benefit of dual-use technologies.

But I want governments to do more. I want them to use their buying power to improve my security. I want them to offer countrywide contracts for software, both security and non-security, that have explicit security requirements. If these contracts are big enough, companies will work to modify their products to meet those requirements. And again, we all benefit from the security improvements.

The only example of this model I know about is a U.S. government-wide procurement competition for full-disk encryption, but this can certainly be done with firewalls, intrusion detection systems, databases, networking hardware, even operating systems.

When it comes to IT technologies, the equities issue should be a no-brainer. The good uses of our common hardware, software, operating systems, network protocols, and everything else vastly outweigh the bad uses. It's time that the government used its immense knowledge and experience, as well as its buying power, to improve cybersecurity for all of us.

Identity-Theft Disclosure Laws

Originally published in Wired, *20 April 2006*

California was the first state to pass a law requiring companies that keep personal data to disclose when that data is lost or stolen. Since then, many states have followed suit. Now Congress is debating federal legislation that would do the same thing nationwide. *[2008 update: There is still no national legislation.]*

Except that it won't do the same thing: The federal bill has become so watered down that it won't be very effective. I would still be in favor of it—a poor federal law is better than none—if it didn't also pre-empt more-effective state laws, which makes it a net loss.

Identity theft is the fastest-growing area of crime. It's badly named—your identity is the one thing that cannot be stolen—and is better thought of as fraud by impersonation. A criminal collects enough personal information about you to be able to impersonate you to banks, credit card companies, brokerage houses, etc. Posing as you, he steals your money or takes a destructive joyride on your good credit.

Many companies keep large databases of personal data that is useful to these fraudsters. But because the companies don't shoulder the cost of the fraud, they're not economically motivated to secure those databases very well. In fact, if your personal data is stolen from their databases, they would much rather not even tell you: Why deal with the bad publicity?

Disclosure laws force companies to make these security breaches public. This is a good idea for three reasons. One, it is good security practice to notify potential identity theft victims that their personal information has been lost or stolen. Two, statistics on actual data thefts are valuable for research purposes. And three, the potential cost of the notification and the associated bad publicity naturally leads companies to spend more money on protecting personal information—or to refrain from collecting it in the first place.

Think of it as public shaming. Companies will spend money to avoid the PR costs of this shaming, and security will improve. In economic terms, the law reduces the externalities and forces companies to deal with the true costs of these data breaches.

This public shaming needs the cooperation of the press and, unfortunately, there's an attenuation effect going on. The first major breach after California passed its disclosure law—SB1386—was in February 2005, when ChoicePoint sold personal data on 145,000 people to criminals. The event was all over the news, and ChoicePoint was shamed into improving its security.

Then LexisNexis exposed personal data on 300,000 individuals. And Citigroup lost data on 3.9 million individuals. SB1386 worked; the only reason we knew about these security breaches was because of the law. But the breaches came in increasing numbers, and in larger quantities. After a while, it was no longer news. And when the press stopped reporting, the "cost" of these breaches to the companies declined.

Today, the only real cost that remains is the cost of notifying customers and issuing replacement cards. It costs banks about $10 to issue a new card, and that's money they would much rather not have to spend. This is the agenda they brought to the federal bill, cleverly titled the Data Accountability and Trust Act, or DATA.

Lobbyists attacked the legislation in two ways. First, they went after the definition of personal information. Only the exposure of very specific information requires disclosure. For example, the theft of a database that contained people's first *initial*, middle name, last name, Social Security number, bank account number, address, phone number, date of birth, mother's maiden name and password would not have to be disclosed, because "personal information" is defined as "an individual's first and last name in combination with ..." certain other personal data.

Second, lobbyists went after the definition of "breach of security." The latest version of the bill reads: "The term 'breach of security' means the unauthorized acquisition of data in electronic form containing personal information that establishes a reasonable basis to conclude that there is a significant risk of identity theft to the individuals to whom the personal information relates."

Get that? If a company loses a backup tape containing millions of individuals' personal information, it doesn't have to disclose if it believes there is no "significant risk of identity theft." If it leaves a database exposed, and has absolutely no audit logs of who accessed that database, it could claim it has no "reasonable basis" to conclude there is a significant risk. Actually, the company could point to an ID Analytics study that showed the probability of fraud to someone who has been the victim of this kind of data loss to be less than 1 in 1,000—which is not a "significant risk"—and then not disclose the data breach at all.

Even worse, this federal law pre-empts the 23 existing state laws—and others being considered—many of which contain stronger individual protections. So while DATA might look like a law protecting consumers nationwide, it is actually a law protecting companies with large databases *from* state laws protecting consumers.

So in its current form, this legislation would make things worse, not better.

Of course, things are in flux. They're *always* in flux. The language of the bill has changed regularly over the past year, as various committees got their hands on it. There's also another bill, HR3997, which is even worse. And even if something passes, it has to be reconciled with whatever the Senate passes, and then voted on again. So no one really knows what the final language will look like.

But the devil is in the details, and the only way to protect us from lobbyists tinkering with the details is to ensure that the federal bill does not pre-empt any state bills: that the federal law is a minimum, but that states can require more.

That said, disclosure is important, but it's not going to solve identity theft. As I've written previously, the reason theft of personal information is so common is that the data is so valuable. The way to mitigate the risk of fraud due to impersonation is not to make personal information harder to steal, it's to make it harder to use.

Disclosure laws only deal with the economic externality of data brokers protecting your personal information. What we really need are laws prohibiting credit card companies and other financial institutions from granting credit to someone using your name with only a minimum of authentication.

But until that happens, we can at least hope that Congress will refrain from passing bad bills that override good state laws—and helping criminals in the process.

Academic Freedom and Security

Originally published in San Jose Mercury News, *20 September 2004*

Cryptography is the science of secret codes, and it is a primary Internet security tool to fight hackers, cybercrime, and cyberterrorism. CRYPTO is the world's premier cryptography conference. It's held every August in Santa Barbara, California.

This year, 400 people from 30 countries came to listen to dozens of talks. Lu Yi was not one of them. Her paper was accepted at the conference. But because she is a Chinese Ph.D. student in Switzerland, she was not able to get a visa in time to attend the conference.

In the three years since 9/11, the U.S. government has instituted a series of security measures at our borders, all designed to keep terrorists out. One of those measures was to tighten up the rules for foreign visas. Certainly this has hurt the tourism industry in the U.S., but the damage done to academic research is more profound and longer-lasting.

According to a survey by the Association of American Universities, many universities reported a drop of more than 10% in foreign student applications from last year. During the 2003 academic year, student visas were down 9%. Foreign applications to graduate schools were down 32%, according to another study by the Council of Graduate Schools.

There is an increasing trend for academic conferences, meetings and seminars to move outside of the United States simply to avoid visa hassles.

This affects all of high-tech, but ironically it particularly affects the very technologies that are critical in our fight against terrorism.

Also in August, on the other side of the country, the University of Connecticut held the second International Conference on Advanced Technologies for Homeland Security. The attendees came from a variety of disciplines—chemical trace detection, communications compatibility, X-ray scanning, sensors of various types, data mining, HAZMAT clothing, network intrusion detection, bomb diffusion, remote-controlled drones—and illustrate the enormous breadth of scientific know-how that can usefully be applied to counterterrorism.

It's wrong to believe that the U.S. can conduct the research we need alone. At the Connecticut conference, the researchers presenting results included many foreigners studying at U.S. universities. Only 30% of the papers at CRYPTO had only U.S. authors. The most important discovery of the conference, a weakness in a mathematical function that protects the integrity of much of the critical information on the Internet, was made by four researchers from China.

Every time a foreign scientist can't attend a U.S. technology conference, our security suffers. Every time we turn away a qualified technology graduate student, our security suffers. Technology is one of our most potent weapons in the war on terrorism, and we're not fostering the international cooperation and development that is crucial for U.S. security.

Security is always a trade-off, and specific security countermeasures affect everyone, both the bad guys and the good guys. The new U.S. immigration rules may affect the few terrorists trying to enter the United States on visas, but they also affect honest people trying to do the same.

All scientific disciplines are international, and free and open information exchange—both in conferences and in academic programs at universities—will result in the maximum advance in the technologies vital to homeland security. The Soviet Union tried to restrict academic freedom along national lines, and it didn't do the country any good. We should try not to follow in those footsteps.

Sensitive Security Information (SSI)

Originally published in Crypto-Gram, *15 March 2005*

For decades, the U.S. government has had systems in place for dealing with military secrets. Information is classified as either Confidential, Secret, Top Secret, or one of many "compartments" of information above Top Secret. Procedures for dealing with classified information were rigid: classified topics could not be discussed on unencrypted phone lines, classified information could not be processed on insecure computers, classified documents had to be stored in locked safes, and so on. The procedures were extreme because the assumed adversary was highly motivated, well-funded, and technically adept: the Soviet Union.

You might argue with the government's decision to classify this and not that, or the length of time information remained classified, but if you assume the information needed to remain secret, than the procedures made sense.

In 1993, the U.S. government created a new classification of information—Sensitive Security Information. The information under this category, as defined by a D.C. court, was limited to information related to the safety of air passengers. This was greatly expanded in 2002, when Congress deleted two words, "air" and "passengers," and changed "safety" to "security." Currently, there's a lot of information covered under this umbrella.

Again, you might argue with what the government chooses to place under this classification, and whether this classification is more designed to hide the inner workings of government from the public, but that's a separate discussion. You can't discuss the mechanics of a lock without discussing what the lock is supposed to protect, but you can discuss the lock and what it protects without discussing whether protecting it is a good idea. SSI is designed to protect information against a terrorist threat. Assume for a moment that there is information that needs to be protected, and that terrorists are who it needs to be protected from.

The rules for SSI information are much more relaxed than the rules for traditional classified information. Before someone can have access to classified information, he must get a government clearance. Before someone can have access to SSI, he simply must sign an NDA. If someone discloses classified information, he faces criminal penalties. If someone discloses SSI, he faces civil penalties.

SSI can be sent unencrypted in e-mail; a simple password-protected attachment is enough. A person can take SSI home with him, read it on an airplane, and talk about it in public places. People entrusted with SSI information shouldn't disclose it to those unauthorized to know it, but it's really up to the individual to make sure that doesn't happen. It's really more like confidential corporate information than government military secrets.

Of course, SSI information is easier to steal than traditional classified information. That's the security trade-off. The threat is less, so the security countermeasures are less.

The U.S. government really had no choice but to establish this classification level, given the kind of information they needed to work with. for example, the terrorist "watch" list is SSI. If the list falls into the wrong hands, it would be bad for national security. But think about the number of people who need access to the list. Every airline needs a copy, so they can determine if any of their passengers are on the list. That's not just domestic airlines, but foreign airlines as well—including foreign airlines that may not agree with American foreign policy. Police departments, both within this country and abroad, need access to the list. My guess is that more than 10,000 people have access to this list, and there's no possible way to give all them a security clearance. Either the U.S. government relaxes the rules about who can have access to the list, or the list doesn't get used in the way the government wants.

On the other hand, the threat is completely different. Military classification levels and procedures were developed during the Cold War, and reflected the Soviet threat. The terrorist adversary is much more diffuse, much less well-funded, much less technologically advanced. SSI rules really make more sense in dealing with this kind of adversary than the military rules.

I'm impressed with the U.S. government SSI rules. You can always argue about whether a particular piece of information needs to be kept secret, and how classifications like SSI can be used to conduct government in secret. Just about everything that the government keeps secret should not be kept secret, and openness actually improves security in most cases. But if you take secrecy as an assumption, SSI defines a reasonable set of secrecy rules against a new threat.

Fingerprinting Foreigners

Originally published in Newsday, *14 January 2004*

Imagine that you're going on vacation to some exotic country. You get your visa, plan your trip, and take a long flight. How would you feel if, at the border, you were photographed and fingerprinted? How would you feel if your biometrics stayed in that country's computers for years? If your fingerprints could be sent back to your home country? Would you feel welcomed by that country, or would you feel like a criminal?

This week, the U.S. government began doing just that to an expected 23 million visitors to the U.S. The US-VISIT program is designed to capture biometric information at our borders. Only citizens of 27 countries who don't need a visa to enter the U.S., mostly in Europe, are exempt. *[2008 update: Visitors eligible for the Visa Waiver Program are also required to use the US-VISIT program. The only exception is Canada.]* Currently all 115 international airports and 14 seaports are covered, and over the next three years this program will be expanded to cover at least 50 land crossings, and also to screen for-eigners exiting the country.

None of this comes cheaply. The program cost $380 million in 2003 and will cost at least the same in 2004. But that's just the start; the Department of Homeland Security's total cost estimate nears $10 billion.

According to the Bush administration, the measures are designed to com-bat terrorism. As a security expert, it's hard for me to see how. The 9/11 ter-rorists would not have been deterred by this system; many of them entered the country legally on valid passports and visas. We have a 5,500-mile-long border with Canada, and another 2,000-mile-long border with Mexico. Two-to-three-hundred-thousand people enter the country illegally each year from Mexico. Two-to-three-million people enter the country legally each year and overstay their visas. Capturing the biometric information of everyone enter-ing the country doesn't make us safer.

And even if we could completely seal our borders, fingerprinting everyone still wouldn't keep terrorists out. It's not as if we can identify terrorists in advance. The border guards can't say "this fingerprint is safe; it's not in our database" because there is no comprehensive fingerprint database for sus-pected terrorists.

More dangerous is the precedent this program sets. Today, the program only affects foreign visitors with visas. The next logical step is to fingerprint all visitors to the U.S., and then everybody, including U.S. citizens.

Following this train of thought quickly leads to sinister speculation. There's no reason why the program should be restricted to entering and exit-ing the country; why shouldn't every airline flight be "protected"? Perhaps the program can be extended to train rides, bus rides, entering and exiting gov-ernment buildings. Ultimately the government will have a biometric database of every U.S. citizen—face and fingerprints—and will be able to track their movements. Do we want to live in that kind of society?

Retaliation is another worry. Brazil is now fingerprinting Americans who visit that country, and other countries are expected to follow suit. All over the world, totalitarian governments will use our fingerprinting regime to justify fingerprinting Americans who enter their countries. This means that your prints are going to end up on file with every tin-pot dictator from Sierra Leone to Uzbekistan. And Tom Ridge has already pledged to share security informa-tion with other countries.

Security is a trade-off. When deciding whether to implement a security measure, we must balance the costs against the benefits. Large-scale finger-printing is something that doesn't add much to our security against terrorism, costs an enormous amount of money that could be better spent elsewhere. Allocating the funds on compiling, sharing, and enforcing the terrorist watch list would be a far better security investment. As a security consumer, I'm getting swindled.

America's security comes from our freedoms and our liberty. For over two centuries we have maintained a delicate balance between freedom and the opportunity for crime. We deliberately put laws in place that hamper police investigations, because we know we are more secure because of them. We know that laws regulating wiretapping, search and seizure, and interrogation make us all safer, even if they make it harder to convict criminals.

The U.S. system of government has a basic unwritten rule: The government should be granted only limited power, and for limited purposes, because of the certainty that government power will be abused. We've already seen the USA PATRIOT Act powers granted to the government to combat terrorism directed against common crimes. Allowing the government to create the infrastructure to collect biometric information on everyone it can is not a power we should grant the government lightly. It's something we would have expected in former East Germany, Iraq, or the Soviet Union. In all of these countries, greater government control meant less security for citizens, and the results in the U.S. will be no different. It's bad civic hygiene to build an infra-structure that can be used to facilitate a police state.

U.S. Medical Privacy Law Gutted

Originally published in Crypto-Gram, *15 June 2005*

In the U.S., medical privacy is largely governed by a 1996 law called HIPAA. Among many other provisions, HIPAA regulates the privacy and security sur-rounding electronic medical records. HIPAA specifies civil penalties against companies that don't comply with the regulations, as well as criminal penal-ties against individuals and corporations who knowingly steal or misuse patient data.

The civil penalties have long been viewed as irrelevant by the healthcare industry. Now the criminal penalties have been gutted. The Justice Department has ruled that the criminal penalties apply to insurers, doctors, hospitals, and other providers—but not necessarily their employees or outsiders who steal personal health data. This means that if an employee mishandles personal data, he cannot be prosecuted under HIPAA unless his boss told him to do it. And the provider cannot be prosecuted unless it is official organization policy.

This is a complicated issue. Peter Swire worked extensively on this bill as President Clinton's Chief Counselor for Privacy, and I am going to quote him extensively. First, a story about someone who was convicted under the criminal part of this statute.

"In 2004 the U.S. Attorney in Seattle announced that Richard Gibson was being indicted for violating the HIPAA privacy law. Gibson was a phlebotomist a lab assistant in a hospital. While at work he accessed the medical records of a person with a terminal cancer condition. Gibson then got credit cards in the patient's name and ran up over $9,000 in charges, notably for video game purchases. In a statement to the court, the patient said he 'lost a year of life both mentally and physically dealing with the stress' of dealing with collection agencies and other results of Gibson's actions. Gibson signed a plea agreement and was sentenced to 16 months in jail."

According to this Justice Department ruling, Gibson was wrongly convicted. I presume his attorney is working on the matter, and I hope he can be re-tried under our identity theft laws. But because Gibson (or someone else like him) was working in his official capacity, he cannot be prosecuted under HIPAA. And because Gibson (or someone like him) was doing something not authorized by his employer, the hospital cannot be prosecuted under HIPAA.

The healthcare industry has been opposed to HIPAA from the beginning, because it puts constraints on their business in the name of security and privacy. This ruling comes after intense lobbying by the industry at the Department of Heath and Human Services and the Justice Department, and is the result of an HHS request for an opinion.

From Swire's analysis of the Justice Department ruling: "For a law professor who teaches statutory interpretation, the OLC opinion is terribly frustrating to read. The opinion reads like a brief for one side of an argument. Even worse, it reads like a brief that knows it has the losing side but has to come out with a predetermined answer."

I've been to my share of HIPAA security conferences. To the extent that big health is following the HIPAA law—and to a large extent, they're waiting to see how it's enforced—they are doing so because of the criminal penalties. They know that the civil penalties aren't that large, and are a cost of doing business. But the criminal penalties were real. Now that they're gone, the pressure on big health to protect patient privacy is greatly diminished.

Again Swire: "The simplest explanation for the bad OLC opinion is politics. Parts of the health care industry lobbied hard to cancel HIPAA in 2001. When President Bush decided to keep the privacy rule quite possibly based on his sincere personal views the industry efforts shifted direction. Industry pressure has stopped HHS from bringing a single civil case out of the 13,000 complaints. Now, after a U.S. Attorney's office had the initiative to prosecute Mr. Gibson, senior officials in Washington have clamped down on criminal enforcement. The participation of senior political officials in the interpretation of a statute, rather than relying on staff attorneys, makes this political theory even more convincing."

This kind of thing is bigger than the security of the healthcare data of Americans. Our administration is trying to collect more data in its attempt to fight terrorism. Part of that is convincing people—both Americans and foreigners—that this data will be protected. When we gut privacy protections because they might inconvenience business, we're telling the world that privacy isn't one of our core concerns.

If the administration doesn't believe that we need to follow its medical data privacy rules, what makes you think they're following the FISA rules?

3 Airline Travel

Airport Passenger Screening

Originally published in Wired, 23 March 2006

 t seems like every time someone tests airport security, airport security fails. In tests between November 2001 and February 2002, screeners missed 70% of knives, 30% of guns, and 60% of (fake) bombs. And recently, testers were able to smuggle bomb-making parts through airport security in 21 of 21 attempts. It makes you wonder why we're all putting our laptops in a separate bin and taking off our shoes. (Although we should all be glad that Richard Reid wasn't the "underwear bomber.")

The failure to detect bomb-making parts is easier to understand. Break something into small enough parts, and it's going to slip past the screeners pretty easily. The explosive material won't show up on the metal detector, and the associated electronics can look benign when disassembled. This isn't even a new problem. It's widely believed that the Chechen women who blew up the two Russian planes in August 2004 probably smuggled their bombs aboard the planes in pieces.

But guns and knives? That surprises most people.

Airport screeners have a difficult job, primarily because the human brain isn't naturally adapted to the task. We're wired for visual pattern matching, and are great at picking out something we know to look for—for example, a lion in a sea of tall grass.

But we're much less adept at detecting random exceptions in uniform data. Faced with an endless stream of identical objects, the brain quickly concludes that everything is identical and there's no point in paying attention. By the time the exception comes around, the brain simply doesn't notice it. This psychological phenomenon isn't just a problem in airport screening: It's been identified in inspections of all kinds, and is why casinos move their dealers around so often. The tasks are simply mind-numbing.

To make matters worse, the smuggler can try to exploit the system. He can position the weapons in his baggage just so. He can try to disguise them by adding other metal items to distract the screeners. He can disassemble bomb parts so they look nothing like bombs. Against a bored screener, he has the upper hand.

And, as has been pointed out again and again in essays on the ludicrousness of post-9/11 airport security, improvised weapons are a huge problem. A rock, a battery for a laptop, a belt, the extension handle off a wheeled suitcase, fishing line, the bare hands of someone who knows karate...the list goes on and on.

Technology can help. X-ray machines already randomly insert "test" bags into the stream—keeping screeners more alert. Computer-enhanced displays are making it easier for screeners to find contraband items in luggage, and eventually the computers will be able to do most of the work. It makes sense: Computers excel at boring repetitive tasks. They should do the quick sort, and let the screeners deal with the exceptions.

Sure, there'll be a lot of false alarms, and some bad things will still get through. But it's better than the alternative.

And it's likely good enough. Remember the point of passenger screening. We're not trying to catch the clever, organized, well-funded terrorists. We're trying to catch the amateurs and the incompetent. We're trying to catch the unstable. We're trying to catch the copycats. These are all legitimate threats, and we're smart to defend against them. Against the professionals, we're just trying to add enough uncertainty into the system that they'll choose other targets instead.

The terrorists' goals have nothing to do with airplanes; their goals are to cause terror. Blowing up an airplane is just a particular attack designed to achieve that goal. Airplanes deserve some additional security because they have catastrophic failure properties: If there's even a small explosion, everyone on the plane dies. But there's a diminishing return on investments in airplane security. If the terrorists switch targets from airplanes to shopping malls, we haven't really solved the problem.

What that means is that a basic cursory screening is good enough. If I were investing in security, I would fund significant research into computer-assisted screening equipment for both checked and carry-on bags, but wouldn't spend a lot of money on invasive screening procedures and secondary screening. I would much rather have well-trained security personnel wandering around the airport, both in and out of uniform, looking for suspicious actions.

When I travel in Europe, I never have to take my laptop out of its case or my shoes off my feet. Those governments have had far more experience with terrorism than the U.S. government, and they know when passenger screening has reached the point of diminishing returns. (They also implemented checked-baggage security measures decades before the United States did—again recognizing the real threat.)

And if I were investing in security, I would invest in intelligence and investigation. The best time to combat terrorism is before the terrorist tries to get on an airplane. The best countermeasures have value, regardless of the nature of the terrorist plot or the particular terrorist target.

In some ways, if we're relying on airport screeners to prevent terrorism, it's already too late. After all, we can't keep weapons out of prisons. How can we ever hope to keep them out of airports?

No-Fly List

Originally published in Newsday, *25 August 2004*

Imagine a list of suspected terrorists so dangerous that we can't ever let them fly, yet so innocent that we can't arrest them—even under the draconian provisions of the USA PATRIOT Act.

This is the federal government's "No-Fly List." First circulated in the weeks after 9/11 as a counterterrorist tool, its details are shrouded in secrecy. But because the list is filled with inaccuracies and ambiguities, thousands of innocent, law-abiding Americans have been subjected to lengthy interrogations and invasive searches every time they fly, and sometimes forbidden to board airplanes. It also has been a complete failure, and has not been responsible for a single terrorist arrest anywhere.

Instead, the list has snared Asif Iqbal, a Rochester, New York, businessman who shares a name with a suspected terrorist currently in custody in Guantanamo. It's snared a 71-year-old retired English teacher. A man with a top-secret government clearance. A woman whose name is similar to that of an Australian man 20 years younger. Anyone with the name David Nelson is on the list. And recently it snared Senator Ted Kennedy, who had the unfortunate luck to share a name with "T Kennedy," an alias once used by a person someone decided should be on the list.

There is no recourse for those on the list, and their stories quickly take on a Kafkaesque tone. People can be put on the list for any reason; no standards exist. There's no ability to review any evidence against you, or even confirm that you are actually on the list. And for most people, there's no way to get off the list or to "prove" once and for all that they're not whoever the list is really looking for. It took Senator Kennedy three weeks to get his name off the list. People without his political pull have spent years futilely trying to clear their names.

There's something distinctly un-American about a secret government blacklist, with no right of appeal or judicial review. Even worse, there's evidence that it's being used as a political harassment tool: Environmental activists, peace protestors, and anti-free-trade activists have all found themselves on the list.

But security is always a trade-off, and some might make the reasonable argument that these kinds of civil liberty abuses are required if we are to successfully fight terrorism in our country. The problem is that the no-fly list doesn't protect us from terrorism.

It's not just that terrorists are not stupid enough to fly under recognized names. It's that the very problems with the list that make it such an affront to civil liberties also make it less effective as a counterterrorist tool.

Any watch list where it's easy to put names on and difficult to take names off will quickly fill with false positives. These false positives eventually overwhelm any real information on the list, and soon the list does nothing more than flag innocents—which is what we see happening today, and why the list hasn't resulted in any arrests.

A quick search through an Internet phone book shows 3,400 listings for "T Kennedy" in the United States. Since many couples only have one phone book entry, many "T Kennedy's" are unlisted spouses—that translates to about 5,000 people total. Adding "T Kennedy" to the no-fly list is irresponsible, especially since it was known to be an alias.

Even worse, this behavior suggests an easy terrorist tactic: use common American names to refer to co-conspirators in your communications. This will make the list even less effective as a security tool, and more effective as a random harassment tool. There might be 5,000 people named "T Kennedy" in the U.S., but there are 54,000 listings for "J. Brown."

Watch lists can be good security, but they need to be implemented properly. It should be harder than it currently is to add names to the list. It should be possible to add names to the list for short periods of time. It should be easy to take names off the list, and to add qualifiers to the list. There needs to be a legal appeals process for people on the list who want to clear their name. For a watch list to be a part of good security, there needs to be a notion of maintaining the list.

This isn't new, and this isn't hard. The police deal with this problem all the time, and they do it well. We do worse identifying potential terrorists than the police do identifying crime suspects. Imagine if all the police did when having a witness identify a suspect was asking whether the names "sounded about right." No suspect picture book. No line up.

In a country built on the principles of due process, the current no-fly list is an affront to our freedoms and liberties. And it's lousy security to boot.

Trusted Traveler Program

Originally published in The Boston Globe, *24 August 2004*

If you fly out of Logan Airport and don't want to take off your shoes for the security screeners and get your bags opened up, pay attention. The U.S. government is testing its "Trusted Traveler" program, and Logan is the fourth test airport. Currently only American Airlines frequent fliers are eligible, but if all goes well the program will be opened up to more people and more airports.

Participants provide their name, address, phone number, and birth date, a set of fingerprints, and a retinal scan. That information is matched against law enforcement and intelligence databases. If the applicant is not on any terrorist watch list, and is otherwise an upstanding citizen, he gets a card that allows him access to a special security lane. The lane doesn't bypass the metal detector or X-ray machine for carry-on bags, but avoids more intensive secondary screening unless there's an alarm of some kind.

Unfortunately, this program won't make us more secure. Some terrorists will be able to get Trusted Traveler cards, and they'll know in advance that they'll be subjected to less-stringent security.

Since 9/11, airport security has been subjecting people to special screening: sometimes randomly, and sometimes based on profile criteria as analyzed by computer. For example, people who buy one-way tickets, or pay with cash, are more likely to be flagged for this extra screening.

Sometimes the results are bizarre. Screeners have searched children and people in wheelchairs. In 2002, Al Gore was randomly stopped and searched twice in one week. And just last month, Senator Ted Kennedy was flagged—and denied boarding—because the computer decided he was on some no-fly list.

Why waste precious time making Grandma Lillie from Worchester empty her purse, when you can search the carry-on items of Anwar, a twenty-six-year-old who arrived last month from Egypt and is traveling without luggage?

The reason is security. Imagine you're a terrorist plotter with half a dozen potential terrorists at your disposal. They all apply for a card, and three get one. Guess which three are going on the mission? And they'll buy round-trip tickets with credit cards, and have a "normal" amount of luggage with them.

What the Trusted Traveler program does is create two different access paths into the airport: high security and low security. The intent is that only good guys will take the low-security path, and the bad guys will be forced to take the high-security path, but it rarely works out that way. You have to assume that the bad guys will find a way to take the low-security path.

The Trusted Traveler program is based on the dangerous myth that terrorists match a particular profile, and that we can somehow pick terrorists out of a crowd if we only can identify everyone. That's simply not true. Most of the 9/11 terrorists were unknown, and not on any watch list. Timothy McVeigh was an upstanding U.S. citizen before he blew up the Oklahoma City Federal Building. Palestinian suicide bombers in Israel are normal, nondescript people. Intelligence reports indicate that al-Qaeda is recruiting non-Arab terrorists for U.S. operations. Airport security is best served by intelligent guards watching for suspicious behavior, and not dumb guards blindly following the results of a Trusted Traveler program.

Moreover, there's no need for the program. Frequent fliers and first-class travelers already have access to special lanes that bypass long lines at security checkpoints, and the computers never seem to flag them for special screening. And even the long lines aren't very long. I've flown out of Logan repeatedly, and I've never had to wait more than ten minutes at security. The people who could use the card don't need one, and infrequent travelers are unlikely to take the trouble—or pay the fee—to get one.

As counterintuitive as it may seem, it's smarter security to randomly screen people than it is to screen solely based on profile. And it's smarter still to do a little bit of both: random screening and profile-based screening. But to create a low-security path, one that guarantees someone on it less rigorous screening, is to invite the bad guys to use that path.

Screening People with Clearances

Originally published in Wired, *5 October 2006*

Why should we waste time at airport security, screening people with U.S. government security clearances? This perfectly reasonable question was asked recently by Robert Poole, director of transportation studies at The Reason Foundation, as he and I were interviewed by WOSU Radio in Ohio.

Poole argued that people with government security clearances, people who are entrusted with U.S. national security secrets, are trusted enough to be allowed through airport security with only a cursory screening. They've already gone through background checks, he said, and it would be more efficient to concentrate screening resources on everyone else.

To someone not steeped in security, it makes perfect sense. But it's a terrible idea, and understanding why teaches us some important security lessons.

The first lesson is that security is a system. Identifying someone's security clearance is a complicated process. People with clearances don't have special ID cards, and they can't just walk into any secured facility. A clearance is held by a particular organization—usually the organization the person works for—and is transferred by a classified message to other organizations when that person travels on official business.

Airport security checkpoints are not set up to receive these clearance messages, so some other system would have to be developed.

Of course, it makes no sense for the cleared person to have his office send a message to every airport he's visiting, at the time of travel. Far easier is to have a centralized database of people who are cleared. But now you have to build this database. And secure it. And ensure that it's kept up to date.

Or maybe we can create a new type of ID card: one that identifies people with security clearances. But that also requires a backend database and a card that can't be forged. And clearances can be revoked at any time, so there needs to be some way of invalidating cards automatically and remotely.

Whatever you do, you need to implement a new set of security procedures at airport security checkpoints to deal with these people. The procedures need to be good enough that people can't spoof it. Screeners need to be trained. The system needs to be tested.

What starts out as a simple idea—don't waste time searching people with government security clearances—rapidly becomes a complicated security system with all sorts of new vulnerabilities.

The second lesson is that security is a trade-off. We don't have infinite dollars to spend on security. We need to choose where to spend our money, and we're best off if we spend it in ways that give us the most security for our dollar.

Given that very few Americans have security clearances, and that speeding them through security wouldn't make much of a difference to anyone else standing in line, wouldn't it be smarter to spend the money elsewhere? Even if you're just making trade-offs about airport security checkpoints, I would rather take the hundreds of millions of dollars this kind of system could cost and spend it on more security screeners and better training for existing security screeners. We could both speed up the lines and make them more effective.

The third lesson is that security decisions are often based on subjective agenda. My guess is that Poole has a security clearance—he was a member of the Bush–Cheney transition team in 2000—and is annoyed that he is being subjected to the same screening procedures as the other (clearly less trusted) people he is forced to stand in line with. From his perspective, not screening people like him is obvious. But objectively it's not.

This issue is no different than searching airplane pilots, something that regularly elicits howls of laughter among amateur security watchers. What they don't realize is that the issue is not whether we should trust pilots, airplane maintenance technicians, or people with clearances. The issue is whether we should trust people who are dressed as pilots, wear airplane-maintenance-tech IDs, or claim to have clearances.

We have two choices: Either build an infrastructure to verify their claims, or assume that they're false. And with apologies to pilots, maintenance techs, and people with clearances, it's cheaper, easier, and more secure to search you all.

Forge Your Own Boarding Pass

Originally published in Wired, *2 November 2006*

Last week, Christopher Soghoian created a Fake Boarding Pass Generator website, allowing anyone to create a fake Northwest Airlines boarding pass: any name, airport, date, flight. This action got him a visit from the FBI, who later came back, smashed open his front door, and seized his computers and other belongings. It resulted in calls for his arrest—the most visible by Representative Edward Markey (D-Massachusetts)—who has since recanted. And it's gotten him more publicity than he ever dreamed of.

All for demonstrating a known and obvious vulnerability in airport security involving boarding passes and IDs.

This vulnerability is nothing new. There was an article on CSOonline from February 2006. There was an article on Slate from February 2005. Senator Chuck Schumer spoke about it in 2005 as well. I wrote about it in the August 2003 issue of *Crypto-Gram*. It's possible I was the first person to publish it, but I certainly wasn't the first person to think of it.

It's kind of obvious, really. If you can make a fake boarding pass, you can get through airport security with it. Big deal; we know.

You can also use a fake boarding pass to fly on someone else's ticket. The trick is to have two boarding passes: one legitimate, in the name the reservation is under, and another phony one that matches the name on your photo ID. Use the fake boarding pass in your name to get through airport security, and the real ticket in someone else's name to board the plane.

This means that a terrorist on the no-fly list can get on a plane: He buys a ticket in someone else's name, perhaps using a stolen credit card, and uses his own photo ID and a fake ticket to get through airport security. Since the ticket is in an innocent's name, it won't raise a flag on the no-fly list.

You can also use a fake boarding pass instead of your real one if you have the "SSSS" mark and want to avoid secondary screening, or if you don't have a ticket but want to get into the gate area.

Historically, forging a boarding pass was difficult. It required special paper and equipment. But since Alaska Airlines started the trend in 1999, most airlines now allow you to print your boarding pass using your home computer and bring it with you to the airport. This program was temporarily suspended after 9/11, but was quickly brought back because of pressure from the airlines. People who print the boarding passes at home can go directly to airport security, and that means fewer airline agents are required.

Airline websites generate boarding passes as graphics files, which means anyone with a little bit of skill can modify them in a program like Photoshop. All Soghoian's website did was automate the process with a single airline's boarding passes.

Soghoian claims that he wanted to demonstrate the vulnerability. You could argue that he went about it in a stupid way, but I don't think what he did is substantively worse than what I wrote in 2003. Or what Schumer described in 2005. Why is it that the person who demonstrates the vulnerability is vilified while the person who describes it is ignored? Or, even worse, the organization that causes it is ignored? Why are we shooting the messenger instead of discussing the problem?

As I wrote in 2005: "The vulnerability is obvious, but the general concepts are subtle. There are three things to authenticate: the identity of the traveler, the boarding pass and the computer record. Think of them as three points on the triangle. Under the current system, the boarding pass is compared to the traveler's identity document, and then the boarding pass is compared with the computer record. But because the identity document is never compared with the computer record—the third leg of the triangle—it's possible to create two different boarding passes and have no one notice. That's why the attack works."

The way to fix it is equally obvious: Verify the accuracy of the boarding passes at the security checkpoints. If passengers had to scan their boarding passes as they went through screening, the computer could verify that the boarding pass already matched to the photo ID also matched the data in the computer. Close the authentication triangle and the vulnerability disappears.

But before we start spending time and money and Transportation Security Administration agents, let's be honest with ourselves: The photo ID requirement is no more than security theater. Its only security purpose is to check names against the no-fly list, which would still be a joke even if it weren't so easy to circumvent. Identification is not a useful security measure here.

Interestingly enough, while the photo ID requirement is presented as an antiterrorism security measure, it is really an airline-business security measure. It was first implemented after the explosion of TWA Flight 800 over the Atlantic in 1996. The government originally thought a terrorist bomb was responsible, but the explosion was later shown to be an accident.

Unlike every other airplane security measure—including reinforcing cockpit doors, which could have prevented 9/11—the airlines didn't resist this one, because it solved a business problem: the resale of non-refundable tickets. Before the photo ID requirement, these tickets were regularly advertised in classified pages: "Round trip, New York to Los Angeles, 11/21–11/30, male, $100." Since the airlines never checked IDs, anyone of the correct gender could use the ticket. Airlines hated that, and tried repeatedly to shut that market down. In 1996, the airlines were finally able to solve that problem and blame it on the FAA and terrorism.

So business is why we have the photo ID requirement in the first place, and business is why it's so easy to circumvent it. Instead of going after someone who demonstrates an obvious flaw that is already public, let's focus on the organizations that are actually responsible for this security failure and have failed to do anything about it for all these years. Where's the TSA's response to all this?

The problem is real, and the Department of Homeland Security and TSA should either fix the security or scrap the system. What we've got now is the worst security system of all: one that annoys everyone who is innocent while failing to catch the guilty.

4 Privacy and Surveillance

Our Data, Ourselves

Originally published in Wired, *15 May 2008*

In the information age, we all have a data shadow. We leave data everywhere we go. It's not just our bank accounts and stock portfolios, or our itemized bills, listing every credit card purchase and telephone call we make. It's automatic road toll collection systems, supermarket affinity cards, ATMs, and so on.

It's also our lives. Our love letters and friendly chat. Our personal e-mails and SMS messages. Our business plans, strategies, and offhand conversations. Our political leanings and positions. And this is just the data we interact with. We all have shadow selves living in the data banks of hundreds of corporations and information brokers—information about us that is both surprisingly personal and uncannily complete—except for the errors that you can neither see nor correct.

What happens to our data happens to ourselves.

This shadow self doesn't just sit there: It's constantly touched. It's examined and judged. When we apply for a bank loan, it's our data that determines whether or not we get it. When we try to board an airplane, it's our data that determines how thoroughly we get searched—or whether we get to board at all. If the government wants to investigate us, they're more likely to go through our data than they are to search our homes; for a lot of that data, they don't even need a warrant.

Who controls our data controls our lives.

It's true. Whoever controls our data can decide whether we can get a bank loan, on an airplane, or into a country. Or what sort of discount we get from a merchant, or even how we're treated by customer support. A potential employer can, illegally in the U.S., examine our medical data and decide whether or not to offer us a job. The police can mine our data and decide whether or not we're a terrorist risk. If a criminal can get hold of enough of our data, he can open credit cards in our names, siphon money out of our investment accounts, even sell our property. Identity theft is the ultimate proof that control of our data means control of our life.

We need to take back our data.

Our data is a part of us. It's intimate and personal, and we have basic rights to it. It should be protected from unwanted touch.

We need a comprehensive data privacy law. This law should protect all information about us, and not be limited merely to financial or health information. It should limit others' ability to buy and sell our information without our knowledge and consent. It should allow us to see information about us held by others, and correct any inaccuracies we find. It should prevent the government from going after our information without judicial oversight. It should enforce data deletion, and limit data collection, where necessary. And we need more than token penalties for deliberate violations.

This is a tall order, and it will take years for us to get there. It's easy to do nothing and let the market take over. But as we see with things like grocery store club cards and click-through privacy policies on websites, most people either don't realize the extent their privacy is being violated or don't have any real choice. And businesses, of course, are more than happy to collect, buy, and sell our most intimate information. But the long-term effects of this on society are toxic; we give up control of ourselves.

The Value of Privacy

Originally published in Wired, *18 May 2006*

Last month, revelation of yet another NSA surveillance effort against the American people rekindled the privacy debate. Those in favor of these programs have trotted out the same rhetorical question we hear every time privacy advocates oppose ID checks, video cameras, massive databases, data mining, and other wholesale surveillance measures: "If you aren't doing anything wrong, what do you have to hide?"

Some clever answers: "If I'm not doing anything wrong, then you have no cause to watch me." "Because the government gets to define what's wrong, and they keep changing the definition." "Because you might do something wrong with my information." My problem with quips like these—as right as they are—is that they accept the premise that privacy is about hiding a wrong. It's not. Privacy is an inherent human right, and a requirement for maintaining the human condition with dignity and respect.

Two proverbs say it best: "*Quis custodiet ipsos custodes?*" ("Who watches the watchers?") and "Absolute power corrupts absolutely."

Cardinal Richelieu understood the value of surveillance when he famously said, "If one would give me six lines written by the hand of the most honest man, I would find something in them to have him hanged." Watch someone long enough, and you'll find something to arrest—or just blackmail—him with. Privacy is important because without it, surveillance information will be abused: to peep, to sell to marketers, and to spy on political enemies—whoever they happen to be at the time.

Privacy protects us from abuses by those in power, even if we're doing nothing wrong at the time of surveillance.

We do nothing wrong when we make love or go to the bathroom. We are not deliberately hiding anything when we seek out private places for reflection or conversation. We keep private journals, sing in the privacy of the shower, and write letters to secret lovers and then burn the letters. Privacy is a basic human need.

A future in which privacy would face constant assault was so alien to the framers of the Constitution that it never occurred to them to call out privacy as an explicit right. Privacy was inherent to the nobility of their being and their cause. Of course being watched in your own home was unreasonable. Watching at all was an act so unseemly as to be inconceivable among gentlemen in their day. You watched convicted criminals, not free citizens. You ruled your own home. It's intrinsic to the concept of liberty.

For if we are observed in all matters, we are constantly under threat of correction, judgment, criticism, even plagiarism of our own uniqueness. We become children, fettered under watchful eyes, constantly fearful that—either now or in the uncertain future—patterns we leave behind will be brought back to implicate us, by whatever authority has now become focused upon our once-private and innocent acts. We lose our individuality, because everything we do is observable and recordable.

How many of us have paused during conversations in the past four-and-a-half years, suddenly aware that we might be eavesdropped on? Probably it was a phone conversation, although maybe it was an e-mail or instant message exchange or a conversation in a public place. Maybe the topic was terrorism, or politics, or Islam. We stop suddenly, momentarily afraid that our words might be taken out of context, then we laugh at our paranoia and go on. But our demeanor has changed, and our words are subtly altered.

This is the loss of freedom we face when our privacy is taken from us. This was life in the former East Germany and life in Saddam Hussein's Iraq. And it's our future as we allow an ever-intrusive eye into our personal, private lives.

Too many wrongly characterize the debate as "security versus privacy." The real choice is liberty versus control. Tyranny, whether it arises under threat of foreign physical attack or under constant domestic authoritative scrutiny, is still tyranny. Liberty requires security without intrusion, security plus privacy. Widespread police surveillance is the very definition of a police state. And that's why we should champion privacy even when we have nothing to hide.

The Future of Privacy

Originally published in Minneapolis Star Tribune, *5 March 2006*

Over the past 20 years, there's been a sea change in the battle for personal privacy.

The pervasiveness of computers has resulted in the almost constant surveillance of everyone, with profound implications for our society and our freedoms. Corporations and the police are both using this new trove of surveillance data. We as a society need to understand the technological trends and discuss their implications. If we ignore the problem and leave it to the "market," we'll all find that we have almost no privacy left.

Most people think of surveillance in terms of police procedure: Follow that car, watch that person, listen in on his phone conversations. This kind of surveillance still occurs. But today's surveillance is more like the NSA's model, recently turned against Americans: Eavesdrop on every phone call, listening for certain keywords. It's still surveillance, but it's wholesale surveillance.

Wholesale surveillance is a whole new world. It's not "follow that car," it's "follow every car." The NSA can eavesdrop on every phone call, looking for patterns of communication or keywords that might indicate a conversation between terrorists. Many airports collect the license plates of every car in their parking lots, and can use that database to locate suspicious or abandoned cars. Several cities have stationary or car-mounted license-plate scanners that keep records of every car that passes, and save that data for later analysis.

More and more, we leave a trail of electronic footprints as we go through our daily lives. We used to walk into a bookstore, browse, and buy a book with cash. Now we visit Amazon, and all of our browsing and purchases are recorded. We used to throw a quarter in a toll booth; now E-ZPass records the date and time our car passed through the booth. Data about us are collected when we make a phone call, send an e-mail message, make a purchase with our credit card, or visit a website.

Much has been written about RFID chips and how they can be used to track people. People can also be tracked by their cell phones, their Bluetooth devices, and their WiFi-enabled computers. In some cities, video cameras capture our image hundreds of times a day.

The common thread here is computers. Computers are involved more and more in our transactions, and data are byproducts of these transactions. As computer memory becomes cheaper, more and more of these electronic footprints are being saved. And as processing becomes cheaper, more and more of it is being cross-indexed and correlated, and then used for secondary purposes.

Information about us has value. It has value to the police, but it also has value to corporations. The Justice Department wants details of Google searches, so they can look for patterns that might help find child pornographers. Google uses that same data so it can deliver context-sensitive advertising messages. The city of Baltimore uses aerial photography to surveil every house, looking for building permit violations. A national lawn-care company uses the same data to better market its services. The phone company keeps detailed call records for billing purposes; the police use them to catch bad guys.

In the dot-com bust, the customer database was often the only salable asset a company had. Companies like Experian and Acxiom are in the business of buying and reselling this sort of data, and their customers are both corporate and government.

Computers are getting smaller and cheaper every year, and these trends will continue. Here's just one example of the digital footprints we leave:

It would take about 100 megabytes of storage to record everything the fastest typist input to his computer in a year. That's a single flash memory chip today, and one could imagine computer manufacturers offering this as a reliability feature. Recording everything the average user does on the Internet requires more memory: 4 to 8 gigabytes a year. That's a lot, but "record everything" is Gmail's model, and it's probably only a few years before ISPs offer this service.

The typical person uses 500 cell phone minutes a month; that translates to 5 gigabytes a year to save it all. My iPod can store 12 times that data. A "life recorder" you can wear on your lapel that constantly records is still a few generations off: 200 gigabytes/year for audio and 700 gigabytes/year for video. It'll be sold as a security device, so that no one can attack you without being recorded. When that happens, will not wearing a life recorder be used as evidence that someone is up to no good, just as prosecutors today use the fact that someone left his cell phone at home as evidence that he didn't want to be tracked?

In a sense, we're living in a unique time in history. Identification checks are common, but they still require us to whip out our ID. Soon it'll happen automatically, either through an RFID chip in our wallet or face-recognition from cameras. And those cameras, now visible, will shrink to the point where we won't even see them.

We're never going to stop the march of technology, but we can enact legislation to protect our privacy: comprehensive laws regulating what can be done with personal information about us, and more privacy protection from the police. Today, personal information about you is not yours; it's owned by the collector. There are laws protecting specific pieces of personal data—videotape rental records, health care information—but nothing like the broad privacy protection laws you find in European countries. That's really the only solution; leaving the market to sort this out will result in even more invasive wholesale surveillance.

Most of us are happy to give out personal information in exchange for specific services. What we object to is the surreptitious collection of personal information, and the secondary use of information once it's collected: the buying and selling of our information behind our back.

In some ways, this tidal wave of data is the pollution problem of the information age. All information processes produce it. If we ignore the problem, it will stay around forever. And the only way to successfully deal with it is to pass laws regulating its generation, use, and eventual disposal.

Privacy and Power

Originally published in Wired, *6 March 2008*

When I write and speak about privacy, I am regularly confronted with the mutual disclosure argument. Explained in books like David Brin's *The Transparent Society*, the argument goes something like this: In a world of ubiquitous surveillance, you'll know all about me, but I will also know all about you. The government will be watching us, but we'll also be watching the government. This is different than before, but it's not automatically worse. And because I know your secrets, you can't use my secrets as a weapon against me.

This might not be everybody's idea of utopia—and it certainly doesn't address the inherent value of privacy—but this theory has a glossy appeal, and could easily be mistaken for a way out of the problem of technology's continuing erosion of privacy. Except it doesn't work, because it ignores the crucial dissimilarity of power.

You cannot evaluate the value of privacy and disclosure unless you account for the relative power levels of the discloser and the disclosee.

If I disclose information to you, your power with respect to me increases. One way to address this power imbalance is for you to similarly disclose information to me. We both have less privacy, but the balance of power is maintained. But this mechanism fails utterly if you and I have different power levels to begin with.

An example will make this clearer. You're stopped by a police officer, who demands to see identification. Divulging your identity will give the officer enormous power over you: He or she can search police databases using the information on your ID; he or she can create a police record attached to your name; he or she can put you on this or that secret terrorist watch list. Asking to see the officer's ID in return gives you no comparable power over him or her. The power imbalance is too great, and mutual disclosure does not make it OK.

You can think of your existing power as the exponent in an equation that determines the value, to you, of more information. The more power you have, the more additional power you derive from the new data.

Another example: When your doctor says "Take off your clothes," it makes no sense for you to say, "You first, doc." The two of you are not engaging in an interaction of equals.

This is the principle that should guide decision-makers when they consider installing surveillance cameras or launching data-mining programs. It's not enough to open the efforts to public scrutiny. All aspects of government work best when the relative power between the governors and the governed remains as small as possible—when liberty is high and control is low. Forced openness in government reduces the relative power differential between the two, and is generally good. Forced openness in laypeople increases the relative power, and is generally bad.

Seventeen-year-old Erik Crespo was arrested in 2005 in connection with a shooting in a New York City elevator. There's no question that he committed the shooting; it was captured on surveillance-camera videotape. But he claimed that while being interrogated, Detective Christopher Perino tried to talk him out of getting a lawyer, and told him that he had to sign a confession before he could see a judge.

Perino denied, under oath, that he ever questioned Crespo. But Crespo had received an MP3 player as a Christmas gift, and surreptitiously recorded the questioning. The defense brought a transcript and CD into evidence. Shortly thereafter, the prosecution offered Crespo a better deal than originally proffered (seven years rather than 15). Crespo took the deal, and Perino was separately indicted on charges of perjury.

Without that recording, it was the detective's word against Crespo's. And who would believe a murder suspect over a New York City detective? That power imbalance was reduced only because Crespo was smart enough to press the "record" button on his MP3 player. Why aren't all interrogations recorded? Why don't defendants have the right to those recordings, just as they have the right to an attorney? Police routinely record traffic stops from their squad cars for their own protection; that video record shouldn't stop once the suspect is no longer a threat.

Cameras make sense when trained on police, and in offices where lawmakers meet with lobbyists, and wherever government officials wield power over the people. Open-government laws, giving the public access to government records and meetings of governmental bodies, also make sense. These all foster liberty.

Ubiquitous surveillance programs that affect everyone without probable cause or warrant, like the NSA's warrantless eavesdropping programs or various proposals to monitor everything on the Internet, foster control. And no one is safer in a political system of control.

Security vs. Privacy

Originally published in Wired, *24 January 2008*

If there's a debate that sums up post-9/11 politics, it's security versus privacy. Which is more important? How much privacy are you willing to give up for security? Can we even afford privacy in this age of insecurity? Security versus privacy: It's the battle of the century, or at least its first decade.

In a January 21 *New Yorker* article, Director of National Intelligence Michael McConnell discusses a proposed plan to monitor all—that's right, *all*—Internet communications for security purposes, an idea so extreme that the word "Orwellian" feels too mild.

The article contains this passage: "In order for cyberspace to be policed, Internet activity will have to be closely monitored. Ed Giorgio, who is working with McConnell on the plan, said that would mean giving the government the authority to examine the content of any e-mail, file transfer or Web search. 'Google has records that could help in a cyber-investigation,' he said. Giorgio warned me, 'We have a saying in this business: "Privacy and security are a zero-sum game."'"

I'm sure they have that saying in their business. And it's precisely why, when people in their business are in charge of government, it becomes a police state. If privacy and security really were a zero-sum game, we would have seen mass immigration into the former East Germany and modern-day China. While it's true that police states like those have less street crime, no one argues that their citizens are fundamentally more secure.

We've been told we have to trade off security and privacy so often—in debates on security versus privacy, writing contests, polls, reasoned essays and political rhetoric—that most of us don't even question the fundamental dichotomy.

But it's a false one.

Security and privacy are not opposite ends of a seesaw; you don't have to accept less of one to get more of the other. Think of a door lock, a burglar alarm, and a tall fence. Think of guns, anti-counterfeiting measures on currency and that dumb liquid ban at airports. Security affects privacy only when it's based on identity, and there are limitations to that sort of approach.

Since 9/11, approximately three things have potentially improved airline security: reinforcing the cockpit doors, passengers realizing they have to fight back, and—possibly—sky marshals. Everything else—all the security measures that affect privacy—is just security theater and a waste of effort.

By the same token, many of the anti-privacy "security" measures we're seeing—national ID cards, warrantless eavesdropping, massive data mining, and so on—do little to improve, and in some cases harm, security. And government claims of their success are either wrong, or against fake threats.

The debate isn't security versus privacy. It's liberty versus control.

You can see it in comments by government officials: "Privacy no longer can mean anonymity," says Donald Kerr, principal deputy director of national intelligence. "Instead, it should mean that government and businesses properly safeguard people's private communications and financial information." Did you catch that? You're expected to give up control of your privacy to others, who—presumably—get to decide how much of it you deserve. That's what loss of liberty looks like.

It should be no surprise that people choose security over privacy: 51% to 29% in a recent poll. Even if you don't subscribe to Maslow's hierarchy of needs, it's obvious that security is more important. Security is vital to survival, not just of people but of every living thing. Privacy is unique to humans, but it's a social need. It's vital to personal dignity, to family life, to society—to what makes us uniquely human—but not to survival.

If you set up the false dichotomy, of course people will choose security over privacy—especially if you scare them first. But it's still a false dichotomy. There is no security without privacy. And liberty requires both security and privacy. The famous quote attributed to Benjamin Franklin reads: "Those who would give up essential liberty to purchase a little temporary safety, deserve neither liberty nor safety." It's also true that those who would give up privacy for security are likely to end up with neither.

Is Big Brother a Big Deal?

Originally published in Information Security, *May 2007*

Big Brother isn't what he used to be. George Orwell extrapolated his totalitarian state from the 1940s. Today's information society looks nothing like Orwell's world, and watching and intimidating a population today isn't anything like what Winston Smith experienced.

Data collection in *1984* was deliberate; today's is inadvertent. In the information society, we generate data naturally. In Orwell's world, people were naturally anonymous; today, we leave digital footprints everywhere.

1984's police state was centralized; today's is decentralized. Your phone company knows who you talk to, your credit card company knows where you shop, and Netflix knows what you watch. Your ISP can read your email, your cell phone can track your movements, and your supermarket can monitor your purchasing patterns. There's no single government entity bringing this together, but there doesn't have to be. As Neal Stephenson said, the threat is no longer Big Brother, but instead thousands of Little Brothers.

1984's Big Brother was run by the state; today's Big Brother is market driven. Data brokers like ChoicePoint and credit bureaus like Experian aren't trying to build a police state; they're just trying to turn a profit. Of course these companies will take advantage of a national ID; they'd be stupid not to. And the correlations, data mining and precise categorizing they can do is why the U.S. government buys commercial data from them.

1984-style police states required lots of people. East Germany employed one informant for every 66 citizens. Today, there's no reason to have anyone watch anyone else; computers can do the work of people.

1984-style police states were expensive. Today, data storage is constantly getting cheaper. If some data is too expensive to save today, it'll be affordable in a few years.

And finally, the police state of *1984* was deliberately constructed, while today's is naturally emergent. There's no reason to postulate a malicious police force and a government trying to subvert our freedoms. Computerized processes naturally throw off personalized data; companies save it for marketing purposes, and even the most well-intentioned law-enforcement agency will make use of it.

Of course, Orwell's Big Brother had a ruthless efficiency that's hard to imagine in a government today. But that completely misses the point. A sloppy and inefficient police state is no reason to cheer; watch the movie *Brazil* and see how scary it can be. You can also see hints of what it might look like in our completely dysfunctional "no-fly" list and useless projects to secretly categorize people according to potential terrorist risk. Police states are inherently inefficient. There's no reason to assume today's will be any more effective.

The fear isn't an Orwellian government deliberately creating the ultimate totalitarian state, although with the U.S.'s programs of phone-record surveillance, illegal wiretapping, massive data mining, a national ID card no one wants, and USA PATRIOT Act abuses, one can make that case. It's that we're doing it ourselves, as a natural byproduct of the information society. We're building the computer infrastructure that makes it easy for governments, corporations, criminal organizations, and even teenage hackers to record everything we do, and—yes—even change our votes. And we will continue to do so unless we pass laws regulating the creation, use, protection, resale, and disposal of personal data. It's precisely the attitude that trivializes the problem that creates it.

How to Fight

Originally published in Crypto-Gram, *15 July 2003*

I landed in Los Angeles at 11:30 PM, and it took me another hour to get to my hotel. The city was booked, and I had been lucky to get a reservation where I did. When I checked in, the clerk insisted on making a photocopy of my driver's license. I tried fighting, but it was no use. I needed the hotel room. There was nowhere else I could go. The night clerk didn't really care if he rented the room to me or not. He had rules to follow, and he was going to follow them.

My wife needed a prescription filled. Her doctor called it in to a local pharmacy, and when she went to pick it up the pharmacist refused to fill it unless she disclosed her personal information for his database. The pharmacist even showed my wife the rule book. She found the part where it said that "a reasonable effort must be made by the pharmacy to obtain, record, and maintain at least the following information," and the part where it said: "If a patient does not want a patient profile established, the patient shall state it in writing to the pharmacist. The pharmacist shall not then be required to prepare a profile as otherwise would be required by this part." Despite this, the pharmacist refused. My wife was stuck. She needed the prescription filled. She didn't want to wait the few hours for her doctor to phone the prescription in somewhere else. The pharmacist didn't care; he wasn't going to budge.

I had to travel to Japan last year, and found a company that rented local cell phones to travelers. The form required either a Social Security number or a passport number. When I asked the clerk why, he said the absence of either sent up red flags. I asked how he could tell a real-looking fake number from an actual number. He said that if I didn't care to provide the number as requested, I could rent my cell phone elsewhere, and hung up on me. I went through another company to rent, but it turned out that they contracted through this same company, and the man declined to deal with me, even at a remove. I eventually got the cell phone by going back to the first company and giving a different name (my wife's), a different credit card, and a made-up passport number. Honor satisfied all around, I guess.

It's stupid security season. If you've flown on an airplane, entered a government building, or done any one of dozens of other things, you've encountered security systems that are invasive, counterproductive, egregious, or just plain annoying. You've met people—guards, officials, minimum-wage workers—who blindly force you to follow the most inane security rules imaginable.

Is there anything you can do?

In the end, all security is a negotiation among affected players: governments, industries, companies, organizations, individuals, etc. The players get to decide what security they want, and what they're willing to trade off in order to get it. But it sometimes seems that we as individuals are not part of that negotiation. Security is more something that is done to us.

Our security largely depends on the actions of others and the environment we're in. For example, the tamper resistance of food packaging depends more on government packaging regulations than on our purchasing choices. The security of a letter mailed to a friend depends more on the ethics of the workers who handle it than on the brand of envelope we choose to use. How safe an airplane is from being blown up has little to do with our actions at the airport and while on the plane. (Shoe-bomber Richard Reid provided the rare exception to this.) The security of the money in our bank accounts, the crime rate in our neighborhoods, and the honesty and integrity of our police departments are out of our direct control. We simply don't have enough power in the negotiations to make a difference.

I had no leverage when trying to check in without giving up a photocopy of my driver's license. My wife had no leverage when she tried to fill her prescription without divulging a bunch of optional personal information. The only reason I had leverage renting a phone in Japan was because I deliberately sneaked around the system. If I try to protest airline security, I'm definitely going to miss my flight, and I might get myself arrested. There's no parity, because those who implement the security have no interest in changing it and no power to do so. They're not the ones who control the security system; it's best to think of them as nearly mindless robots. (The security system relies on them behaving this way, replacing the flexibility and adaptability of human judgment with a three-ring binder of "best practices" and procedures.)

It would be different if the pharmacist were the owner of the pharmacy, or if the person behind the registration desk owned the hotel. Or even if the policeman were a neighborhood beat cop. In those cases, there's more parity. I can negotiate my security, and he can decide whether or not to modify the rules for me. But modern society is more often faceless corporations and mindless governments. It's implemented by people and machines that have enormous power, but only power to implement what they're told to implement. And they have no real interest in negotiating. They don't need to. They don't care.

But there's a paradox. We're not only individuals; we're also consumers, citizens, taxpayers, voters, and—if things get bad enough—protestors and sometimes even angry mobs. Only in the aggregate do we have power, and the more we organize, the more power we have.

Even an airline president, while making his way through airport security, has no power to negotiate the level of security he'll receive and the trade-offs he's willing to make. In an airport and on an airplane, we're all nothing more than passengers: an asset to be protected from a potential attacker. The only way to change security is to step outside the system and negotiate with the people in charge. It's only outside the system that each of us has power: sometimes as an asset owner, but more often as another player. And it is outside the system that we will do our best negotiating.

Outside the system we have power, and outside the system we can negotiate with the people who have power over the security system we want to change. After my hotel stay, I wrote to the hotel management and told them that I was never staying there again. (Unfortunately, I am collecting an ever-longer list of hotels I will never stay in again.) My wife has filed a complaint against that pharmacist with the Minnesota Board of Pharmacy. John Gilmore has gone further: He hasn't flown since 9/11, and is suing the government for the constitutional right to fly within the U.S. without showing a photo ID. *[2008 update: He lost the suit; the district court dismissed the case, and appeal was denied.]*

Three points about fighting back. First, one-on-one negotiations—customer and pharmacy owner, for example—can be effective, but they also allow all kinds of undesirable factors like class and race to creep in. It's unfortunate but true that I'm a lot more likely to engage in a successful negotiation with a policeman than a black person is. For this reason, more stylized complaints or protests are often more effective than one-on-one negotiations.

Second, naming and shaming doesn't work. Just as it doesn't make sense to negotiate with a clerk, it doesn't make sense to insult him. Instead say: "I know you didn't make the rule, but if the people who did ever ask you how it's going, tell them the customers think the rule is stupid and insulting and ineffective." While it's very hard to change one institution's mind when it is in the middle of a fight, it is possible to affect the greater debate. Other companies are making the same security decisions; they need to know that it's not working.

Third, don't forget the political process. Elections matter; political pressure by elected officials on corporations and government agencies has a real impact. One of the most effective forms of protest is to vote for candidates who share your ideals.

The more we band together, the more power we have. A large-scale boycott of businesses that demand photo IDs would bring about a change. (Conference organizers have more leverage with hotels than individuals. The USENIX conferences won't use hotels that demand ID from guests, for example.) A large group of single-issue voters supporting candidates who worked against stupid security would make a difference.

Sadly, I believe things will get much worse before they get better. Many people seem not to be bothered by stupid security; it even makes some feel safer. In the U.S., people are now used to showing their ID everywhere; it's the new security reality post-9/11. They're used to intrusive security, and they believe those who say that it's necessary.

It's important that we pick our battles. My guess is that most of the effort fighting stupid security is wasted. No hotel has changed its practice because of my strongly worded letters or loss of business. Gilmore's suit will, unfortunately, probably lose in court. My wife will probably make that pharmacist's life miserable for a while, but the practice will probably continue at that chain pharmacy. If I need a cell phone in Japan again, I'll just give a fake passport number right away without trying to fight the policy. Fighting might brand you as a troublemaker, which might lead to more trouble.

Still, we can make a difference. Gilmore's suit is generating all sorts of press, and raising public awareness. The Boycott Delta campaign had a real impact: Passenger profiling is being revised because of public complaints. And due to public outrage, Poindexter's Terrorism (Total) Information Awareness program, while not out of business, is looking shaky.

When you see counterproductive, invasive, or just plain stupid security, don't let it slip by. Write the letter. Create a website. File a FOIA request. Make some noise. You don't have to join anything; noise need not be more than individuals standing up for themselves.

You don't win every time. But you do win sometimes.

Toward Universal Surveillance

Originally published in CNet, 30 January 2004

Last month, the Supreme Court let stand the Justice Department's right to secretly arrest non-citizen residents. Combined with the government's power to designate foreign prisoners of war as "enemy combatants" in order to ignore international treaties regulating their incarceration, and their power to indefinitely detain U.S. citizens without charge or access to an attorney, the United States is looking more and more like a police state.

Since 9/11, the Justice Department has asked for, and largely received, additional powers that allow it to perform an unprecedented amount of surveillance of American citizens and visitors. The USA PATRIOT Act, passed in haste after 9/11, started the ball rolling. In December, a provision slipped into an appropriations bill allowing the FBI to obtain personal financial information from banks, insurance companies, travel agencies, real estate agents, stockbrokers, the U.S. Postal Service, jewelry stores, casinos, and car dealerships without a warrant—because they're all construed as financial institutions. Starting this year, the U.S. government is photographing and fingerprinting foreign visitors into this country from all but 27 other countries. *[2008 update: Except for Canadians, everyone is photographed and fingerprinted.]*

The litany continues. CAPPS-II, the government's vast computerized system for probing the backgrounds of all passengers boarding flights, will be fielded this year. Total Information Awareness, a program that would link diverse databases and allow the FBI to collate information on all Americans, was halted at the federal level after a huge public outcry, but is continuing at a state level with federal funding. Over New Year's, the FBI collected the names of 260,000 people staying at Las Vegas hotels. More and more, at every level of society, the "Big Brother is Watching You" style of total surveillance is slowly becoming a reality.

Security is a trade-off. It makes no sense to ask whether a particular security system is effective or not—otherwise you'd all be wearing bulletproof vests and staying immured in your home. The proper question to ask is whether the trade-off is worth it. Is the level of security gained worth the costs, whether in money, in liberties, in privacy, or in convenience?

This is a personal decision, and one greatly influenced by the situation. For most of us, bulletproof vests are not worth the cost and inconvenience. For some of us, home burglar alarm systems are. And most of us lock our doors at night.

Terrorism is no different. We need to weigh each security countermeasure. Is the additional security against the risks worth the costs? Are there smarter things we can be spending our money on? How does the risk of terrorism compare with the risks in other aspects of our lives: automobile accidents, domestic violence, industrial pollution, and so on? Are there costs that are just too expensive for us to bear?

Unfortunately, it's rare to hear this level of informed debate. Few people remind us how minor the terrorist threat really is. Rarely do we discuss how little identification has to do with security, and how broad surveillance of everyone doesn't really prevent terrorism. And where's the debate about what's more important: the freedoms and liberties that have made America great or some temporary security?

Instead, the DOJ (fueled by a strong police mentality inside the Administration) is directing our nation's political changes in response to 9/11. And it's making trade-offs from its own subjective perspective: trade-offs that benefit it even if they are to the detriment of others.

From the point of view of the DOJ, judicial oversight is unnecessary and unwarranted; doing away with it is a better trade-off. They think collecting information on everyone is a good idea, because they are less concerned with the loss of privacy and liberty. Expensive surveillance and data mining systems are a good trade-off for them because more budget means even more power. And from their perspective, secrecy is better than openness; if the police are absolutely trustworthy, then there's nothing to be gained from a public process.

If you put the police in charge of security, the trade-offs they make result in measures that resemble a police state.

This is wrong. The trade-offs are larger than the FBI or the DOJ. Just as a company would never put a single department in charge of its own budget, someone above the narrow perspective of the DOJ needs to be balancing the country's needs and making decisions about these security trade-offs.

The laws limiting police power were put in place to protect us from police abuse. Privacy protects us from threats by government, corporations, and individuals. And the greatest strength of our nation comes from our freedoms, our openness, our liberties, and our system of justice. Ben Franklin is credited as saying: "Those who would give up essential liberty for temporary safety deserve neither liberty nor safety." Since 9/11 Americans have squandered an enormous amount of liberty, and we didn't even get any temporary safety in return.

Kafka and the Digital Person

Originally published in Crypto-Gram, *15 December 2004*

Last week I stayed at the St. Regis hotel in Washington, DC. It was my first visit, and the management gave me a questionnaire, asking me things like my birthday, my spouse's name and birthday, my anniversary, and my favorite fruits, drinks, and sweets. The purpose was clear; the hotel wanted to be able to offer me a more personalized service the next time I visited. And it was a purpose I agreed with; I wanted more personalized service. But I was very uneasy about filling out the form.

It wasn't that the information was particularly private. I make no secret of my birthday, or anniversary, or food preferences. Much of that information is even floating around the Web somewhere. Secrecy wasn't the issue.

The issue was control. In the United States, information about a person is owned by the person who collects it, not by the person it is about. There are specific exceptions in the law, but they're few and far between. There are no broad data protection laws, as you find in the European Union. There are no Privacy Commissioners, as you find in Canada. Privacy law in the United States is largely about secrecy: If the information is not secret, there's little you can do to control its dissemination.

As a result, enormous databases exist that are filled with personal information. These databases are owned by marketing firms, credit bureaus, and the government. Amazon knows what books we buy. Our supermarket knows what foods we eat. Credit card companies know quite a lot about our purchasing habits. Credit bureaus know about our financial history, and what they don't know is contained in bank records. Health insurance records contain details about our health and well-being. Government records contain our Social Security numbers, birthdates, addresses, mother's maiden names, and a host of other things. Many drivers license records contain digital pictures.

All of this data is being combined, indexed, and correlated. And it's being used for all sorts of things. Targeted marketing campaigns are just the tip of the iceberg. This information is used by potential employers to judge our suitability as employees, by potential landlords to determine our suitability as renters, and by the government to determine our likelihood of being a terrorist.

Some stores are beginning to use our data to determine whether we are desirable customers or not. If customers take advantage of too many discount offers or make too many returns, they may be profiled as "bad" customers and be treated differently from the "good" customers.

And with alarming frequency, our data is being abused by identity thieves. The businesses that gather our data don't care much about keeping it secure. So identity theft is a problem where those who suffer from it—the individuals—are not in a position to improve security, and those who are in a position to improve security don't suffer from the problem.

The issue here is not about secrecy, it's about control. The issue is that both government and commercial organizations are building "digital dossiers" about us, and that these dossiers are being used to judge and categorize us through some secret process.

A new book by George Washington University Law Professor Daniel Solove examines the problem of the growing accumulation of personal information in enormous databases. The book is called *The Digital Person: Technology and Privacy in the Information Age*, and it is a fascinating read.

Solove's book explores this problem from a legal perspective, explaining what the problem is, how current U.S. law fails to deal with it, and what we should do to protect privacy today. It's an unusually perceptive discussion of one of the most vexing problems of the digital age—our loss of control over our personal information. It's a fascinating journey into the almost surreal ways personal information is hoarded, used, and abused in the digital age.

Solove argues that our common conceptualization of the privacy problem is Big Brother—some faceless organization knowing our most intimate secrets—is only one facet of the issue. A better metaphor can be found in Franz Kafka's *The Trial*. In the book, a vast faceless bureaucracy constructs a vast dossier about a person, who can't find out what information exists about him in the dossier, why the information has been gathered, or what it will be used for. Privacy is not about intimate secrets; it's about who has control of the millions of pieces of personal data that we leave like droppings as we go through our daily life. And until the U.S. legal system recognizes this fact, Americans will continue to live in an world where they have little control over their digital person.

In the end, I didn't complete the questionnaire from the St. Regis Hotel. While I was fine with the St. Regis in Washington DC having that information in order to make my subsequent stays a little more personal, and was probably fine with that information being shared among other St. Regis hotels, I wasn't comfortable with the St. Regis doing whatever they wanted with that information. I wasn't comfortable with them selling the information to a marketing database. I wasn't comfortable with anyone being able to buy that information. I wasn't comfortable with that information ending up in a database of my habits, my preferences, my proclivities. It wasn't the primary use of that information that bothered me, it was the secondary uses.

Solove has done much more thinking about this issue than I have. His book provides a clear account of the social problems involving information privacy, and haunting predictions of current U.S. legal policies. Even more importantly, the legal solutions he provides are compelling and worth serious consideration. I recommend his book highly.

CCTV Cameras

Originally published in The Guardian, *26 June 2008*

Pervasive security cameras don't substantially reduce crime. There are exceptions, of course, and that's what gets the press. Most famously, CCTV cameras helped catch James Bulger's murderers in 1993. And earlier this year, they helped convict Steve Wright of murdering five women in the Ipswich, England area. But these are the well-publicized exceptions. Overall, CCTV cameras aren't very effective.

This fact has been demonstrated again and again: by a comprehensive study for the Home Office in 2005, by several studies in the U.S., and again with new data announced last month by New Scotland Yard. Cameras actually solve very few crimes, and their deterrent effect is minimal.

Conventional wisdom predicts the opposite. But if that were true, then camera-happy London, with something like 500,000, would be the safest city on the planet. It isn't, of course, because of technological limitations of cameras, organizational limitations of police, and the adaptive abilities of criminals.

To some, it's comforting to imagine vigilant police monitoring every camera, but the truth is very different. Most CCTV footage is never looked at until well after a crime is committed. When it is examined, it's very common for the viewers not to identify suspects. Lighting is bad and images are grainy, and criminals tend not to stare helpfully at the lens. Cameras break far too often. The best camera systems can still be thwarted by sunglasses or hats. Even when they afford quick identification—think of the 2005 London transport bombers and the 9/11 terrorists—police are often able to identify suspects without the cameras. Cameras afford a false sense of security, encouraging laziness when we need police to be vigilant.

The solution isn't for police to watch the cameras. Unlike an officer walking the street, cameras only look in particular directions at particular locations. Criminals know this, and can easily adapt by moving their crimes to someplace not watched by a camera—and there will always be such places. Additionally, while a police officer on the street can respond to a crime in progress, the same officer in front of a CCTV screen can only dispatch another officer to arrive much later. By their very nature, cameras result in underused and misallocated police resources.

Cameras aren't completely ineffective, of course. In certain circumstances, they're effective in reducing crime in enclosed areas with minimal foot traffic. Combined with adequate lighting, they substantially reduce both personal attacks and auto-related crime in car parks. And from some perspectives, simply moving crime around is good enough. If a local Tesco supermarket installs cameras in its store, and a robber targets the store next door as a result, that's money well spent by Tesco. But it doesn't reduce the overall crime rate, so it is a waste of money to the township.

But the question really isn't whether cameras reduce crime; the question is whether they're worth it. And given their cost (£500 million in the past 10 years), their limited effectiveness, the potential for abuse (spying on naked women in their own homes, sharing nude images, selling best-of videos, and even spying on national politicians), and their Orwellian effects on privacy and civil liberties, most of the time they're not. The funds spent on CCTV cameras would be far better spent on hiring experienced police officers.

We live in a unique time in our society: the cameras are everywhere, and we can still see them. Ten years ago, cameras were much rarer than they are today. And in ten years, they'll be so small you won't even notice them. Already, companies like L-1 Security Solutions are developing police-state CCTV surveillance technologies like facial recognition for China, technology that will find its way into countries like the U.K. The time to address appropriate limits on this technology is before the cameras fade from notice.

Anonymity and Accountability

Originally published in Wired, *12 January 2006*

In a recent essay, Kevin Kelly warns of the dangers of anonymity. It's OK in small doses, he maintains, but too much of it is a problem: "(I)n every system that I have seen where anonymity becomes common, the system fails. The recent taint in the honor of Wikipedia stems from the extreme ease which anonymous declarations can be put into a very visible public record. Communities infected with anonymity will either collapse, or shift the anonymous to pseudo-anonymous, as in eBay, where you have a traceable identity behind an invented nickname."

Kelly has a point, but it comes out all wrong. Anonymous systems are inherently easier to abuse and harder to secure, as his eBay example illustrates. In an anonymous commerce system—where the buyer does not know who the seller is and vice versa—it's easy for one to cheat the other. This cheating, even if only a minority engaged in it, would quickly erode confidence in the marketplace, and eBay would be out of business. The auction site's solution was brilliant: a feedback system that attached an ongoing "reputation" to those anonymous user names, and made buyers and sellers accountable for their actions.

And that's precisely where Kelly makes his mistake. The problem isn't anonymity; it's accountability. If someone isn't accountable, then knowing his name doesn't help. If you have someone who is completely anonymous, yet just as completely accountable, then—heck, just call him Fred.

History is filled with bandits and pirates who amass reputations without anyone knowing their real names.

EBay's feedback system doesn't work because there's a traceable identity behind that anonymous nickname. EBay's feedback system works because each anonymous nickname comes with a record of previous transactions attached, and if someone cheats someone else then everybody knows it.

Similarly, Wikipedia's veracity problems are not a result of anonymous authors adding fabrications to entries. They're an inherent property of an information system with distributed accountability. People think of Wikipedia as an encyclopedia, but it's not. We all trust Britannica entries to be correct because we know the reputation of that company and, by extension, its editors and writers. On the other hand, we all should know that Wikipedia will contain a small amount of false information because no particular person is accountable for accuracy—and that would be true even if you could mouse over each sentence and see the name of the person who wrote it.

Historically, accountability has been tied to identity, but there's no reason why it has to be so. My name doesn't have to be on my credit card. I could have an anonymous photo ID that proved I was of legal drinking age. There's no reason for my e-mail address to be related to my legal name.

This is what Kelly calls pseudo-anonymity. In these systems, you hand your identity to a trusted third party that promises to respect your anonymity to a limited degree. For example, I have a credit card in another name from my credit card company. It's tied to my account, but it allows me to remain anonymous to merchants I do business with.

The security of pseudo-anonymity inherently depends on how trusted that "trusted third party" is. Depending on both local laws and how much they're respected, pseudo-anonymity can be broken by corporations, the police, or the government. It can be broken by the police collecting a whole lot of information about you, or by ChoicePoint collecting billions of tiny pieces of information about everyone and then making correlations. Pseudo-anonymity is only limited anonymity. It's anonymity from those without power, and not from those with power. Remember that anon.penet.fi couldn't stay up in the face of government.

In a perfect world, we wouldn't need anonymity. It wouldn't be necessary for commerce, since no one would ostracize or blackmail you based on what you purchased. It wouldn't be necessary for Internet activities, because no one would blackmail or arrest you based on who you corresponded with or what you read. It wouldn't be necessary for AIDS patients, members of fringe political parties, or people who call suicide hotlines. Yes, criminals use anonymity, just like they use everything else society has to offer. But the benefits of anonymity—extensively discussed in an excellent essay by Gary T. Marx—far outweigh the risks.

In Kelly's world—a perfect world—limited anonymity is enough because the only people who would harm you are individuals who cannot learn your identity, not those in power who can.

We do not live in a perfect world. We live in a world where information about our activities—even ones that are perfectly legal—can easily be turned against us. Recent news reports have described a student being hounded by his college because he said uncomplimentary things in his blog, corporations filing SLAPP lawsuits against people who criticize them, and people being profiled based on their political speech.

We live in a world where the police and the government are made up of less-than-perfect individuals who can use personal information about people, together with their enormous power, for imperfect purposes. Anonymity protects all of us from the powerful by the simple measure of not letting them get our personal information in the first place.

Facebook and Data Control

Originally published in Wired, *21 September 2006*

Earlier this month, the popular social networking site Facebook learned a hard lesson in privacy. It introduced a new feature called "News Feeds" that shows an aggregation of everything members do on the site: added and deleted friends, a change in relationship status, a new favorite song, a new interest, etc. Instead of a member's friends having to go to his page to view any changes, these changes were all presented to them automatically.

The outrage was enormous. One group, Students Against Facebook News Feeds, amassed more than 700,000 members. Members planned to protest at the company's headquarters. Facebook's founder was completely stunned, and the company scrambled to add some privacy options.

Welcome to the complicated and confusing world of privacy in the information age. Facebook didn't think there would be any problem; all it did was take available data and aggregate it in a novel way for what it perceived was its customers' benefit. Facebook members instinctively understood that making this information easier to display was an enormous difference, and that privacy is more about control than about secrecy.

But on the other hand, Facebook members are just fooling themselves if they think they can control information they give to third parties.

Privacy used to be about secrecy. Someone defending himself in court against the charge of revealing someone else's personal information could use as a defense the fact that it was not secret. But clearly, privacy is more complicated than that. Just because you tell your insurance company something doesn't mean you don't feel violated when that information is sold to a data broker. Just because you tell your friend a secret doesn't mean you're happy when he tells others. Same with your employer, your bank, or any company you do business with.

But as the Facebook example illustrates, privacy is much more complex. It's about who you choose to disclose information to, how, and for what purpose. And the key word there is "choose." People are willing to share all sorts of information, as long as they are in control.

When Facebook unilaterally changed the rules about how personal information was revealed, it reminded people that they weren't in control. Its 8 million members put their personal information on the site based on a set of rules about how that information would be used. It's no wonder those members—high school and college kids who traditionally don't care much about their own privacy—felt violated when Facebook changed the rules.

Unfortunately, Facebook can change the rules whenever it wants. Its Privacy Policy is 2,800 words long, and ends with a notice that it can change at any time. How many members ever read that policy, let alone read it regularly and check for changes? Not that a privacy policy is the same as a contract. Legally, Facebook owns all data members upload to the site. It can sell the data to advertisers, marketers, and data brokers. (Note: There is no evidence that Facebook does any of this.) It can allow the police to search its databases upon request. It can add new features that change who can access what personal data, and how.

But public perception is important. The lesson here for Facebook and other companies—for Google and MySpace and AOL and everyone else who hosts our e-mails and webpages and chat sessions—is that people believe they own their data. Even though the user agreement might technically give companies the right to sell the data, change the access rules to that data, or otherwise own that data, we—the users—believe otherwise. And when we who are affected by those actions start expressing our views—watch out.

What Facebook should have done was add the feature as an option, and allow members to opt in if they wanted to. Then, members who wanted to share their information via News Feeds could do so, and everyone else wouldn't have felt that they had no say in the matter. This is definitely a gray area, and it's hard to know beforehand which changes need to be implemented slowly and which won't matter. Facebook, and others, need to talk to its members openly about new features. Remember: Members want control.

The lesson for Facebook members might be even more jarring: If they think they have control over their data, they're only deluding themselves. They can rebel against Facebook for changing the rules, but the rules have changed, regardless of what the company does.

Whenever you put data on a computer, you lose some control over it. And when you put it on the Internet, you lose a lot of control over it. News Feeds brought Facebook members face-to-face with the full implications of putting their personal information on Facebook. It had just been an accident of the user interface that it was difficult to aggregate the data from multiple friends into a single place. And even if Facebook eliminates News Feeds entirely, a third party could easily write a program that does the same thing. Facebook could try to block the program, but would lose that technical battle in the end.

We're all still wrestling with the privacy implications of the Internet, but the balance has tipped in favor of more openness. Digital data is just too easy to move, copy, aggregate, and display. Companies like Facebook need to respect the social rules of their sites, to think carefully about their default settings—they have an enormous impact on the privacy mores of the online world—and to give users as much control over their personal information as they can.

But we all need to remember that much of that control is illusory.

The Death of Ephemeral Conversation

Originally published in Forbes, *18 October 2006*

The political firestorm over former U.S. Representative Mark Foley's salacious instant messages hides another issue, one about privacy. We are rapidly turning into a society where our intimate conversations can be saved and made public later. This represents an enormous loss of freedom and liberty, and the only way to solve the problem is through legislation.

Everyday conversation used to be ephemeral. Whether face-to-face or by phone, we could be reasonably sure that what we said disappeared as soon as we said it. Of course, organized crime bosses worried about phone taps and room bugs, but that was the exception. Privacy was the default assumption.

This has changed. We now type our casual conversations. We chat in e-mail, with instant messages on our computer and SMS messages on our cell phones, and in comments on social networking websites like Friendster, LiveJournal, and MySpace. These conversations—with friends, lovers, colleagues, fellow employees—are not ephemeral; they leave their own electronic trails.

We know this intellectually, but we haven't truly internalized it. We type on, engrossed in conversation, forgetting that we're being recorded.

Foley's instant messages were saved by the young men he talked to, but they could have also been saved by the instant messaging service. There are tools that allow both businesses and government agencies to monitor and log IM conversations. E-mail can be saved by your ISP or by the IT department in your corporation. Gmail, for example, saves everything, even if you delete it.

And these conversations can come back to haunt people—in criminal prosecutions, divorce proceedings, or simply as embarrassing disclosures. During the 1998 Microsoft anti-trust trial, the prosecution pored over masses of e-mail, looking for a smoking gun. Of course they found things; everyone says things in conversation that, taken out of context, can prove anything.

The moral is clear: If you type it and send it, prepare to explain it in public later.

And voice is no longer a refuge. Face-to-face conversations are still safe, but we know that the NSA is monitoring everyone's international phone calls. (They said nothing about SMS messages, but one can assume they were monitoring those, too.) Routine recording of phone conversations is still rare—certainly the NSA has the capability—but will become more common as telephone calls continue migrating to the IP network.

If you find this disturbing, you should. Fewer conversations are ephemeral, and we're losing control over the data. We trust our ISPs, employers, and cell phone companies with our privacy, but again and again they've proven they can't be trusted. Identity thieves routinely gain access to these repositories of our information. Paris Hilton and other celebrities have been the victims of hackers breaking into their cell phone providers' networks. Google reads our Gmail and inserts context-dependent ads.

Even worse, normal constitutional protections don't apply to much of this. The police need a court-issued warrant to search our papers or eavesdrop on our communications, but can simply issue a subpoena—or ask nicely or threateningly—for data of ours that is held by a third party, including stored copies of our communications.

The Justice Department wants to make this problem even worse, by forcing ISPs and others to save our communications—just in case we're someday the target of an investigation. This is not only bad privacy and security, it's a blow to our liberty as well. A world without ephemeral conversation is a world without freedom.

We can't turn back technology; electronic communications are here to stay. But as technology makes our conversations less ephemeral, we need laws to step in and safeguard our privacy. We need a comprehensive data privacy law, protecting our data and communications regardless of where it is stored or how it is processed. We need laws forcing companies to keep it private and to delete it as soon as it is no longer needed.

And we need to remember, whenever we type and send, we're being watched.

Foley is an anomaly. Most of us do not send instant messages in order to solicit sex with minors. Law enforcement might have a legitimate need to access Foley's IMs, e-mails, and cell phone calling logs, but that's why there are warrants supported by probable cause—they help ensure that investigations are properly focused on suspected pedophiles, terrorists and other criminals. We saw this in the recent U.K. terrorist arrests; focused investigations on suspected terrorists foiled the plot, not broad surveillance of everyone without probable cause.

Without legal privacy protections, the world becomes one giant airport security area, where the slightest joke—or comment made years before—lands you in hot water. The world becomes one giant market-research study, where we are all life-long subjects. The world becomes a police state, where we all are assumed to be Foleys and terrorists in the eyes of the government.

Automated Targeting System

Originally published in Forbes, *8 January 2007*

If you've traveled abroad recently, you've been investigated. You've been assigned a score indicating what kind of terrorist threat you pose. That score is used by the government to determine the treatment you receive when you return to the U.S. and for other purposes as well.

Curious about your score? You can't see it. Interested in what information was used? You can't know that. Want to clear your name if you've been wrongly categorized? You can't challenge it. Want to know what kind of rules the computer is using to judge you? That's secret, too. So is when and how the score will be used.

U.S. customs agencies have been quietly operating this system for several years. Called Automated Targeting System, it assigns a "risk assessment" score to people entering or leaving the country, or engaging in import or export activity. This score, and the information used to derive it, can be shared with federal, state, local, and even foreign governments. It can be used if you apply for a government job, grant, license, contract, or other benefit. It can be shared with nongovernmental organizations and individuals in the course of an investigation. In some circumstances private contractors can get it, even those outside the country. And it will be saved for 40 years.

Little is known about this program. Its bare outlines were disclosed in the Federal Register in October. We do know that the score is partially based on details of your flight record—where you're from, how you bought your ticket, where you're sitting, any special meal requests—or on motor vehicle records, as well as on information from crime, watch-list and other databases.

Civil liberties groups have called the program Kafkaesque. But I have an even bigger problem with it. It's a waste of money.

The idea of feeding a limited set of characteristics into a computer, which then somehow divines a person's terrorist leanings, is farcical. Uncovering terrorist plots requires intelligence and investigation, not large-scale processing of everyone.

Additionally, any system like this will generate so many false alarms as to be completely unusable. In 2005, Customs & Border Protection processed 431 million people. Assuming an unrealistic model that identifies terrorists (and innocents) with 99.9% accuracy, that's still 431,000 false alarms annually.

The number of false alarms will be much higher than that. The no-fly list is filled with inaccuracies; we've all read about innocent people named David Nelson who can't fly without hours-long harassment. Airline data, too, are riddled with errors.

The odds of this program's being implemented securely, with adequate privacy protections, are not good. Last year I participated in a government working group to assess the security and privacy of a similar program developed by the Transportation Security Administration, called Secure Flight. After five years and $100 million spent, the program still can't achieve the simple task of matching airline passengers against terrorist watch lists.

In 2002 we learned about yet another program, called Total Information Awareness, for which the government would collect information on every American and assign him or her a terrorist risk score. Congress found the idea so abhorrent that it halted funding for the program. Two years ago, and again this year, Secure Flight was also banned by Congress until it could pass a series of tests for accuracy and privacy protection.

In fact, the Automated Targeting System is arguably illegal as well (a point several congressmen made recently); all recent Department of Homeland Security appropriations bills specifically prohibit the department from using profiling systems against persons not on a watch list.

There is something un-American about a government program that uses secret criteria to collect dossiers on innocent people and shares that information with various agencies, all without any oversight. It's the sort of thing you'd expect from the former Soviet Union or East Germany or China. And it doesn't make us any safer from terrorism.

Anonymity and the Netflix Dataset

Originally published in Wired, *13 December 2007*

Last year, Netflix published 10 million movie rankings by 500,000 customers, as part of a challenge for people to come up with better recommendation systems than the one the company was using. The data was anonymized by removing personal details and replacing names with random numbers, to protect the privacy of the recommenders.

Arvind Narayanan and Vitaly Shmatikov, researchers at the University of Texas at Austin, de-anonymized some of the Netflix data by comparing rankings and timestamps with public information in the Internet Movie Database, or IMDb.

Their research illustrates some inherent security problems with anonymous data, but first it's important to explain what they did and did not do.

They did *not* reverse the anonymity of the entire Netflix dataset. What they did was reverse the anonymity of the Netflix dataset for those sampled users who also entered some movie rankings, under their own names, in the IMDb. (While IMDb's records are public, crawling the site to get them is against the IMDb's terms of service, so the researchers used a representative few to prove their algorithm.)

The point of the research was to demonstrate how little information is required to de-anonymize information in the Netflix dataset.

On one hand, isn't that sort of obvious? The risks of anonymous databases have been written about before, such as in this 2001 paper published in an IEEE journal. The researchers working with the anonymous Netflix data didn't painstakingly figure out people's identities—as others did with the AOL search database last year—they just compared it with an already identified subset of similar data: a standard data-mining technique.

But as opportunities for this kind of analysis pop up more frequently, lots of anonymous data could end up at risk.

Someone with access to an anonymous dataset of telephone records, for example, might partially de-anonymize it by correlating it with a catalog merchant's telephone order database. Or Amazon's online book reviews could be the key to partially de-anonymizing a public database of credit card purchases, or a larger database of anonymous book reviews.

Google, with its database of users' Internet searches, could easily de-anonymize a public database of Internet purchases, or zero in on searches of medical terms to de-anonymize a public health database. Merchants who maintain detailed customer and purchase information could use their data to partially de-anonymize any large search engine's data, if it were released in an anonymized form. A data broker holding databases of several companies might be able to de-anonymize most of the records in those databases.

What the University of Texas researchers demonstrate is that this process isn't hard, and doesn't require a lot of data. It turns out that if you eliminate the top 100 movies everyone watches, our movie-watching habits are all pretty individual. This would certainly hold true for our book reading habits, our Internet shopping habits, our telephone habits, and our web searching habits.

The obvious countermeasures for this are, sadly, inadequate. Netflix could have randomized its dataset by removing a subset of the data, changing the timestamps or adding deliberate errors into the unique ID numbers it used to replace the names. It turns out, though, that this only makes the problem slightly harder. Narayanan's and Shmatikov's de-anonymization algorithm is surprisingly robust, and works with partial data, data that has been perturbed, even data with errors in it.

With only eight movie ratings (two of which may be completely wrong), and dates that may be up to two weeks in error, they can uniquely identify 99% of the records in the dataset. After that, all they need is a little bit of identifiable data: from the IMDb, from your blog, from anywhere. The moral is that it takes only a small named database for someone to pry the anonymity off a much larger anonymous database.

Other research reaches the same conclusion. Using public anonymous data from the 1990 census, Latanya Sweeney found that 87% of the population in the United States—216 million of 248 million—could likely be uniquely identified by their five-digit ZIP code, combined with their gender and date of birth. About half of the U.S. population is likely identifiable by gender, date of birth, and the city, town, or municipality in which the person resides. Expanding the geographic scope to an entire county reduces that to a still-significant 18%. "In general," the researchers wrote, "few characteristics are needed to uniquely identify a person."

Stanford University researchers reported similar results using 2000 census data. It turns out that date of birth, which (unlike birthday month and day alone) sorts people into thousands of different buckets, is incredibly valuable in disambiguating people.

This has profound implications for releasing anonymous data. On one hand, anonymous data is an enormous boon for researchers—AOL did a good thing when it released its anonymous dataset for research purposes, and it's sad that the CTO resigned and an entire research team was fired after the public outcry. Large anonymous databases of medical data are enormously valuable to society: for large-scale pharmacology studies, long-term follow-up studies, and so on. Even anonymous telephone data makes for fascinating research.

On the other hand, in the age of wholesale surveillance, where everyone collects data on us all the time, anonymization is very fragile and riskier than it initially seems.

Like everything else in security, anonymity systems shouldn't be fielded before being subjected to adversarial attacks. We all know that it's folly to implement a cryptographic system before it's rigorously attacked; why should we expect anonymity systems to be any different? And, like everything else in security, anonymity is a trade-off. There are benefits, and there are corresponding risks.

Narayanan and Shmatikov are currently working on developing algorithms and techniques that enable the secure release of anonymous datasets like Netflix's. That's a research result we can all benefit from.

Does Secrecy Help Protect Personal Information?

Originally published in Information Security, *January 2007*

Personal information protection is an economic problem, not a security problem. And the problem can be easily explained: The organizations we trust to protect our personal information do not suffer when information gets exposed. On the other hand, individuals who suffer when personal information is exposed don't have the capability to protect that information.

There are actually two problems here: Personal information is easy to steal, and it's valuable once stolen. We can't solve one problem without solving the other. The solutions aren't easy, and you're not going to like them.

First, fix the economic problem. Credit card companies make more money extending easy credit and making it trivial for customers to use their cards than they lose from fraud. They won't improve their security as long as you (and not they) are the one who suffers from identity theft. It's the same for banks and brokerages: As long as you're the one who suffers when your account is hacked, they don't have any incentive to fix the problem. And data brokers like ChoicePoint are worse; they don't suffer if they reveal your information. You don't have a business relationship with them; you can't even switch to a competitor in disgust.

Credit card security works as well as it does because the 1968 Truth in Lending Law limits consumer liability for fraud to $50. If the credit card companies could pass fraud losses on to the consumers, they would be spending far less money to stop those losses. But once Congress forced them to suffer the costs of fraud, they invented all sorts of security measures—real-time transaction verification, expert systems patrolling the transaction database and so on—to prevent fraud. The lesson is clear: Make the party in the best position to mitigate the risk responsible for the risk. What this will do is enable the capitalist innovation engine. Once it's in the financial interest of financial institutions to protect us from identity theft, they will.

Second, stop using personal information to authenticate people. Watch how credit cards work. Notice that the store clerk barely looks at your signature, or how you can use credit cards remotely where no one can check your signature. The credit card industry learned decades ago that authenticating people has only limited value. Instead, they put most of their effort into authenticating the transaction, and they're much more secure because of it.

This won't solve the problem of securing our personal information, but it will greatly reduce the threat. Once the information is no longer of value, you only have to worry about securing the information from voyeurs rather than the more common—and more financially motivated—fraudsters.

And third, fix the other economic problem: Organizations that expose our personal information aren't hurt by that exposure. We need a comprehensive privacy law that gives individuals ownership of their personal information and allows them to take action against organizations that don't care for it properly.

"Passwords" like credit card numbers and mother's maiden name used to work, but we've forever left the world where our privacy comes from the obscurity of our personal information and the difficulty others have in accessing it. We need to abandon security systems that are based on obscurity and difficulty, and build legal protections to take over where technological advances have left us exposed.

Risks of Data Reuse

Originally published in Wired, *28 June 2007*

We learned the news in March: Contrary to decades of denials, the U.S. Census Bureau used individual records to round up Japanese-Americans during World War II.

The Census Bureau normally is prohibited by law from revealing data that could be linked to specific individuals; the law exists to encourage people to answer census questions accurately and without fear. And while the Second War Powers Act of 1942 temporarily suspended that protection in order to locate Japanese-Americans, the Census Bureau had maintained that it only provided general information about neighborhoods.

New research proves they were lying.

The whole incident serves as a poignant illustration of one of the thorniest problems of the information age: data collected for one purpose and then used for another, or "data reuse."

When we think about our personal data, what bothers us most is generally not the initial collection and use, but the secondary uses. I personally appreciate it when Amazon suggests books that might interest me, based on books I have already bought. I like it that my airline knows what type of seat and meal I prefer, and my hotel chain keeps records of my room preferences. I don't mind that my automatic road-toll collection tag is tied to my credit card, and that I get billed automatically. I even like the detailed summary of my purchases that my credit card company sends me at the end of every year. What I don't want, though, is any of these companies selling that data to brokers, or for law enforcement to be allowed to paw through those records without a warrant.

There are two bothersome issues about data reuse. First, we lose control of our data. In all of the examples above, there is an implied agreement between the data collector and me: It gets the data in order to provide me with some sort of service. Once the data collector sells it to a broker, though, it's out of my hands. It might show up on some telemarketer's screen, or in a detailed report to a potential employer, or as part of a data-mining system to evaluate my personal terrorism risk. It becomes part of my data shadow, which always follows me around but I can never see.

This, of course, affects our willingness to give up personal data in the first place. The reason U.S. census data was declared off-limits for other uses was to placate Americans' fears and assure them that they could answer questions truthfully. How accurate would you be in filling out your census forms if you knew the FBI would be mining the data, looking for terrorists? How would it affect your supermarket purchases if you knew people were examining them and making judgments about your lifestyle? I know many people who engage in data poisoning: deliberately lying on forms in order to propagate erroneous data. I'm sure many of them would stop that practice if they could be sure that the data was only used for the purpose for which it was collected.

The second issue about data reuse is error rates. All data has errors, and different uses can tolerate different amounts of error. The sorts of marketing databases you can buy on the web, for example, are notoriously error-filled. That's OK; if the database of ultra-affluent Americans of a particular ethnicity you just bought has a 10% error rate, you can factor that cost into your marketing campaign. But that same database, with that same error rate, might be useless for law enforcement purposes.

Understanding error rates and how they propagate is vital when evaluating any system that reuses data, especially for law enforcement purposes. A few years ago, the Transportation Security Administration's follow-on watch list system, Secure Flight, was going to use commercial data to give people a terrorism risk score and determine how much they were going to be questioned or searched at the airport. People rightly rebelled against the thought of being judged in secret, but there was much less discussion about whether the commercial data from credit bureaus was accurate enough for this application.

An even more egregious example of error-rate problems occurred in 2000, when the Florida Division of Elections contracted with Database Technologies (since merged with ChoicePoint) to remove convicted felons from the voting rolls. The databases used were filled with errors and the matching procedures were sloppy, which resulted in thousands of disenfranchised voters—mostly black—and almost certainly changed a presidential election result.

Of course, there are beneficial uses of secondary data. Take, for example, personal medical data. It's personal and intimate, yet valuable to society in aggregate. Think of what we could do with a database of everyone's health information: massive studies examining the long-term effects of different drugs and treatment options, different environmental factors, different lifestyle choices. There's an enormous amount of important research potential hidden in that data, and it's worth figuring out how to get at it without compromising individual privacy.

This is largely a matter of legislation. Technology alone can never protect our rights. There are just too many reasons not to trust it, and too many ways to subvert it. Data privacy ultimately stems from our laws, and strong legal protections are fundamental to protecting our information against abuse. But at the same time, technology is still vital.

Both the Japanese internment and the Florida voting-roll purge demonstrate that laws can change—and sometimes change quickly. We need to build systems with privacy-enhancing technologies that limit data collection wherever possible. Data that is never collected cannot be reused. Data that is collected anonymously, or deleted immediately after it is used, is much harder to reuse. It's easy to build systems that collect data on everything—it's what computers naturally do—but it's far better to take the time to understand what data is needed and why, and only collect that.

History will record what we, here in the early decades of the information age, did to foster freedom, liberty, and democracy. Did we build information technologies that protected people's freedoms even during times when society tried to subvert them? Or did we build technologies that could easily be modified to watch and control? It's bad civic hygiene to build an infrastructure that can be used to facilitate a police state.

5 ID Cards and Security

National ID Cards

Originally published in Minneapolis Star Tribune, *1 April 2004*

As a security technologist, I regularly encounter people who say the United States should adopt a national ID card. How could such a program not make us more secure, they ask?

The suggestion, when it's made by a thoughtful civic-minded person like Nicholas Kristof in *The New York Times*, often takes on a tone that is regretful and ambivalent: Yes, indeed, the card would be a minor invasion of our privacy, and undoubtedly it would add to the growing list of interruptions and delays we encounter every day; but we live in dangerous times, we live in a new world....

It all sounds so reasonable, but there's a lot to disagree with in such an attitude.

The potential privacy encroachments of an ID card system are far from minor. And the interruptions and delays caused by incessant ID checks could easily proliferate into a persistent traffic jam in office lobbies and airports and hospital waiting rooms and shopping malls.

But my primary objection isn't the totalitarian potential of national IDs, nor the likelihood that they'll create a whole immense new class of social and economic dislocations. Nor is it the opportunities they will create for colossal boondoggles by government contractors. My objection to the national ID card, at least for the purposes of this essay, is much simpler.

It won't work. It won't make us more secure.

In fact, everything I've learned about security over the last 20 years tells me that once it is put in place, a national ID card program will actually make us less secure.

My argument may not be obvious, but it's not hard to follow, either. It centers around the notion that security must be evaluated not based on how it works, but on how it fails.

It doesn't really matter how well an ID card works when used by the hundreds of millions of honest people that would carry it. What matters is how the system might fail when used by someone intent on subverting that system: how it fails naturally, how it can be made to fail, and how failures might be exploited.

The first problem is the card itself. No matter how unforgeable we make it, it will be forged. And even worse, people will get legitimate cards in fraudulent names.

Two of the 9/11 terrorists had valid Virginia driver's licenses in fake names. And even if we could guarantee that everyone who issued national ID cards couldn't be bribed, initial cardholder identity would be determined by other identity documents...all of which would be easier to forge.

Not that there would ever be such thing as a single ID card. Currently about 20% of all identity documents are lost per year. An entirely separate security system would have to be developed for people who lost their card, a system that itself would be capable of abuse.

Additionally, any ID system involves people...people who regularly make mistakes. We all have stories of bartenders falling for obviously fake IDs, or sloppy ID checks at airports and government buildings. It's not simply a matter of training; checking IDs is a mind-numbingly boring task, one that is guaranteed to have failures. Biometrics such as thumbprints show some promise here, but bring with them their own set of exploitable failure modes.

But the main problem with any ID system is that it requires the existence of a database. In this case, it would have to be an immense database of private and sensitive information on every American—one widely and instantaneously accessible from airline check-in stations, police cars, schools, and so on.

The security risks are enormous. Such a database would be a kludge of existing databases; databases that are incompatible, full of erroneous data, and unreliable. As computer scientists, we do not know how to keep a database of this magnitude secure, whether from outside hackers or the thousands of insiders authorized to access it.

And when the inevitable worms, viruses, or random failures happen and the database goes down, what then? Is America supposed to shut down until it's restored?

Proponents of national ID cards want us to assume all these problems, and the tens of billions of dollars such a system would cost—for what? For the promise of being able to identify someone?

What good would it have been to know the names of Timothy McVeigh, the Unabomber, or the DC snipers before they were arrested? Palestinian suicide bombers generally have no history of terrorism. The goal is here is to know someone's intentions, and their identity has very little to do with that.

And there are security benefits in having a variety of different ID documents. A single national ID is an exceedingly valuable document, and accordingly, there's greater incentive to forge it. There is more security in alert guards paying attention to subtle social cues than bored minimum-wage guards blindly checking IDs.

That's why, when someone asks me to rate the security of a national ID card on a scale of one to 10, I can't give an answer. It doesn't even belong on a scale.

REAL-ID: Costs and Benefits

Originally published in The Bulletin of Atomic Scientists, *March/April 2007*

The argument was so obvious it hardly needed repeating. Some thought we would all be safer—from terrorism, from crime, even from inconvenience—if we had a better ID card. A good, hard-to-forge national ID is a no-brainer (or so the argument goes), and it's ridiculous that a modern country like the United States doesn't have one.

Still, most Americans have been and continue to be opposed to a national ID card. Even just after 9/11, polls showed a bare majority (51%) in favor—and that quickly became a minority opinion again. As such, both political parties came out against the card, which meant that the only way it could become law was to sneak it through.

Republican Cong. F. James Sensenbrenner of Wisconsin did just that. In February 2005, he attached the Real ID Act to a defense appropriations bill. No one was willing to risk not supporting the troops by holding up the bill, and it became law. No hearings. No floor debate. With nary a whisper, the United States had a national ID.

By forcing all states to conform to common and more stringent rules for issuing driver's licenses, the Real ID Act turns these licenses into a de facto national ID. It's a massive, unfunded mandate imposed on the states, and—naturally— the states have resisted. The detailed rules and timetables are still being worked out by the Department of Homeland Security, and it's the details that will determine exactly how expensive and onerous the program actually is.

It is against this backdrop that the National Governors Association, the National Conference of State Legislatures, and the American Association of Motor Vehicle Administrators together tried to estimate the cost of this initiative. "The Real ID Act: National Impact Analysis" is a methodical and detailed report, and everything after the executive summary is likely to bore anyone but the most dedicated bean counters. But rigor is important because states want to use this document to influence both the technical details and timetable of Real ID. The estimates are conservative, leaving no room for problems, delays, or unforeseen costs, and yet the total cost is $11 billion over the first five years of the program.

If anything, it's surprisingly cheap: only $37 each for an estimated 295 million people who would get a new ID under this program. But it's still an enormous amount of money. The question to ask is, of course: Is the security benefit we all get worth the $11 billion price tag? We have a cost estimate; all we need now is a security estimate.

I'm going to take a crack at it.

When most people think of ID cards, they think of a small plastic card with their name and photograph. This isn't wrong, but it's only a small piece of any ID program. What starts out as a seemingly simple security device—a card that binds a photograph with a name—becomes a complex security system.

It doesn't really matter how well a Real ID works when used by the hundreds of millions of honest people who would carry it. What matters is how the system might fail when used by someone intent on subverting that system: how it fails naturally, how it can be made to fail, and how failures might be exploited.

The first problem is the card itself. No matter how unforgeable we make it, it will be forged. We can raise the price of forgery, but we can't make it impossible. Real IDs will be forged.

Even worse, people will get legitimate cards in fraudulent names. Two of the 9/11 terrorists had valid Virginia driver's licenses in fake names. And even if we could guarantee that everyone who issued national ID cards couldn't be bribed, cards are issued based on other identity documents—all of which are easier to forge.

And we can't assume that everyone will always have a Real ID. Currently about 20% of all identity documents are lost per year. An entirely separate security system would have to be developed for people who lost their card, a system that itself would be susceptible to abuse.

Additionally, any ID system involves people: people who regularly make mistakes. We've all heard stories of bartenders falling for obviously fake IDs, or sloppy ID checks at airports and government buildings. It's not simply a matter of training; checking IDs is a mind-numbingly boring task, one that is guaranteed to have failures. Biometrics such as thumbprints could help, but bring with them their own set of exploitable failure modes.

All of these problems demonstrate that identification checks based on Real ID won't be nearly as secure as we might hope. But the main problem with any strong identification system is that it requires the existence of a database. In this case, it would have to be 50 linked databases of private and sensitive information on every American—one widely and instantaneously accessible from airline check-in stations, police cars, schools, and so on.

The security risks of this database are enormous. It would be a kludge of existing databases that are incompatible, full of erroneous data, and unreliable. Computer scientists don't know how to keep a database of this magnitude secure, whether from outside hackers or the thousands of insiders authorized to access it.

But even if we could solve all these problems, and within the putative $11 billion budget, we still wouldn't be getting very much security. A reliance on ID cards is based on a dangerous security myth, that if only we knew who everyone was, we could pick the bad guys out of the crowd.

In an ideal world, what we would want is some kind of ID that denoted intention. We'd want all terrorists to carry a card that said "evildoer" and everyone else to carry a card that said "honest person who won't try to hijack or blow up anything." Then security would be easy. We could just look at people's IDs, and, if they were evildoers, we wouldn't let them on the airplane or into the building.

This is, of course, ridiculous; so we rely on identity as a substitute. In theory, if we know who you are, and if we have enough information about you, we can somehow predict whether you're likely to be an evildoer. But that's almost as ridiculous.

Even worse, as soon as you divide people into two categories—more-trusted and less-trusted people—you create a third, and very dangerous, category: untrustworthy people whom we have no reason to mistrust. Oklahoma City bomber Timothy McVeigh; the Washington, DC, snipers; the London subway bombers; and many of the 9/11 terrorists had no previous links to terrorism. Evildoers can also steal the identity—and profile—of an honest person. Profiling can result in less security by giving certain people an easy way to skirt security.

There's another, even more dangerous, failure mode for these systems: honest people who fit the evildoer profile. Because evildoers are so rare, almost everyone who fits the profile will turn out to be a false alarm. Think of all the problems with the government's no-fly list. That list, which is what Real IDs will be checked against, not only wastes investigative resources that might be better spent elsewhere, but it also causes grave harm to those innocents who fit the profile.

Enough of terrorism; what about more mundane concerns like identity theft? Perversely, a hard-to-forge ID card can actually increase the risk of identity theft. A single ubiquitous ID card will be trusted more and used in more applications. Therefore, someone who does manage to forge one—or get one issued in someone else's name—can commit much more fraud with it. A centralized ID system is a far greater security risk than a decentralized one with various organizations issuing ID cards according to their own rules for their own purposes.

Security is always a trade-off; it must be balanced with the cost. We all do this intuitively. Few of us walk around wearing bulletproof vests. It's not because they're ineffective, it's because for most of us the trade-off isn't worth it. It's not worth the cost, the inconvenience, or the loss of fashion sense. If we were living in a war-torn country like Iraq, we might make a different trade-off.

Real ID is another lousy security trade-off. It'll cost the United States at least $11 billion, and we won't get much security in return. The report suggests a variety of measures designed to ease the financial burden on the states: extend compliance deadlines, allow manual verification systems, and so on. But what it doesn't suggest is the simple change that would do the most good: scrap the Real ID program altogether. For the price, we're not getting anywhere near the security we should.

RFID Passports

Originally published in The International Herald Tribune, *4 October 2004, with a longer version published in* Crypto-Gram, *15 October 2004*

Since 9/11, the Bush administration—specifically, the Department of Homeland Security—has wanted the world to standardize on machine-readable passports. Future U.S. passports, currently being tested, will include an embedded computer chip. This chip will allow the passport to contain much more information than a simple machine-readable character font, and will allow passport officials to quickly and easily read that information. That's a reasonable requirement, and a good idea for bringing passport technology into the 21st century. But the administration is advocating radio frequency identification (RFID) chips for both U.S. and foreign passports, and that's a very bad thing.

RFID chips are like smart cards, but they can be read from a distance. A receiving device can "talk" to the chip remotely, without any need for physical contact, and get whatever information is on it. Passport officials envision being able to download the information on the chip simply by bringing it within a few centimeters of a reader.

Unfortunately, RFID chips can be read by any reader, not just the ones at passport control. The upshot of this is that anyone carrying around an RFID passport is broadcasting his identity.

Think about what that means for a minute. It means that a passport holder is continuously broadcasting his name, nationality, age, address, and whatever else is on the RFID chip. It means that anyone with a reader can learn that information, without the passport holder's knowledge or consent. It means that pickpockets, kidnappers, and terrorists can easily—and surreptitiously—pick Americans out of a crowd.

It's a clear threat to both privacy and personal safety. Quite simply, it's a bad idea.

The administration claims that the chips can only be read from a few centimeters away, so there's no potential for abuse. This is a spectacularly naive claim. All wireless protocols can work at much longer ranges than specified. In tests, RFID chips have been read by receivers 20 meters away. Improvements in technology are inevitable.

Security is always a trade-off. If the benefits of RFID outweigh the risks, then maybe it's worth it. Certainly there isn't a significant benefit when people present their passport to a customs official. If that customs official is going to take the passport and bring it near a reader, why can't he go those extra few centimeters that a contact chip would require?

The administration is deliberately choosing a less secure technology without justification. If there were a good reason to choose that technology, then it might make sense. But there isn't. There's a large cost in security and privacy, and no benefit. Any rational analysis will conclude that there isn't any reason to choose an RFID chip over a conventional chip.

Unfortunately, there is a reason. At least, it's the only reason I can think of for the administration wanting RFID chips in passports: They want surreptitious access themselves. They want to be able to identify people in crowds. They want to pick out the Americans, and pick out the foreigners. They want to do the very thing that they insist, despite demonstrations to the contrary, can't be done.

Normally I am very careful before I ascribe such sinister motives to a government agency. Incompetence is the norm, and malevolence is much rarer. But this seems like a clear case of the government putting its own interests above the security and privacy of its citizens, and then lying about it.

The Security of RFID Passports

Originally published in Wired, *3 November 2005*

In 2004, when the U.S. State Department first started talking about embedding RFID chips in passports, the outcry from privacy advocates was huge. When the State Department issued its draft regulation in February, it got 2,335 comments, 98.5% negative. In response, the final State Department regulations, issued last month, contain two features that attempt to address security and privacy concerns. But one serious problem remains.

Before I describe the problem, some context on the surrounding controversy may be helpful. RFID chips are passive, and broadcast information to any reader that queries the chip. So critics, myself included, were worried that the new passports would reveal your identity without your consent or even your knowledge. Thieves could collect the personal data of people as they walk down a street, criminals could scan passports looking for Westerners to kidnap or rob, and terrorists could rig bombs to explode only when four Americans are nearby. The police could use the chips to conduct surveillance on an individual; stores could use the technology to identify customers without their knowledge.

RFID privacy problems are larger than passports and identity cards. The RFID industry envisions these chips embedded everywhere: in the items we buy, for example. But even a chip that only contains a unique serial number could be used for surveillance. And it's easy to link the serial number with an identity—when you buy the item using a credit card, for example—and from then on it can identify you. Data brokers like ChoicePoint will certainly maintain databases of RFID numbers and associated people; they'd do a disservice to their stockholders if they didn't.

The State Department downplayed these risks by insisting that the RFID chips only work at short distances. In fact, last month's publication claims: "The proximity chip technology utilized in the electronic passport is designed to be read with chip readers at ports of entry only when the document is placed within inches of such readers." The issue is that they're confusing three things: the designed range at which the chip is specified to be read, the maximum range at which the chip could be read, and the eavesdropping range or the maximum range the chip could be read with specialized equipment. The first is indeed inches, but the second was demonstrated earlier this year to be 69 feet. The third is significantly longer.

And remember, technology always gets better—it never gets worse. It's simply folly to believe that these ranges won't get longer over time.

To its credit, the State Department listened to the criticism. As a result, RFID passports will now include a thin radio shield in their covers, protecting the chips when the passports are closed. Although some have derided this as a tinfoil hat for passports, the fact is the measure will prevent the documents from being snooped when closed.

However, anyone who travels knows that passports are used for more than border crossings. You often have to show your passport at hotels and airports, and while changing money. More and more it's an identity card; new Italian regulations require foreigners to show their passports when using an Internet cafe.

Because of this, the State Department added a second, and more-important, feature: access control. The data on the chip will be encrypted, and the key is printed on the passport. A customs officer swipes the passport through an optical reader to get the key, and then the RFID reader uses the key to communicate with the RFID chip.

This means that the passport holder can control who gets access to the information on the chip, and someone cannot skim information from the passport without first opening it up and reading the information inside. This also means that a third party can't eavesdrop on the communication between the card and the reader, because it's encrypted.

By any measure, these features are exemplary, and should serve as a role model for any RFID identity-document applications. Unfortunately, there's still a problem.

RFID chips, including the ones specified for U.S. passports, can still be uniquely identified by their radio behavior. Specifically, these chips have a unique identification number used for collision avoidance. It's how the chips avoid communications problems if you put a bagful of them next to a reader. This is something buried deep within the chip, and has nothing to do with the data or application on the chip.

Chip manufacturers don't like to talk about collision IDs or how they work, but researchers have shown how to uniquely identify RFID chips by querying them and watching how they behave. And since these queries access a lower level of the chip than the passport application, an access-control mechanism doesn't help.

To fix this, the State Department needs to require that the chips used in passports implement a collision-avoidance system not based on unique serial numbers. The RFID spec—ISO 14443A is its name—allows for a random system, but I don't believe any manufacturer implements it this way.

Adding chips to passports can inarguably be good for security. Initial chips will only contain the information printed on the passport, but this system has always envisioned adding digital biometrics like photographs or even fingerprints, which will make passports harder to forge, and stolen passports harder to use.

But the State Department's contention that they need an RFID chip, that smartcard-like contact chips won't work, is much less convincing. Even with all this security, RFID should be the design choice of last resort.

The State Department has done a great job addressing specific security and privacy concerns, but its lack of technical skills is hurting it. The collision-avoidance ID issue is just one example of where, apparently, the State Department didn't have enough of the expertise it needed to do this right.

Of course it can fix the problem, but the real issue is how many other problems like this are lurking in the details of its design? We don't know, and I doubt the State Department knows, either. The only way to vet its design, and to convince us that RFID is necessary, would be to open it up to public scrutiny.

The State Department's plan to issue RFID passports by October 2006 is both precipitous and risky. It made a mistake designing this behind closed doors. There needs to be some pretty serious quality assurance and testing before deploying this system, and this includes careful security evaluations by independent security experts. Right now the State Department has no intention of doing that; it's already committed to a scheme before knowing if it even works or if it protects privacy.

Multi-Use ID Cards

Originally published in Wired, *9 February 2006*

I don't know about your wallet, but mine contains a driver's license, three credit cards, two bank ATM cards, frequent-flier cards for three airlines and frequent-guest cards for three hotel chains, memberships cards to two airline clubs, a library card, a AAA card, a Costco membership, and a bunch of other ID-type cards.

Any technologist who looks at the pile would reasonably ask: Why all those cards? Most of them are not intended to be hard-to-forge identification cards; they're simply ways of carrying around unique numbers that are pointers into a database. Why does Visa bother issuing credit cards in the first place? Clearly you don't need the physical card in order to complete the transaction, as anyone who has bought something over the phone or the Internet knows. Your bank could just use your driver's license number as an account number.

The same with those airline, hotel, and rental car affinity cards. Or any of the discount cards given out by supermarkets, office supply stores, hardware stores and—it seems—everyone else. They could use any of your existing account numbers. Or simply your name and address. In fact, if you forget your card, they'll look up your account number if you give them your phone number. Why go to the trouble and expense of issuing unique cards at all?

A single, centralized authentication system has long been the dream of many technologists. Those involved in computer security will remember the promise of public-key infrastructure, or PKI. Everyone was going to have a single digital "certificate" that would be accepted by all sorts of different applications. It never happened.

And today, the most far-reaching proposals for national ID cards—including a recent South African proposal—envision a world where a single ID would be used for everything. It won't happen, either.

And neither will a world of biometrics. It's the obvious next step: Why carry a driver's license? Use your face or fingerprint.

But the truth is, neither a national ID nor a biometric system will ever replace the decks of plastic and paper that crowd our wallets.

For starters, the uniqueness of the cards provides important security to the issuers. Everyone has different rules for card issuance, expiration, and revocation, and everyone wants to be in control of his own cards. If you lose control, you lose security. So airline clubs ask for a photo ID with your membership card, and merchants want to see it when you use your credit card, but neither will replace their cards with that photo ID.

Another reason is reliability. Your credit card company doesn't want your ability to make purchases disappear if you have your driver's license revoked. Your airline doesn't want your frequent-flier account to depend on a particular credit card. And no company wants the liability of having its application depend on someone else's infrastructure, or having its infrastructure support someone else's application.

But security and reliability are only secondary concerns. If it made smart business sense for companies to piggyback on existing cards, they would find a way around the security concerns. The reason they don't boils down to one word: branding.

My airline wants a card with its logo on it in my wallet. So does my rental car company, my supermarket, and everyone else I do business with. My credit card company wants me to open up my wallet and notice its card; I'm far more likely to use a physical card than a virtual one that I have to remember is attached to my driver's license number. And I'm more likely to feel important if I have a card, especially a card that recognizes me as a frequent flier or a preferred customer.

Some years ago, when credit cards with embedded chips were new, the card manufacturers designed a secure, multi-application operating system for these smartcards. The idea was that a single physical card could be used for everything: multiple credit card accounts, airline affinity memberships, public-transportation payment cards, etc. Nobody bought into the system: not because of security concerns, but because of branding concerns. Whose logo would get to be on the card? When the manufacturers envisioned a card with multiple small logos, one for each application, everyone wanted to know: Whose logo would be first? On top? In color?

The companies give you their own card partly because they want complete control of the rules around their own system, but mostly because they want you to carry around a small piece of advertising in your wallet. An American Express Gold Card is supposed to make you feel powerful and everyone else feel green. They want you to wave it around.

That's why you still have a dozen different cards in your wallet. And countries that have national IDs give their citizens yet another card to carry around in their wallets—and not a replacement for something else.

Giving Driver's Licenses to Illegal Immigrants

Originally published in Detroit Free Press, *7 February 2008*

Many people say that allowing illegal aliens to obtain state driver's licenses helps them and encourages them to remain illegally in this country. Michigan Attorney General Mike Cox late last year issued an opinion that licenses could be issued only to legal state residents, calling it "one more tool in our initiative to bolster Michigan's border and document security."

In reality, we are a much more secure nation if we do issue driver's licenses and/or state IDs to every resident who applies, regardless of immigration status. Issuing them doesn't make us any less secure, and refusing puts us at risk.

The state driver's license databases are the only comprehensive databases of U.S. residents. They're more complete, and contain more information—including photographs and, in some cases, fingerprints—than the IRS database, the Social Security database, or state birth certificate databases. As such, they are an invaluable police tool—for investigating crimes, tracking down suspects, and proving guilt.

Removing the 8 million to 15 million illegal immigrants from these databases would only make law enforcement harder. Of course, the unlicensed won't pack up and leave. They will drive without licenses, increasing insurance premiums for everyone. They will use fake IDs, buy real IDs from crooked DMV employees—as several of the 9/11 terrorists did—forge "breeder documents" to get real IDs (another 9/11 terrorist trick), or resort to identity theft. These millions of people will continue to live and work in this country, invisible to any government database and therefore the police.

Assuming that denying licenses to illegals will make them leave is head-in-the-sand thinking.

Of course, even an attempt to deny licenses to illegal immigrants puts DMV clerks in the impossible position of verifying immigration status. This is expensive and time-consuming; furthermore, it won't work. The law is complicated, and it can take hours to verify someone's status, only to get it wrong. Paperwork can be easy to forge, far easier than driver's licenses, meaning many illegal immigrants will get these licenses that now "prove" immigrant status.

Even more legal immigrants will be mistakenly denied licenses, resulting in lawsuits and additional government expense.

Some states have considered a tiered license system, one that explicitly lists immigration status on the licenses. Of course, this won't work either. Illegal immigrants are far more likely to take their chances being caught than admit their immigration status to the DMV.

We are all safer if everyone in society trusts and respects law enforcement. A society where illegal immigrants are afraid to talk to police because of fear of deportation is a society where fewer people come forward to report crimes, aid police investigations, and testify as witnesses.

And finally, denying driver's licenses to illegal immigrants will not protect us from terrorism. Contrary to popular belief, a driver's license is not required to board a plane. You can use any government-issued photo ID, including a foreign passport. And if you're willing to undergo secondary screening, you can board a plane without an ID at all. This is probably how anybody on the no-fly list gets around these days.

A 2003 American Association of Motor Vehicle Administrators report concludes: "Digital images from driver's licenses have significantly aided law enforcement agencies charged with homeland security. The 19 (9/11) terrorists obtained driver licenses from several states, and federal authorities relied heavily on these images for the identification of the individuals responsible."

Whether it's the DHS trying to protect the nation from terrorism, or local, state, and national law enforcement trying to protect the nation from crime, we are all safer if we encourage every adult in America to get a driver's license.

6 Election Security

Voting Technology and Security

Originally published in Forbes.com, 13 November 2006

L ast week in Florida's 13th Congressional district, the victory margin was only 386 votes out of 153,000. There'll be a mandatory lawyered-up recount, but it won't include the almost 18,000 votes that seem to have disappeared. The electronic voting machines didn't include them in their final tallies, and there's no backup to use for the recount. The district will pick a winner to send to Washington, but it won't be because they are sure the majority voted for him. Maybe the majority did, and maybe it didn't. There's no way to know.

Electronic voting machines represent a grave threat to fair and accurate elections, a threat that every American—Republican, Democrat or independent—should be concerned about. Because they're computer-based, the deliberate or accidental actions of a few can swing an entire election. The solution: Paper ballots, which can be verified by voters and recounted if necessary.

To understand the security of electronic voting machines, you first have to consider election security in general. The goal of any voting system is to capture the intent of each voter and collect them all into a final tally. In practice, this occurs through a series of transfer steps. When I voted last week, I transferred my intent onto a paper ballot, which was then transferred to a tabulation machine via an optical scan reader; at the end of the night, the individual machine tallies were transferred by election officials to a central facility and combined into a single result I saw on television.

All election problems are errors introduced at one of these steps, whether it's voter disenfranchisement, confusing ballots, broken machines, or ballot stuffing. Even in normal operations, each step can introduce errors. Voting accuracy, therefore, is a matter of 1) minimizing the number of steps, and 2) increasing the reliability of each step.

Much of our election security is based on "security by competing interests." Every step, with the exception of voters completing their single anonymous ballots, is witnessed by someone from each major party; this ensures that any partisan shenanigans—or even honest mistakes—will be caught by the other observers. This system isn't perfect, but it's worked pretty well for a couple hundred years.

Electronic voting is like an iceberg; the real threats are below the waterline where you can't see them. Paperless electronic voting machines bypass that security process, allowing a small group of people—or even a single hacker—to affect an election. The problem is software—programs that are hidden from view and cannot be verified by a team of Republican and Democrat election judges, programs that can drastically change the final tallies. And because all that's left at the end of the day are those electronic tallies, there's no way to verify the results or to perform a recount. Recounts are important.

This isn't theoretical. In the U.S., there have been hundreds of documented cases of electronic voting machines distorting the vote to the detriment of candidates from both political parties: machines losing votes, machines swapping the votes for candidates, machines registering more votes for a candidate than there were voters, machines not registering votes at all. I would like to believe these are all mistakes and not deliberate fraud, but the truth is that we can't tell the difference. And these are just the problems we've caught; it's almost certain that many more problems have escaped detection because no one was paying attention.

This is both new and terrifying. For the most part, and throughout most of history, election fraud on a massive scale has been hard; it requires very public actions or a highly corrupt government—or both. But electronic voting is different: A lone hacker can affect an election. He can do his work secretly before the machines are shipped to the polling stations. He can affect an entire area's voting machines. And he can cover his tracks completely, writing code that deletes itself after the election.

And that assumes well-designed voting machines. The actual machines being sold by companies like Diebold, Sequoia Voting Systems, and Election Systems & Software are much worse. The software is badly designed. Machines are "protected" by hotel minibar keys. Vote tallies are stored in easily changeable files. Machines can be infected with viruses. Some voting software runs on

Microsoft Windows, with all the bugs and crashes and security vulnerabilities that introduces. The list of inadequate security practices goes on and on.

The voting machine companies counter that such attacks are impossible because the machines are never left unattended (they're not), the memory cards that hold the votes are carefully controlled (they're not), and everything is supervised (it isn't). Yes, they're lying, but they're also missing the point.

We shouldn't—and don't—have to accept voting machines that might someday be secure only if a long list of operational procedures are followed precisely. We need voting machines that are secure regardless of how they're programmed, handled, and used, and that can be trusted even if they're sold by a partisan company, or a company with possible ties to Venezuela.

Sounds like an impossible task, but in reality, the solution is surprisingly easy. The trick is to use electronic voting machines as ballot-generating machines. Vote by whatever automatic touch-screen system you want: a machine that keeps no records or tallies of how people voted, but only generates a paper ballot. The voter can check it for accuracy, then process it with an optical-scan machine. The second machine provides the quick initial tally, while the paper ballot provides for recounts when necessary. And absentee and backup ballots can be counted the same way.

You can even do away with the electronic vote-generation machines entirely and hand-mark your ballots like we do in Minnesota. Or run a 100% mail-in election like Oregon does. Again, paper ballots are the key.

Paper? Yes, paper. A stack of paper is harder to tamper with than a number in a computer's memory. Voters can see their vote on paper, regardless of what goes on inside the computer. And most important, everyone understands paper. We get into hassles over our cell phone bills and credit card mischarges, but when was the last time you had a problem with a $20 bill? We know how to count paper. Banks count it all the time. Both Canada and the U.K. count paper ballots with no problems, as do the Swiss. We can do it, too. In today's world of computer crashes, worms, and hackers, a low-tech solution is the most secure.

Secure voting machines are just one component of a fair and honest election, but they're an increasingly important part. They're where a dedicated attacker can most effectively commit election fraud (and we know that changing the results can be worth millions). But we shouldn't forget other voter suppression tactics: telling people the wrong polling place or election date, taking registered voters off the voting rolls, having too few machines at polling places, or making it onerous for people to register. (Oddly enough, ineligible people voting isn't a problem in the U.S., despite political rhetoric to the contrary; every study shows their numbers to be so small as to be insignificant. And photo ID requirements actually cause more problems than they solve.)

Voting is as much a perception issue as it is a technological issue. It's not enough for the result to be mathematically accurate; every citizen must also be confident that it is correct. Around the world, people protest or riot after an election not when their candidate loses, but when they think their candidate lost unfairly. It is vital for a democracy that an election both accurately determine the winner and adequately convince the loser. In the U.S., we're losing the perception battle.

The current crop of electronic voting machines fail on both counts. The results from Florida's 13th Congressional district are neither accurate nor convincing. As a democracy, we deserve better. We need to refuse to vote on electronic voting machines without a voter-verifiable paper ballot, and to continue to pressure our legislatures to implement voting technology that works.

Computerized and Electronic Voting

Originally published in Crypto-Gram, *15 December 2003*

There are dozens of stories about computerized voting machines producing erroneous results. Votes mysteriously appear or disappear. Votes cast for one person are credited to another. Here are two from the most recent election: One candidate in Virginia found that the computerized election machines failed to register votes for her, and in fact subtracted a vote for her, in about "one out of a hundred tries." And in Indiana, 5,352 voters in a district of 19,000 managed to cast 144,000 ballots on a computerized machine.

These problems were only caught because their effects were obvious—and obviously wrong. Subtle problems remain undetected, and for every problem we catch—even though their effects often can't be undone—there are probably dozens that escape our notice.

Computers are fallible and software is unreliable; election machines are no different than your home computer.

Even more frightening than software mistakes is the potential for fraud. The companies producing voting machine software use poor computer-security practices. They leave sensitive code unprotected on networks. They install patches and updates without proper security auditing. And they use the law to prohibit public scrutiny of their practices. When damning memos from Diebold became public, the company sued to suppress them. Given these shoddy security practices, what confidence do we have that someone didn't break into the company's network and modify the voting software?

And because elections happen all at once, there would be no means of recovery. Imagine if, in the next presidential election, someone hacked the vote in New York. Would we let New York vote again in a week? Would we redo the entire national election? Would we tell New York that their votes didn't count?

Any discussion of computerized voting necessarily leads to Internet voting. Why not just do away with voting machines entirely, and let everyone vote remotely?

Online voting schemes have even more potential for failure and abuse. Internet systems are extremely difficult to secure, as evidenced by the never-ending stream of computer vulnerabilities and the widespread effect of Internet worms and viruses. It might be convenient to vote from your home computer, but it would also open new opportunities for people to play Hack the Vote.

And any remote voting scheme has its own problems. The voting booth provides security against coercion. I may be bribed or threatened to vote a certain way, but when I enter the privacy of the voting booth I can vote the way I want. Remote voting, whether by mail or by Internet, removes that security. The person buying my vote can be sure that he's buying a vote by taking my blank ballot from me and completing it himself.

In the U.S., we believe that allowing absentees to vote is more important than this added security, and that it is probably a good trade-off. And people like the convenience. In California, for example, over 25% vote by mail.

Voting is particularly difficult in the United States for two reasons. One, we vote on dozens of different things at one time. And two, we demand final results before going to sleep at night.

What we need are simple voting systems—paper ballots that can be counted even in a blackout. We need technology to make voting easier, but it has to be reliable and verifiable.

My suggestion is simple, and it's one echoed by many computer security researchers. All computerized voting machines need a paper audit trail. Build any computerized machine you want. Have it work any way you want. The voter votes on it, and when he's done the machine prints out a paper receipt, much like an ATM does. The receipt is the voter's real ballot. He looks it over, and then drops it into a ballot box. The ballot box contains the official votes, which are used for any recount. The voting machine has the quick initial tally.

This system isn't perfect, and doesn't address many security issues surrounding voting. It's still possible to deny individuals the right to vote, stuff machines and ballot boxes with pre-cast votes, lose machines and ballot boxes, intimidate voters, etc. Computerized machines don't make voting completely secure, but machines with paper audit trails prevent all sorts of new avenues of error and fraud.

Why Election Technology is Hard

Originally published in San Francisco Chronicle, *31 October 2004*

Four years after the Florida debacle of 2000 and two years after Congress passed the Help America Vote Act, voting problems are again in the news: confusing ballots, malfunctioning voting machines, problems over who's registered and who isn't. All this brings up a basic question: Why is it so hard to run an election?

A fundamental requirement for a democratic election is a secret ballot, and that's the first reason. Computers regularly handle multimillion-dollar financial transactions, but much of their security comes from the ability to audit the transactions after the fact and correct problems that arise. Much of what they do can be done the next day if the system is down. Neither of these solutions works for elections.

American elections are particularly difficult because they're so complicated. One ballot might have 50 different things to vote on, all but one different in each state and many different in each district. It's much easier to hold national elections in India, where everyone casts a single vote, than in the United States. Additionally, American election systems need to be able to handle 100 million voters in a single day—an immense undertaking in the best of circumstances.

Speed is another factor. Americans demand election results before they go to sleep; we won't stand for waiting more than two weeks before knowing who won, as happened in India and Afghanistan this year.

To make matters worse, voting systems are used infrequently, at most a few times a year. Systems that are used every day improve because people familiarize themselves with them, discover mistakes, and figure out improvements. It seems as if we all have to relearn how to vote every time we do it.

It should be no surprise that there are problems with voting. What's surprising is that there aren't more problems. So how to make the system work better?

- Simplicity: This is the key to making voting better. Registration should be as simple as possible. The voting process should be as simple as possible. Ballot designs should be simple, and they should be tested. The computer industry understands the science of user-interface—that knowledge should be applied to ballot design.
- Uniformity: Simplicity leads to uniformity. The United States doesn't have one set of voting rules or one voting system. It has 51 different sets of voting rules—one for every state and the District of Columbia—and even more systems. The more systems are standardized around the country, the more we can learn from each other's mistakes.
- Verifiability: Computerized voting machines might have a simple user interface, but complexity hides behind the screen and keyboard. To avoid even more problems, these machines should have a voter-verifiable paper ballot. This isn't a receipt; it's not something you take home with you. It's a paper "ballot" with your votes—one that you verify for accuracy and then put in a ballot box. The machine provides quick tallies, but the paper is the basis for any recounts.
- Transparency: All computer code used in voting machines should be public. This allows interested parties to examine the code and point out errors, resulting in continually improving security. Any voting-machine company that claims its code must remain secret for security reasons is lying. Security in computer systems comes from transparency—open systems that pass public scrutiny—and not secrecy.

But those are all solutions for the future. If you're a voter this year, your options are fewer. My advice is to vote carefully. Read the instructions carefully, and ask questions if you are confused. Follow the instructions carefully, checking every step as you go. Remember that it might be impossible to correct a problem once you've finished voting. In many states—including California—you can request a paper ballot if you have any worries about the voting machine.

And be sure to vote. This year, thousands of people are watching and waiting at the polls to help voters make sure their vote counts.

Electronic Voting Machines

Originally published in openDemocracy.com, 9 November 2004

In the aftermath of the U.S.'s 2004 election, electronic voting machines are again in the news. Computerized machines lost votes, subtracted votes instead of adding them, and doubled votes. Because many of these machines have no paper audit trails, a large number of votes will never be counted. And while it is unlikely that deliberate voting-machine fraud changed the result of the presidential election, the Internet is buzzing with rumors and allegations of fraud in a number of different jurisdictions and races. It is still too early to tell if any of these problems affected any individual elections. Over the next several weeks we'll see whether any of the information crystallizes into something significant.

The U.S has been here before. After 2000, voting machine problems made international headlines. The government appropriated money to fix the problems nationwide. Unfortunately, electronic voting machines—although presented as the solution—have largely made the problem worse. This doesn't mean that these machines should be abandoned, but they need to be designed to increase both their accuracy, and people's trust in their accuracy. This is difficult, but not impossible.

Before I can discuss electronic voting machines, I need to explain why voting is so difficult. Basically, a voting system has four required characteristics:

- Accuracy. The goal of any voting system is to establish the intent of each individual voter, and translate those intents into a final tally. To the extent that a voting system fails to do this, it is undesirable. This characteristic also includes security: It should be impossible to change someone else's vote, ballot stuff, destroy votes, or otherwise affect the accuracy of the final tally.
- Anonymity. Secret ballots are fundamental to democracy, and voting systems must be designed to facilitate voter anonymity.
- Scalability. Voting systems need to be able to handle very large elections. One hundred million people vote for president in the United States. About 372 million people voted in India's June elections, and more than 115 million in Brazil's October elections. The complexity

of an election is another issue. Unlike many countries where the national election is a single vote for a person or a party, a United States voter is faced with dozens of individual elections: national, local, and everything in between.

- Speed. Voting systems should produce results quickly. This is particularly important in the United States, where people expect to learn the results of the day's election before bedtime. It's less important in other countries, where people don't mind waiting days—or even weeks—before the winner is announced.

Through the centuries, different technologies have done their best. Stones and pot shards dropped in Greek vases gave way to paper ballots dropped in sealed boxes. Mechanical voting booths, punch cards, and then optical scan machines replaced hand-counted ballots. New computerized voting machines promise even more efficiency, and Internet voting even more convenience.

But in the rush to improve speed and scalability, accuracy has been sacrificed. And to reiterate: accuracy is not how well the ballots are counted by, for example, a punch-card reader. It's not how the tabulating machine deals with hanging chads, pregnant chads, or anything like that. Accuracy is how well the process translates voter intent into properly counted votes.

Technologies get in the way of accuracy by adding steps. Each additional step means more potential errors, simply because no technology is perfect. Consider an optical-scan voting system. The voter fills in ovals on a piece of paper, which is fed into an optical-scan reader. The reader senses the filled-in ovals and tabulates the votes. This system has several steps: voter to ballot to ovals to optical reader to vote tabulator to centralized total.

At each step, errors can occur. If the ballot is confusing, then some voters will fill in the wrong ovals. If a voter doesn't fill them in properly, or if the reader is malfunctioning, then the sensor won't sense the ovals properly. Mistakes in tabulation—either in the machine or when machine totals get aggregated into larger totals—also cause errors. A manual system—tallying the ballots by hand, and then doing it again to double-check—is more accurate simply because there are fewer steps.

The error rates in modern systems can be significant. Some voting technologies have a 5% error rate: One in twenty people who vote using the system don't have their votes counted properly. This system works anyway because most of the time errors don't matter. If you assume that the errors are uniformly distributed—in other words, that they affect each candidate with equal probability—then they won't affect the final outcome except in very close races. So we're willing to sacrifice accuracy to get a voting system that will more quickly handle large and complicated elections. In close races, errors can affect the outcome, and that's the point of a recount. A recount is an alternate system of tabulating votes: one that is slower (because it's manual), simpler (because it just focuses on one race), and therefore more accurate.

Note that this is only true if everyone votes using the same machines. If parts of town that tend to support candidate A use a voting system with a higher error rate than the voting system used in parts of town that tend to support candidate B, then the results will be skewed against candidate A. This is an important consideration in voting accuracy, although tangential to the topic of this essay.

With this background, the issue of computerized voting machines becomes clear. Actually, "computerized voting machines" is a bad choice of words. Many of today's voting technologies involve computers. Computers tabulate both punch-card and optical-scan machines. The current debate centers around all-computer voting systems, primarily touch-screen systems, called Direct Record Electronic (DRE) machines. (The voting system used in India's most recent election—a computer with a series of buttons—is subject to the same issues.) In these systems the voter is presented with a list of choices on a screen, perhaps multiple screens if there are multiple elections, and he indicates his choice by touching the screen. These machines are easy to use, produce final tallies immediately after the polls close, and can handle very complicated elections. They also can display instructions in different languages and allow for the blind or otherwise handicapped to vote without assistance.

They're also more error-prone. The very same software that makes touch-screen voting systems so friendly also makes them inaccurate. And even worse, they're inaccurate in precisely the worst possible way.

Bugs in software are commonplace, as any computer user knows. Computer programs regularly malfunction, sometimes in surprising and subtle ways. This is true for all software, including the software in computerized voting machines. For example:

In Fairfax County, Virginia, in 2003, a programming error in the electronic voting machines caused them to mysteriously subtract 100 votes from one particular candidate's totals.

In San Bernardino County, California, in 2001, a programming error caused the computer to look for votes in the wrong portion of the ballot in 33 local elections, which meant that no votes registered on those ballots for that election. A recount was done by hand.

In Volusia County, Floridca, in 2000, an electronic voting machine gave Al Gore a final vote count of negative 16,022 votes.

The 2003 election in Boone County, IA, had the electronic vote-counting equipment showing that more than 140,000 votes had been cast in the November 4 municipal elections. The county has only 50,000 residents and less than half of them were eligible to vote in this election.

There are literally hundreds of similar stories.

What's important about these problems is not that they resulted in a less accurate tally, but that the errors were not uniformly distributed; they affected one candidate more than the other. This means that you can't assume that errors will cancel each other out and not affect the election; you have to assume that any error will skew the results significantly.

Another issue is that software can be hacked. That is, someone can deliberately introduce an error that modifies the result in favor of his preferred candidate. This has nothing to do with whether the voting machines are hooked up to the Internet on election day. The threat is that the computer code could be modified while it is being developed and tested, either by one of the programmers or a hacker who gains access to the voting machine company's network. It's much easier to surreptitiously modify a software system than a hardware system, and it's much easier to make these modifications undetectable.

A third issue is that these problems can have further-reaching effects in software. A problem with a manual machine just affects that machine. A software problem, whether accidental or intentional, can affect many thousands of machines—and skew the results of an entire election.

Some have argued in favor of touch-screen voting systems, citing the millions of dollars that are handled every day by ATMs and other computerized financial systems. That argument ignores another vital characteristic of voting systems: anonymity. Computerized financial systems get most of their security from audit. If a problem is suspected, auditors can go back through the records of the system and figure out what happened. And if the problem turns out to be real, the transaction can be unwound and fixed. Because elections are anonymous, that kind of security just isn't possible.

None of this means that we should abandon touch-screen voting; the benefits of DRE machines are too great to throw away. But it does mean that we need to recognize its limitations, and design systems that can be accurate despite them.

Computer security experts are unanimous on what to do. (Some voting experts disagree, but I think we're all much better off listening to the computer security experts. The problems here are with the computer, not with the fact that the computer is being used in a voting application.) And they have two recommendations:

DRE machines must have a voter-verifiable paper audit trails (sometimes called a voter-verified paper ballot). This is a paper ballot printed out by the voting machine, which the voter is allowed to look at and verify. He doesn't take it home with him. Either he looks at it on the machine behind a glass screen, or he takes the paper and puts it into a ballot box. The point of this is twofold. One, it allows the voter to confirm that his vote was recorded in the manner he intended. And two, it provides the mechanism for a recount if there are problems with the machine.

Software used on DRE machines must be open to public scrutiny. This also has two functions. One, it allows any interested party to examine the software and find bugs, which can then be corrected. This public analysis improves security. And two, it increases public confidence in the voting process. If the software is public, no one can insinuate that the voting system has unfairness built into the code. (Companies that make these machines regularly argue that they need to keep their software secret for security reasons. Don't believe them. In this instance, secrecy has nothing to do with security.)

Computerized systems with these characteristics won't be perfect—no piece of software is—but they'll be much better than what we have now. We need to start treating voting software like we treat any other high-reliability system. The auditing that is conducted on slot machine software in the U.S. is significantly more meticulous than what is done to voting software. The development process for mission-critical airplane software makes voting software look like a slapdash affair. If we care about the integrity of our elections, this has to change.

Proponents of DREs often point to successful elections as "proof" that the systems work. That completely misses the point. The fear is that errors in the software—either accidental or deliberately introduced—can undetectably alter the final tallies. An election without any detected problems is no more a proof the system is reliable and secure than a night that no one broke into your house is proof that your door locks work. Maybe no one tried, or maybe someone tried and succeeded…and you don't know it.

Even if we get the technology right, we still won't be done. If the goal of a voting system is to accurately translate voter intent into a final tally, the voting machine is only one part of the overall system. In the 2004 U.S. election, problems with voter registration, untrained poll workers, ballot design, and procedures for handling problems resulted in far more votes not being counted than problems with the technology. But if we're going to spend money on new voting technology, it makes sense to spend it on technology that makes the problem easier instead of harder.

Revoting

Originally published in Wired, *16 November 2006*

In the world of voting, automatic recount laws are not uncommon. Virginia, where George Allen lost to James Webb in the Senate race by 7,800 out of more than 2.3 million votes, or 0.33%, is an example. If the margin of victory is 1% or less, the loser is allowed to ask for a recount. If the margin is 0.5% or less, the government pays for it. If the margin is between 0.5% and 1%, the loser pays for it.

We have recounts because vote counting is—to put it mildly—sloppy. Americans like their election results fast, before they go to bed at night. So we're willing to put up with inaccuracies in our tallying procedures, and ignore the fact that the numbers we see on television correlate only roughly with reality.

Traditionally, it didn't matter very much, because most voting errors were "random errors."

There are two basic types of voting errors: random errors and systemic errors. Random errors are just that, random—equally likely to happen to anyone. In a close race, random errors won't change the result because votes intended for candidate A that mistakenly go to candidate B happen at the same rate as votes intended for B that mistakenly go to A. (Mathematically, as candidate A's margin of victory increases, random errors slightly decrease it.)

This is why, historically, recounts in close elections rarely change the result. The recount will find the few percent of the errors in each direction, and they'll cancel each other out. In an extremely close election, a careful recount will yield a different result—but that's a rarity.

The other kind of voting error is a systemic error. These are errors in the voting process—the voting machines, the procedures—that cause votes intended for A to go to B at a different rate than the reverse.

An example would be a voting machine that mysteriously recorded more votes for A than there were voters. (Sadly, this kind of thing is not uncommon with electronic voting machines.) Another example would be a random error that only occurs in voting equipment used in areas with strong A support. Systemic errors can make a dramatic difference in an election, because they can easily shift thousands of votes from A to B without any counterbalancing shift from B to A.

Even worse, systemic errors can introduce errors out of proportion to any actual randomness in the vote-counting process. That is, the closeness of an election is not any indication of the presence or absence of systemic errors.

When a candidate has evidence of systemic errors, a recount can fix a wrong result—but only if the recount can catch the error. With electronic voting machines, all too often there simply isn't the data: there are no votes to recount.

This year's election in Florida's 13th Congressional district is such an example. The winner won by a margin of 373 out of 237,861 total votes, but as many as 18,000 votes were not recorded by the electronic voting machines. These votes came from areas where the loser was favored over the winner, and would have likely changed the result.

Or imagine this—as far as we know—hypothetical situation: After the election, someone discovers rogue software in the voting machines that flipped some votes from A to B. Or someone gets caught vote tampering—changing the data on electronic memory cards. The problem is that the original data is lost forever; all we have is the hacked vote.

Faced with problems like this, we can do one of two things. We can certify the result anyway, regretful that people were disenfranchised but knowing that we can't undo that wrong. Or, we can tell everyone to come back and vote again.

To be sure, the very idea of revoting is rife with problems. Elections are a snapshot in time—election day—and a revote will not reflect that. If Virginia revoted for the Senate this year, the election would not just be for the junior senator from Virginia, but for control of the entire Senate. Similarly, in the 2000 presidential election in Florida and the 2004 presidential election in Ohio, single-state revotes would have decided the presidency.

And who should be allowed to revote? Should only people in those precincts where there were problems revote, or should the entire election be rerun? In either case, it is certain that more voters will find their way to the polls, possibly changing the demographic and swaying the result in a direction different than that of the initial set of voters. Is that a bad thing, or a good thing?

Should only people who actually voted—records are kept—or who could demonstrate that they were erroneously turned away from the polls be allowed to revote? In this case, the revote will almost certainly have fewer voters, as some of the original voters will be unable to vote a second time. That's probably a bad thing—but maybe it's not.

The only analogy we have for this are run-off elections, which are required in some jurisdictions if the winning candidate didn't get 50% of the vote. But it's easy to know when you need to have a run-off. Who decides, and based on what evidence, that you need to have a revote?

I admit that I don't have the answers here. They require some serious thinking about elections, and what we're trying to achieve. But smart election security not only tries to prevent vote hacking—or even systemic electronic voting-machine errors—it prepares for recovery after an election has been hacked. We have to start discussing these issues now, when they're non-partisan, instead of waiting for the inevitable situation, and the pre-drawn battle lines those results dictate.

Hacking the Papal Election

Originally published in Crypto-Gram, *15 April 2005*

As the College of Cardinals prepares to elect a new pope, people like me wonder about the election process. How does it work, and just how hard is it to hack the vote?

Of course I'm not advocating voter fraud in the papal election. Nor am I insinuating that a cardinal might perpetrate fraud. But people who work in security can't look at a system without trying to figure out how to break it; it's an occupational hazard.

The rules for papal elections are steeped in tradition, and were last codified on 22 February, 1996: "Universi Dominici Gregis on the Vacancy of the Apostolic See and the Election of the Roman Pontiff." The document is well-thought-out, and filled with details.

The election takes place in the Sistine Chapel, directed by the Church Chamberlain. The ballot is entirely paper-based, and all ballot counting is done by hand. Votes are secret, but everything else is done in public.

First there's the "pre-scrutiny" phase. "At least two or three" paper ballots are given to each cardinal (115 will be voting), presumably so that a cardinal has extras in case he makes a mistake. Then nine election officials are randomly selected: three "Scrutineers" who count the votes, three "Revisers," who verify the results of the Scrutineers, and three "Infirmarii" who collect the votes from those too sick to be in the room. (These officials are chosen randomly for each ballot.)

Each cardinal writes his selection for Pope on a rectangular ballot paper "as far as possible in handwriting that cannot be identified as his." He then folds the paper lengthwise and holds it aloft for everyone to see.

When everyone is done voting, the "scrutiny" phase of the election begins. The cardinals proceed to the altar one by one. On the altar is a large chalice with a paten (the shallow metal plate used to hold communion wafers during mass) resting on top of it. Each cardinal places his folded ballot on the paten. Then he picks up the paten and slides his ballot into the chalice.

If a cardinal cannot walk to the altar, one of the Scrutineers—in full view of everyone—does this for him. If any cardinals are too sick to be in the chapel, the Scrutineers give the Infirmarii a locked empty box with a slot, and the three Infirmarii together collect those votes. (If a cardinal is too sick to write, he asks one of the Infirmarii to do it for him.) The box is opened and the ballots are placed onto the paten and into the chalice, one at a time.

When all the ballots are in the chalice, the first Scrutineer shakes it several times in order to mix them. Then the third Scrutineer transfers the ballots, one by one, from one chalice to another, counting them in the process. If the total number of ballots is not correct, the ballots are burned, and everyone votes again.

To count the votes, each ballot is opened, and the vote is read by each Scrutineer in turn, the third one aloud. Each Scrutineer writes the vote on a tally sheet. This is all done in full view of the cardinals. The total number of votes cast for each person is written on a separate sheet of paper.

Then there's the "post-scrutiny" phase. The Scrutineers tally the votes and determine if there's a winner. Then the Revisers verify the entire process: ballots, tallies, everything. And then the ballots are burned. (That's where the smoke comes from: white if a Pope has been elected, black if not.)

How hard is this to hack? The first observation is that the system is entirely manual, making it immune to the sorts of technological attacks that make modern voting systems so risky. The second observation is that the small group of voters—all of whom know each other—makes it impossible for an outsider to affect the voting in any way. The chapel is cleared and locked before voting. No one is going to dress up as a cardinal and sneak into the Sistine Chapel. In effect, the voter verification process is about as perfect as you're ever going to find.

Eavesdropping on the process is certainly possible, although the rules explicitly state that the chapel is to be checked for recording and transmission devices "with the help of trustworthy individuals of proven technical ability." I read that the Vatican is worried about laser microphones, as there are windows near the chapel's roof.

That leaves us with insider attacks. Can a cardinal influence the election? Certainly the Scrutineers could potentially modify votes, but it's difficult. The counting is conducted in public, and there are multiple people checking every step. It's possible for the first Scrutineer, if he's good at sleight of hand, to swap one ballot paper for another before recording it. Or for the third Scrutineer to swap ballots during the counting process.

A cardinal can't stuff ballots when he votes. The complicated paten-and-chalice ritual ensures that each cardinal votes once—his ballot is visible—and also keeps his hand out of the chalice holding the other votes.

Making the ballots large would make these attacks harder. So would controlling the blank ballots better, and only distributing one to each cardinal per vote. Presumably cardinals change their mind more often during the voting process, so distributing extra blank ballots makes sense.

Ballots from previous votes are burned, which makes it harder to use one to stuff the ballot box. But there's one wrinkle: "If however a second vote is to take place immediately, the ballots from the first vote will be burned only at the end, together with those from the second vote." I assume that's done so there's only one plume of smoke for the two elections, but it would be more secure to burn each set of ballots before the next round of voting. (Although the stack of ballots are pierced with a needle and thread and tied together, which 1) marks them as used, and 2) makes them harder to reuse.)

And lastly, the cardinals are in "choir dress" during the voting, which has translucent lace sleeves under a short red cape; much harder for sleight-of-hand tricks.

It's possible for one Scrutineer to misrecord the votes, but with three Scrutineers, the discrepancy would be quickly detected. I presume a recount would take place, and the correct tally would be verified. Two or three Scrutineers in cahoots with each other could do more mischief, but since the Scrutineers are chosen randomly, the probability of a cabal being selected is very low. And then the Revisers check everything.

More interesting is to try and attack the system of selecting Scrutineers, which isn't well-defined in the document. Influencing the selection of Scrutineers and Revisers seems a necessary first step towards influencing the election.

Ballots with more than one name (overvotes) are void, and I assume the same is true for ballots with no name written on them (undervotes). Illegible or ambiguous ballots are much more likely, and I presume they are discarded. The rules do have a provision for multiple ballots by the same cardinal: "If during the opening of the ballots the Scrutineers should discover two ballots folded in such a way that they appear to have been completed by one elector, if these ballots bear the same name they are counted as one vote; if however they bear two different names, neither vote will be valid; however, in neither of the two cases is the voting session annulled." This surprises me, although I suppose it has happened by accident.

If there's a weak step, it's the counting of the ballots. There's no real reason to do a pre-count, and it gives the Scrutineer doing the transfer a chance to swap legitimate ballots with others he previously stuffed up his sleeve. I like the idea of randomizing the ballots, but putting the ballots in a wire cage and spinning it around would accomplish the same thing more securely, albeit with less reverence.

And if I were improving the process, I would add some kind of white-glove treatment to prevent a Scrutineer from hiding a pencil lead or pen tip under his fingernails. Although the requirement to write out the candidate's name in full gives more resistance against this sort of attack.

The recent change in the process that lets the cardinals go back and forth from the chapel into their dorm rooms—instead of being locked in the chapel the whole time as was done previously—makes the process slightly less secure. But I'm sure it makes it a lot more comfortable.

Lastly, there's the potential for one of the Infirmarii to do what he wants when transcribing the vote of an infirm cardinal, but there's no way to prevent that. If the cardinal is concerned, he could ask all three Infirmarii to witness the ballot.

There's also enormous social—religious, actually—disincentives to hacking the vote. The election takes place in a chapel, at an altar. They also swear an oath as they are casting their ballot—further discouragement. And the Scrutineers are explicitly exhorted not to form any sort of cabal or make any plans to sway the election under pain of excommunication: "The Cardinal electors shall further abstain from any form of pact, agreement, promise or other commitment of any kind which could oblige them to give or deny their vote to a person or persons."

I'm sure there are negotiations and deals and influencing—cardinals are mortal men, after all, and such things are part of how humans come to agreement.

What are the lessons here? First, open systems conducted within a known group make voting fraud much harder. Every step of the election process is observed by everyone, and everyone knows everyone, which makes it harder for someone to get away with anything. Second, small and simple elections are easier to secure. This kind of process works to elect a Pope or a club president, but quickly becomes unwieldy for a large-scale election. The only way manual systems work is through a pyramid-like scheme, with small groups reporting their manually obtained results up the chain to more central tabulating authorities.

And a third and final lesson: when an election process is left to develop over the course of a couple thousand years, you end up with something surprisingly good.

7

Security and Disasters

First Responders

Originally published in Wired, *23 August 2007*

I live in Minneapolis, so the collapse of the Interstate 35W bridge over the Mississippi River earlier this month hit close to home, and was covered in both my local and national news.

Much of the initial coverage consisted of human interest stories, centered on the victims of the disaster and the incredible bravery shown by first responders: the policemen, firefighters, EMTs, divers, National Guard soldiers, and even ordinary people, who all risked their lives to save others. (Just two weeks later, three rescue workers died in their almost-certainly-futile attempt to save six miners in Utah.)

Perhaps the most amazing aspect of these stories is that there's nothing particularly amazing about them. No matter what the disaster—hurricane, earthquake, terrorist attack—the nation's first responders get to the scene soon after.

Which is why it's such a crime when these people can't communicate with each other.

Historically, police departments, fire departments, and EMTs have all had their own independent communications equipment, so when there's a disaster that involves them all, they can't communicate with each other. A 1996 government report said this about the *first* World Trade Center bombing in 1993: "Rescuing victims of the World Trade Center bombing, who were caught between floors, was hindered when police officers could not communicate with firefighters on the very next floor."

And we all know that police and firefighters had the same problem on 9/11. You can read details in firefighter Dennis Smith's book and 9/11 Commission testimony. The *9/11 Commission Report* discusses this as well: Chapter 9 talks about the first responders' communications problems, and commission recommendations for improving emergency-response communications are included in Chapter 12 (pp. 396-397).

In some cities, this communication gap is beginning to close. Homeland Security money has flowed into communities around the country. And while some wasted it on measures like cameras, armed robots, and things having nothing to do with terrorism, others spent it on interoperable communications capabilities. Minnesota did that in 2004.

It worked. Hennepin County Sheriff Rich Stanek told the *St. Paul Pioneer-Press* that lives were saved by disaster planning that had been fine-tuned and improved with lessons learned from 9/11:

"'We have a unified command system now where everyone—police, fire, the sheriff's office, doctors, coroners, local and state and federal officials—operate under one voice,' said Stanek, who is in charge of water recovery efforts at the collapse site.

"'We all operate now under the 800 (megahertz radio frequency system), which was the biggest criticism after 9/11,' Stanek said, 'and to have 50 to 60 different agencies able to speak to each other was just fantastic.'"

Others weren't so lucky. Louisiana's first responders had catastrophic communications problems in 2005, after Hurricane Katrina. According to *National Defense Magazine*: "Police could not talk to firefighters and emergency medical teams. Helicopter and boat rescuers had to wave signs and follow one another to survivors. Sometimes, police and other first responders were out of touch with comrades a few blocks away. National Guard relay runners scurried about with scribbled messages as they did during the Civil War."

A congressional report on preparedness and response to Katrina said much the same thing.

In 2004, the U.S. Conference of Mayors issued a report on communications interoperability. In 25% of the 192 cities surveyed, the police couldn't communicate with the fire department. In 80% of cities, municipal authorities couldn't communicate with the FBI, FEMA, and other federal agencies.

The source of the problem is a basic economic one, called the "collective action problem." A collective action is one that needs the coordinated effort of several entities in order to succeed. The problem arises when each individual entity's needs diverge from the collective needs, and there is no mechanism to ensure that those individual needs are sacrificed in favor of the collective need.

Jerry Brito of George Mason University shows how this applies to first-responder communications. Each of the nation's 50,000 or so emergency-response organizations—local police department, local fire department, etc.—buys its own communications equipment. As you'd expect, they buy equipment as closely suited to their needs as they can. Ensuring interoperability with other organizations' equipment benefits the common good, but sacrificing their unique needs for that compatibility may not be in the best immediate interest of any of those organizations. There's no central directive to ensure interoperability, so there ends up being none.

This is an area where the federal government can step in and do good. Too much of the money spent on terrorism defense has been overly specific: effective only if the terrorists attack a particular target or use a particular tactic. Money spent on emergency response is different: It's effective regardless of what the terrorists plan, and it's also effective in the wake of natural or infrastructure disasters.

No particular disaster, whether intentional or accidental, is common enough to justify spending a lot of money on preparedness for a specific emergency. But spending money on preparedness in general will pay off again and again.

Accidents and Security Incidents

Originally published in Crypto-Gram, *15 September 2003*

On August 14 at 4:00 p.m., the power went out in New York City and across much of the Northeast. As many as 50 million people were without power, some for days. Although there were some initial rumors of terrorism—only a few, thankfully—it was an accident.

At a time when we're worried about attacks—by terrorists, hackers, and ordinary criminals—it's worth spending some time talking about accidents.

Some years ago computer-security researcher Ross Anderson described the difference as Murphy vs. Satan. Defending against accidents, he said, means designing and engineering in a world ruled by Murphy's Law. Things go wrong because, well, because things go wrong. When you're designing for safety, you're designing for a world where random faults occur. You're designing a bridge that will not collapse if there's an earthquake, bed sheets that won't burst into flames if there's a fire, computer systems that will still work—or at least fail gracefully—in a power blackout. Sometimes you're designing for large-scale events—tornadoes, earthquakes, and other natural disasters—and sometimes you're designing for individual events: someone slipping on the bathroom floor, a child sticking a fork into something (accidental from the parent's point of view, even though the child may have done it on purpose), a tree falling on a building's roof.

Security is different. In addition to worrying about accidents, you also have to think about nonrandom events. Defending against attacks means engineering in a world ruled by Satan's Law. Things go wrong because there is a malicious and intelligent adversary trying to force things to go wrong, at the very worst time, with the very worst results. The differences between attacks and accidents are intent, intelligence, and control.

Here are some examples:

Safety: You can predict how many fire stations a town needs to handle all the random fires that are likely to break out. *Security*: A pyromaniac can deliberately set off more fire alarms than the town's fire stations can handle so as to make his attacks more effective.

Safety: Knives are accidentally left in airplane carry-on luggage and can be spotted by airport X-ray machines. *Security*: An attacker tries to sneak through a knife made of a material hard to detect with an X-ray machine, and then deliberately positions it in her luggage to make it even harder to detect with the X-ray machine.

Safety: Building engineers calculate how many fire doors are required for safe evacuation in an emergency. *Security*: Those doors are deliberately barricaded before murderers set fire to the building. (This happened in a Rwandan convent in 1994.)

A few years ago, a colleague of mine was showing off his company's network security operations center. He was confident his team could respond to any computer intrusion. "What happens if the hacker calls a bomb threat in to this building before attacking your network?" I asked. He hadn't thought of that. The problem is, attackers do think of these things. The adolescent murderers at the Westside Middle School in Jonesboro, Arkansas, in 1998 set off the fire alarm and killed five and wounded ten others as they all funneled outside.

In an accident, the attacker is fate, luck, or Mother Nature. In an attack, the attacker is both intelligent and deliberate. Attackers can deliberately force faults at precisely the most opportune time and in precisely the most opportune way. Attackers can exploit other people's accidents. And when an attacker finds a vulnerability, he can exploit it again and again. The odds of a natural fire are very low in most industrial countries, but an arsonist can create a fire on demand. Buffer overflows can happen in computers by accident, but they hardly ever do; an attacker can force a buffer overflow that does maximum damage to a computer system. It is the notion of an attacker that separates safety and security engineering. In security, intelligent opposition is trying to make security fail. And a safety failure caused by an attacker becomes a security failure.

The two are also very similar. Regardless of whether you were stabbed by a mugger or the knife slipped in kitchen accident, the emergency room will respond the same way. The response by firemen, policemen, and other rescue personnel after 9/11 would have been no different had the planes lost their bearings in fog and accidentally flown into the Twin Towers (as a plane flew into the Empire State Building in 1945). Backup procedures are the same regardless of whether someone accidentally deleted a file or a worm deleted the file as part of its programming.

Defenses are largely the same: countermeasures to defend the systems, and reactive measures after the events. Better isolation of individual power plants stops blackouts from spreading, regardless of the cause. The rarity of blackouts, which led to inexperience in dealing with them, exacerbated the problem. Disaster recovery works against both floods and bombs. Securing the weakest link, defense in depth, compartmentalization—all the techniques I talk about to improve security—also help prevent accidents.

And, in both cases—security failures and accidents—it's a series of failures that makes for spectacular results. The power blackout started as a small accident and then cascaded into a large-scale blackout. The 9/11 terrorist attack started out as a relatively small security failure (taking over the airplanes), turned into a large disaster (crashing them into the World Trade Center), and then cascaded into an enormous disaster (lives lost, buildings collapsed, loss of communications, etc.). In neither case could the final results have been predicted based only on the initial failure; the systems were just too complicated.

It's because of the interconnectedness of our systems that these events turned into large-scale disasters. It happens rarely—neither the blackout nor the terrorist attacks were common events—but sometimes things are aligned in just the perfect way so that everything comes out wrong. But if an intelligent and malicious attacker is trying to steer events, disaster is more likely.

Security at the Olympics

Originally published in Sydney Morning Herald, *26 August 2004*

If you watched the Olympic games on television, you saw the unprecedented security surrounding the 2004 Olympics. You saw shots of guards and soldiers, and gunboats and frogmen patrolling the harbors. But there was a lot more security behind the scenes. Olympic press materials state that there was a system of 1,250 infrared and high-resolution surveillance cameras mounted on concrete poles. Additional surveillance data was collected from sensors on 12 patrol boats, 4,000 vehicles, 9 helicopters, 4 mobile command centers, and a blimp. It wasn't only images; microphones collected conversations, speech-recognition software converted them to text, and then sophisticated pattern-matching software looked for suspicious patterns. Seventy thousand people were involved in Olympic security, about seven per athlete or one for every 76 spectators.

The Greek government reportedly spent $1.5 billion on security during the Olympics. But aside from the impressive-looking guards and statistics, was the money well-spent? In many ways, Olympic security is a harbinger of what life could be like in the U.S. If the Olympics are going to be a security test bed, it's worth exploring how well the security actually worked.

Unfortunately, that's not easy to do. We have press materials, but the security details remain secret. We know, for example, that SAIC developed the massive electronic surveillance system, but we have to take their word for it that it actually works. Now, SAIC is no slouch; it was one of the contractors that built the NSA's ECHELON electronics eavesdropping system, and presumably has some tricks up its sleeves. But how well does the system detect suspicious conversations or objects, and how often does it produce false alarms? We have no idea.

But while we can't examine the inner workings of Olympic security, we do have some glimpses of security in action.

A reporter from the *Sunday Mirror*, a newspaper in Britain, reported all sorts of problems with security. First, he got a job as a driver with a British contractor. He provided no references, underwent no formal interview or background check, and was immediately given access to the main stadium. He found that his van was never thoroughly searched, and that he could have brought in anything. He was able to plant three packages that were designed to look like bombs, all of which went undetected during security sweeps. He was able to get within 60 feet of dozens of heads of state during the opening ceremonies.

In a separate incident, a man wearing a tutu and clown shoes managed to climb a diving platform, dive into the water, and swim around for several minutes before officials pulled him out. He claimed that he wanted to send a message to his wife, but the name of an online gambling website printed on his chest implied a more commercial motive.

And on the last day of the Olympics, a Brazilian runner who was leading the men's marathon, with only a few miles to go, was shoved off the course into the crowd by a costumed intruder from Ireland. He ended up coming in third; his lead was narrowing before the incident, but it's impossible to tell how much the episode might have cost him.

These three incidents are anecdotal, but they illustrate an important point about security at this kind of event: It's pretty much impossible to stop a lone operator intent on making mischief. It doesn't matter how many cameras and listening devices you've installed. It doesn't matter how many badge checkers and gun-toting security personnel you've hired. It doesn't matter how many billions of dollars you've spent.

A lone gunman or a lone bomber can always find a crowd of people.

This is not to say that guards and cameras are useless, only that they have their limits. Money spent on them rapidly reaches the point of diminishing returns, and after that, more is just wasteful.

Far more effective would have been to spend most of that $1.5 billion on intelligence and on emergency response. Intelligence is an invaluable tool against terrorism, and it works regardless of what the terrorists are plotting—even if the plots have nothing to do with the Olympics. Emergency response preparedness is no less valuable, and it too works regardless of what terrorists manage to pull off—before, during, or after the Olympics.

No major security incidents happened this year at the Olympics. As a result, major security contractors will tout that result as proof that $1.5 billion was well-spent on security. What it really shows is how quickly $1.5 billion can be wasted on security. Now that the Olympics are over and everyone has gone home, the world will be no safer for spending all the money. That's a shame, because that $1.5 billion could have bought the world a lot of security if spent properly.

Blaster and the August 14th Blackout ▬▬▬▬▬

Originally published in News.com, 9 December 2003

Did Blaster cause the August 14th blackout? The official analysis says "no," but I'm not so sure.

According to the "Interim Report: Causes of the August 14th Blackout in the United States and Canada," published in November and based on detailed research by a panel of government and industry officials, the blackout was caused by a series of failures.

The chain of events began at FirstEnergy, a power company in Ohio. There, a series of human and computer failures turned a small problem into a major one. And because critical alarm systems failed, workers at FirstEnergy did not stop the cascade because they did not know what was happening.

This is where I think Blaster may have been involved. The report gives a specific timeline for the failures. At 14:14 EDT, the "alarm and logging software" at FirstEnergy's control room failed. This alarm software "provided audible and visual indications when a significant piece of equipment changed from an acceptable to problematic condition." Of course, no one knew that it failed.

Six minutes later, "several" remote control consoles failed. At 14:41, the primary server computer that hosted the alarm function failed. Its functions were passed to a backup computer, which failed at 14:54.

Doesn't this sound like a computer worm wending its way through FirstEnergy's operational computers?

According to the report, "...for over an hour no one in FE's control room grasped that their computer systems were not operating properly, even though FE's Information Technology support staff knew of the problems and were working to solve them..."

Doesn't this sound like IT working to clean a worm out of its network?

This massive computer failure was critical to the cascading power failure. The report continues: "Power system operators rely heavily on audible and on-screen alarms, plus alarm logs, to reveal any significant changes in their system's conditions. After 14:14 EDT on August 14, FE's operators were working under a significant handicap without these tools. However, they were in further jeopardy because they did not know that they were operating without alarms, so that they did not realize that system conditions were changing."

Other computer glitches are mentioned in the report. At the Midwest Independent Transmission System Operator, a regional agency that oversees power distribution, there's something called a "state estimator." It's a computer used to determine whether the power grid is in trouble. This computer also failed, at 12:15. According to the report, a technician tried to repair it and forgot to turn it back on when he went to lunch.

The Blaster worm first appeared on August 11, and infected more than a million computers in the days following. It targeted a vulnerability in the Microsoft operating system. Infected computers, in turn, tried to infect other computers, and in this way the worm automatically spread from computer to computer and network to network. Although the worm didn't perform any malicious actions on the computers it infected, its mere existence drained resources and often caused the host computer to crash. To remove the worm a system administrator had to run a program that erased the malicious code; then the administrator had to patch the vulnerability so that the computer would not get re-infected.

According to research by Stuart Staniford, Blaster was a random-start sequential-scanner, and scanned at about 11 IPs/second. A given scanner would cover a Class B network in about 1 hour and 40 minutes. The FirstEnergy computer-failure times are fairly consistent with a series of computers with addresses dotted around a class B being compromised by a scan of the class B, probably by an infected instance on the same network. (Note that it was not necessary for the FirstEnergy network to be on the Internet; Blaster infected many internal networks.)

The coincidence of the timing is too obvious to ignore. At 14:14 EDT, the Blaster Worm was dropping systems all across North America. The report doesn't explain why so many computers—both primary and backup systems—at FirstEnergy were failing at around the same time, but Blaster is certainly a reasonable suspect.

Unfortunately, the report doesn't directly address the Blaster worm and its effects on FirstEnergy's computers. The closest I could find was this paragraph, on page 99: "Although there were a number of worms and viruses impacting the Internet and Internet connected systems and networks in North America before and during the outage, the SWG's preliminary analysis provides no indication that worm/virus activity had a significant effect on the power generation and delivery systems. Further SWG analysis will test this finding."

Why the tortured prose? The writers take pains to assure us that "the power generation and delivery systems" were not affected by Blaster. But what about the alarm systems? Clearly they were all affected by something, and all at the same time.

This wouldn't be the first time a Windows epidemic swept through FirstEnergy. The company has admitted it was hit by Slammer in January.

Let's be fair. I don't know that Blaster caused the blackout. The report doesn't say that Blaster caused the blackout. Conventional wisdom is that Blaster did not cause the blackout. But it seems more and more likely that Blaster was one of the many causes of the blackout.

Regardless of the answer, there's a very important moral here. As networked computers infiltrate more and more of our critical infrastructure, that infrastructure is vulnerable not only to attacks but also to sloppy software and sloppy operations. And these vulnerabilities are invariably not the obvious ones. The computers that directly control the power grid are well-protected. It's the peripheral systems that are less protected and more likely to be vulnerable. And a direct attack is unlikely to cause our infrastructure to fail, because the connections are too complex and too obscure. It's only by accident—Blaster affecting systems at just the wrong time, allowing a minor failure to become a major one—that these massive failures occur.

We've seen worms knock out 911 telephone service. We've seen worms disable ATMs. None of this was predictable beforehand, but all of it is preventable. I believe that this sort of thing will become even more common in the future.

Avian Flu and Disaster Planning

Originally published in Wired, *26 July 2007*

If an avian flu pandemic broke out tomorrow, would your company be ready for it?

Computerworld published a series of articles on that question last year, prompted by a presentation analyst firm Gartner gave at a conference last November. Among Gartner's recommendations: "Store 42 gallons of water per data center employee—enough for a six-week quarantine—and don't forget about food, medical care, cooking facilities, sanitation and electricity."

And Gartner's conclusion, over half a year later: Pretty much no organizations are ready.

This doesn't surprise me at all. It's not that organizations don't spend enough effort on disaster planning, although that's true; it's that this really isn't the sort of disaster worth planning for.

Disaster planning is critically important for individuals, families, organizations large and small, and governments. For the individual, it can be as simple as spending a few minutes thinking about how he or she would respond to a disaster. For example, I've spent a lot of time thinking about what I would do if I lost the use of my computer, whether by equipment failure, theft, or government seizure. As a result, I have a pretty complex backup and encryption system, ensuring that 1) I'd still have access to my data, and 2) no one else would. On the other hand, I haven't given any serious thought to family disaster planning, although others have.

For an organization, disaster planning can be much more complex. What would it do in the case of fire, flood, earthquake, and so on? How would its business survive? The resultant disaster plan might include backup data centers, temporary staffing contracts, planned degradation of services, and a host of other products and services—and consultants to tell you how to use it all.

And anyone who does this kind of thing knows that planning isn't enough: Testing your disaster plan is critical. Far too often the backup software fails when it has to do an actual restore, or the diesel-powered emergency generator fails to kick in. That's also the flaw with emergency kit links given below; if you don't know how to use a compass or first-aid kit, having one in your car won't do you much good.

But testing isn't valuable just because it reveals practical problems with a plan. It also has enormous ancillary benefits for your organization in terms of communication and team building. There's nothing like a good crisis to get people to rely on each other. Sometimes I think companies should forget about those team-building exercises that involve climbing trees and building fires, and instead pretend that a flood has taken out the primary data center.

It really doesn't matter what disaster scenario you're testing. The real disaster won't be like the test, regardless of what you do, so just pick one and go. Whether you're an individual trying to recover from a simulated virus attack, or an organization testing its response to a hypothetical shooter in the building, you'll learn a lot about yourselves and your organization, as well as your plan.

There is a sweet spot, though, in disaster preparedness. Some disasters are too small or too common to worry about. ("We're out of paper clips!? Call the Crisis Response Team together. I'll get the Paper Clip Shortage Readiness Program Directive Manual Plan.") And others are too large or too rare.

It makes no sense to plan for total annihilation of the continent, whether by nuclear or meteor strike—that's obvious. But depending on the size of the planner, many other disasters are also too large to plan for. People can stockpile food and water to prepare for a hurricane that knocks out services for a few days, but not for a Katrina-like flood that knocks out services for months. Organizations can prepare for losing a data center due to a flood, fire, or hurricane, but not for a Black Death–scale epidemic that would wipe out a third of the population. No one can fault bond trading firm Cantor Fitzgerald, which lost two thirds of its employees in the 9/11 attack on the World Trade Center, for not having a plan in place to deal with that possibility.

Another consideration is scope. If your corporate headquarters burns down, it's actually a bigger problem for you than a citywide disaster that does much more damage. If the whole San Francisco Bay Area were taken out by an earthquake, customers of affected companies would be far more likely to forgive lapses in service, or would go the extra mile to help out. Think of the nationwide response to 9/11; the human "just deal with it" social structures kicked in, and we all muddled through.

In general, you can only reasonably prepare for disasters that leave your world largely intact. If a third of the country's population dies, it's a different world. The economy is different, the laws are different—the world is different. You simply can't plan for it; there's no way you can know enough about what the new world will look like. Disaster planning only makes sense within the context of existing society.

What all of this means is that any bird flu pandemic will very likely fall outside the corporate disaster-planning sweet spot. We're just guessing on its infectiousness, of course, but (despite the alarmism from two and three years ago), likely scenarios are either moderate to severe absenteeism because people are staying home for a few weeks—any organization ought to be able to deal with that—or a major disaster of proportions that dwarf the concerns of any organization. There's not much in between.

Honestly, if you think you're heading toward a world where you need to stash six weeks' worth of food and water in your company's closets, do you really believe that it will be enough to see you through to the other side?

A blogger commented on what I said in one article: "Schneier is using what I would call the nuclear war argument for doing nothing. If there's a nuclear war nothing will be left anyway, so why waste your time stockpiling food or building fallout shelters? It's entirely out of your control. It's someone else's responsibility. Don't worry about it."

Almost. Bird flu, pandemics, and disasters in general—whether man-made like 9/11, natural like bird flu, or a combination like Katrina—are definitely things we should worry about. The proper place for bird flu planning is at the government level. (These are also the people who should worry about nuclear and meteor strikes.) But real disasters don't exactly match our plans, and we are best served by a bunch of generic disaster plans and a smart, flexible organization that can deal with anything.

The key is preparedness. Much more important than planning, preparedness is about setting up social structures so that people fall into doing something sensible when things go wrong. Think of all the wasted effort—and even more wasted *desire*—to do something after Katrina because there was no way for most people to help. Preparedness is about getting people to react when there's a crisis. It's something the military trains its soldiers for.

This advice holds true for organizations, families, and individuals as well. And remember, despite what you read about nuclear accidents, suicide terrorism, genetically engineered viruses, and mutant man-eating badgers, you live in the safest society in the history of mankind.

8 Economics of Security

Economics and Information Security

Originally published in Wired, *29 June 2006*

I'm sitting in a conference room at Cambridge University, trying to simultaneously finish this article for Wired News and pay attention to the presenter onstage.

I'm in this awkward situation because 1) this article is due tomorrow, and 2) I'm attending the fifth Workshop on the Economics of Information Security, or: WEIS—to my mind, the most interesting computer security conference of the year.

The idea that economics has anything to do with computer security is relatively new. Ross Anderson and I seem to have stumbled upon the idea independently. He in his brilliant article from 2001, "Why Information Security Is Hard—An Economic Perspective," and me in various essays and presentations from that same period.

WEIS began a year later at the University of California at Berkeley and has grown ever since. It's the only workshop where technologists get together with economists and lawyers and try to understand the problems of computer security.

And economics has a lot to teach computer security. We generally think of computer security as a problem of technology, but often systems fail because of misplaced economic incentives: The people who could protect a system are not the ones who suffer the costs of failure.

When you start looking, economic considerations are everywhere in computer security. Hospitals' medical-records systems provide comprehensive billing-management features for the administrators who specify them, but are not so good at protecting patients' privacy. ATMs suffered from fraud in countries like the United Kingdom and the Netherlands, where poor regulation left banks without sufficient incentive to secure their systems, and allowed them to pass the cost of fraud along to their customers. And one reason the Internet is insecure is that liability for attacks is so diffuse.

In all of these examples, the economic considerations of security are more important than the technical considerations.

More generally, many of the most basic security questions are at least as much economic as technical. Do we spend enough on keeping hackers out of our computer systems? Or do we spend too much? For that matter, do we spend appropriate amounts on police and Army services? And are we spending our security budgets on the right things? In the shadow of 9/11, questions like these have a heightened importance.

Economics can actually explain many of the puzzling realities of Internet security. Firewalls are common, e-mail encryption is rare: not because of the relative effectiveness of the technologies, but because of the economic pressures that drive companies to install them. Corporations rarely publicize information about intrusions; that's because of economic incentives against doing so. And an insecure operating system is the international standard, in part, because its economic effects are largely borne not by the company that builds the operating system, but by the customers that buy it.

Some of the most controversial cyberpolicy issues also sit squarely between information security and economics. For example, the issue of digital rights management: Is copyright law too restrictive—or not restrictive enough—to maximize society's creative output? And if it needs to be more restrictive, will DRM technologies benefit the music industry or the technology vendors? Is Microsoft's Trusted Computing Initiative a good idea, or just another way for the company to lock its customers into Windows, Media Player and Office? Any attempt to answer these questions becomes rapidly entangled with both information security and economic arguments.

WEIS encourages papers on these and other issues in economics and computer security. We heard papers presented on the economics of digital forensics of cell phones—if you have an uncommon phone, the police probably don't have the tools to perform forensic analysis—and the effect of stock spam on stock prices: It actually works in the short term. We learned that more-educated wireless network users are not more likely to secure their access points, and that the best predictor of wireless security is the default configuration of the router.

Other researchers presented economic models to explain patch management, peer-to-peer worms, investment in information security technologies, and opt-in versus opt-out privacy policies. There was a field study that tried to estimate the cost to the U.S. economy for information infrastructure failures: less than you might think. And one of the most interesting papers looked at economic barriers to adopting new security protocols, specifically DNS Security Extensions.

This is all heady stuff. In the early years, there was a bit of a struggle as the economists and the computer security technologists tried to learn each others' languages. But now it seems that there's a lot more synergy, and more collaboration between the two camps.

I've long said that the fundamental problems in computer security are no longer about technology; they're about applying technology. Workshops like WEIS are helping us understand why good security technologies fail and bad ones succeed, and that kind of insight is critical if we're going to improve security in the information age.

Aligning Interest with Capability

Originally published in Wired, *1 June 2006*

Have you ever been to a retail store and seen this sign on the register: "Your purchase free if you don't get a receipt"? You almost certainly didn't see it in an expensive or high-end store. You saw it in a convenience store, or a fast-food restaurant, or maybe a liquor store. That sign is a security device, and a clever one at that. And it illustrates a very important rule about security: It works best when you align interests with capability.

If you're a store owner, one of your security worries is employee theft. Your employees handle cash all day, and dishonest ones will pocket some of it for themselves. The history of the cash register is mostly a history of preventing this kind of theft. Early cash registers were just boxes with a bell attached. The bell rang when an employee opened the box, alerting the store owner— who was presumably elsewhere in the store—that an employee was handling money.

The register tape was an important development in security against employee theft. Every transaction is recorded in write-only media, in such a way that it's impossible to insert or delete transactions. It's an audit trail. Using that audit trail, the store owner can count the cash in the drawer, and compare the amount with the register tape. Any discrepancies can be docked from the employee's paycheck.

If you're a dishonest employee, you have to keep transactions off the register. If someone hands you money for an item and walks out, you can pocket that money without anyone being the wiser. And, in fact, that's how employees steal cash in retail stores.

What can the store owner do? He can stand there and watch the employee, of course. But that's not very efficient; the whole point of having employees is so that the store owner can do other things. The customer is standing there anyway, but the customer doesn't care one way or another about a receipt.

So here's what the employer does: he hires the customer. By putting up a sign saying, "Your purchase free if you don't get a receipt," the employer is getting the customer to guard the employee. The customer makes sure the employee gives him a receipt, and employee theft is reduced accordingly.

There is a general rule in security to align interest with capability. The customer has the capability of watching the employee; the sign gives him the interest.

In *Beyond Fear*, I wrote about ATM fraud; you can see the same mechanism at work:

"When ATM cardholders in the U.S. complained about phantom withdrawals from their accounts, the courts generally held that the banks had to prove fraud. Hence, the banks' agenda was to improve security and keep fraud low, because they paid the costs of any fraud. In the U.K., the reverse was true: The courts generally sided with the banks and assumed that any attempts to repudiate withdrawals were cardholder fraud, and the cardholder had to prove otherwise. This caused the banks to have the opposite agenda; they didn't care about improving security, because they were content to blame the problems on the customers and send them to jail for complaining. The result was that in the U.S., the banks improved ATM security to forestall additional losses—most of the fraud actually was not the cardholder's fault—while in the U.K., the banks did nothing."

The banks had the capability to improve security. In the U.S., they also had the interest. But in the U.K., only the customer had the interest. It wasn't until the U.K. courts reversed themselves and aligned interest with capability that ATM security improved.

Computer security is no different. For years I have argued in favor of software liabilities. Software vendors are in the best position to improve software security; they have the capability. But, unfortunately, they don't have much interest. Features, schedule, and profitability are far more important. Software liabilities will change that. They'll align interest with capability, and they'll improve software security.

One last story. In Italy, tax fraud used to be a national hobby. (It may still be; I don't know.) The government was tired of retail stores not reporting sales and paying taxes, so they passed a law regulating the customers. Customers having just purchased an item and stopped within a certain distance of a retail store had to produce a receipt or they would be fined. Just as in the "Your purchase free if you don't get a receipt" story, the law turned the customers into tax inspectors. They demanded receipts from merchants, which in turn forced the merchants to create a paper audit trail for the purchase and pay the required tax.

This was a great idea, but it didn't work very well. Customers, especially tourists, didn't like to be stopped by police. People started demanding that the police prove they just purchased the item. Threatening people with fines if they didn't guard merchants wasn't as effective an enticement as offering people a reward if they didn't get a receipt.

Interest must be aligned with capability, but you need to be careful how you generate interest.

National Security Consumers

Originally published in News.com, 4 May 2004

National security is a hot political topic right now, as both presidential candidates are asking us to decide which one of them is better fit to secure the country.

Many large and expensive government programs—the CAPPS II airline profiling system, the US-VISIT program that fingerprints foreigners entering our country, and the various data-mining programs in research and development—take as a given the need for more security.

At the end of 2005, when many provisions of the controversial USA PATRIOT Act expire, we will again be asked to sacrifice certain liberties for security, as many legislators seek to make those provisions permanent.

As a security professional, I see a vital component missing from the debate. It's important to discuss different security measures, and determine which ones will be most effective. But that's only half of the equation; it's just as important to discuss the costs. Security is always a trade-off, and herein lies the real question: "Is this security countermeasure worth it?"

As Americans, and as citizens of the world, we need to think of ourselves as security consumers. Just as a smart consumer looks for the best value for his dollar, we need to do the same. Many of the countermeasures being proposed and implemented cost billions. Others cost in other ways: convenience, privacy, civil liberties, fundamental freedoms, greater danger of other threats. As consumers, we need to get the most security we can for what we spend.

The invasion of Iraq, for example, is presented as an important move for national security. It may be true, but it's only half of the argument. Invading Iraq has cost the United States enormously. The monetary bill is more than $100 billion, and the cost is still rising. The cost in American lives is more than 600, and the number is still rising. The cost in world opinion is considerable. There's a question that needs to be addressed: "Was this the best way to spend all of that? As security consumers, did we get the most security we could have for that $100 billion, those lives, and those other things?"

If it was, then we did the right thing. But if it wasn't, then we made a mistake. Even though a free Iraq is a good thing in the abstract, we would have been smarter spending our money, and lives and good will, in the world elsewhere.

That's the proper analysis, and it's the way everyone thinks when making personal security choices. Even people who say that we must do everything possible to prevent another 9/11 don't advocate permanently grounding every aircraft in this country. Even though that would be an effective countermeasure, it's ridiculous. It's not worth it. Giving up commercial aviation is far too large a price to pay for the increase in security that it would buy. Only a foolish security consumer would do something like that.

Oddly, when I first wrote this essay for CNet, I received a comment accusing me of being a pacifist. To me, this completely misses the point. I am not espousing a political philosophy; I am espousing a decision-making methodology. Whether you are a pacifist or a militarist, a Republican or a Democrat, an American or European...you're a security consumer. Different consumers will make different trade-offs, since much of this decision is subjective, but they'll use the same analysis.

We need to bring the same analysis to bear when thinking about other security countermeasures. Is the added security from the CAPPS-II airline profiling system worth the billions of dollars it will cost, both in dollars and in the systematic stigmatization of certain classes of Americans? Would we be smarter to spend our money on hiring Arabic translators within the FBI and the CIA, or on emergency response capabilities in our cities and towns?

As security consumers, we get to make this choice. America doesn't have infinite money or freedoms. If we're going to spend them to get security, we should act like smart consumers and get the most security we can.

The efficacy of a security countermeasure is important, but it's never the only consideration. Almost none of the people reading this essay wear bullet-proof vests. It's not because they don't work—in fact, they do—but because most people don't believe that wearing the vest is worth the cost. It's not worth the money, or the inconvenience, or the lack of style. The risk of being shot is low. As security consumers, we don't believe that a bulletproof vest is a good security trade-off.

Similarly, much of what is being proposed as national security is a bad security trade-off. It's not worth it, and as consumers we're getting ripped off.

Being a smart security consumer is hard, just as being a good citizen is hard. Why? Because both require thoughtful consideration of trade-offs and alterna-tives. But in this election year, it is vitally important. We need to learn about the issues. We need to turn to experts who are nonpartisan—who are not try-ing to get elected or stay elected. We need to become informed. Otherwise it's no different from walking into a car dealership without knowing anything about the different models and prices—we're going to get ripped off.

Liability and Security

Originally published in IEEE Computer, *April 2004*

Today, computer security is at a crossroads. It's failing, regularly, and with increasingly serious results. I believe it will improve eventually. In the near term, the consequences of insecurity will get worse before they get better. And when they get better, the improvement will be slow and will be met with con-siderable resistance. The engine of this improvement will be liability—hold-ing software manufacturers accountable for the security and, more generally, the quality of their products—and the timetable for improvement depends wholly on how quickly security liability permeates cyberspace.

Network security is not a problem that technology can solve. Security has a technological component, but businesses approach security as they do any other business risk: in terms of risk management. Organizations optimize their activities to minimize their cost–risk product, and understanding those motivations is key to understanding computer security today.

For example, most organizations don't spend a lot of money on network security. Why? Because the costs are significant: time, expense, reduced functionality, frustrated end users. On the other hand, the costs of ignoring security and getting hacked are small: the possibility of bad press and angry customers, maybe some network downtime, none of which is permanent. And there's some regulatory pressure, from audits or lawsuits, that add additional costs. The result: a smart organization does what everyone else does, and no more.

The same economic reasoning explains why software vendors don't spend a lot of effort securing their products. The costs of adding good security are significant—large expenses, reduced functionality, delayed product releases, annoyed users—while the costs of ignoring security are minor: occasional bad press, and maybe some users switching to competitors' products. Any smart software vendor will talk big about security, but do as little as possible.

Think about why firewalls succeeded in the marketplace. It's not because they're effective; most firewalls are installed so poorly as not to be effective, and there are many more effective security products that have never seen widespread deployment. Firewalls are ubiquitous because auditors started demanding firewalls. This changed the cost equation for businesses. The cost of adding a firewall was expense and user annoyance, but the cost of not having a firewall was failing an audit. And even worse, a company without a firewall could be accused of not following industry best practices in a lawsuit. The result: Everyone has a firewall, whether it does any good or not.

Network security is a business problem, and the only way to fix it is to concentrate on the business motivations. We need to change the costs; security needs to affect an organization's bottom line in an obvious way. In order to improve computer security, the CEO must care. In order for the CEO to care, it must affect the stock price and the shareholders.

I have a three-step program towards improving computer and network security. None of the steps has anything to do with the technology; they all have to do with businesses, economics, and people.

Step one: Enforce liabilities. This is essential. Today there are no real consequences for having bad security, or for having low-quality software of any kind. In fact, the marketplace rewards low quality. More precisely, it rewards early releases at the expense of almost all quality. If we expect CEOs to spend significant resources on security—especially the security of their customers—

they must be liable for mishandling their customers' data. If we expect software vendors to reduce features, lengthen development cycles, and invest in secure software development processes, they must be liable for security vulnerabilities in their products.

Legislatures could impose liability on the computer industry, by forcing software manufacturers to live with the same product liability laws that affect other industries. If software manufacturers produced a defective product, they would be liable for damages. Even without this, courts could start imposing liability-like penalties on software manufacturers and users. This is starting to happen. A U.S. judge forced the Department of Interior to take its network offline, because it couldn't guarantee the safety of American Indian data it was entrusted with. Several cases have resulted in penalties against companies who used customer data in violation of their privacy promises, or who collected that data using misrepresentation or fraud. And judges have issued restraining orders against companies with insecure networks that are used as conduits for attacks against others.

However it happens, liability changes everything. Currently, there is no reason for a software company not to offer more features, more complexity. Liability forces software companies to think twice before changing something. Liability forces companies to protect the data they're entrusted with.

Step two: Allow parties to transfer liabilities. This will happen automatically, because this is what insurance companies do. The insurance industry turns variable-cost risks into fixed expenses. They're going to move into cyber-insurance in a big way. And when they do, they're going to drive the computer security industry...just like they drive the security industry in the brick-and-mortar world.

A company doesn't buy security for its warehouse—strong locks, window bars, or an alarm system—because it makes it feel safe. It buys that security because its insurance rates go down. The same thing will hold true for computer security. Once enough policies are being written, insurance companies will start charging different premiums for different levels of security. Even without legislated liability, the CEO will start noticing how his insurance rates change. And once the CEO starts buying security products based on his insurance premiums, the insurance industry will wield enormous power in the marketplace. They will determine which security products are ubiquitous, and which are ignored. And since the insurance companies pay for the actual liability, they have a great incentive to be rational about risk analysis and the effectiveness of security products.

And software companies will take notice, and will increase security in order to make the insurance for their products affordable.

Step three: Provide mechanisms to reduce risk. This will happen automatically and be entirely market driven, because it's what the insurance industry wants. Moreover, they want it done in standard models that they can build policies around. They're going to look to security processes: processes of secure software development before systems are released, and processes of protection, detection, and response for corporate networks and systems. And more and more, they're going to look towards outsourced services.

The insurance industry prefers security outsourcing, because they can write policies around those services. It's much easier to design insurance around a standard set of security services delivered by an outside vendor than it is to customize a policy for each individual network.

Actually, this isn't a three-step program. It's a one-step program with two inevitable consequences. Enforce liability, and everything else will flow from it. It has to.

Much of Internet security is a common—an area used by a community as a whole. Like all commons, keeping it working benefits everyone, but any individual can benefit from exploiting it. (Think of the criminal justice system in the real world.) In our society, we protect our commons—our environment, healthy working conditions, safe food and drug practices, lawful streets, sound accounting practices—by legislating those goods and by making companies liable for taking undue advantage of those commons. This kind of thinking is what gives us bridges that don't collapse, clean air and water, and sanitary restaurants. We don't live in a "buyer beware" society; we hold companies liable for taking advantage of buyers.

There's no reason to treat software any differently from other products. Today Firestone can produce a tire with a single systemic flaw and they're liable, but Microsoft can produce an operating system with multiple systemic flaws discovered per week and not be liable. This makes no sense, and it's the primary reason security is so bad today.

Liabilities and Software Vulnerabilities

Originally published in Wired, *20 October 2005*

At a security conference last month, Howard Schmidt, the former White House cybersecurity adviser, took the bold step of arguing that software developers should be held personally accountable for the security of the code they write.

He's on the right track, but he's made a dangerous mistake. It's the software *manufacturers* that should be held liable, not the individual programmers. Getting this one right will result in more-secure software for everyone; getting it wrong will simply result in a lot of messy lawsuits.

To understand the difference, it's necessary to understand the basic economic incentives of companies, and how businesses are affected by liabilities. In a capitalist society, businesses are profit-making ventures, and they make decisions based on both short- and long-term profitability. They try to balance the costs of more-secure software—extra developers, fewer features, longer time to market—against the costs of insecure software: expense to patch, occasional bad press, potential loss of sales.

The result is what you see all around you: lousy software. Companies find it's cheaper to weather the occasional press storm, spend money on PR campaigns touting good security, and fix public problems after the fact than to design security right from the beginning.

The problem with this analysis is that most of the costs of insecure software fall on the users. In economics, this is known as an externality: an effect of a decision not borne by the decision maker.

Normally, you would expect users to respond by favoring secure products over insecure products—after all, they're making their own buying decisions based on the same capitalist model. But that's not generally possible. In some cases, software monopolies limit the available product choice; in other cases, the "lock-in effect" created by proprietary file formats or existing infrastructure or compatibility requirements makes it harder to switch; and in still other cases, none of the competing companies have made security a differentiating characteristic. In all cases, it's hard for an average buyer to distinguish a truly secure product from an insecure product with a "boy, are we secure" marketing campaign.

The end result is that insecure software is common. But because users, not software manufacturers, pay the price, nothing improves. Making software manufacturers liable fixes this externality.

Watch the mechanism work. If end users can sue software manufacturers for product defects, then the cost of those defects to the software manufacturers rises. Manufacturers are now paying the true economic cost for poor software, and not just a piece of it. So when they're balancing the cost of making their software secure versus the cost of leaving their software insecure, there are more costs on the latter side. This will provide an incentive for them to make their software more secure.

To be sure, making software more secure will cost money, and manufacturers will have to pass those costs on to users in the form of higher prices. But users are already paying extra costs for insecure software: costs of third-party security products, costs of consultants and security-services companies, direct and indirect costs of losses. Making software manufacturers liable moves those costs around and, as a byproduct, causes the quality of software to improve.

This is why Schmidt's idea won't work. He wants individual software developers to be liable, and not the corporations. This will certainly give pissed-off users someone to sue, but it won't reduce the externality and it won't result in more-secure software.

Computer security isn't a technological problem—it's an economic problem. Socialists might imagine that companies will improve software security out of the goodness of their hearts, but capitalists know that it needs to be in companies' economic best interest. We'll have fewer vulnerabilities when the entities that have the capability to reduce those vulnerabilities have the economic incentive to do so. And this is why solutions like liability and regulation work.

Lock-In

Originally published in Wired, *7 February 2008*

Buying an iPhone isn't the same as buying a car or a toaster. Your iPhone comes with a complicated list of rules about what you can and can't do with it. You can't install unapproved third-party applications on it. You can't unlock it and use it with the cell phone carrier of your choice. And Apple is serious about these rules: A software update released in September 2007 erased unauthorized software and—in some cases—rendered unlocked phones unusable.

"Bricked" is the term, and Apple isn't the least bit apologetic about it.

Computer companies want more control over the products they sell you, and they're resorting to increasingly draconian security measures to get that control. The reasons are economic.

Control allows a company to limit competition for ancillary products. With Mac computers, anyone can sell software that does anything. But Apple gets to decide who can sell what on the iPhone. It can foster competition when it wants and reserve itself a monopoly position when it wants. And it can dictate terms to any company that wants to sell iPhone software and accessories.

This increases Apple's bottom line. But the primary benefit of all this control for Apple is that it increases lock-in. "Lock-in" is an economic term for the difficulty of switching to a competing product. For some products—cola, for example—there's no lock-in. I can drink a Coke today and a Pepsi tomorrow—no big deal. But for other products, it's harder.

Switching word processors, for example, requires installing a new application, learning a new interface and a new set of commands, converting all the files (which may not convert cleanly) and custom software (which will certainly require rewriting), and possibly even buying new hardware. If Coke stops satisfying me for even a moment, I'll switch—something Coke learned the hard way in 1985 when it changed the formula and started marketing New Coke. But my word processor has to really piss me off for a good long time before I'll even consider going through all that work and expense.

Lock-in isn't new. It's why all gaming-console manufacturers make sure their game cartridges don't work on any other console, and how they can price the consoles at a loss and make up the profit by selling games. It's why Microsoft never wants to open up its file formats so other applications can read them. It's why music purchased from Apple for your iPod won't work on other brands of music players. It's why every U.S. cell phone company fought against phone number portability. It's why Facebook sues any company that tries to scrape its data and put it on a competing website. It explains airline frequent flyer programs, supermarket affinity cards, and the My Coke Rewards program.

With enough lock-in, a company can protect its market share even as it reduces customer service, raises prices, refuses to innovate, and otherwise abuses its customer base. It should be no surprise that this sounds like pretty much every experience you've had with IT companies: Once the industry discovered lock-in, everyone started figuring out how to get as much of it as they can.

Economists Carl Shapiro and Hal Varian even proved that the value of a software company is the total lock-in. Here's the logic: Assume, for example, you have 100 people in a company using MS Office at a cost of $500 each. If it cost the company less than $50,000 to switch to Open Office, they would. If it cost the company more than $50,000, Microsoft would increase its prices.

Mostly, companies increase their lock-in through security mechanisms. Sometimes patents preserve lock-in, but more often it's copy protection, digital rights management (DRM), code signing, or other security mechanisms. These security features aren't what we normally think of as security: They don't protect us from some outside threat, they protect the companies from *us*.

Microsoft has been planning this sort of control-based security mechanism for years. First called Palladium and now NGSCB (Next-Generation Secure Computing Base), the idea is to build a control-based security system into the computing hardware. The details are complicated, but the results range from only allowing a computer to boot from an authorized copy of the OS to prohibiting the user from accessing "unauthorized" files or running unauthorized software. The competitive benefits to Microsoft are enormous,

Of course, that's not how Microsoft advertises NGSCB. The company has positioned it as a security measure, protecting users from worms, Trojans, and other malware. But control does not equal security; and this sort of control-based security is very difficult to get right, and sometimes makes us more vulnerable to other threats. Perhaps this is why Microsoft is quietly killing NGSCB—we've gotten BitLocker, and we might get some other security features down the line—despite the huge investment hardware manufacturers made when incorporating special security hardware into their motherboards.

I've previously written about the security-versus-privacy debate, and how it's actually a debate about liberty versus control. Here we see the same dynamic, but in a commercial setting. By confusing control and security, companies are able to force control measures that work against our interests by convincing us they are doing it for our own safety.

As for Apple and the iPhone, I don't know what they're going to do. On one hand, there's this analyst report that claims there are over a million unlocked iPhones, costing Apple between $300 million and $400 million in revenue. On the other hand, Apple is planning to release a software development kit this month, reversing its earlier restriction and allowing third-party vendors to write iPhone applications. Apple will attempt to keep control through a secret application key that will be required by all "official" third-party applications, but of course it's already been leaked.

And the security arms race goes on...

Third Parties Controlling Information

Originally published in Wired, *21 February 2008*

Wine Therapy is a web bulletin board for serious wine geeks. It's been active since 2000, and its database of back posts and comments is a wealth of information: tasting notes, restaurant recommendations, stories, and so on. Late last year, someone hacked the board software, got administrative privileges, and deleted the database. There was no backup.

Of course the board's owner should have been making backups all along, but he has been very sick for the past year and wasn't able to. And the Internet Archive has been only somewhat helpful.

More and more, information we rely on—either created by us or by others—is out of our control. It's out there on the Internet, on someone else's website and being cared for by someone else. We use those websites, sometimes daily, and don't even think about their reliability.

Bits and pieces of the web disappear all the time. It's called "link rot," and we're all used to it. A friend saved 65 links in 1999 when he planned a trip to Tuscany; only half of them still work today. In *Crypto-Gram* and in my own blog, essays and news articles and websites that I link to regularly disappear.

It may be because of a site's policies—some newspapers only have a couple of weeks on their website—or it may be more random: Position papers disappear off a politician's website after he changes his mind on an issue, corporate literature disappears from the company's website after an embarrassment, etc. The ultimate link rot is "site death," where entire websites disappear: Olympic and World Cup events after the games are over, political candidates' websites after the elections are over, corporate websites after the funding runs out, and so on.

Mostly, we ignore the issue. Sometimes I save a copy of a good recipe I find, or an article relevant to my research, but mostly I trust that whatever I want will be there next time. Were I planning a trip to Tuscany, I would rather search for relevant articles today than rely on a nine-year-old list anyway. Most of the time, link rot and site death aren't really a problem.

This is changing in a Web 2.0 world, with websites that are less about information and more about community. We help build these sites, with our posts or our comments. We visit them regularly and get to know others who also visit regularly. They become part of our socialization on the Internet and the loss of them affects us differently, as Greatest Journal users discovered in January when their site died.

Few, if any, of the people who made Wine Therapy their home kept backup copies of their own posts and comments. I'm sure they didn't even think of it. I don't think of it when I post to the various boards and blogs and forums I frequent. Of course I know better, but I think of these forums as extensions of my own computer—until they disappear.

As we rely on others to maintain our writings and our relationships, we lose control over their availability. Of course, we also lose control over their security, as MySpace users learned last month when a 17-GB file of half a million supposedly private photos was uploaded to a BitTorrent site.

In the early days of the web, I remember feeling giddy over the wealth of information out there and how easy it was to get to. "The Internet is my hard drive," I told newbies. It's even more true today; I don't think I could write without so much information so easily accessible. But it's a pretty damned unreliable hard drive.

The Internet is my hard drive, but only if my needs are immediate and my requirements can be satisfied inexactly. It was easy for me to search for information about the MySpace photo hack. And it was easy to look up, and respond to, comments to this essay, both on Wired.com and on my own website. Wired.com is a commercial venture, so there is advertising value in keeping everything accessible. My site is not at all commercial, but there is personal value in keeping everything accessible. By that analysis, all sites should be up on the Internet forever, although that's certainly not true. What is true is that there's no way to predict what will disappear when.

Unfortunately, there's not much we can do about it. The security measures largely aren't in our hands. We can save copies of important web pages locally, and copies of anything important we post. The Internet Archive is remarkably valuable in saving bits and pieces of the Internet. And recently, we've started seeing tools for archiving information and pages from social networking sites. But what's really important is the whole community, and we don't know which bits we want until they're no longer there.

And about Wine Therapy? I *think* it started in 2000. It might have been 2001. I can't check, because someone erased the archives.

Who Owns Your Computer?

Originally published in Wired, *4 May 2006*

When technology serves its owners, it is liberating. When it is designed to serve others, over the owner's objection, it is oppressive. There's a battle raging on your computer right now—one that pits you against worms and viruses, Trojans, spyware, automatic update features, and digital rights-management technologies. It's the battle to determine who owns your computer.

You own your computer, of course. You bought it. You paid for it. But how much control do you really have over what happens on your machine? Technically you might have bought the hardware and software, but you have less control over what it's doing behind the scenes.

Using the hacker sense of the term, your computer is "owned" by other people.

It used to be that only malicious hackers were trying to own your computers. Whether through worms, viruses, Trojans, or other means, they would try to install some kind of remote-control program onto your system. Then they'd use your computers to sniff passwords, make fraudulent bank transactions, send spam, initiate phishing attacks and so on. Estimates are that somewhere between hundreds of thousands and millions of computers are members of remotely controlled "bot" networks. Owned.

Now, things are not so simple. There are all sorts of interests vying for control of your computer. There are media companies that want to control what you can do with the music and videos they sell you. There are companies that use software as a conduit to collect marketing information, deliver advertising, or do whatever it is their real owners require. And there are software companies that are trying to make money by pleasing not only their customers, but other companies they ally themselves with. All these companies want to own your computer.

Some examples:

- Entertainment software: In October 2005, it emerged that Sony had distributed a rootkit with several music CDs—the same kind of software that crackers use to own people's computers. This rootkit secretly installed itself when the music CD was played on a computer. Its purpose was to prevent people from doing things with the music that Sony didn't approve of: It was a DRM system. If the exact same piece of software had been installed secretly by a hacker, this would have been an illegal act. But Sony believed that it had legitimate reasons for wanting to own its customers' machines.

- Antivirus: You might have expected your antivirus software to detect Sony's rootkit. After all, that's why you bought it. But initially, the security programs sold by Symantec and others did not detect it, because Sony had asked them not to. You might have thought that the software you bought was working for you, but you would have been wrong.

- Internet services: Hotmail allows you to blacklist certain e-mail addresses, so that mail from them automatically goes into your spam trap. Have you ever tried blocking all that incessant marketing e-mail from Microsoft? You can't.

- Application software: Internet Explorer users might have expected the program to incorporate easy-to-use cookie handling and pop-up blockers. After all, other browsers do, and users have found them useful in defending against Internet annoyances. But Microsoft isn't just selling software to you; it sells Internet advertising as well. It isn't in the company's best interest to offer users features that would adversely affect its business partners.

- Spyware: Spyware is nothing but someone else trying to own your computer. These programs eavesdrop on your behavior and report back to their real owners—sometimes without your knowledge or consent—about your behavior.

- Update: Automatic update features are another way software companies try to own your computer. While they can be useful for improving security, they also require you to trust your software vendor not to disable your computer for nonpayment, breach of contract or other presumed infractions.

Adware, software-as-a-service and Google Desktop search are all examples of some other company trying to own your computer. And Trusted Computing will only make the problem worse.

There is an inherent insecurity to technologies that try to own people's computers: They allow individuals other than the computers' legitimate owners to enforce policy on those machines. These systems invite attackers to assume the role of the third party and turn a user's device against him.

Remember the Sony story: The most insecure feature in that DRM system was a cloaking mechanism that gave the rootkit control over whether you could see it executing or spot its files on your hard disk. By taking ownership away from you, it reduced your security.

If left to grow, these external control systems will fundamentally change your relationship with your computer. They will make your computer much less useful by letting corporations limit what you can do with it. They will make your computer much less reliable because you will no longer have control of what is running on your machine, what it does, and how the various software components interact. At the extreme, they will transform your computer into a glorified boob tube.

You can fight back against this trend by only using software that respects your boundaries. Boycott companies that don't honestly serve their customers, that don't disclose their alliances, that treat users like marketing assets. Use open-source software—software created and owned by users, with no hidden agendas, no secret alliances, and no back-room marketing deals.

Just because computers were a liberating force in the past doesn't mean they will be in the future. There is enormous political and economic power behind the idea that you shouldn't truly own your computer or your software, despite having paid for it.

A Security Market for Lemons

Originally published in Wired, *19 April 2007*

More than a year ago, I wrote about the increasing risks of data loss because more and more data fits in smaller and smaller packages. Today I use a 4-GB USB memory stick for backup while I am traveling. I like the convenience, but if I lose the tiny thing, I risk all my data.

Encryption is the obvious solution for this problem—I use PGPdisk—but Secustick sounds even better: It automatically erases itself after a set number of bad password attempts. The company makes a bunch of other impressive claims: The product was commissioned, and eventually approved, by the French intelligence service; it is used by many militaries and banks; its technology is revolutionary.

Unfortunately, the only impressive aspect of Secustick is its hubris, which was revealed when Tweakers.net completely broke its security. There's no data self-destruct feature. The password protection can easily be bypassed. The data isn't even encrypted. As a secure storage device, Secustick is pretty useless.

On the surface, this is just another snake-oil security story. But there's a deeper question: Why are there so many bad security products out there? It's not just that designing good security is hard—although it is—and it's not just that anyone can design a security product that he himself cannot break. Why do mediocre security products beat the good ones in the marketplace?

In 1970, American economist George Akerlof wrote a paper called "The Market for 'Lemons,'" which established asymmetrical information theory. He eventually won a Nobel Prize for his work, which looks at markets where the seller knows a lot more about the product than the buyer.

Akerlof illustrated his ideas with a used-car market. A used-car market includes both good cars and lousy ones (lemons). The seller knows which is which, but the buyer can't tell the difference—at least until he's made his purchase. I'll spare you the math, but what ends up happening is that the buyer bases his purchase price on the value of a used car of average quality.

This means that the best cars don't get sold; their prices are too high. Which means that the owners of these best cars don't put their cars on the market. And then this starts spiraling. The removal of the good cars from the market reduces the average price buyers are willing to pay, and then the very good cars no longer sell, and disappear from the market. And then the good cars, and so on until only the lemons are left.

In a market where the seller has more information about the product than the buyer, bad products can drive the good ones out of the market.

The computer security market has a lot of the same characteristics of Akerlof's lemons market. Take the market for encrypted USB memory sticks. Several companies make encrypted USB drives—Kingston Technology sent me one in the mail a few days ago—but even I couldn't tell you if Kingston's offering is better than Secustick. Or if it's better than any other encrypted USB drives. They use the same encryption algorithms. They make the same security claims. And if I can't tell the difference, most consumers won't be able to either.

Of course, it's more expensive to make an actually secure USB drive. Good security design takes time, and necessarily means limiting functionality. Good security testing takes even more time, especially if the product is any good. This means the less-secure product will be cheaper, sooner to market, and have more features. In this market, the more-secure USB drive is going to lose out.

I see this kind of thing happening over and over in computer security. In the late 1980s and early 1990s, there were more than a hundred competing firewall products. The few that "won" weren't the most secure firewalls; they were the ones that were easy to set up, easy to use, and didn't annoy users too much. Because buyers couldn't base their buying decision on the relative security merits, they based them on these other criteria. The intrusion detection system, or IDS, market evolved the same way, and before that the antivirus market. The few products that succeeded weren't the most secure, because buyers couldn't tell the difference.

How do you solve this? You need what economists call a "signal," a way for buyers to tell the difference. Warranties are a common signal. Alternatively, an independent auto mechanic can tell good cars from lemons, and a buyer can hire his expertise. The Secustick story demonstrates this. If there is a consumer advocate group that has the expertise to evaluate different products, then the lemons can be exposed.

Secustick, for one, seems to have been withdrawn from sale.

But security testing is both expensive and slow, and it just isn't possible for an independent lab to test everything. Unfortunately, the exposure of Secustick is an exception. It was a simple product, and easily exposed once someone bothered to look. A complex software product—a firewall, an IDS—is very hard to test well. And, of course, by the time you have tested it, the vendor has a new version on the market.

In reality, we have to rely on a variety of mediocre signals to differentiate the good security products from the bad. Standardization is one signal. The widely used AES encryption standard has reduced, although not eliminated, the number of lousy encryption algorithms on the market. Reputation is a more common signal; we choose security products based on the reputation of the company selling them, the reputation of some security wizard associated with them, magazine reviews, recommendations from colleagues, or general buzz in the media.

All these signals have their problems. Even product reviews, which should be as comprehensive as the Tweakers' Secustick review, rarely are. Many firewall comparison reviews focus on things the reviewers can easily measure, like packets per second, rather than how secure the products are. In IDS comparisons, you can find the same bogus "number of signatures" comparison. Buyers lap that stuff up; in the absence of deep understanding, they happily accept shallow data.

With so many mediocre security products on the market, and the difficulty of coming up with a strong quality signal, vendors don't have strong incentives to invest in developing good products. And the vendors that do tend to die a quiet and lonely death.

Websites, Passwords, and Consumers

Originally published in IEEE Security and Privacy,
July/August 2004

Criminals follow the money. Today, more and more money is on the Internet. Millions of people manage their bank accounts, PayPal accounts, stock portfolios, or other payment accounts online. It's a tempting target: If a criminal can gain access to one of these accounts, he can steal money.

And almost all these accounts are protected only by passwords.

If you're reading this essay, you probably already know that passwords are insecure. In my book *Secrets and Lies* (way back in 2000), I wrote: "Over the past several decades, Moore's Law has made it possible to brute-force larger and larger entropy keys. At the same time, there is a maximum to the entropy that the average computer user (or even the above-average computer user) is willing to remember.... These two numbers have crossed; password crackers can now break anything that you can reasonably expect a user to memorize."

On the Internet, password security is actually much better than that, because dictionary attacks work best offline. It's one thing to test every possible key on your own computer when you have the actual ciphertext, but it's a much slower process when you have to do it remotely across the Internet. And if the website is halfway clever, it'll shut down an account if there are too many—5? 10?—incorrect password attempts in a row. If you shut accounts down soon enough, you can even make four-digit PINs work on websites.

This is why the criminals have taken to stealing passwords instead.

Phishing is now a very popular attack, and it's amazingly effective. Think about how the attack works. You get an e-mail from your bank. It has a plausible message body and contains a URL that looks like it's from your bank. You click on it, and up pops your bank website. When asked for your username and password, you type it in. Okay, maybe you or I are aware enough not to type it in. But the average home banking customer doesn't stand a chance against this kind of social engineering attack.

And in June 2004, a Trojan horse appeared that captured passwords. It looked like an image file, but it was actually an executable that installed an add-on to Internet Explorer. That add-on monitored and recorded outbound connections to the websites of several dozen major financial institutions and then sent usernames and passwords to a computer in Russia. Using SSL didn't help; the Trojan monitored keystrokes before they were encrypted.

The computer security industry has several solutions that are better than passwords: secure tokens that provide one-time passwords, biometric readers, etc. But issuing hardware to millions of electronic banking customers is prohibitively expensive, both in initial cost and in customer support. And customers hate these systems. If you're a bank, the last thing you want to do is to annoy your customers.

But having money stolen out of your account is even more annoying, and banks are increasingly fielding calls from customer victims. Even though the security problem has nothing to do with the bank, and even though the customer is the one who made the security mistake, banks are having to make good on the customers' losses. It's one of the most important lessons of Internet security: sometimes your biggest security problems are ones that you have no control over.

The problem is serious. In a May survey report, Gartner estimated that about 3 million Americans have fallen victim to phishing attacks. "Direct losses from identity theft fraud against phishing attack victims—including new-account, checking account, and credit card account fraud—cost U.S. banks and credit card issuers about $1.2 billion last year" (in 2003). Keyboard sniffers and Trojans will help make this number even greater in 2004.

Even if financial institutions reimburse customers, the inevitable result is that people will begin to distrust the Internet. The average Internet user doesn't understand security; he thinks that a gold lock icon in the lower-right-hand corner of his browser means that he's secure. If it doesn't—and we all know that it doesn't—he'll stop using Internet financial websites and applications.

The solutions are not easy. The never-ending stream of Windows vulnerabilities limits the effectiveness of any customer-based software solution—digital certificates, plug-ins, and so on—and the ease with which malicious software can run on Windows limits the effectiveness of other solutions. Point solutions might force attackers to change tactics, but won't solve the underlying insecurities. Computer security is an arms race, and money creates very motivated attackers. Unsolved, this type of security problem can change the way people interact with the Internet. It'll prove that the naysayers were right all along, that the Internet isn't safe for electronic commerce.

9

Psychology of Security

The Feeling and Reality of Security

Originally published in Wired, *3 April 2008*

S ecurity is both a feeling and a reality, and they're different. You can feel secure even though you're not, and you can be secure even though you don't feel it. There are two different concepts mapped onto the same word—the English language isn't working very well for us here—and it can be hard to know which one we're talking about when we use the word.

There is considerable value in separating out the two concepts: in explaining how the two are different, and understanding when we're referring to one and when the other. There is value as well in recognizing when the two converge, understanding why they diverge, and knowing how they can be made to converge again.

Some fundamentals first. Viewed from the perspective of economics, security is a trade-off. There's no such thing as absolute security, and any security you get has some cost: in money, in convenience, in capabilities, in insecurities somewhere else, whatever. Every time people make decisions about security—computer security, community security, national security—they make trade-offs.

People make these trade-offs as individuals. We all get to decide, individually, if the expense and inconvenience of having a home burglar alarm is worth the security. We all get to decide if wearing a bulletproof vest is worth the cost and tacky appearance. We all get to decide if we're getting our money's worth from the billions of dollars we're spending combating terrorism, and if invading Iraq was the best use of our counterterrorism resources. We might not have the power to *implement* our opinion, but we get to decide if we think it's worth it.

Now we may or may not have the expertise to make those trade-offs intelligently, but we make them anyway. All of us. People have a natural intuition about security trade-offs, and we make them, large and small, dozens of times throughout the day. We can't help it: It's part of being alive.

Imagine a rabbit, sitting in a field eating grass. And he sees a fox. He's going to make a security trade-off: Should he stay or should he flee? Over time, the rabbits that are good at making that trade-off will tend to reproduce, while the rabbits that are bad at it will tend to get eaten or starve.

So, as a successful species on the planet, you'd expect that human beings would be really good at making security trade-offs. Yet, at the same time, we can be hopelessly bad at it. We spend more money on terrorism than the data warrants. We fear flying and choose to drive instead. Why?

The short answer is that people make most trade-offs based on the *feeling* of security and not the reality.

I've written a lot about how people get security trade-offs wrong, and the cognitive biases that cause us to make mistakes. Humans have developed these biases because they make evolutionary sense. And most of the time, they work.

Most of the time—and this is important—our feeling of security matches the reality of security. Certainly, this is true of prehistory. Modern times are harder. Blame technology, blame the media, blame whatever. Our brains are much better optimized for the security trade-offs endemic to living in small family groups in the East African highlands in 100,000 B.C. than to those endemic to living in 2008 New York.

If we make security trade-offs based on the feeling of security rather than the reality, we choose security that makes us *feel* more secure over security that actually makes us more secure. And that's what governments, companies, family members, and everyone else provide. Of course, there are two ways to make people feel more secure. The first is to make people actually more secure, and hope they notice. The second is to make people feel more secure without making them actually more secure, and hope they don't notice.

The key here is whether we notice. The feeling and reality of security tend to converge when we take notice, and diverge when we don't. People notice when 1) there are enough positive and negative examples to draw a conclusion, and 2) there isn't too much emotion clouding the issue.

Both elements are important. If someone tries to convince us to spend money on a new type of home burglar alarm, we as society will know pretty quickly if he's got a clever security device or if he's a charlatan; we can monitor crime rates. But if that same person advocates a new national antiterrorism system, and there weren't any terrorist attacks before it was implemented, and there weren't any after it was implemented, how do we know if his system was effective?

People are more likely to realistically assess these incidents if they don't contradict preconceived notions about how the world works. For example: It's obvious that a wall keeps people out, so arguing against building a wall across America's southern border to keep illegal immigrants out is harder to do.

The other thing that matters is agenda. There are lots of people, politicians, companies, and so on who deliberately try to manipulate your feeling of security for their own gain. They try to cause fear. They invent threats. They take minor threats and make them major. And when they talk about rare risks with only a few incidents to base an assessment on—terrorism is the big example here—they are more likely to succeed.

Unfortunately, there's no obvious antidote. Information is important. We can't understand security unless we understand it. But that's not enough: Few of us really understand cancer, yet we regularly make security decisions based on its risk. What we do is accept that there are experts who understand the risks of cancer, and trust them to make the security trade-offs for us.

There are some complex feedback loops going on here, between emotion and reason, between reality and our knowledge of it, between feeling and familiarity, and between the understanding of how we reason and feel about security and our analyses and feelings. We're never going to stop making security trade-offs based on the feeling of security, and we're never going to completely prevent those with specific agendas from trying to take care of us. But the more we know, the better trade-offs we'll make.

Behavioral Assessment Profiling

Originally published in The Boston Globe, *24 November 2004*

On December 14, 1999, Ahmed Ressam tried to enter the United States from Canada at Port Angeles, Washington. He had a suitcase bomb in the trunk of his car. A U.S. customs agent, Diana Dean, questioned him at the border. He was fidgeting, sweaty, and jittery. He avoided eye contact. In Dean's own words, he was acting "hinky." Ressam's car was eventually searched, and he was arrested.

It wasn't any one thing that tipped Dean off; it was everything encompassed in the slang term "hinky." But it worked. The reason there wasn't a bombing at Los Angeles International Airport around Christmas 1999 was because a trained, knowledgeable security person was paying attention.

This is "behavioral assessment" profiling. It's what customs agents do at borders all the time. It's what the Israeli police do to protect their airport and airplanes. And it's a new pilot program in the United States at Boston's Logan Airport. Behavioral profiling is dangerous because it's easy to abuse, but it's also the best thing we can do to improve the security of our air passenger system.

Behavioral profiling is not the same as computerized passenger profiling. The latter has been in place for years. It's a secret system, and it's a mess. Sometimes airlines decided who would undergo secondary screening, and they would choose people based on ticket purchase, frequent-flyer status, and similarity to names on government watch lists. CAPPS-2 was to follow, evaluating people based on government and commercial databases and assigning a "risk" score. This system was scrapped after public outcry, but another profiling system called Secure Flight will debut next year. Again, details are secret.

The problem with computerized passenger profiling is that it simply doesn't work. Terrorists don't fit a profile and cannot be plucked out of crowds by computers. Terrorists are European, Asian, African, Hispanic, and Middle Eastern, male and female, young and old. Richard Reid, the shoe bomber, was British with a Jamaican father. Jose Padilla, arrested in Chicago in 2002 as a "dirty bomb" suspect, was a Hispanic-American. Timothy McVeigh was a white American. So was the Unabomber, who once taught mathematics at the University of California, Berkeley. The Chechens who blew up two Russian planes last August were female. Recent reports indicate that al-Qaeda is recruiting Europeans for further attacks on the United States.

Terrorists can buy plane tickets—either one way or round trip—with cash or credit cards. Mohamed Atta, the leader of the 9/11 plot, had a frequent-flyer gold card. They are a surprisingly diverse group of people, and any computer profiling system will just make it easier for those who don't meet the profile.

Behavioral assessment profiling is different. It cuts through all of those superficial profiling characteristics and centers on the person. State police are trained as screeners in order to look for suspicious conduct such as furtiveness or undue anxiety. Already at Logan Airport, the program has caught 20 people who were either in the country illegally or had outstanding warrants of one kind or another.

Earlier this month, the ACLU of Massachusetts filed a lawsuit challenging the constitutionality of behavioral assessment profiling. The lawsuit is unlikely to succeed; the principle of "implied consent" that has been used to uphold the legality of passenger and baggage screening will almost certainly be applied in this case as well.

But the ACLU has it wrong. Behavioral assessment profiling isn't the problem. Abuse of behavioral profiling is the problem, and the ACLU has correctly identified where it can go wrong. If policemen fall back on naive profiling by race, ethnicity, age, gender—characteristics not relevant to security—they're little better than a computer. Instead of "driving while black," the police will face accusations of harassing people for the infraction of "flying while Arab." Their actions will increase racial tensions and make them less likely to notice the real threats. And we'll all be less safe as a result.

Behavioral assessment profiling isn't a "silver bullet." It needs to be part of a layered security system, one that includes passenger baggage screening, airport employee screening, and random security checks. It's best implemented not by police but by specially trained federal officers. These officers could be deployed at airports, sports stadiums, political conventions—anywhere terrorism is a risk because the target is attractive. Done properly, this is the best thing to happen to air passenger security since reinforcing the cockpit door.

In Praise of Security Theater

Originally published in Wired, *25 January 2007*

While visiting some friends and their new baby in the hospital last week, I noticed an interesting bit of security. To prevent infant abduction, all babies had RFID tags attached to their ankles by a bracelet. There are sensors on the doors to the maternity ward, and if a baby passes through, an alarm goes off.

Infant abduction is rare, but still a risk. In the last 22 years, about 233 such abductions have occurred in the United States. Approximately 4 million babies are born each year, which means that a baby has a 1-in-375,000 chance of being abducted. Compare this with the infant mortality rate in the U.S.—one in 145—and it becomes clear where the real risks are.

And the 1-in-375,000 chance is not today's risk. Infant abduction rates have plummeted in recent years, mostly due to education programs at hospitals.

So why are hospitals bothering with RFID bracelets? I think they're primarily to reassure the mothers. Many times during my friends' stay at the hospital, the doctors had to take the baby away for this or that test. Millions of years of evolution have forged a strong bond between new parents and new baby; the RFID bracelets are a low-cost way to ensure that the parents are more relaxed when their baby was out of their sight.

Security is both a reality and a feeling. The reality of security is mathematical, based on the probability of different risks and the effectiveness of different countermeasures. We know the infant abduction rates and how well the bracelets reduce those rates. We also know the cost of the bracelets, and can thus calculate whether they're a cost-effective security measure or not. But security is also a feeling, based on individual psychological reactions to both the risks and the countermeasures. And the two things are different: You can be secure even though you don't feel secure, and you can feel secure even though you're not really secure.

The RFID bracelets are what I've come to call security theater: security primarily designed to make you *feel* more secure. I've regularly maligned security theater as a waste, but it's not always, and not entirely, so.

It's only a waste if you consider the reality of security exclusively. There are times when people feel less secure than they actually are. In those cases—like with mothers and the threat of baby abduction—a palliative countermeasure that primarily increases the feeling of security is just what the doctor ordered.

Tamper-resistant packaging for over-the-counter drugs started to appear in the 1980s, in response to some highly publicized poisonings. As a countermeasure, it's largely security theater. It's easy to poison many foods and over-the-counter medicines right through the seal—with a syringe, for example—or to open and replace the seal well enough that an unwary consumer won't detect it. But in the 1980s, there was a widespread fear of random poisonings in over-the-counter medicines, and tamper-resistant packaging brought people's perceptions of the risk more in line with the actual risk: minimal.

Much of the post-9/11 security can be explained by this as well. I've often talked about the National Guard troops in airports right after the terrorist attacks, and the fact that they had no bullets in their guns. As a security countermeasure, it made little sense for them to be there. They didn't have the training necessary to improve security at the checkpoints, or even to be another useful pair of eyes. But to reassure a jittery public that it's OK to fly, it was probably the right thing to do.

Security theater also addresses the ancillary risk of lawsuits. Lawsuits are ultimately decided by juries or settled because of the threat of jury trial, and juries are going to decide cases based on their feelings as well as the facts. It's not enough for a hospital to point to infant abduction rates and rightly claim that RFID bracelets aren't worth it; the other side is going to put a weeping mother on the stand and make an emotional argument. In these cases, security theater provides real security against the legal threat.

Like real security, security theater has a cost. It can cost money, time, concentration, freedoms, and so on. It can come at the cost of reducing the things we can do. Most of the time security theater is a bad trade-off, because the costs far outweigh the benefits. But there are instances when a little bit of security theater makes sense.

We make smart security trade-offs—and by this I mean trade-offs for genuine security—when our feeling of security closely matches the reality. When the two are out of alignment, we get security wrong. Security theater is no substitute for security reality, but, used correctly, security theater can be a way of raising our feeling of security so that it more closely matches the reality of security. It makes us feel more secure handing our babies off to doctors and nurses, buying over-the-counter medicines, and flying on airplanes—closer to how secure we should feel if we had all the facts and did the math correctly.

Of course, too much security theater and our feeling of security becomes greater than the reality, which is also bad. And others—politicians, corporations, and so on—can use security theater to make us feel more secure without doing the hard work of actually making us secure. That's the usual way security theater is used, and why I so often malign it.

But to write off security theater completely is to ignore the feeling of security. And as long as people are involved with security trade-offs, that's never going to work.

CYA Security

Originally published in Wired, *22 February 2007*

Since 9/11, we've spent hundreds of billions of dollars defending ourselves from terrorist attacks. Stories about the ineffectiveness of many of these security measures are common, but less so are discussions of *why* they are so ineffective.

In short: much of our country's counterterrorism security spending is not designed to protect us from the terrorists, but instead to protect our public officials from criticism when another attack occurs.

Boston, January 31: As part of a guerilla marketing campaign, a series of amateur-looking blinking signs depicting characters from Aqua Teen Hunger Force, a show on the Cartoon Network, were placed on bridges, near a medical center, underneath an interstate highway, and in other crowded public places.

Police mistook these signs for bombs and shut down parts of the city, eventually spending over $1M sorting it out. Authorities blasted the stunt as a terrorist hoax, while others ridiculed the Boston authorities for overreacting. Almost no one looked beyond the finger pointing and jeering to discuss exactly why the Boston authorities overreacted so badly. They overreacted because the signs were weird.

If someone left a backpack full of explosives in a crowded movie theater, or detonated a truck bomb in the middle of a tunnel, no one would demand to know why the police hadn't noticed it beforehand. But if a weird device with blinking lights and wires turned out to be a bomb—what every movie bomb looks like—there would be inquiries and demands for resignations. It took the police two weeks to notice the Mooninite blinkies, but once they did, they overreacted because their jobs were at stake.

This is "Cover Your Ass" security, and unfortunately it's very common.

Airplane security seems to forever be looking backwards. Pre-9/11, it was bombs, guns, and knives. Then it was small blades and box cutters. Richard Reid tried to blow up a plane, and suddenly we all have to take off our shoes. And after last summer's liquid plot, we're stuck with a series of nonsensical bans on liquids and gels.

Once you think about this in terms of CYA, it starts to make sense. The TSA wants to be sure that if there's another airplane terrorist attack, it's not held responsible for letting it slip through. One year ago, no one could blame the TSA for not detecting liquids. But since everything seems obvious in hindsight, it's basic job preservation to defend against what the terrorists tried last time.

We saw this kind of CYA security when Boston and New York City randomly checked bags on the subways after the London bombing, or when buildings started sprouting concrete barriers after the Oklahoma City bombing. We also see it in ineffective attempts to detect nuclear bombs; authorities employ CYA security against the media-driven threat so they can say "we tried."

At the same time, we're ignoring threat possibilities that don't make the news as much—against chemical plants, for example. But if there were ever an attack, that would change quickly.

CYA also explains the TSA's inability to take anyone off the no-fly list, no matter how innocent. No one is willing to risk his career on removing someone from the no-fly list who might—no matter how remote the possibility— turn out to be the next terrorist mastermind.

Another form of CYA security is the overly specific countermeasures we see during big events like the Olympics and the Oscars, or in protecting small towns. In all those cases, those in charge of the specific security don't dare return the money with a message "use this for more effective general counter-measures." If they were wrong and something happened, they'd lose their jobs.

And finally, we're seeing CYA security on the national level, from our politicians. We might be better off as a nation funding intelligence gathering and Arabic translators, but it's a better re-election strategy to fund something visible but ineffective, like a national ID card or a wall between the U.S. and Mexico.

Securing our nation from threats that are weird, threats that either happened before or captured the media's imagination, and overly specific threats are all examples of CYA security. It happens not because the authorities involved—the Boston police, the TSA, and so on—are not competent, or not doing their job. It happens because there isn't sufficient national oversight, planning, and coordination.

People and organizations respond to incentives. We can't expect the Boston police, the TSA, the guy who runs security for the Oscars, or local public officials to balance their own security needs against the security of the nation. They're all going to respond to the particular incentives imposed from above. What we need is a coherent antiterrorism policy at the national level: one based on real threat assessments, instead of fear-mongering, re-election strategies, or pork-barrel politics.

Sadly, though, there might not be a solution. All the money is in fear-mongering, re-election strategies, and pork-barrel politics. And, like so many things, security follows the money.

Copycats

Originally published in Wired, *8 March 2007*

It's called "splash-and-grab," and it's a new way to rob convenience stores. (Okay; it's not really new. It was used on the TV show *The Shield* in 2005. But it's back in the news.) Two guys walk into a store, and one comes up to the counter with a cup of hot coffee or cocoa. He pays for it, and when the clerk opens the cash drawer, he throws the coffee in the clerk's face. The other one grabs the cash drawer, and they both run.

Crimes never change, but tactics do. This tactic is new; someone just invented it. But now that it's in the news, copycats are repeating the trick. There have been at least 19 such robberies in Delaware, Pennsylvania, and New Jersey. (Some arrests have been made since then.)

Here's another example: On November 24, 1971, someone with the alias Dan Cooper invented a new way to hijack an aircraft. Claiming he had a bomb, he forced a plane to land and then exchanged the passengers and flight attendants for $200,000 and four parachutes. (I leave it as exercise for the reader to explain why asking for more than one parachute is critical to the plan's success.) Taking off again, he told the pilots to fly to 10,000 feet. He then lowered the plane's back stairs and parachuted away. He was never caught, and the FBI still doesn't know who he is or whether he survived.

After this story hit the press, there was an epidemic of copycat attacks. In 31 hijackings the following year, half of the hijackers demanded parachutes. It got so bad that the FAA required Boeing to install a special latch—the Cooper Vane—on the back staircases of its 727s so they couldn't be lowered in the air.

The Internet is filled with copycats. Green-card lawyers invented spam; now everyone does it. Other people invented phishing, pharming, spear phishing. The virus, the worm, the Trojan: It's hard to believe that these ubiquitous Internet attack tactics were, until comparatively recently, tactics that no one had thought of.

Most attackers are copycats. They aren't clever enough to invent a new way to rob a convenience store, use the web to steal money, or hijack an airplane. They try the same attacks again and again, or read about a new attack in the newspaper and decide they can try it, too.

In combating threats, it makes sense to focus on copycats when there is a population of people already willing to commit the crime, who will migrate to a new tactic once it has been demonstrated to be successful. In instances where there aren't many attacks or attackers, and they're smarter—al-Qaeda-style terrorism comes to mind—focusing on copycats is less effective because the bad guys will respond by modifying their attacks accordingly.

Compare that to suicide bombings in Israel, which are mostly copycat attacks. The authorities basically know what a suicide bombing looks like, and do a pretty good job defending against the particular tactics they tend to see again and again. It's still an arms race, but there is a lot of security gained by defending against copycats.

But even so, it's important to understand which aspect of the crime will be adopted by copycats. Splash-and-grab crimes have nothing to do with convenience stores; copycats can target any store where hot coffee is easily available and there is only one clerk on duty. And the tactic doesn't necessarily need coffee; one copycat used bleach. The new idea is to throw something painful and damaging in a clerk's face, grab the valuables, and run.

Similarly, when a suicide bomber blows up a restaurant in Israel, the authorities don't automatically assume the copycats will attack other restaurants. They focus on the particulars of the bomb, the triggering mechanism and the way the bomber arrived at his target. Those are the tactics that copycats will repeat. The next target may be a theater or a hotel or any other crowded location.

The lesson for counterterrorism in America: Stay flexible. We're not threatened by a bunch of copycats, so we're best off expending effort on security measures that will work regardless of the tactics or the targets: intelligence, investigation, and emergency response. By focusing too much on specifics—what the terrorists did last time—we're wasting valuable resources that could be used to keep us safer.

Rare Risk and Overreactions

Originally published in Wired, *17 May 2007*

Everyone had a reaction to the horrific events of the Virginia Tech shootings. Some of those reactions were rational. Others were not.

A high school student was suspended for customizing a first-person shooter game with a map of his school. A contractor was fired from his government job for talking about a gun, and then visited by the police when he created a comic about the incident. A dean at Yale banned realistic stage weapons from the university theaters—a policy that was reversed within a day. And some teachers terrorized a sixth-grade class by staging a fake gunman attack, without telling them it was a drill.

These things all happened, even though shootings like this are incredibly rare; even though—for all the press—less than 1% of homicides and suicides of children ages 5 to 19 occur in schools. In fact, these overreactions occurred, not despite these facts, but *because* of them.

The Virginia Tech massacre is precisely the sort of event we humans tend to overreact to. Our brains aren't very good at probability and risk analysis, especially when it comes to rare occurrences. We tend to exaggerate spectacular, strange and rare events, and downplay ordinary, familiar and common ones. There's a lot of research in the psychological community about how the brain responds to risk—some of it I have already written about—but the gist is this: Our brains are much better at processing the simple risks we've had to deal with throughout most of our species' existence, and much poorer at evaluating the complex risks society forces us to face today.

Novelty plus dread equals overreaction.

We can see the effects of this all the time. We fear being murdered, kidnapped, raped and assaulted by strangers, when it's far more likely that the perpetrator of such offenses is a relative or a friend. We worry about airplane crashes and rampaging shooters instead of automobile crashes and domestic violence—both far more common.

In the United States, dogs, snakes, bees, and pigs each kill more people per year than sharks. In fact, dogs kill more humans than any animal except for other humans. Sharks are more dangerous than dogs, yes, but we're far more likely to encounter dogs than sharks.

Our greatest recent overreaction to a rare event was our response to the terrorist attacks of 9/11. I remember then-Attorney General John Ashcroft giving a speech in Minnesota—where I live—in 2003, and claiming that the fact there were no new terrorist attacks since 9/11 was proof that his policies were working. I thought: "There were no terrorist attacks in the two years preceding 9/11, and you didn't have any policies. What does that prove?"

What it proves is that terrorist attacks are very rare, and maybe our reaction wasn't worth the enormous expense, loss of liberty, attacks on our Constitution, and damage to our credibility on the world stage. Still, overreacting was the natural thing for us to do. Yes, it's security theater, but it makes us feel safer.

People tend to base risk analysis more on personal story than on data, despite the old joke that "the plural of anecdote is not data." If a friend gets mugged in a foreign country, that story is more likely to affect how safe you feel traveling to that country than abstract crime statistics.

We give storytellers we have a relationship with more credibility than strangers, and stories that are close to us more weight than stories from foreign lands. In other words, proximity of relationship affects our risk assessment. And who is everyone's major storyteller these days? Television. (Nassim Nicholas Taleb's great book, *The Black Swan: The Impact of the Highly Improbable*, discusses this.)

Consider the reaction to another event from last month: professional baseball player Josh Hancock got drunk and died in a car crash. As a result, several baseball teams are banning alcohol in their clubhouses after games. Aside from this being a ridiculous reaction to an incredibly rare event (2,430 baseball games per season, 35 people per clubhouse, two clubhouses per game. And how often has this happened?), it makes no sense as a solution. Hancock didn't get drunk in the clubhouse; he got drunk at a bar. But Major League Baseball needs to be seen as doing *something*, even if that something doesn't make sense—even if that something actually increases risk by forcing players to drink at bars instead of at the clubhouse, where there's more control over the practice.

I tell people that if it's in the news, don't worry about it. The very definition of "news" is "something that hardly ever happens." It's when something isn't in the news, when it's so common that it's no longer news—car crashes, domestic violence—that you should start worrying.

But that's not the way we think. Psychologist Scott Plous said it well in *The Psychology of Judgment and Decision Making*:

"In very general terms: (1) The more available an event is, the more frequent or probable it will seem; (2) the more vivid a piece of information is, the more easily recalled and convincing it will be; and (3) the more salient something is, the more likely it will be to appear causal."

So, when faced with a very available and highly vivid event like 9/11 or the Virginia Tech shootings, we overreact. And when faced with all the salient related events, we assume causality. We pass the USA PATRIOT Act. We think if we give guns out to students, or maybe make it harder for students to get guns, we'll have solved the problem. We don't let our children go to playgrounds unsupervised. We stay out of the ocean because we read about a shark attack somewhere.

It's our brains again. We need to "do something," even if that something doesn't make sense; even if it is ineffective. And we need to do something directly related to the details of the actual event. So instead of implementing effective, but more general, security measures to reduce the risk of terrorism, we ban box cutters on airplanes. And we look back on the Virginia Tech massacre with 20-20 hindsight and recriminate ourselves about the things we *should* have done.

Lastly, our brains need to find someone or something to blame. (Jon Stewart has an excellent bit on the Virginia Tech scapegoat search, and media coverage in general.) But sometimes there is no scapegoat to be found; sometimes we did everything right, but just got unlucky. We simply can't prevent a lone nutcase from shooting people at random; there's no security measure that would work.

As circular as it sounds, rare events are rare primarily because they don't occur very often, not because of any preventive security measures. And implementing security measures to make these rare events even rarer is like the joke about the guy who stomps around his house to keep the elephants away.

"Elephants? There are no elephants in this neighborhood," says a neighbor.

"See how well it works!"

If you want to do something that makes security sense, figure out what's common among a bunch of rare events, and concentrate your countermeasures there. Focus on the general risk of terrorism, and not the specific threat of airplane bombings using liquid explosives. Focus on the general risk of troubled young adults, and not the specific threat of a lone gunman wandering around a college campus. Ignore the movie-plot threats, and concentrate on the real risks.

Tactics, Targets, and Objectives

Originally published in Wired, *31 May 2007*

If you encounter an aggressive lion, stare him down. But not a leopard; avoid his gaze at all costs. In both cases, back away slowly; don't run. If you stumble on a pack of hyenas, run and climb a tree; hyenas can't climb trees. But don't do that if you're being chased by an elephant; he'll just knock the tree down. Stand still until he forgets about you.

I spent the last few days on safari in a South African game park, and this was just some of the security advice we were all given. What's interesting about this advice is how well-defined it is. The defenses might not be terribly effective—you still might get eaten, gored, or trampled—but they're your best hope. Doing something else isn't advised, because animals do the same things over and over again. These are security countermeasures against specific tactics.

Lions and leopards learn tactics that work for them, and I was taught tactics to defend myself. Humans are intelligent, and that means we are more adaptable than animals. But we're also, generally speaking, lazy and stupid; and, like a lion or hyena, we will repeat tactics that work. Pickpockets use the same tricks over and over again. So do phishers, and school shooters. If improvised explosive devices didn't work often enough, Iraqi insurgents would do something else.

So security against people generally focuses on tactics as well.

A friend of mine recently asked me where she should hide her jewelry in her apartment, so that burglars wouldn't find it. Burglars tend to look in the same places all the time—dresser tops, night tables, dresser drawers, bathroom counters—so hiding valuables somewhere else is more likely to be effective, especially against a burglar who is pressed for time. Leave decoy cash and jewelry in an obvious place so a burglar will think he's found your stash and then leave. Again, there's no guarantee of success, but it's your best hope.

The key to these countermeasures is to find the pattern: the common attack tactic that is worth defending against. That takes data. A single instance of an attack that didn't work—liquid bombs, shoe bombs—or one instance that did—9/11—is not a pattern. Implementing defensive tactics against them is the same as my safari guide saying: "We've only ever heard of one tourist encountering a lion. He stared it down and survived. Another tourist tried the same thing with a leopard, and he got eaten. So when you see a lion...." The advice I was given was based on thousands of years of collective wisdom from people encountering African animals again and again.

Compare this with the Transportation Security Administration's approach. With every unique threat, TSA implements a countermeasure with no basis to say that it helps, or that the threat will ever recur.

Furthermore, human attackers can adapt more quickly than lions. A lion won't learn that he should ignore people who stare him down, and eat them anyway. But people will learn. Burglars now know the common "secret" places people hide their valuables—the toilet, cereal boxes, the refrigerator and freezer, the medicine cabinet, under the bed—and look there. I told my friend to find a different secret place, and to put decoy valuables in a more obvious place.

This is the arms race of security. Common attack tactics result in common countermeasures. Eventually, those countermeasures will be evaded and new attack tactics developed. These, in turn, require new countermeasures. You can easily see this in the constant arms race that is credit card fraud, ATM fraud, or automobile theft.

The result of these tactic-specific security countermeasures is to make the attacker go elsewhere. For the most part, the attacker doesn't particularly care about the target. Lions don't care who or what they eat; to a lion, you're just a conveniently packaged bag of protein. Burglars don't care which house they rob, and terrorists don't care who they kill. If your countermeasure makes the lion attack an impala instead of you, or if your burglar alarm makes the burglar rob the house next door instead of yours, that's a win for you.

Tactics matter less if the attacker is after you personally. If, for example, you have a priceless painting hanging in your living room and the burglar knows it, he's not going to rob the house next door instead—even if you have a burglar alarm. He's going to figure out how to defeat your system. Or he'll stop you at gunpoint and force you to open the door. Or he'll pose as an air-conditioner repairman. What matters is the target, and a good attacker will consider a variety of tactics to reach his target.

This approach requires a different kind of countermeasure, but it's still well-understood in the security world. For people, it's what alarm companies, insurance companies and bodyguards specialize in. President Bush needs a different level of protection against targeted attacks than Bill Gates does, and I need a different level of protection than either of them. It would be foolish of me to hire bodyguards in case someone is targeting me for robbery or kidnapping. Yes, I would be more secure, but it's not a good security trade-off.

Al-Qaeda terrorism is different yet again. The goal is to terrorize. It doesn't care about the target, but it doesn't have any pattern of tactic, either. Given that, the best way to spend our counterterrorism dollar is on intelligence, investigation, and emergency response. And to refuse to be terrorized.

These measures are effective because they don't assume any particular tactic, and they don't assume any particular target. We should only apply specific countermeasures when the cost-benefit ratio makes sense (reinforcing airplane cockpit doors) or when a specific tactic is repeatedly observed (lions attacking people who don't stare them down). Otherwise, general countermeasures are far more effective a defense.

The Security Mindset

Originally published in Wired, *20 March 2008*

Uncle Milton Industries has been selling ant farms to children since 1956. Some years ago, I remember opening one up with a friend. There were no actual ants included in the box. Instead, there was a card that you filled in with your address, and the company would mail you some ants. My friend expressed surprise that you could get ants sent to you in the mail.

I replied: "What's really interesting is that these people will send a tube of live ants to anyone you tell them to."

Security requires a particular mindset. Security professionals—at least the good ones—see the world differently. They can't walk into a store without noticing how they might shoplift. They can't use a computer without wondering about the security vulnerabilities. They can't vote without trying to figure out how to vote twice. They just can't help it.

SmartWater is a liquid with a unique identifier linked to a particular owner. "The idea is for me to paint this stuff on my valuables as proof of ownership," I wrote when I first learned about the idea. "I think a better idea would be for me to paint it on your valuables, and then call the police."

Really, we can't help it.

This kind of thinking is not natural for most people. It's not natural for engineers. Good engineering involves thinking about how things can be made to work; the security mindset involves thinking about how things can be made to fail. It involves thinking like an attacker, an adversary or a criminal. You don't have to exploit the vulnerabilities you find, but if you don't see the world that way, you'll never notice most security problems.

I've often speculated about how much of this is innate, and how much is teachable. In general, I think it's a particular way of looking at the world, and that it's far easier to teach someone domain expertise—cryptography or software security or safecracking or document forgery—than it is to teach someone a security mindset.

Which is why CSE 484, an undergraduate computer-security course taught this quarter at the University of Washington, is so interesting to watch. Professor Tadayoshi Kohno is trying to teach a security mindset.

You can see the results in the blog the students are keeping. They're encouraged to post security reviews about random things: smart pill boxes,

Quiet Care Elder Care monitors, Apple's Time Capsule, GM's OnStar, traffic lights, safe deposit boxes, and dorm room security.

One recent post is about an automobile dealership. The poster described how she was able to retrieve her car after service just by giving the attendant her last name. Now any normal car owner would be happy about how easy it was to get her car back, but someone with a security mindset immediately thinks: "Can I really get a car just by knowing the last name of someone whose car is being serviced?"

The rest of the blog post speculates on how someone could steal a car by exploiting this security vulnerability, and whether it makes sense for the dealership to have this lax security. You can quibble with the analysis—I'm curious about the liability that the dealership has, and whether their insurance would cover any losses—but that's all domain expertise. The important point is to notice, and then question, the security in the first place.

The lack of a security mindset explains a lot of bad security out there: voting machines, electronic payment cards, medical devices, ID cards, Internet protocols. The designers are so busy making these systems work that they don't stop to notice how they might fail or be made to fail, and then how those failures might be exploited. Teaching designers a security mindset will go a long way toward making future technological systems more secure.

That part's obvious, but I think the security mindset is beneficial in many more ways. If people can learn how to think outside their narrow focus and see a bigger picture, whether in technology or politics or their everyday lives, they'll be more sophisticated consumers, more skeptical citizens, less gullible people.

If more people had a security mindset, services that compromise privacy wouldn't have such a sizable market share—and Facebook would be totally different. Laptops wouldn't be lost with millions of unencrypted Social Security numbers on them, and we'd all learn a lot fewer security lessons the hard way. The power grid would be more secure. Identity theft would go way down. Medical records would be more private. If people had the security mindset, they wouldn't have tried to look at Britney Spears' medical records, since they would have realized that they would be caught.

There's nothing magical about this particular university class; anyone can exercise his security mindset simply by trying to look at the world from an attacker's perspective. If I wanted to evade this particular security device, how would I do it? Could I follow the letter of this law but get around the spirit?

If the person who wrote this advertisement, essay, article, or television documentary were unscrupulous, what could he have done? And then, how can I protect myself from these attacks?

The security mindset is a valuable skill that everyone can benefit from, regardless of career path.

Business of Security

My Open Wireless Network

Originally published in Wired, *10 January 2008*

Whenever I talk or write about my own security setup, the one thing that surprises people—and attracts the most criticism—is the fact that I run an open wireless network at home. There's no password. There's no encryption. Anyone with wireless capability who can see my network can use it to access the Internet.

To me, it's basic politeness. Providing Internet access to guests is kind of like providing heat and electricity, or a hot cup of tea. But to some observers, it's both wrong and dangerous.

I'm told that uninvited strangers may sit in their cars in front of my house, and use my network to send spam, eavesdrop on my passwords, and upload and download everything from pirated movies to child pornography. As a result, I risk all sorts of bad things happening to me, from seeing my IP address blacklisted to having the police crash through my door.

While this is technically true, I don't think it's much of a risk. I can count five open wireless networks in coffee shops within a mile of my house, and any potential spammer is far more likely to sit in a warm room with a cup of coffee and a scone than in a cold car outside my house. And yes, if someone did commit a crime using my network the police might visit, but what better defense is there than the fact that I have an open wireless network? If I enabled wireless security on my network and someone hacked it, I would have a far harder time proving my innocence.

This is not to say that the new wireless security protocol, WPA, isn't very good. It is. But there are going to be security flaws in it; there always are.

I spoke to several lawyers about this, and in their lawyerly way they outlined several other risks with leaving your network open.

While none thought you could be successfully prosecuted just because someone else used your network to commit a crime, any investigation could be time-consuming and expensive. You might have your computer equipment seized, and if you have any contraband of your own on your machine, it could be a delicate situation. Also, prosecutors aren't always the most technically savvy bunch, and you might end up being charged despite your innocence. The lawyers I spoke with say most defense attorneys will advise you to reach a plea agreement rather than risk going to trial on child-pornography charges.

In a less far-fetched scenario, the Recording Industry Association of America is known to sue copyright infringers based on nothing more than an IP address. The accused's chance of winning is higher than in a criminal case, because in civil litigation the burden of proof is lower. And again, lawyers argue that even if you win it's not worth the risk or expense, and that you should settle and pay a few thousand dollars.

I remain unconvinced of this threat, though. The RIAA has conducted about 26,000 lawsuits, and there are more than 15 million music downloaders. Mark Mulligan of Jupiter Research said it best: "If you're a file sharer, you know that the likelihood of you being caught is very similar to that of being hit by an asteroid."

I'm also unmoved by those who say I'm putting my own data at risk, because hackers might park in front of my house, log on to my open network, and eavesdrop on my Internet traffic or break into my computers. This is true, but my computers are much more at risk when I use them on wireless networks in airports, coffee shops, and other public places. If I configure my computer to be secure regardless of the network it's on, then it simply doesn't matter. And if my computer isn't secure on a public network, securing my own network isn't going to reduce my risk very much.

Yes, computer security is hard. But if your computers leave your house, you have to solve it anyway. And any solution will apply to your desktop machines as well.

Finally, critics say someone might steal bandwidth from me. Despite isolated court rulings that this is illegal, my feeling is that they're welcome to it. I really don't mind if neighbors use my wireless network when they need it, and I've heard several stories of people who have been rescued from connectivity emergencies by open wireless networks in the neighborhood.

Similarly, I appreciate an open network when I am otherwise without bandwidth. If someone were using my network to the point that it affected my own traffic or if some neighbor kid were dinking around, I might want to do something about it; but as long as we're all polite, why should this concern me? Pay it forward, I say.

Certainly this does concern ISPs. Running an open wireless network will often violate your terms of service. But despite the occasional cease-and-desist letter and providers getting pissy at people who exceed some secret bandwidth limit, this isn't a big risk either. The worst that will happen to you is that you'll have to find a new ISP.

A company called Fon has an interesting approach to this problem. Fon wireless access points have two wireless networks: a secure one for you, and an open one for everyone else. You can configure your open network in either "Bill" or "Linus" mode. In the former, people pay you to use your network, and you have to pay to use any other Fon wireless network. In Linus mode, anyone can use your network, and you can use any other Fon wireless network for free. It's a really clever idea.

Security is always a trade-off. I know people who rarely lock their front door, who drive in the rain (and while using a cell phone), and who talk to strangers. In my opinion, securing my wireless network isn't worth it. And I appreciate everyone else who keeps an open wireless network, including all the coffee shops, bars, and libraries I have visited in the past, the Dayton International Airport where I started writing this, and the Four Points Sheraton where I finished. You all make the world a better place.

Debating Full Disclosure

Originally published in CSO Online, *January 2007*

Full disclosure—the practice of making the details of security vulnerabilities public—is a damned good idea. Public scrutiny is the only reliable way to improve security, while secrecy only makes us less secure.

Unfortunately, secrecy *sounds* like a good idea. Keeping software vulnerabilities secret, the argument goes, keeps them out of the hands of the hackers. The problem, according to this position, is less the vulnerability itself and more the information about the vulnerability.

But that assumes that hackers can't discover vulnerabilities on their own, and that software companies will spend time and money fixing secret vulnerabilities. Both of those assumptions are false. Hackers have proven to be quite adept at discovering secret vulnerabilities, and full disclosure is the only reason vendors routinely patch their systems.

To understand why the second assumption isn't true, you need to understand the underlying economics. To a software company, vulnerabilities are largely an externality. That is, they affect you—the user—much more than they affect it. A smart vendor treats vulnerabilities less as a software problem, and more as a PR problem. So if we, the user community, want software vendors to patch vulnerabilities, we need to make the PR problem more acute.

Full disclosure does this. Before full disclosure was the norm, researchers would discover vulnerabilities in software and send details to the software companies—who would ignore them, trusting in the security of secrecy. Some would go so far as to threaten the researchers with legal action if they disclosed the vulnerabilities.

Later on, researchers announced that particular vulnerabilities existed, but did not publish details. Software companies would then call the vulnerabilities "theoretical" and deny they actually existed. Of course, they would still ignore the problems, and occasionally threaten the researcher with legal action. Then, of course, some hacker would create an exploit using the vulnerability—and the company would release a really quick patch, apologize profusely, and go on to explain that the whole thing was entirely the fault of the evil, vile hackers.

It wasn't until researchers published complete details of the vulnerabilities that the software companies started fixing them.

Of course, the software companies hated this. They received bad PR every time a vulnerability was made public, and the only way to get some good PR was to quickly release a patch. For a large company like Microsoft, this was very expensive.

So a bunch of software companies, and some security researchers, banded together and invented "responsible disclosure." The basic idea was that the threat of publishing the vulnerability is almost as good as actually publishing it. A responsible researcher would quietly give the software vendor a head start on patching its software, before releasing the vulnerability to the public.

This was a good idea—and these days it's normal procedure—but one that was possible only because full disclosure was the norm. And it remains a good idea only as long as full disclosure is the threat.

The moral here doesn't just apply to software; it's very general. Public scrutiny is how security improves, whether we're talking about software or airport security or government counterterrorism measures. Yes, there are trade-offs. Full disclosure means that the bad guys learn about the vulnerability at the same time as the rest of us—unless, of course, they knew about it beforehand—but most of the time the benefits far outweigh the disadvantages.

Secrecy prevents people from accurately assessing their own risk. Secrecy precludes public debate about security, and inhibits security education that leads to improvements. Secrecy doesn't improve security; it stifles it.

I'd rather have as much information as I can to make an informed decision about security, whether it's a buying decision about a software product or an election decision about two political parties. I'd rather have the information I need to pressure vendors to improve security.

I don't want to live in a world where companies can sell me software they know is full of holes or where the government can implement security measures without accountability. I much prefer a world where I have all the information I need to assess and protect my own security.

Doping in Professional Sports

Originally published in Wired, *10 August 2006*

The big news in professional bicycle racing is that Floyd Landis has been stripped of his Tour de France title because he tested positive for a banned performance-enhancing drug. Sidestepping the entire issue of whether professional athletes should be allowed to take performance-enhancing drugs, how dangerous those drugs are, and what constitutes a performance-enhancing drug in the first place, I'd like to talk about the security and economic issues surrounding the issue of doping in professional sports.

Drug testing is a security issue. Various sports federations around the world do their best to detect illegal doping, and players do their best to evade the tests. It's a classic security arms race: Improvements in detection technologies lead to improvements in drug-detection evasion, which in turn spur the development of better detection capabilities. Right now, it seems that the drugs are winning; in places, these drug tests are described as "intelligence tests": If you can't get around them, you don't deserve to play.

But unlike many security arms races, the detectors have the ability to look into the past. Last year, a laboratory tested Lance Armstrong's urine and found traces of the banned substance EPO. What's interesting is that the urine sample tested wasn't from 2005; it was from 1999. Back then, there weren't any good tests for EPO in urine. Today there are, and the lab took a frozen urine sample—who knew that labs save urine samples from athletes?—and tested it. He was later cleared—the lab procedures were sloppy—but I don't think the real ramifications of the episode were ever well understood. Testing can go back in time.

This has two major effects. One, doctors who develop new performance-enhancing drugs may know exactly what sorts of tests the anti-doping laboratories are going to run, and they can test their ability to evade drug detection beforehand. But they cannot know what sorts of tests will be developed in the future, and athletes cannot assume that just because a drug is undetectable today it will remain so years later.

Two, athletes accused of doping based on years-old urine samples have no way of defending themselves. They can't resubmit to testing; it's too late. If I were an athlete worried about these accusations, I would deposit my urine "in escrow" on a regular basis to give me some ability to contest an accusation.

The doping arms race will continue because of the incentives. It's a classic Prisoner's Dilemma. Consider two competing athletes: Alice and Bob. Both Alice and Bob have to individually decide if they are going to take drugs or not.

Imagine Alice evaluating her two options:

"If Bob doesn't take any drugs," she thinks, "then it will be in my best interest to take them. They will give me a performance edge against Bob. I have a better chance of winning.

"Similarly, if Bob takes drugs, it's also in my interest to agree to take them. At least that way Bob won't have an advantage over me.

"So even though I have no control over what Bob chooses to do, taking drugs gives me the better outcome, regardless of what his action might be."

Unfortunately, Bob goes through exactly the same analysis. As a result, they both take performance-enhancing drugs and neither has the advantage over the other. If they could just trust each other, they could refrain from taking the drugs and maintain the same non-advantage status—without any legal or physical danger. But competing athletes can't trust each other, and everyone feels he has to dope—and continues to search out newer and more undetectable drugs—in order to compete. And the arms race continues.

Some sports are more vigilant about drug detection than others. European bicycle racing is particularly vigilant; so are the Olympics. American professional sports are far more lenient, often trying to give the appearance of vigilance while still allowing athletes to use performance-enhancing drugs. They know that their fans want to see beefy linebackers, powerful sluggers, and lightning-fast sprinters. So, with a wink and a nod, they only test for the easy stuff.

For example, look at baseball's current debate on human growth hormone: HGH. They have serious tests, and penalties, for steroid use, but everyone knows that players are now taking HGH because there is no urine test for it. There's a blood test in development, but it's still some time away from working. The way to stop HGH use is to take blood tests now and store them for future testing, but the players' union has refused to allow it and the baseball commissioner isn't pushing it.

In the end, doping is all about economics. Athletes will continue to dope because the Prisoner's Dilemma forces them to do so. Sports authorities will either improve their detection capabilities or continue to pretend to do so—depending on their fans and their revenues. And as technology continues to improve, professional athletes will become more like deliberately designed racing cars.

University Networks and Data Security

Originally published in IEEE Security and Privacy,
September/October 2006

In general, the problems of securing a university network are no different than those of securing any other large corporate network. But when it comes to data security, universities have their own unique problems. It's easy to point fingers at students—a large number of potentially adversarial transient insiders. Yet that's really no different from a corporation dealing with an assortment of employees and contractors—the difference is the culture.

Universities are edge-focused; central policies tend to be weak, by design, with maximum autonomy for the edges. This means they have natural tendencies against centralization of services. Departments and individual professors are used to being semiautonomous. Because these institutions were established long before the advent of computers, when networking did begin to infuse universities, it developed within existing administrative divisions. Some universities have academic departments with separate IT departments, budgets, and staff, with a central IT group providing bandwidth but little or no oversight. Unfortunately, these smaller IT groups don't generally count policy development and enforcement as part of their core competencies.

The lack of central authority makes enforcing uniform standards challenging, to say the least. Most university CIOs have much less power than their corporate counterparts; university mandates can be a major obstacle in enforcing any security policy. This leads to an uneven security landscape.

There's also a cultural tendency for faculty and staff to resist restrictions, especially in the area of research. Because most research is now done online—or, at least, involves online access—restricting the use of or deciding on appropriate uses for information technologies can be difficult. This resistance also leads to a lack of centralization and an absence of IT operational procedures such as change control, change management, patch management, and configuration control.

The result is that there's rarely a uniform security policy. The centralized servers—the core where the database servers live—are generally more secure, whereas the periphery is a hodgepodge of security levels.

So, what to do? Unfortunately, solutions are easier to describe than implement. First, universities should take a top-down approach to securing their infrastructure. Rather than fighting an established culture, they should concentrate on the core infrastructure.

Then they should move personal, financial, and other comparable data into that core. Leave information important to departments and research groups to them, and centrally store information that's important to the university as a whole. This can be done under the auspices of the CIO. Laws and regulations can help drive consolidation and standardization.

Next, enforce policies for departments that need to connect to the sensitive data in the core. This can be difficult with older legacy systems, but establishing a standard for best practices is better than giving up. All legacy technology is upgraded eventually.

Finally, create distinct segregated networks within the campus. Treat networks that aren't under the IT department's direct control as untrusted. Student networks, for example, should be firewalled to protect the internal core from them. The university can then establish levels of trust commensurate with the segregated networks' adherence to policies. If a research network claims it can't have any controls, then let the university create a separate virtual network for it, outside the university's firewalls, and let it live there. Note, though, that if something or someone on that network wants to connect to sensitive data within the core, it's going to have to agree to whatever security policies that level of data access requires.

Securing university networks is an excellent example of the social problems surrounding network security being harder than the technical ones. But harder doesn't mean impossible, and there is a lot that can be done to improve security.

Do We Really Need a Security Industry?

Originally published in Wired, *3 May 2007*

Last week, I attended the Infosecurity Europe conference in London. Like at the RSA Conference in February, the show floor was chockablock full of network, computer and information security companies. As I often do, I mused about what it means for the IT industry that there are thousands of dedicated security products on the market: some good, more lousy, many difficult even to describe. Why aren't IT products and services naturally secure, and what would it mean for the industry if they were?

I mentioned this in an interview with Silicon.com, and the published article seems to have caused a bit of a stir. Rather than letting people wonder what I really meant, I thought I should explain.

The primary reason the IT security industry exists is because IT products and services aren't naturally secure. If computers were already secure against viruses, there wouldn't be any need for antivirus products. If bad network traffic couldn't be used to attack computers, no one would bother buying a firewall. If there were no more buffer overflows, no one would have to buy products to protect against their effects. If the IT products we purchased were secure out of the box, we wouldn't have to spend billions every year making them secure.

Aftermarket security is actually a very inefficient way to spend our security dollars; it may compensate for insecure IT products, but doesn't help improve their security. Additionally, as long as IT security is a separate industry, there will be companies making money based on insecurity—companies who will lose money if the Internet becomes more secure.

Fold security into the underlying products, and the companies marketing those products will have an incentive to invest in security upfront, to avoid having to spend more cash obviating the problems later. Their profits would rise in step with the overall level of security on the Internet. Initially we'd still be spending a comparable amount of money per year on security—on secure development practices, on embedded security and so on—but some of that money would be going into improving the quality of the IT products we're buying, and would reduce the amount we spend on security in future years.

I know this is a utopian vision that I probably won't see in my lifetime, but the IT services market is pushing us in this direction. As IT becomes more of a utility, users are going to buy a whole lot more services than products. And by nature, services are more about results than technologies. Service customers—whether home users or multinational corporations—care less and less about the specifics of security technologies, and increasingly expect their IT to be integrally secure.

Eight years ago, I formed Counterpane Internet Security on the premise that end users (big corporate users, in this case) really don't want to have to deal with network security. They want to fly airplanes, produce pharmaceuticals, or do whatever their core business is. They don't want to hire the expertise to monitor their network security, and will gladly farm it out to a company that can do it for them. We provided an array of services that took day-to-day security out of the hands of our customers: security monitoring, security-device management, incident response. Security was something our customers purchased, but they purchased results, not details.

Last year, BT bought Counterpane, further embedding network security services into the IT infrastructure. BT has customers that don't want to deal with network management at all; they just want it to work. They want the Internet to be like the phone network, or the power grid, or the water system; they want it to be a utility. For these customers, security isn't even something they purchase: It's one small part of a larger IT services deal. It's the same reason IBM bought ISS: to be able to have a more integrated solution to sell to customers.

This is where the IT industry is headed, and when it gets there, there'll be no point in user conferences like Infosec and RSA. They won't go away; they'll simply become industry conferences. If you want to measure progress, look at the demographics of these conferences. A shift toward infrastructure-geared attendees is a measure of success.

Of course, security products won't disappear— at least, not in my lifetime. There'll still be firewalls, antivirus software and everything else. There'll still be startup companies developing clever and innovative security technologies. But the end user won't care about them. They'll be embedded within the services sold by large IT outsourcing companies like BT, EDS and IBM, or ISPs like EarthLink and Comcast. Or they'll be a check-box item somewhere in the core switch.

IT security is getting harder—increasing complexity is largely to blame— and the need for aftermarket security products isn't disappearing anytime soon. But there's no earthly reason why users need to know what an intrusion-detection system with stateful protocol analysis is, or why it's helpful in spotting SQL injection attacks. The whole IT security industry is an accident—an artifact of how the computer industry developed. As IT fades into the background and becomes just another utility, users will simply expect it to work— and the details of how it works won't matter.

Basketball Referees and Single Points of Failure

Originally published in Wired, *6 September 2007*

Sports referees are supposed to be fair and impartial. They're not supposed to favor one team over another. And they're most certainly not supposed to have a financial interest in the outcome of a game.

Tim Donaghy, referee for the National Basketball Association, has been accused of both betting on basketball games and fixing games for the mob. He has confessed to far less—gambling in general, and selling inside information on players, referees, and coaches to a big-time professional gambler named James "Sheep" Battista. But the investigation continues, and the whole scandal is an enormous black eye for the sport. Fans like to think that the game is fair and that the winning team really is the winning team.

The details of the story are fascinating and well worth reading. But what interests me more are its general lessons about risk and audit.

What sorts of systems—IT, financial, NBA games, or whatever—are most at risk of being manipulated? The ones where the smallest change can have the greatest impact, and the ones where trusted insiders can make that change.

Of all major sports, basketball is the most vulnerable to manipulation. There are only five players on the court per team, fewer than in other professional team sports; thus, a single player can have a much greater effect on a basketball game than he can in the other sports. Star players like Michael Jordan, Kobe Bryant, and LeBron James can carry an entire team on their shoulders. Even baseball great Alex Rodriguez can't do that.

Because individual players matter so much, a single referee can affect a basketball game more than he can in any other sport. Referees call fouls. Contact occurs on nearly every play, any of which could be called as a foul. They're called "touch fouls," and they are mostly, but not always, ignored. The refs get to decide which ones to call.

Even more drastically, a ref can put a star player in foul trouble immediately—and cause the coach to bench him longer throughout the game—if he wants the other side to win. He can set the pace of the game, low-scoring or high-scoring, based on how he calls fouls. He can decide to invalidate a basket by calling an offensive foul on the play, or give a team the potential for some extra points by calling a defensive foul. There's no formal instant replay. There's no second opinion. A ref's word is law—there are only three of them—and a crooked ref has enormous power to control the game.

It's not just that basketball referees are single points of failure, it's that they're both trusted insiders and single points of catastrophic failure.

These sorts of vulnerabilities exist in many systems. Consider what a terrorist-sympathizing Transportation Security Administration screener could do to airport security. Or what a criminal CFO could embezzle. Or what a dishonest computer repair technician could do to your computer or network. The same goes for a corrupt judge, police officer, customs inspector, border-control officer, food-safety inspector, and so on.

The best way to catch corrupt trusted insiders is through audit. The particular components of a system that have the greatest influence on the performance of that system need to be monitored and audited, even if the probability of compromise is low. It's after the fact, but if the likelihood of detection is high and the penalties (fines, jail time, public disgrace) are severe, it's a pretty strong deterrent. Of course, the counterattack is to target the auditing system. Hackers routinely try to erase audit logs that contain evidence of their intrusions.

Even so, audit is the reason we want open source code reviews and verifiable paper trails in voting machines; otherwise, a single crooked programmer could single-handedly change an election. It's also why the Securities and

Exchange Commission closely monitors trades by brokers: They are in an ideal position to get away with insider trading. The NBA claims it monitors referees for patterns that might indicate abuse; there's still no answer to why it didn't detect Donaghy.

Most companies focus the bulk of their IT-security monitoring on external threats, but they should be paying more attention to internal threats. While a company may inherently trust its employees, those trusted employees have far greater power to affect corporate systems and are often single points of failure. And trusted employees can also be compromised by external elements, as Tom Donaghy was by Battista and possibly the Mafia.

All systems have trusted insiders. All systems have catastrophic points of failure. The key is recognizing them, and building monitoring and audit systems to secure them.

Chemical Plant Security and Externalities

Originally published in Wired, *18 October 2007*

It's not true that no one worries about terrorists attacking chemical plants, it's just that our politics seem to leave us unable to deal with the threat.

Toxins such as ammonia, chlorine, propane, and flammable mixtures are constantly being produced or stored in the United States as a result of legitimate industrial processes. Chlorine gas is particularly toxic; in addition to bombing a plant, someone could hijack a chlorine truck or blow up a railcar. Phosgene is even more dangerous. According to the Environmental Protection Agency, there are 7,728 chemical plants in the United States where an act of sabotage—or an accident—could threaten more than 1,000 people. Of those, 106 facilities could threaten more than a million people.

The problem of securing chemical plants against terrorism—or even accidents—is actually simple once you understand the underlying economics. Normally, we leave the security of something up to its owner. The basic idea is that the owner of each chemical plant 1) best understands the risks, and 2) is the one who loses out if security fails. Any outsider—i.e., regulatory agency—is just going to get it wrong. It's the basic free-market argument, and in most instances it makes a lot of sense.

And chemical plants do have security. They have fences and guards (which might or might not be effective). They have fail-safe mechanisms built into their operations. For example, many large chemical companies use hazardous substances like phosgene, methyl isocyanate, and ethylene oxide in their plants, but don't ship them between locations. They minimize the amounts that are stored as process intermediates. In rare cases of extremely hazardous materials, no significant amounts are stored; instead they are only present in pipes connecting the reactors that make them with the reactors that consume them.

This is all good and right, and what free-market capitalism dictates. The problem is, it isn't enough.

Any rational chemical plant owner will only secure the plant up to its value to him. That is, if the plant is worth $100 million, then it makes no sense to spend $200 million on securing it. If the odds of it being attacked are less than 1%, it doesn't even make sense to spend $1 million on securing it. The math is more complicated than this, because you have to factor in such things as the reputational cost of having your name splashed all over the media after an incident, but that's the basic idea.

But to society, the cost of an actual attack can be much, much greater. If a terrorist blows up a particularly toxic plant in the middle of a densely populated area, deaths could be in the tens of thousands and damage could be in the hundreds of millions. Indirect economic damage could be in the billions. The owner of the chlorine plant would pay none of these potential costs.

Sure, the owner could be sued. But he's not at risk for more than the value of his company, and—in any case—he'd probably be smarter to take the chance. Expensive lawyers can work wonders, courts can be fickle, and the government could step in and bail him out (as it did with airlines after 9/11). And a smart company can often protect itself by spinning off the risky asset in a subsidiary company, or selling it off completely. The overall result is that our nation's chemical plants are secured to a much smaller degree than the risk warrants.

In economics, this is called an *externality*: an effect of a decision not borne by the decision maker. The decision maker in this case, the chemical plant owner, makes a rational economic decision based on the risks and costs *to him*.

If we—whether we're the community living near the chemical plant or the nation as a whole—expect the owner of that plant to spend money for increased security to account for those externalities, we're going to have to pay for it. And we have three basic ways of doing that. One, we can do it ourselves, stationing government police or military or contractors around the chemical plants. Two, we can pay the owners to do it, subsidizing some sort of security standard.

Or three, we could regulate security and force the companies to pay for it themselves. There's no free lunch, of course. "We," as in society, still pay for it in increased prices for whatever the chemical plants are producing, but the cost is paid for by the product's consumers rather than by taxpayers in general.

Personally, I don't care very much which method is chosen—that's politics, not security. But I do know we'll have to pick one, or some combination of the three. Asking nicely just isn't going to work. It can't; not in a free-market economy.

We taxpayers pay for airport security, and not the airlines, because the overall effects of a terrorist attack against an airline are far greater than their effects to the particular airline targeted. We pay for port security because the effects of bringing a large weapon into the country are far greater than the concerns of the port's owners. And we should pay for chemical plant, train and truck security for exactly the same reasons.

Thankfully, after years of hoping the chemical industry would do it on its own, this April the Department of Homeland Security started regulating chemical plant security. Some complain that the regulations don't go far enough, but at least it's a start.

11

Cybercrime and Cyberwar

Mitigating Identity Theft

Originally published in CNet, *14 April 2005*

Identity theft is the new crime of the information age. A criminal collects enough personal data on someone to impersonate a victim to banks, credit card companies, and other financial institutions. Then he racks up debt in the person's name, collects the cash, and disappears. The victim is left holding the bag. While some of the losses are absorbed by financial institutions—credit card companies in particular—the credit-rating damage is borne by the victim. It can take years for the victim to clear his name.

Unfortunately, the solutions being proposed in Congress won't help. To see why, we need to start with the basics. The very term "identity theft" is an oxymoron. Identity is not a possession that can be acquired or lost; it's not a thing at all. Someone's identity is the one thing about a person that cannot be stolen.

The real crime here is fraud; more specifically, impersonation leading to fraud. Impersonation is an ancient crime, but the rise of information-based credentials gives it a modern spin. A criminal impersonates a victim online and steals money from his account. He impersonates a victim in order to deceive financial institutions into granting credit to the criminal in the victim's name. He impersonates a victim to the Post Office and gets the victim's address changed. He impersonates a victim in order to fool the police into arresting the wrong man. No one's identity is stolen; identity information is being misused to commit fraud.

The crime involves two very separate issues. The first is the privacy of personal data. Personal privacy is important for many reasons, one of which is impersonation and fraud. As more information about us is collected, correlated, and sold, it becomes easier for criminals to get their hands on the data they need to commit fraud. This is what's been in the news recently: ChoicePoint, LexisNexis, Bank of America, and so on. But data privacy is more than just fraud. Whether it is the books we take out of the library, the websites we visit, or the contents of our text messages, most of us have personal data on third-party computers that we don't want made public. The posting of Paris Hilton's phonebook on the Internet is a celebrity example of this.

The second issue is the ease with which a criminal can use personal data to commit fraud. It doesn't take much personal information to apply for a credit card in someone else's name. It doesn't take much to submit fraudulent bank transactions in someone else's name. It's surprisingly easy to get an identification card in someone else's name. Our current culture, where identity is verified simply and sloppily, makes it easier for a criminal to impersonate his victim.

Proposed fixes tend to concentrate on the first issue—making personal data harder to steal—whereas the real problem is the second. If we're ever going to manage the risks and effects of electronic impersonation, we must concentrate on preventing and detecting fraudulent transactions.

Fraudulent transactions have nothing to do with the legitimate account holders. Criminals impersonate legitimate users to financial institutions. That means that any solution can't involve the account holders. That leaves only one reasonable answer: Financial institutions need to be liable for fraudulent transactions. They need to be liable for sending erroneous information to credit bureaus based on fraudulent transactions.

They can't claim that the user must keep his password secure or his machine virus free. They can't require the user to monitor his accounts for fraudulent activity, or his credit reports for fraudulently obtained credit cards. Those aren't reasonable requirements for most users. The bank must be made responsible, regardless of what the user does.

If you think this won't work, look at credit cards. Credit card companies are liable for all but the first $50 of fraudulent transactions. They're not hurting for business; and they're not drowning in fraud, either. They've developed and fielded an array of security technologies designed to detect and prevent fraudulent transactions. They've pushed most of the actual costs onto the merchants. And almost no security centers around trying to authenticate the cardholder.

That's an important lesson. Identity theft solutions focus much too much on authenticating the person. Whether it's two-factor authentication, ID cards, biometrics, or whatever, there's a widespread myth that authenticating the person is the way to prevent these crimes. But once you understand that the problem is fraudulent transactions, you quickly realize that authenticating the person isn't the way to proceed.

Again, think about credit cards. Store clerks barely verify signatures when people use cards. People can use credit cards to buy things by mail, phone, or Internet, where no one verifies the signature or even that you have possession of the card. Even worse, no credit card company mandates secure storage requirements for credit cards. They don't demand that cardholders secure their wallets in any particular way. Credit card companies simply don't worry about verifying the cardholder or putting requirements on what he does. They concentrate on verifying the transaction.

This same sort of thinking needs to be applied to other areas where criminals use impersonation to commit fraud. I don't know what the final solutions will look like, but I do know that once financial institutions are liable for losses due to these types of fraud, they will find solutions. Maybe there'll be a daily withdrawal limit, like there is on ATMs. Maybe large transactions will be delayed for a period of time, or will require a call-back from the bank or brokerage company. Maybe people will no longer be able to open a credit card account by simply filling out a bunch of information on a form. Likely the solution will be a combination of solutions that reduces fraudulent transactions to a manageable level, but we'll never know until the financial institutions have the financial incentive to put them in place.

Right now, the economic incentives result in financial institutions that are so eager to allow transactions—new credit cards, cash transfers, whatever— that they're not paying enough attention to fraudulent transactions. They've pushed the costs for fraud onto the merchants. But if they're liable for losses and damages to legitimate users, they'll pay more attention. And they'll mitigate the risks. Security can do all sorts of things, once the economic incentives to apply them are there.

By focusing on the fraudulent use of personal data, I do not mean to minimize the harm caused by third-party data and violations of privacy. I believe that the U.S. would be well-served by a comprehensive Data Protection Act like the one the European Union had implemented. However, I do not believe that a law of this type would significantly reduce the risk of fraudulent impersonation. To mitigate that risk, we need to concentrate on detecting and preventing fraudulent transactions. We need to make the entity that is in the best position to mitigate the risk to be responsible for that risk. And that means making the financial institutions liable for fraudulent transactions.

Doing anything less simply won't work.

LifeLock and Identity Theft

Originally published in Wired, *12 June 2008*

LifeLock, one of the companies that offers identity-theft protection in the United States, has been taking quite a beating recently. They're being sued by credit bureaus, competitors, and lawyers in several states that are launching class-action lawsuits. And the stories in the media...it's like a piranha feeding frenzy.

There are also a lot of errors and misconceptions. With its aggressive advertising campaign and a CEO who publishes his Social Security number and dares people to steal his identity—Todd Davis, 457-55-5462—LifeLock is a company that's easy to hate. But the company's story has some interesting security lessons, and it's worth understanding in some detail.

In December 2003, as part of the Fair and Accurate Credit Transactions Act, or FACTA, credit bureaus were forced to allow you to put a fraud alert on their credit reports, requiring lenders to verify your identity before issuing a credit card in your name. This alert is temporary, and expires after 90 days. Several companies have sprung up—LifeLock, Debix, LoudSiren, TrustedID—that automatically renew these alerts and effectively make them permanent.

This service pisses off the credit bureaus and their financial customers. The reason lenders don't routinely verify your identity before issuing you credit is that it takes time, costs money, and is one more hurdle between you and another credit card. (Buy, buy, buy—it's the American way.) So in the eyes of credit bureaus, LifeLock's customers are inferior goods; selling their data isn't as valuable. LifeLock also opts its customers out of pre-approved credit card offers, further making them less valuable in the eyes of credit bureaus.

And so began a smear campaign on the part of the credit bureaus. You can read their points of view in a *New York Times* article, written by a reporter who didn't do much more than regurgitate their talking points. And the class-action lawsuits have piled on, accusing LifeLock of deceptive business practices, fraudulent advertising, and so on. The biggest smear is that LifeLock didn't even protect Todd Davis, and that his identity was allegedly stolen.

It wasn't. Someone in Texas used Davis's Social Security number to get a $500 advance against his paycheck. It worked because the loan operation didn't check with any of the credit bureaus before approving the loan—perfectly reasonable for an amount this small. The payday-loan operation called Davis to collect, and LifeLock cleared up the problem. His credit report remains spotless.

The Experian credit bureau's lawsuit basically claims that fraud alerts are only for people who have been victims of identity theft. This seems spurious; the text of the law states that anyone "who asserts a good faith suspicion that the consumer has been or is about to become a victim of fraud or related crime" can request a fraud alert. It seems to me that includes anybody who has ever received one of those notices about their financial details being lost or stolen, which is everybody.

As to deceptive business practices and fraudulent advertising—those just seem like class-action lawyers piling on. LifeLock's aggressive fear-based marketing doesn't seem any worse than a lot of other similar advertising campaigns. My guess is that the class-action lawsuits won't go anywhere.

In reality, forcing lenders to verify identity before issuing credit is exactly the sort of thing we need to do to fight identity theft. Basically, there are two ways to deal with identity theft: Make personal information harder to steal, or make stolen personal information harder to use. We all know the former doesn't work, so that leaves the latter. If Congress wanted to solve the problem for real, one of the things it would do is make fraud alerts permanent for everybody. But the credit industry's lobbyists would never allow that.

LifeLock does a bunch of other clever things. They monitor the national address database, and alert you if your address changes. They look for your credit and debit card numbers on hacker and criminal websites and such, and assist you in getting a new number if they see it. They have a million-dollar service guarantee—for complicated legal reasons, they can't call it insurance—to help you recover if your identity is ever stolen.

But even with all of this, I am not a LifeLock customer. At $120 a year, it's just not worth it. You wouldn't know it from the press attention, but dealing with identity theft has become easier and more routine. Sure, it's a pervasive problem. The Federal Trade Commission reported that 8.3 million Americans were identity-theft victims in 2005. But that includes things like someone stealing your credit card and using it, something that rarely costs you any money and that LifeLock doesn't protect against. New account fraud is much less common, affecting 1.8 million Americans per year, or 0.8% of the adult population. The FTC hasn't published detailed numbers for 2006 or 2007, but the rate seems to be declining.

New card fraud is also not very damaging. The median amount of fraud the thief commits is $1,350, but you're not liable for that. Some spectacularly horrible identity theft stories notwithstanding, the financial industry is pretty good at quickly cleaning up the mess. The victim's median out-of-pocket cost for new account fraud is only $40, plus 10 hours of grief to clean up the problem. Even assuming your time is worth $100 an hour, LifeLock isn't worth more than $8 a year.

And it's hard to get any data on how effective LifeLock really is. They've been in business three years and have about a million customers, but most of them have joined up in the last year. They've paid out on their service guarantee 113 times, but a lot of those were for things that happened before their customers became customers. (It was easier to pay than argue, I assume.) But they don't know how often the fraud alerts actually catch an identity thief in the act. My guess is that it's less than the 0.8% fraud rate above.

LifeLock's business model is based more on the fear of identity theft than the actual risk.

It's pretty ironic of the credit bureaus to attack LifeLock on its marketing practices, since they know all about profiting from the fear of identity theft. FACTA also forced the credit bureaus to give Americans a free credit report once a year upon request. Through deceptive marketing techniques, they've turned this requirement into a multimillion-dollar business.

Get LifeLock if you want, or one of its competitors if you prefer. But remember that you can do most of what these companies do yourself. You can put a fraud alert on your own account, but you have to remember to renew it every three months. You can also put a credit freeze on your account, which is more work for the average consumer but more effective if you're a privacy wonk—and the rules differ by state. And maybe someday Congress will do the right thing and put LifeLock out of business by forcing lenders to verify identity every time they issue credit in someone's name.

Phishing

Originally published in Wired, *6 October 2005*

Earlier this month, California became the first state to enact a law specifically addressing phishing. Phishing, for those of you who have been away from the

Internet for the past few years, is when an attacker sends you an e-mail falsely claiming to be a legitimate business in order to trick you into giving away your account info—passwords, mostly. When this is done by hacking DNS, it's called pharming.

Financial companies have until now avoided taking on phishers in a serious way, because it's cheaper and simpler to pay the costs of fraud. That's unacceptable, however, because consumers who fall prey to these scams pay a price that goes beyond financial losses, in inconvenience, stress and, in some cases, blots on their credit reports that are hard to eradicate. As a result, lawmakers need to do more than create new punishments for wrongdoers—they need to create tough new incentives that will effectively force financial companies to change the status quo and improve the way they protect their customers' assets. Unfortunately, the California law does nothing to address this.

The new legislation was enacted because phishing is a new crime. But the law won't help, because phishing is just a tactic. Criminals phish in order to get your passwords, so they can make fraudulent transactions in your name. The real crime is an ancient one: financial fraud.

These attacks prey on the gullibility of people. This distinguishes them from worms and viruses, which exploit vulnerabilities in computer code. In the past, I've called these attacks examples of "semantic attacks" because they exploit human meaning rather than computer logic. The victims are people who get e-mails and visit websites, and generally believe that these e-mails and websites are legitimate.

These attacks take advantage of the inherent unverifiability of the Internet. Phishing and pharming are easy because authenticating businesses on the Internet is hard. While it might be possible for a criminal to build a fake bricks-and-mortar bank in order to scam people out of their signatures and bank details, it's much easier for the same criminal to build a fake website or send a fake e-mail. And while it might be technically possible to build a security infrastructure to verify both websites and e-mail, both the cost and user unfriendliness means that it'd only be a solution for the geekiest of Internet users.

These attacks also leverage the inherent scalability of computer systems. Scamming someone in person takes work. With e-mail, you can try to scam millions of people per hour. And a one-in-a-million success rate might be good enough for a viable criminal enterprise.

In general, two Internet trends affect all forms of identity theft. The widespread availability of personal information has made it easier for a thief to get his hands on it. At the same time, the rise of electronic authentication and online transactions—you don't have to walk into a bank, or even use a bank card, in order to withdraw money now—has made that personal information much more valuable.

The problem of phishing cannot be solved solely by focusing on the first trend: the availability of personal information. Criminals are clever people, and if you defend against a particular tactic such as phishing, they'll find another. In the space of just a few years, we've seen phishing attacks get more sophisticated. The newest variant, called "spear phishing," involves individually targeted and personalized e-mail messages that are even harder to detect. And there are other sorts of electronic fraud that aren't technically phishing.

The actual problem to be solved is that of fraudulent transactions. Financial institutions make it too easy for a criminal to commit fraudulent transactions, and too difficult for the victims to clear their names. The institutions make a lot of money because it's easy to make a transaction, open an account, get a credit card and so on. For years I've written about how economic considerations affect security problems. Institutions can put security countermeasures in place to prevent fraud, detect it quickly and allow victims to clear themselves. But all of that's expensive. And it's not worth it to them.

It's not that financial institutions suffer no losses. Because of something called Regulation E, they already pay most of the direct costs of identity theft. But the costs in time, stress, and hassle are entirely borne by the victims. And in one in four cases, the victims have not been able to completely restore their good name.

In economics, this is known as an externality: It's an effect of a business decision that is not borne by the person or organization making the decision. Financial institutions have no incentive to reduce those costs of identity theft because they don't bear them.

Push the responsibility—all of it—for identity theft onto the financial institutions, and phishing will go away. This fraud will go away not because people will suddenly get smart and quit responding to phishing e-mails, because California has new criminal penalties for phishing, or because ISPs will recognize and delete the e-mails. It will go away because the information a criminal can get from a phishing attack won't be enough for him to commit fraud—because the companies won't stand for all those losses.

If there's one general precept of security policy that is universally true, it is that security works best when the entity that is in the best position to mitigate the risk is responsible for that risk. Making financial institutions responsible for losses due to phishing and identity theft is the only way to deal with the problem. And not just the direct financial losses—they need to make it less painful to resolve identity theft issues, enabling people to truly clear their names and credit histories. Money to reimburse losses is cheap compared with the expense of redesigning their systems, but anything less won't work.

Bot Networks

Originally published in Wired, *27 July 2006*

What could you do if you controlled a network of thousands of computers—or, at least, could use the spare processor cycles on those machines? You could perform massively parallel computations: model nuclear explosions or global weather patterns, factor large numbers or find Mersenne primes, or break cryptographic problems.

All of these are legitimate applications. And you can visit distributed.net and download software that allows you to donate your spare computer cycles to some of these projects. (You can help search for Optimal Golomb Rulers—even if you have no idea what they are.) You've got a lot of cycles to spare. There's no reason that your computer can't help search for extraterrestrial life as it, for example, sits idly waiting for you to read this essay.

The reason these things work is that they are consensual; none of these projects download software onto your computer without your knowledge. None of these projects control your computer without your consent. But there are lots of software programs that do just that.

The term used for a computer remotely controlled by someone else is a "bot." A group of computers—thousands or even millions—controlled by someone else is a bot network. Estimates are that millions of computers on the Internet today are part of bot networks, and the largest bot networks have over 1.5 million machines.

Initially, bot networks were used for just one thing: denial-of-service attacks. Hackers would use them against each other, fighting hacker feuds in cyberspace by attacking each other's computers. The first widely publicized use of a distributed intruder tool—technically not a botnet, but practically the same thing—was in February 2000, when Canadian hacker Mafiaboy directed an army of compromised computers to flood CNN.com, Amazon.com, eBay,

Dell Computer, and other sites with debilitating volumes of traffic. Every newspaper carried that story.

These days, bot networks are more likely to be controlled by criminals than by hackers. The important difference is the motive: profit. Networks are being used to send phishing e-mails and other spam. They're being used for click fraud. They're being used as an extortion tool: Pay up or we'll DDoS you!

Mostly, they're being used to collect personal data for fraud—commonly called "identity theft." Modern bot software doesn't just attack other computers; it attacks its hosts as well. The malware is packed with keystroke loggers to steal passwords and account numbers. In fact, many bots automatically hunt for financial information, and some botnets have been built solely for this purpose—to gather credit card numbers, online banking passwords, PayPal accounts, and so on, from compromised hosts.

Swindlers are also using bot networks for click fraud. Google's anti-fraud systems are sophisticated enough to detect thousands of clicks by one computer; it's much harder to determine if a single click by each of thousands of computers is fraud, or just popularity.

And, of course, most bots constantly search for other computers that can be infected and added to the bot network. (A 1.5 million-node bot network was discovered in the Netherlands last year. The command-and-control system was dismantled, but some of the bots are still active, infecting other computers and adding them to this defunct network.)

Modern bot networks are remotely upgradeable, so the operators can add new functionality to the bots at any time, or switch from one bot program to another. Bot authors regularly upgrade their botnets during development, or to evade detection by anti-virus and malware cleanup tools.

One application of bot networks that we haven't seen all that much of is to launch a fast-spreading worm. Much has been written about "flash worms" that can saturate the Internet in 15 minutes or less. The situation gets even worse if 10 thousand bots synchronize their watches and release the worm at exactly the same time. Why haven't we seen more of this? My guess is because there isn't any profit in it.

There's no real solution to the botnet problem, because there's no single problem. There are many different bot networks, controlled in many different ways, consisting of computers infected through many different vulnerabilities. Really, a bot network is nothing more than an attacker taking advantage of 1) one or more software vulnerabilities, and 2) the economies of scale that computer networks bring. It's the same thing as distributed.net or SETI@home, only the attacker doesn't ask your permission first.

As long as networked computers have vulnerabilities—and that'll be for the foreseeable future—there'll be bot networks. It's a natural side-effect of a computer network with bugs.

Cyber-Attack

Originally published in Wired, *5 April 2007*

Last month, Marine General James Cartwright told the House Armed Services Committee that the best cyber defense is a good offense.

As reported in *Federal Computer Week*, Cartwright said: "History teaches us that a purely defensive posture poses significant risks," and that if "we apply the principle of warfare to the cyberdomain, as we do to sea, air and land, we realize the defense of the nation is better served by capabilities enabling us to take the fight to our adversaries, when necessary, to deter actions detrimental to our interests."

The general isn't alone. In 2003, the entertainment industry tried to get a law passed giving them the right to attack any computer suspected of distributing copyrighted material. And there probably isn't a sysadmin in the world who doesn't want to strike back at computers that are blindly and repeatedly attacking their networks.

Of course, the general is correct from his point of view. But his reasoning illustrates perfectly why peacetime and wartime are different, and why generals don't make good police chiefs.

A cyber-security policy that condones both active deterrence and retaliation—without any judicial determination of wrongdoing—is attractive, but it's wrongheaded, not least because it ignores the line between war, where those involved are permitted to determine when counterattack is required, and crime, where only impartial third parties (judges and juries) can impose punishment.

In warfare, the notion of counterattack is extremely powerful. Going after the enemy—its positions, its supply lines, its factories, its infrastructure—is an age-old military tactic. But in peacetime, we call it revenge, and consider it dangerous. Anyone accused of a crime deserves a fair trial. The accused has the right to defend himself, to face his accuser, to be represented by an attorney, and to be presumed innocent until proven guilty.

Both vigilante counterattacks and pre-emptive attacks fly in the face of these rights. They punish people who haven't been found guilty. It's the same whether it's an angry lynch mob stringing up a suspect, the MPAA disabling the computer of someone it believes made an illegal copy of a movie, or a corporate security officer launching a denial-of-service attack against someone he believes is targeting his company over the net.

In all of these cases, the attacker could be wrong. This has been true for lynch mobs, and on the Internet it's even harder to know who's attacking you. Just because my computer looks like the source of an attack doesn't mean it is. And even if it is, it might be a zombie controlled by yet another computer; I might be a victim, too. The goal of a government's legal system is justice; the goal of a vigilante is expediency.

I understand the frustrations of General Cartwright, just as I do the frustrations of the entertainment industry, and the world's sysadmins. Justice in cyberspace can be difficult. It can be hard to figure out who is attacking you, and it can take a long time to make them stop. It can be even harder to prove anything in court. The international nature of many attacks exacerbates the problems; more and more cybercriminals are jurisdiction shopping: attacking from countries with ineffective computer crime laws, easily bribable police forces, and no extradition treaties.

Revenge is appealingly straightforward, and treating the whole thing as a military problem is easier than working within the legal system.

But that doesn't make it right. In 1789, the Declaration of the Rights of Man and of the Citizen declared: "No person shall be accused, arrested, or imprisoned except in the cases and according to the forms prescribed by law. Any one soliciting, transmitting, executing, or causing to be executed any arbitrary order shall be punished."

I'm glad General Cartwright thinks about offensive cyberwar; it's how generals are supposed to think. I even agree with Richard Clarke's threat of military-style reaction in the event of a cyber-attack by a foreign country or a terrorist organization. But short of an act of war, we're far safer with a legal system that respects our rights.

Counterattack

Originally published in Crypto-Gram, *15 December 2002*

This must be an idea whose time has come, because I'm seeing it talked about everywhere. The entertainment industry floated a bill that would give it the ability to break into other people's computers if they are suspected of copyright violation. Several articles have been written on the notion of automated law enforcement, where both governments and private companies use computers to automatically find and target suspected criminals. And finally, Tim Mullen and other security researchers start talking about "strike back," where the victim of a computer assault automatically attacks back at the perpetrator.

The common theme here is vigilantism: citizens and companies taking the law into their own hands and going after their assailants. Viscerally, it's an appealing idea. But it's a horrible one, and one that society after society has eschewed.

Our society does not give us the right of revenge, and wouldn't work very well if it did. Our laws give us the right to justice, in either the criminal or civil context. Justice is all we can expect if we want to enjoy our constitutional freedoms, personal safety, and an orderly society.

Anyone accused of a crime deserves a fair trial. He deserves the right to defend himself, the right to face his accuser, the right to an attorney, and the right to be held innocent until proven guilty.

Vigilantism flies in the face of these rights. It punishes people before they have been found guilty. Angry mobs lynching someone suspected of murder is wrong, even if that person is actually guilty. The MPAA disabling someone's computer because he's suspected of copying a movie is wrong, even if the movie was copied. Revenge is a basic human emotion, but revenge only becomes justice if carried out by the State.

And the State has more motivation to be fair. The RIAA sent a cease-and-desist letter to an ISP asking them to remove certain files that were the copyrighted works of George Harrison. One of the files: "Portrait of mrs. harrison Williams 1943.jpg." The RIAA simply Googled for the string "harrison" and went after everyone who turned up. Vigilantism is wrong because the vigilante could be wrong. The goal of a State legal system is justice; the goal of the RIAA was expediency.

Systems of strike back are much the same. The idea is that if a computer is attacking you—sending you viruses, acting as a DDoS zombie, etc.—you might be able to forcibly shut that computer down or remotely install a patch. Again, a nice idea in theory but one that's legally and morally wrong.

Imagine you're a homeowner, and your neighbor has some kind of device on the outside of his house that makes noise. A lot of noise. All day and all night. Enough noise that any reasonable person would claim it to be a public nuisance. Even so, it is not legal for you to take matters into your own hands and stop the noise.

Destroying property is not a recognized remedy for stopping a nuisance, even if it is causing you real harm. Your remedies are to: 1) call the police and ask them to turn it off, break it, or insist that the neighbor turn it off; or 2) sue the neighbor and ask the court to enjoin him from using that device unless it is repaired properly, and to award you damages for your aggravation. Vigilante justice is simply not an option, no matter how right you believe your cause to be.

This is law, not technology, so there are all sorts of shades of gray to this issue. The interests at stake in the original attack, the nature of the property, liberty or personal safety taken away by the counterattack, the risk of being wrong, and the availability and effectiveness of other measures are all factors that go into the assessment of whether something is morally or legally right. The RIAA bill is at one extreme because copyright is a limited property interest, and there is a great risk of wrongful deprivation of use of the computer, and of the user's privacy and security. A strikeback that disables a dangerous Internet worm is less extreme. Clearly this is something that the courts will have to sort out.

Way back in 1789, the Declaration of the Rights of Man and of the Citizen said that: "No person shall be accused, arrested, or imprisoned except in the cases and according to the forms prescribed by law. Any one soliciting, transmitting, executing, or causing to be executed any arbitrary order shall be punished." And also: "As all persons are held innocent until they shall have been declared guilty, if arrest shall be deemed indispensable, all harshness not essential to the securing of the prisoner s person shall be severely repressed by law."

Neither the interests of sysadmins on the Internet, nor the interests of companies like Disney, should be allowed to trump these rights.

Cyberwar

Originally published in Crypto-Gram, *15 January 2005*

The first problem with any discussion about cyberwar is definitional. I've been reading about cyberwar for years now, and there seem to be as many definitions of the term as there are people who write about the topic. Some people try to limit cyberwar to military actions taken during wartime, while others are so inclusive that they include the script kiddies who deface websites for fun.

I think the restrictive definition is more useful, and would like to define four different terms as follows:

- Cyberwar—Warfare in cyberspace. This includes warfare attacks against a nation's military—forcing critical communications channels to fail, for example—and attacks against the civilian population.
- Cyberterrorism—The use of cyberspace to commit terrorist acts. An example might be hacking into a computer system to cause a nuclear power plant to melt down, a dam to open, or two airplanes to collide. In a previous *Crypto-Gram* essay, I discussed how realistic the cyberterrorism threat is.
- Cybercrime—Crime in cyberspace. This includes much of what we've already experienced: theft of intellectual property, extortion based on the threat of DDOS attacks, fraud based on identity theft, and so on.
- Cybervandalism—The script kiddies who deface websites for fun are technically criminals, but I think of them more as vandals or hooligans. They're like the kids who spray-paint buses: in it more for the thrill than anything else.

At first glance, there's nothing new about these terms except the "cyber" prefix. War, terrorism, crime, even vandalism are old concepts. That's correct, the only thing new is the domain; it's the same old stuff occurring in a new arena. But because the arena of cyberspace is different from other arenas, there are differences worth considering.

One thing that hasn't changed is that the terms overlap: Although the goals are different, many of the tactics used by armies, terrorists, and criminals are the same. Just as all three groups use guns and bombs, all three groups can use cyberattacks. And just as every shooting is not necessarily an act of war, every successful Internet attack, no matter how deadly, is not necessarily an act of cyberwar. A cyberattack that shuts down the power grid might be part of a cyberwar campaign, but it also might be an act of cyberterrorism, cybercrime, or even—if it's done by some fourteen-year-old who doesn't really understand what he's doing—cybervandalism. Which it is will depend on the motivations of the attacker and the circumstances surrounding the attack...just as in the real world.

For it to be cyberwar, it must first be war. And in the 21st century, war will inevitably include cyberwar. For just as war moved into the air with the development of kites and balloons and then aircraft, and war moved into space with the development of satellites and ballistic missiles, war will move into cyberspace with the development of specialized weapons, tactics, and defenses.

The Waging of Cyberwar

There should be no doubt that the smarter and better-funded militaries of the world are planning for cyberwar, both attack and defense. It would be foolish for a military to ignore the threat of a cyberattack and not invest in defensive capabilities, or to disregard the strategic or tactical possibility of launching an offensive cyberattack against an enemy during wartime. And while history has taught us that many militaries are indeed foolish and ignore the march of progress, cyberwar has been discussed too much in military circles to be ignored.

This implies that at least some of our world's militaries have Internet attack tools that they're saving in case of wartime. They could be denial-of-service tools. They could be exploits that would allow military intelligence to penetrate military systems. They could be viruses and worms similar to what we're seeing now, but perhaps country- or network-specific. They could be Trojans that eavesdrop on networks, disrupt network operations, or allow an attacker to penetrate still other networks.

Script kiddies are attackers who run exploit code written by others, but don't really understand the intricacies of what they're doing. Conversely, professional attackers spend an enormous amount of time developing exploits: finding vulnerabilities, writing code to exploit them, figuring out how to cover their tracks. The real professionals don't release their code to the script kiddies; the stuff is much more valuable if it remains secret until it is needed. I believe that militaries have collections of vulnerabilities in common operating systems, generic applications, or even custom military software that their potential enemies are using, and code to exploit those vulnerabilities. I believe that these militaries are keeping these vulnerabilities secret, and that they are saving them in case of wartime or other hostilities. It would be irresponsible for them not to.

The most obvious cyberattack is the disabling of large parts of the Internet, at least for a while. Certainly some militaries have the capability to do this, but in the absence of global war I doubt that they would do so; the Internet is far too useful an asset and far too large a part of the world economy. More interesting is whether they would try to disable national pieces of it. If Country A went to war with Country B, would Country A want to disable Country B's portion of the Internet, or remove connections between Country B's Internet and the rest of the world? Depending on the country, a low-tech solution might be the easiest: Disable whatever undersea cables they're using as access. Could Country A's military turn its own Internet into a domestic-only network if they wanted?

For a more surgical approach, we can also imagine cyberattacks designed to destroy particular organizations' networks; e.g., as the denial-of-service attack against the Al Jazeera website during the recent Iraqi war, allegedly by pro-American hackers but possibly by the government. We can imagine a cyberattack against the computer networks at a nation's military headquarters, or the computer networks that handle logistical information.

One important thing to remember is that destruction is the last thing a military wants to do with a communications network. A military only wants to shut an enemy's network down if they aren't getting useful information from it. The best thing to do is to infiltrate the enemy's computers and networks, spy on them, and surreptitiously disrupt select pieces of their communications when appropriate. The next best thing is to passively eavesdrop. After that, the next best is to perform traffic analysis: Analyze who is talking to whom and the characteristics of that communication. Only if a military can't do any of that do they consider shutting the thing down. Or if, as sometimes but rarely happens, the benefits of completely denying the enemy the communications channel outweigh all of the advantages.

Properties of Cyberwar

Because attackers and defenders use the same network hardware and software, there is a fundamental tension between cyberattack and cyberdefense. The National Security Agency has referred to this as the "equities issue," and it can be summarized as follows. When a military discovers a vulnerability in a common product, they can either alert the manufacturer and fix the vulnerability, or not tell anyone. It's not an easy decision. Fixing the vulnerability gives both the good guys and the bad guys a more secure system. Keeping the vulnerability secret means that the good guys can exploit the vulnerability to attack the bad guys, but it also means that the good guys are vulnerable. As long as everyone uses the same microprocessors, operating systems, network proto-cols, applications software, etc., the equities issue will always be a considera-tion when planning cyberwar.

Cyberwar can take on aspects of espionage, and does not necessarily involve open warfare. (In military talk, cyberwar is not necessarily "hot.") Since much of cyberwar will be about seizing control of a network and eavesdropping on it, there may not be any obvious damage from cyberwar operations. This means that the same tactics might be used in peacetime by national intelli-gence agencies. There's considerable risk here. Just as U.S. U2 flights over the Soviet Union could have been viewed as an act of war, the deliberate penetra-tion of a country's computer networks might be as well.

Cyberattacks target infrastructure. In this way they are no different than conventional military attacks against other networks: power, transportation, communications, etc. All of these networks are used by both civilians and the military during wartime, and attacks against them inconvenience both groups of people. For example, when the Allies bombed German railroad bridges during World War II, that affected both civilian and military transport. And when the United States bombed Iraqi communications links in both the first and second Iraqi Wars, that affected both civilian and military communica-tions. Cyberattacks, even attacks targeted as precisely as today's smart bombs, are likely to have collateral effects.

Cyberattacks can be used to wage information war. Information war is another topic that's received considerable media attention of late, although it is not new. Dropping leaflets on enemy soldiers to persuade them to surren-der is information war. Broadcasting radio programs to enemy troops is infor-mation war. As people get more and more of their information over cyberspace, cyberspace will increasingly become a theater for information war. It's not hard to imagine cyberattacks designed to co-opt the enemy's com-munications channels and use them as a vehicle for information war.

Because cyberwar targets information infrastructure, the waging of it can be more damaging to countries that have significant computer-network infra-structure. The idea is that a technologically poor country might decide that a cyberattack that affects the entire world would disproportionately affect its enemies, because rich nations rely on the Internet much more than poor ones. In some ways this is the dark side of the digital divide, and one of the reasons countries like the United States are so worried about cyberdefense.

Cyberwar is asymmetric, and can be a guerrilla attack. Unlike conventional military offensives involving divisions of men and supplies, cyberattacks are carried out by a few trained operatives. In this way, cyberattacks can be part of a guerrilla warfare campaign.

Cyberattacks also make effective surprise attacks. For years we've heard dire warnings of an "electronic Pearl Harbor." These are largely hyperbole today. I discuss this more in that previous *Crypto-Gram* essay on cyberterrorism, but right now the infrastructure just isn't sufficiently vulnerable in that way.

Cyberattacks do not necessarily have an obvious origin. Unlike other forms of warfare, misdirection is more likely a feature of a cyberattack. It's possible to have damage being done, but not know where it's coming from. This is a significant difference; there's something terrifying about not knowing your opponent—or knowing it, and then being wrong. Imagine if, after Pearl Harbor, we did not know who attacked us?

Cyberwar is a moving target. In the previous paragraph, I said that today the risks of an electronic Pearl Harbor are unfounded. That's true; but this, like all other aspects of cyberspace, is continually changing. Technological improvements affect everyone, including cyberattack mechanisms. And the Internet is becoming critical to more of our infrastructure, making cyberattacks more attractive. There will be a time in the future, perhaps not too far into the future, when a surprise cyberattack becomes a realistic threat.

And finally, cyberwar is a multifaceted concept. It's part of a larger military campaign, and attacks are likely to have both real-world and cyber components. A military might target the enemy's communications infrastructure through both physical attack—bombings of selected communications facilities and transmission cables—and virtual attack. An information warfare campaign might include dropping of leaflets, usurpation of a television channel, and mass sending of e-mail. And many cyberattacks still have easier non-cyber equivalents: A country wanting to isolate another country's Internet might find a low-tech solution, involving the acquiescence of backbone companies like Cable & Wireless, easier than a targeted worm or virus. Cyberwar doesn't replace war; it's just another arena in which the larger war is fought.

People overplay the risks of cyberwar and cyberterrorism. It's sexy, and it gets media attention. And at the same time, people underplay the risks of cybercrime. Today crime is big business on the Internet, and it's getting bigger all the time. But luckily, the defenses are the same. The countermeasures aimed at preventing both cyberwar and cyberterrorist attacks will also defend against cybercrime and cybervandalism. So even if organizations secure their networks for the wrong reasons, they'll do the right thing.

Militaries and Cyberwar

Originally published in Crypto-Gram, *15 January 2003*

Recently I was interviewed by an Iranian newspaper on the subject of computer security. One of the questions I was asked was whether or not the Pentagon had a secret weapon that could disable the Internet.

It's an interesting question. I have no idea what the real answer is, but I can certainly speculate.

There's no doubt that the smarter and better-funded militaries in the world are planning for cyberwar, both attack and defense. It's a multifaceted concept. A military might target the enemy's communications infrastructure through both physical attack—bombings of selected communications facilities and transmission cables—and virtual attack. It would be foolish for a military to ignore the threat and not invest in defensive capabilities, or to ignore the possibility of launching an offensive cyber-attack against an enemy during wartime. And while history has taught us that many militaries are indeed foolish, some are not.

This implies that at least some of our world's militaries have Internet attack tools that they're saving in case of wartime. They could be denial-of-service tools. They could be exploits that would allow military intelligence to penetrate military systems. They could be viruses and worms similar to what we're seeing now, but perhaps country- or network-specific. I can certainly imagine a military finding a new vulnerability in a common operating system or software package and keeping it secret, hoping to use that vulnerability to their advantage in wartime.

So my guess is that the U.S. military could disable large parts of the Internet, at least for a while, if they wanted. But I doubt that they would do so; it's far too useful an asset, and far too large a part of our economy. More interesting is whether they would try to disable pieces of it. If we went to war with country X, would we want to disable their portion of the Internet, or remove connections between their Internet and our Internet? Depending on the country, a low-tech solution might be the easiest: Disable whatever undersea cables they're using as access. Could the U.S. military turn the Internet into a U.S.-only network if they wanted? That seems less likely, although again a low-tech solution involving the acquiescence of companies like Cable & Wireless might be the easiest.

One important thing to remember here is that you only want to shut an enemy's network down if you aren't getting useful information from it. The best thing to do is to infiltrate the enemy's computers and networks, spy on them, and surreptitiously disrupt select pieces of their communications when appropriate. The next best thing is to passively eavesdrop. After that, the next best is to perform traffic analysis. Only if you can't do any of that do you consider shutting the thing down.

When a military discovers a vulnerability in a common product, they can either alert the manufacturer and fix the vulnerability, or not tell anyone. In U.S. military circles, this is called the equities issue. It's not an easy decision. Fixing the vulnerability gives both the good guys and the bad guys a more secure system. Keeping the vulnerability secret means that the good guys can exploit the vulnerability to attack the bad guys, but it also means that the good guys are vulnerable.

Script kiddies are attackers who run exploit code written by others, but don't really understand the intricacies of what they're doing. Professional attackers spend an enormous amount of time developing exploits: finding vulnerabilities, writing code to exploit them, figuring out how to cover their tracks. The real professionals don't release their code to the script kiddies; the stuff is much more valuable if it remains secret. I believe that some militaries have collections of vulnerabilities, and code to exploit those vulnerabilities, that they are saving in case of wartime or other hostilities. It would be irresponsible for them not to.

The Truth About Chinese Hackers

Originally published in Discovery Technology, *19 June 2008*

The popular media concept is that there is a coordinated attempt by the Chinese government to hack into U.S. computers—military, government, corporate—and steal secrets. The truth is a lot more complicated.

There certainly is a lot of hacking coming out of China. Any company that does security monitoring sees it all the time.

These hacker groups seem not to be working for the Chinese government. They don't seem to be coordinated by the Chinese military. They're basically young, male, patriotic Chinese citizens, trying to demonstrate that they're just as good as everyone else. As well as the American networks the media likes to talk about, their targets also include pro-Tibet, pro-Taiwan, Falun Gong, and pro-Uyghur sites.

The hackers are in this for two reasons: fame and glory, and an attempt to make a living. The fame and glory comes from their nationalistic goals. Some of these hackers are heroes in China. They're upholding the country's honor against both anti-Chinese forces like the pro-Tibet movement and larger forces like the United States.

And the money comes from several sources. The groups sell owned computers, malware services, and data they steal on the black market. They sell hacker tools and videos to others wanting to play. They even sell T-shirts, hats, and other merchandise on their websites.

This is not to say that the Chinese military ignores the hacker groups within their country. Certainly the Chinese government knows the leaders of the hacker movement and chooses to look the other way. The government probably buys stolen intelligence from these hackers. It probably recruits for its own organizations from this self-selecting pool of experienced hacking experts. It certainly learns from the hackers.

And some of the hackers are good. Over the years, they have become more sophisticated in both tools and techniques. They're stealthy. They do good network reconnaissance. My guess is what the Pentagon thinks is the problem is only a small percentage of the actual problem.

And they discover their own vulnerabilities. Earlier this year, one security company noticed a unique attack against a pro-Tibet organization. That same attack was also used two weeks earlier against a large multinational defense contractor.

They also hoard vulnerabilities. During the 1999 conflict over the two-states theory, in a heated exchange with a group of Taiwanese hackers, one Chinese group threatened to unleash multiple stockpiled worms at once. There was no reason to disbelieve this threat.

If anything, the fact that these groups aren't being run by the Chinese government makes the problem worse. Without central political coordination, they're likely to take more risks, do more stupid things, and generally ignore the political fallout of their actions.

In this regard, they're more like a non-state actor.

So while I'm perfectly happy that the U.S. government is using the threat of Chinese hacking as an impetus to get its own cybersecurity in order, and I hope it succeeds, I also hope that the U.S. government recognizes that these groups are not acting under the direction of the Chinese military and doesn't treat their actions as officially approved by the Chinese government.

12 Computer and Information Security

Safe Personal Computing

Originally published in CNet, *9 December 2004*

I am regularly asked what average Internet users can do to ensure their security. My first answer is usually, "Nothing—you're screwed."

But that's not true, and the reality is more complicated. You're screwed if you do nothing to protect yourself, but there are many things you can do to increase your security on the Internet.

Two years ago, I published a list of PC security recommendations. The idea was to give home users concrete actions they could take to improve security. This is an update of that list: a dozen things you can do to improve your security.

- General: Turn off the computer when you're not using it, especially if you have an "always on" Internet connection.
- Laptop security: Keep your laptop with you at all times when not at home; treat it as you would a wallet or purse. Regularly purge unneeded data files from your laptop. The same goes for PDAs. People tend to store more personal data—including passwords and PINs—on PDAs than they do on laptops.
- Backups: Back up regularly. Back up to disk, tape, or CD-ROM. There's a lot you can't defend against; a recent backup will at least let you recover from an attack. Store at least one set of backups off-site (a safe-deposit box is a good place) and at least one set on-site. Remember to destroy old backups. The best way to destroy CD-Rs is to microwave them on high for five seconds. You can also break them in half or run them through the better sorts of shredders.

- Operating systems: If possible, don't use Microsoft Windows. Buy a Macintosh or use Linux. If you must use Windows, set up Automatic Update so that you automatically receive security patches. And delete the files "command.com" and "cmd.exe."

- Applications: Limit the number of applications on your machine. If you don't need it, don't install it. If you no longer need it, uninstall it. Look into one of the free office suites as an alternative to Microsoft Office. Regularly check for updates to the applications you use and install them. Keeping your applications patched is important, but don't lose sleep over it.

- Browsing: Don't use Microsoft Internet Explorer, period. Limit use of cookies and applets to those few sites that provide services you need. Set your browser to regularly delete cookies. Don't assume a Web site is what it claims to be, unless you've typed in the URL yourself. Make sure the address bar shows the exact address, not a near-miss.

- Websites: Secure Sockets Layer (SSL) encryption does not provide any assurance that the vendor is trustworthy or that its database of customer information is secure.

  Think before you do business with a website. Limit the financial and personal data you send to websites—don't give out information unless you see a value to you. If you don't want to give out personal information, lie. Opt out of marketing notices. If the website gives you the option of not storing your information for later use, take it. Use a credit card for online purchases, not a debit card.

- Passwords: You can't memorize good enough passwords any more, so don't bother. For high-security websites such as banks, create long random passwords and write them down. Guard them as you would your cash: i.e., store them in your wallet, etc.

  Never reuse a password for something you care about. (It's fine to have a single password for low-security sites, such as for newspaper archive access.) Assume that all PINs can be easily broken and plan accordingly.

  Never type a password you care about, such as for a bank account, into a non-SSL encrypted page. If your bank makes it possible to do that, complain to them. When they tell you that it is OK, don't believe them; they're wrong.

- E-mail: Turn off HTML e-mail. Don't automatically assume that any e-mail is from the "From" address.

Delete spam without reading it. Don't open messages with file attachments, unless you know what they contain; immediately delete them. Don't open cartoons, videos, and similar "good for a laugh" files forwarded by your well-meaning friends; again, immediately delete them. Never click links in e-mail unless you're sure about the e-mail; copy and paste the link into your browser instead. Don't use Outlook or Outlook Express. If you must use Microsoft Office, enable macro virus protection; in Office 2000, set the security level to "high," and don't trust any received files unless you have to. If you're using Windows, turn off the "hide file extensions for known file types" option; it lets Trojan horses masquerade as other types of files. Uninstall the Windows Scripting Host if you can get along without it. If you can't, at least change your file associations, so that script files aren't automatically sent to the Scripting Host if you double-click them.

- Antivirus and anti-spyware software: Use it—either a combined program or two separate programs. Download and install the updates, at least weekly and whenever you read about a new virus in the news. Some antivirus products automatically check for updates. Enable that feature and set it to "daily."
- Firewall: Spend $50 for a Network Address Translator firewall device; it's likely to be good enough in default mode. On your laptop, use personal firewall software. If you can, hide your IP address. There's no reason to allow any incoming connections from anybody.
- Encryption: Install an e-mail and file encryptor (like PGP or TrueCrypt). Encrypting all your e-mail or your entire hard drive is unrealistic, but some mail is too sensitive to send in the clear. Similarly, some files on your hard drive are too sensitive to leave unencrypted. *[2008 update: Full disk encryption is now easy, and you won't notice any latency. Do it.]*

None of the measures I've described are foolproof. If the secret police want to target your data or your communications, no countermeasure on this list will stop them. But these precautions are all good network-hygiene measures, and they'll make you a more difficult target than the computer next door. And even if you only follow a few basic measures, you're unlikely to have any problems.

I'm stuck using Microsoft Windows and Office, but I use Opera for Web browsing and Eudora for e-mail. I use Windows Update to automatically get patches and install other patches when I hear about them. My antivirus software updates itself regularly. I keep my computer relatively clean and delete applications that I don't need. I'm diligent about backing up my data and about storing data files that are no longer needed offline.

I'm suspicious to the point of near-paranoia about e-mail attachments and websites. I delete cookies and spyware. I watch URLs to make sure I know where I am, and I don't trust unsolicited e-mails. I don't care about low-security passwords, but try to have good passwords for accounts that involve money. I still don't do Internet banking. I have my firewall set to deny all incoming connections. And I turn my computer off when I'm not using it.

That's basically it. Really, it's not that hard. The hardest part is developing an intuition about e-mail and websites. But that just takes experience.

How to Secure Your Computer, Disks, and Portable Drives

Originally published in Wired, *29 November 2007*

Computer security is hard. Software, computer and network security are all ongoing battles between attacker and defender. And in many cases the attacker has an inherent advantage: He only has to find one network flaw, while the defender has to find and fix every flaw.

Cryptography is an exception. As long as you don't write your own algorithm, secure encryption is easy. And the defender has an inherent mathematical advantage: Longer keys increase the amount of work the defender has to do linearly, while geometrically increasing the amount of work the attacker has to do.

Unfortunately, cryptography can't solve most computer-security problems. The one problem cryptography *can* solve is the security of data when it's not in use. Encrypting files, archives—even entire disks—is easy.

All of this makes it even more amazing that Her Majesty's Revenue & Customs in the United Kingdom lost two disks with personal data on 25 million British citizens, including dates of birth, addresses, bank-account information, and national insurance numbers. On the one hand, this is no bigger a deal than any of the thousands of other exposures of personal data we've read about in recent years—the U.S. Veteran's Administration loss of personal data of 26 million American veterans is an obvious similar event. But this has turned into Britain's privacy Chernobyl.

Perhaps encryption isn't so easy after all, and some people could use a little primer. This is how I protect my laptop.

There are several whole-disk encryption products on the market. I use PGP Disk's Whole Disk Encryption tool for two reasons. It's easy, and I trust both the company and the developers to write it securely. (Disclosure: I'm also on PGP Corp.'s Technical Advisory Board.)

Setup only takes a few minutes. After that, the program runs in the background. Everything works like before, and the performance degradation is negligible. Just make sure you choose a secure password—PGP's encouragement of passphrases makes this much easier—and you're secure against leaving your laptop in the airport or having it stolen out of your hotel room.

The reason you encrypt your entire disk, and not just key files, is so you don't have to worry about swap files, temp files, hibernation files, erased files, browser cookies, or whatever. You don't need to enforce a complex policy about which files are important enough to be encrypted. And you have an easy answer to your boss or to the press if the computer is stolen: no problem; the laptop is encrypted.

PGP Disk can also encrypt external disks, which means you can also secure that USB memory device you've been using to transfer data from computer to computer. When I travel, I use a portable USB drive for backup. Those devices are getting physically smaller—but larger in capacity—every year, and by encrypting I don't have to worry about losing them.

I recommend one more complication. Whole-disk encryption means that anyone at your computer has access to everything: someone at your unattended computer, a Trojan that infected your computer, and so on. To deal with these and similar threats I recommend a two-tier encryption strategy. Encrypt anything you don't need access to regularly—archived documents, old e-mail, whatever—separately, with a different password. I like to use PGP Disk's encrypted zip files, because it also makes secure backup easier (and lets you secure those files before you burn them on a DVD and mail them across the country), but you can also use the program's virtual-encrypted-disk feature to create a separately encrypted volume. Both options are easy to set up and use.

There are still two scenarios you aren't secure against, though. You're not secure against someone snatching your laptop out of your hands as you're typing away at the local coffee shop. And you're not secure against the authorities telling you to decrypt your data for them.

The latter threat is becoming more real. I have long been worried that someday, at a border crossing, a customs official will open my laptop and ask me to type in my password. Of course I could refuse, but the consequences might be severe—and permanent. And some countries—the United Kingdom, Singapore, Malaysia—have passed laws giving police the authority to demand that you divulge your passwords and encryption keys.

To defend against both of these threats, minimize the amount of data on your laptop. Do you really need 10 years of old e-mails? Does everyone in the company really need to carry around the entire customer database? One of the most incredible things about the Revenue & Customs story is that a low-level government employee mailed a copy of the entire national child database to the National Audit Office in London. Did he have to? Doubtful. The best defense against data loss is to not have the data in the first place.

Failing that, you can try to convince the authorities that you don't have the encryption key. This works better if it's a zipped archive than the whole disk. You can argue that you're transporting the files for your boss, or that you forgot the key long ago. Make sure the time stamp on the files matches your claim, though.

There are other encryption programs out there. If you're a Windows Vista user, you might consider BitLocker. This program, embedded in the operating system, also encrypts the computer's entire drive. But it only works on the C: drive, so it won't help with external disks or USB tokens. And it can't be used to make encrypted zip files. But it's easy to use, and it's free. And many people like the open-source and free program, TrueCrypt. I know nothing about it.

Crossing Borders with Laptops and PDAs

Originally published in The Guardian, *15 May 2008*

Last month, a U.S. court ruled that border agents can search your laptop, or any other electronic device, when you're entering the country. They can take your computer and download its entire contents, or keep it for several days. Customs and Border Patrol has not published any rules regarding this practice, and I and others have written a letter to Congress urging it to investigate and regulate this practice.

But the U.S. is not alone. British customs agents search laptops for pornography. And there are reports on the Internet of this sort of thing happening at other borders, too. You might not like it, but it's a fact. So how do you protect yourself?

Encrypting your entire hard drive, something you should certainly do for security in case your computer is lost or stolen, won't work here. The border agent is likely to start this whole process with a "please type in your password." Of course you can refuse, but the agent can search you further, detain you longer, refuse you entry into the country, and otherwise ruin your day.

You're going to have to hide your data. Set a portion of your hard drive to be encrypted with a different key—even if you also encrypt your entire hard drive—and keep your sensitive data there. Lots of programs allow you to do this. I use PGP Disk (from pgp.com). TrueCrypt (truecrypt.org) is also good, and free.

While customs agents might poke around on your laptop, they're unlikely to find the encrypted partition. (You can make the icon invisible, for some added protection.) And if they download the contents of your hard drive to examine later, you won't care.

Be sure to choose a strong encryption password. Details are too complicated for a quick tip, but basically anything easy to remember is easy to guess. Unfortunately, this isn't a perfect solution. Your computer might have left a copy of the password on the disk somewhere, and smart forensic software will find it.

So your best defense is to clean up your laptop. A customs agent can't read what you don't have. You don't need five years' worth of email and client data. You don't need your old love letters and those photos (you know the ones I'm talking about). Delete everything you don't absolutely need. And use a secure file erasure program to do it. While you're at it, delete your browser's cookies, cache, and browsing history. It's nobody's business what websites you've visited. And turn your computer off—don't just put it to sleep—before you go through customs; that deletes other things. Think of all this as the last thing to do before you stow your electronic devices for landing. Some companies now give their employees forensically clean laptops for travel and have them download any sensitive data over a virtual private network once they've entered the country. They send any work back the same way, and delete everything again before crossing the border to go home. This is a good idea if you can do it.

If you can't, consider putting your sensitive data on a USB drive or even a camera memory card: Even 16GB cards are reasonably priced these days. Encrypt it, of course, because it's easy to lose something that small. Slip it in your pocket, and it's likely to remain unnoticed even if the customs agent pokes through your laptop. If someone does discover it, you can try saying: "I don't know what's on there. My boss told me to give it to the head of the New York office." If you've chosen a strong encryption password, you won't care if he confiscates it.

Lastly, don't forget your phone and PDA. Customs agents can search those too: emails, your phone book, your calendar. Unfortunately, there's nothing you can do here except delete things.

I know this all sounds like work, and that it's easier to just ignore everything here and hope you don't get searched. Today, the odds are in your favor. But new forensic tools are making automatic searches easier and easier, and the recent U.S. court ruling is likely to embolden other countries. It's better to be safe than sorry.

Choosing Secure Passwords

Originally published in Wired, *11 January 2007*

Ever since I wrote about the 34,000 MySpace passwords I analyzed, people have been asking how to choose secure passwords. There's been a lot written on this topic over the years, but most of it seems to be based on anecdotal suggestions rather than actual analytic evidence. What follows is some serious advice.

The attack I'm evaluating against is an offline password-guessing attack. This attack assumes that the attacker either has a copy of your encrypted document or a server's encrypted password file, and can try passwords as fast as he can. There are instances where this attack doesn't make sense. ATM cards, for example, are secure even though they only have four-digit PINs, because you can't do offline password guessing. And the police are more likely to get a warrant for your Hotmail account than to bother trying to crack your e-mail password. Your encryption program's key-escrow system is almost certainly more vulnerable than your password, as is any "secret question" you've set up in case you forget your password.

Offline password guessers have gotten both fast and smart. AccessData sells Password Recovery Toolkit, or PRTK. Depending on the software it's attacking, PRTK can test up to hundreds of thousands of passwords per second, and it tests more common passwords sooner than obscure ones.

So the security of your password depends on two things: any details of the software that slow down password guessing, and in what order programs like PRTK guess different passwords.

Some software includes routines deliberately designed to slow down password guessing. Good encryption software doesn't use your password as the encryption key; there's a process that converts your password into the encryption key. And the software can make this process as slow as it wants.

The results are all over the map. Microsoft Office, for example, has a simple password-to-key conversion, so PRTK can test 350,000 Microsoft Word passwords per second on a 3-GHz Pentium 4, which is a reasonably current benchmark computer. WinZip used to be even worse—well over a million guesses per second for version 7.0—but with version 9.0, the cryptosystem's ramp-up function has been substantially increased: PRTK can only test 900 passwords per second. PGP also makes things deliberately hard for programs like PRTK, also only allowing about 900 guesses per second.

When attacking programs with deliberately slow ramp-ups, it's important to make every guess count. A simple six-character, lowercase, exhaustive character attack, "aaaaaa" through "zzzzzz," has more than 308 million combinations. And it's generally unproductive, because the program spends most of its time testing improbable passwords like "pqzrwj."

According to Eric Thompson of AccessData, a typical password consists of a root plus an appendage. A root isn't necessarily a dictionary word, but it's something pronounceable. An appendage is either a suffix (90% of the time) or a prefix (10% of the time).

So the first attack PRTK performs is to test a dictionary of about 1,000 common passwords, things like "letmein," "password," "123456," and so on. Then it tests them each with about 100 common suffix appendages: "1," "4u," "69," "abc," "!" and so on. Believe it or not, it recovers about 24% of all passwords with these 100,000 combinations.

Then, PRTK goes through a series of increasingly complex root dictionaries and appendage dictionaries. The root dictionaries include:

- Common word dictionary: 5,000 entries
- Names dictionary: 10,000 entries
- Comprehensive dictionary: 100,000 entries
- Phonetic pattern dictionary: 1/10,000 of an exhaustive character search

The phonetic pattern dictionary is interesting. It's not really a dictionary; it's a Markov-chain routine that generates pronounceable English-language strings of a given length. For example, PRTK can generate and test a dictionary of very pronounceable six-character strings, or just-barely pronounceable seven-character strings. They're working on generation routines for other languages.

PRTK also runs a four-character-string exhaustive search. It runs the dictionaries with lowercase (the most common), initial uppercase (the second most common), all uppercase and final uppercase. It runs the dictionaries with common substitutions: "$" for "s," "@" for "a," "1" for "l," and so on. Anything that's "leet speak" is included here, like "3" for "e."

The appendage dictionaries include things like:

- All two-digit combinations
- All dates from 1900 to 2006
- All three-digit combinations
- All single symbols
- All single digit, plus single symbol
- All two-symbol combinations

AccessData's secret sauce is the order in which it runs the various root and appendage dictionary combinations. The company's research indicates that the password sweet spot is a seven- to nine-character root plus a common appendage, and that it's much more likely for someone to choose a hard-to-guess root than an uncommon appendage.

Normally, PRTK runs on a network of computers. Password guessing is a trivially distributable task, and it can easily run in the background. A large organization like the Secret Service can easily have hundreds of computers chugging away at someone's password. A company called Tableau is building a specialized FPGA hardware add-on to speed up PRTK for slow programs like PGP and WinZip: roughly a 150- to 300-times performance increase.

How good is all of this? Eric Thompson estimates that with a couple of weeks' to a month's worth of time, his software breaks 55% to 65% of all passwords. (This depends, of course, very heavily on the application.) Those results are good, but not great.

But that assumes no biographical data. Whenever it can, AccessData collects whatever personal information it can on the subject before beginning. If it can see other passwords, it can make guesses about what types of passwords the subject uses. How big a root is used? What kind of root? Does he put appendages at the end or the beginning? Does he use substitutions? ZIP codes are common appendages, so those go into the file. So do addresses, names from the address book, other passwords and any other personal information. This data ups PRTK's success rate a bit, but more importantly it reduces the time from weeks to days or even hours.

So if you want your password to be hard to guess, you should choose something not on any of the root or appendage lists. You should mix upper and lowercase in the middle of your root. You should add numbers and symbols in the middle of your root, not as common substitutions. Or drop your appendage in the middle of your root. Or use two roots with an appendage in the middle.

Even something lower down on PRTK's dictionary list—the seven-character phonetic pattern dictionary—together with an uncommon appendage, is not going to be guessed. Neither is a password made up of the first letters of a sentence, especially if you throw numbers and symbols in the mix. And yes, these passwords are going to be hard to remember, which is why you should use a program like the free and open-source Password Safe to store them all in. (PRTK can test only 900 Password Safe 3.0 passwords per second.)

Even so, none of this might actually matter. AccessData sells another program, Forensic Toolkit, that, among other things, scans a hard drive for every printable character string. It looks in documents, in the Registry, in e-mail, in swap files, in deleted space on the hard drive … everywhere. And it creates a dictionary from that, and feeds it into PRTK.

And PRTK breaks more than 50% of passwords from this dictionary alone.

What's happening is that the Windows operating system's memory management leaves data all over the place in the normal course of operations. You'll type your password into a program, and it gets stored in memory somewhere. Windows swaps the page out to disk, and it becomes the tail end of some file. It gets moved to some far out portion of your hard drive, and there it'll sit forever. Linux and Mac OS aren't any better in this regard.

I should point out that none of this has anything to do with the encryption algorithm or the key length. A weak 40-bit algorithm doesn't make this attack easier, and a strong 256-bit algorithm doesn't make it harder. These attacks simulate the process of the user entering the password into the computer, so the size of the resultant key is never an issue.

For years, I have said that the easiest way to break a cryptographic product is almost never by breaking the algorithm, that almost invariably there is a programming error that allows you to bypass the mathematics and break the product. A similar thing is going on here. The easiest way to guess a password isn't to guess it at all, but to exploit the inherent insecurity in the underlying operating system.

Authentication and Expiration

Originally published in IEEE Security & Privacy,
January/February 2005

There's a security problem with many Internet authentication systems that's never talked about: There's no way to terminate the authentication.

A couple of months ago, I bought something from an e-commerce site. At the checkout page, I wasn't able to just type in my credit card number and make my purchase. Instead, I had to choose a username and password. Usually I don't like doing that, but in this case I wanted to be able to access my account at a later date. In fact, the password was useful because I needed to return an item I purchased.

Months have passed, and I no longer want an ongoing relationship with the e-commerce site. I don't want a username and password. I don't want them to have my credit card number on file. I've received my purchase, I'm happy, and I'm done. But because that username and password have no expiration date associated with them, they never end. It's not a subscription service, so there's no mechanism to sever the relationship. I will have access to that e-commerce site for as long as it remembers that username and password.

In other words, I am liable for that account forever.

Traditionally, passwords have indicated an ongoing relationship between a user and some computer service. Sometimes it's a company employee and the company's servers. Sometimes it's an account and an ISP. In both cases, both parties want to continue the relationship, so expiring a password and then forcing the user to choose another is a matter of security.

In cases with this ongoing relationship, the security consideration is damage minimization. Nobody wants some bad guy to learn the password, and everyone wants to minimize the amount of damage he can do if he does. Regularly changing your password is a solution to that problem.

This approach works because both sides want it to; they both want to keep the authentication system working correctly, and minimize attacks.

In the case of the e-commerce site, the interests are much more one-sided. The e-commerce site wants me to live in their database forever. They want to market to me, and entice me to come back. They want to sell my information. (This is the kind of information that might be buried in the privacy policy or terms of service, but no one reads those because they're unreadable. And all bets are off if the company changes hands.)

There's nothing I can do about this, but a username and password that never expires is another matter entirely. The e-commerce site wants me to establish an account because it increases the chances that I'll use it again. But I want a way to terminate the business relationship, a way to say: "I am no longer taking responsibility for items purchased using that username and password."

Near as I can tell, the username and password I typed into that e-commerce site puts my credit card at risk until it expires. If the e-commerce site uses a system that debits amounts from my checking account whenever I place an order, I could be at risk forever. (The U.S. has legal liability limits, but they're not that useful. According to Regulation E, the electronic transfers regulation, a fraudulent transaction must be reported within two days to cap liability at $50; within 60 days, it's capped at $500. Beyond that, you're out of luck.)

This is wrong. Every e-commerce site should have a way to purchase items without establishing a username and password. I like sites that allow me to make a purchase as a "guest," without setting up an account.

But just as importantly, every e-commerce site should have a way for customers to terminate their accounts and should allow them to delete their usernames and passwords from the system. It's okay to market to previous customers. It's not okay to needlessly put them at financial risk.

The Failure of Two-Factor Authentication

Originally published in Communications of the ACM, *April 2005*

Two-factor authentication isn't our savior. It won't defend against phishing. It's not going to prevent identity theft. It's not going to secure online accounts from fraudulent transactions. It solves the security problems we had ten years ago, not the security problems we have today.

The problem with passwords is that they're too easy to lose control of. People give them to other people. People write them down, and other people read them. People send them in e-mail, and that e-mail is intercepted. People use them to log into remote servers, and their communications are eavesdropped on. They're also easy to guess. And once any of that happens, the password no longer works as an authentication token because you can't be sure who is typing that password in.

Two-factor authentication mitigates this problem. If your password includes a number that changes every minute, or a unique reply to a random challenge, then it's harder for someone else to intercept. You can't write down the ever-changing part. An intercepted password won't be good the next time it's needed. And a two-factor password is harder to guess. Sure, someone can always give his password and token to his secretary, but no solution is foolproof.

These tokens have been around for at least two decades, but it's only recently that they have gotten mass-market attention. AOL is rolling them out. Some banks are issuing them to customers, and even more are talking about doing it. It seems that corporations are finally waking up to the fact that passwords don't provide adequate security, and are hoping that two-factor authentication will fix their problems.

Unfortunately, the nature of attacks has changed over those two decades. Back then, the threats were all passive: eavesdropping and offline password guessing. Today, the threats are more active: phishing and Trojan horses.

Here are two new active attacks we're starting to see:

- **Man-in-the-Middle Attack.** An attacker puts up a fake bank website and entices user to that website. User types in his password, and the attacker in turn uses it to access the bank's real website. Done right, the user will never realize that he isn't at the bank's website. Then the attacker either disconnects the user and makes any fraudulent transactions he wants, or passes along the user's banking transactions while making his own transactions at the same time.
- **Trojan attack.** Attacker gets Trojan installed on user's computer. When user logs into his bank's website, the attacker piggybacks on that session via the Trojan to make any fraudulent transaction he wants.

See how two-factor authentication doesn't solve anything? In the first case, the attacker can pass the ever-changing part of the password to the bank along with the never-changing part. And in the second case, the attacker is relying on the user to log in.

The real threat is fraud due to impersonation, and the tactics of impersonation will change in response to the defenses. Two-factor authentication will force criminals to modify their tactics, that's all.

Recently I've seen examples of two-factor authentication using two different communications paths: Call it "two-channel authentication." One bank sends a challenge to the user's cell phone via SMS and expects a reply via SMS. If you assume that all your customers have cell phones, then this results in a two-factor authentication process without extra hardware. And even better, the second authentication piece goes over a different communications channel than the first; eavesdropping is much, much harder.

But in this new world of active attacks, no one cares. An attacker using a man-in-the-middle attack is happy to have the user deal with the SMS portion of the log-in, since he can't do it himself. And a Trojan attacker doesn't care, because he's relying on the user to log in anyway.

Two-factor authentication is not useless. It works for local log-in, and it works within some corporate networks. But it won't work for remote authentication over the Internet. I predict that banks and other financial institutions will spend millions outfitting their users with two-factor authentication tokens. Early adopters of this technology may very well experience a significant drop in fraud for a while as attackers move to easier targets, but in the end there will be a negligible drop in the amount of fraud and identity theft.

More on Two-Factor Authentication

Originally published in Network World, *4 April 2005*

Recently I published an essay arguing that two-factor authentication is an ineffective defense against identity theft. For example, issuing tokens to online banking customers won't reduce fraud, because new attack techniques simply ignore the countermeasure. Unfortunately, some took my essay as a condemnation of two-factor authentication in general. This is not true. It's simply a matter of understanding the threats and the attacks.

Passwords just don't work anymore. As computers have gotten faster, password guessing has gotten easier. Ever-more-complicated passwords are required to evade password-guessing software. At the same time, there's an upper limit to how complex a password users can be expected to remember. About five years ago, these two lines crossed: It is no longer reasonable to expect users to have passwords that can't be guessed. For anything that requires reasonable security, the era of passwords is over.

Two-factor authentication solves this problem. It works against passive attacks: eavesdropping and password guessing. It protects against users choosing weak passwords, telling their passwords to their colleagues or writing their passwords on pieces of paper taped to their monitors. For an organization trying to improve access control for its employees, two-factor authentication is a great idea. Microsoft is integrating two-factor authentication into its operating system, another great idea.

What two-factor authentication won't do is prevent identity theft and fraud. It'll prevent certain tactics of identity theft and fraud, but criminals simply will switch tactics. We're already seeing fraud tactics that completely ignore two-factor authentication. As banks roll out two-factor authentication, criminals simply will switch to these new tactics.

One way to think about this is that two-factor authentication solves security problems involving authentication. The current wave of attacks against financial systems are not exploiting vulnerabilities in the authentication system, so two-factor authentication doesn't help.

Security is always an arms race, and you could argue that this situation is simply the cost of treading water. The problem with this reasoning is it ignores countermeasures that permanently reduce fraud. By concentrating on authenticating the individual rather than authenticating the transaction, banks are forced to defend against criminal tactics rather than the crime itself.

Credit cards are a perfect example. Notice how little attention is paid to cardholder authentication. Clerks barely check signatures. People use their cards over the phone and on the Internet, where the card's existence isn't even verified. The credit card companies spend their security dollars authenticating the transaction, not the cardholder.

Two-factor authentication is a long-overdue solution to the problem of passwords. I welcome its increasing popularity, but identity theft and bank fraud are not results of password problems; they stem from poorly authenticated transactions. The sooner people realize that, the sooner they'll stop advocating stronger authentication measures and the sooner security will actually improve.

Home Users: A Public Health Problem?

Originally published in Information Security, *September 2007*

To the average home user, security is an intractable problem. Microsoft has made great strides improving the security of their operating system "out of the box," but there are still a dizzying array of rules, options, and choices that users have to make. How should they configure their anti-virus program? What sort of backup regime should they employ? What are the best settings for their wireless network? And so on and so on and so on.

How is it possible that we in the computer industry have created such a shoddy product? How have we foisted on people a product that is so difficult to use securely, that requires so many add-on products?

It's even worse than that. We have sold the average computer user a bill of goods. In our race for an ever-increasing market, we have convinced every person that he needs a computer. We have provided application after application—IM, peer-to-peer file sharing, eBay, Facebook—to make computers both useful and enjoyable to the home user. At the same time, we've made them so hard to maintain that only a trained sysadmin can do it.

And then we wonder why home users have such problems with their buggy systems, why they can't seem to do even the simplest administrative tasks, and why their computers aren't secure. They're not secure because home users don't know how to secure them.

At work, I have an entire IT department I can call on if I have a problem. They filter my net connection so that I don't see spam, and most attacks are blocked before they even get to my computer. They tell me which updates to install on my system and when. And they're available to help me recover if something untoward does happen to my system. Home users have none of this support. They're on their own.

This problem isn't simply going to go away as computers get smarter and users get savvier. The next generation of computers will be vulnerable to all sorts of different attacks, and the next generation of attack tools will fool users in all sorts of different ways. The security arms race isn't going away any time soon, but it will be fought with ever more complex weapons.

This isn't simply an academic problem; it's a public health problem. In the hyper-connected world of the Internet, everyone's security depends in part on everyone else's. As long as there are insecure computers out there, hackers will use them to eavesdrop on network traffic, send spam, and attack other computers. We are all more secure if all those home computers attached to the Internet via DSL or cable modems are protected against attack. The only question is: What's the best way to get there?

I wonder about those who say "educate the users." Have they tried? Have they ever met an actual user? It's unrealistic to expect home users to be responsible for their own security. They don't have the expertise, and they're not going to learn. And it's not just user actions we need to worry about; these computers are insecure right out of the box.

The only possible way to solve this problem is to force the ISPs to become IT departments. There's no reason why they can't provide home users with the same level of support my IT department provides me with. There's no reason why they can't provide "clean pipe" service to the home. Yes, it will cost home users more. Yes, it will require changes in the law to make this mandatory. But what's the alternative?

In 1991, Walter S. Mossberg debuted his "Personal Technology" column in *The Wall Street Journal* with the words: "Personal computers are just too hard to use, and it isn't your fault." Sixteen years later, the statement is still true—and doubly true when it comes to computer security.

If we want home users to be secure, we need to design computers and networks that are secure out of the box, without any work by the end users. There simply isn't any other way.

Security Products: Suites vs. Best-of-Breed

Originally published in Information Security, *March 2008*

We know what we don't like about buying consolidated product suites: one great product and a bunch of mediocre ones. And we know what we don't like about buying best-of-breed: multiple vendors, multiple interfaces, and multiple products that don't work well together. The security industry has gone back and forth between the two, as a new generation of IT security professionals rediscovers the downsides of each solution.

The real problem is that neither solution really works, and we continually fool ourselves into believing whatever we don't have is better than what we have at the time. And the real solution is to buy results, not products.

Honestly, no one wants to buy IT security. People want to buy whatever they want—connectivity, a Web presence, e-mail, networked applications, whatever—and they want it to be secure. That they're forced to spend money on IT security is an artifact of the youth of the computer industry. And sooner or later the need to buy security will disappear.

It will disappear because IT vendors are starting to realize they have to provide security as part of whatever they're selling. It will disappear because organizations are starting to buy services instead of products, and demanding security as part of those services. It will disappear because the security industry will disappear as a consumer category, and will instead market to the IT industry.

The critical driver here is outsourcing. Outsourcing is the ultimate consolidator, because the customer no longer cares about the details. If I buy my network services from a large IT infrastructure company, I don't care if it secures things by installing the hot new intrusion prevention systems, by configuring the routers and servers so as to obviate the need for network-based security, or if it uses magic security dust given to it by elven kings. I just want a contract that specifies a level and quality of service, and my vendor can figure it out.

IT is infrastructure. Infrastructure is always outsourced. And the details of how the infrastructure works are left to the companies that provide it.

This is the future of IT, and when that happens we're going to start to see a type of consolidation we haven't seen before. Instead of large security companies gobbling up small security companies, both large and small security companies will be gobbled up by non-security companies. It's already starting to happen. In 2006, IBM bought ISS. The same year BT bought my company, Counterpane, and last year it bought INS. These aren't large security companies buying small security companies; these are non-security companies buying large and small security companies.

If I were Symantec and McAfee, I would be preparing myself for a buyer.

This is good consolidation. Instead of having to choose between a single product suite that isn't very good or a best-of-breed set of products that don't work well together, we can ignore the issue completely. We can just find an infrastructure provider that will figure it out and make it work—who cares how?

Separating Data Ownership and Device Ownership

Originally published in Wired, *30 November 2006*

Consider two different security problems. In the first, you store your valuables in a safe in your basement. The threat is burglars, of course. But the safe is yours, and the house is yours, too. You control access to the safe, and probably have an alarm system.

The second security problem is similar, but you store your valuables in someone else's safe. Even worse, it's someone you don't trust. He doesn't know the combination, but he controls access to the safe. He can try to break in at his leisure. He can transport the safe anyplace he needs to. He can use whatever tools he wants. In the first case, the safe needs to be secure, but it's still just a part of your overall home security. In the second case, the safe is the only security device you have.

This second security problem might seem contrived, but it happens regularly in our information society: Data controlled by one person is stored on a device controlled by another. Think of a stored-value smart card: If the person owning the card can break the security, he can add money to the card. Think of a DRM system: Its security depends on the person owning the computer not being able to get at the insides of the DRM security. Think of the RFID chip on a passport. Or a postage meter. Or SSL traffic being sent over a public network.

These systems are difficult to secure, and not just because you give your attacker the device and let him utilize whatever time, equipment and expertise he needs to break it. It's difficult to secure because breaks are generally "class breaks." The expert who figures out how to do it can build hardware—or write software—to do it automatically. Only one person needs to break a given DRM system; the software can break every other device in the same class.

This means that the security needs to be secure not against the average attacker, but against the smartest, most-motivated, and best-funded attacker.

I was reminded of this problem earlier this month, when researchers announced a new attack against implementations of the RSA cryptosystem. The attack exploits the fact that different operations take different times on modern CPUs. By closely monitoring—and actually affecting—the CPU during an RSA operation, an attacker can recover the key. The most obvious applications for this attack are DRM systems that try to use a protected partition in the CPU to prevent the computer's owner from learning the DRM system's cryptographic keys.

These sorts of attacks are not new. In 1995, researchers discovered they could recover cryptographic keys by comparing relative timings on chips. In later years, both power and radiation were used to break cryptosystems. I called these "side-channel attacks," because they made use of information other than the plaintext and ciphertext. And where are they most useful? To recover secrets from smart cards.

Whenever I see security systems with this data/device separation, I try to solve the security problem by removing the separation. This means completely redesigning the system and the security assumptions behind it.

Compare a stored-value card with a debit card. In the former case, the card owner can create money by changing the value on the card. For this system to be secure, the card needs to be protected by a variety of security countermeasures. In the latter case, there aren't any secrets on the card. Your bank doesn't care that you can read the account number off the front of the card, or the data off the magnetic stripe off the back—the real data, and the security, are in the bank's databases.

Or compare a DRM system with a financial model that doesn't care about copying. The former is impossible to secure, the latter easy.

Separating data ownership and device ownership doesn't mean that security is impossible, only much more difficult. You can buy a safe so strong that you can lock your valuables in it and give it to your attacker—with confidence. I'm not so sure you can design a smart card that keeps secrets from its owner, or a DRM system that works on a general-purpose computer—especially because of the problem of class breaks. But in all cases, the best way to solve the security problem is not to have it in the first place.

Assurance

Originally published in Wired, *9 August 2007*

Over the past several months, the state of California conducted the most comprehensive security review yet of electronic voting machines. People I consider to be security experts analyzed machines from three different manufacturers, performing both a red-team attack analysis and a detailed source code review. Serious flaws were discovered in all machines and, as a result, the machines were all decertified for use in California elections.

The reports are worth reading, as is much of the commentary on the topic. The reviewers were given an unrealistic timetable and had trouble getting the required documentation. The fact that major security vulnerabilities were found in all machines is a testament to how poorly they were designed, not to the thoroughness of the analysis. Yet California Secretary of State Debra Bowen has conditionally recertified the machines for use, as long as the makers fix the discovered vulnerabilities and adhere to a lengthy list of security requirements designed to limit future security breaches and failures.

While this is a good effort, it has security completely backward. It begins with a presumption of security: If there are no known vulnerabilities, the system must be secure. If there is a vulnerability, then once it's fixed, the system is again secure. How anyone comes to this presumption is a mystery to me. Is there any version of any operating system anywhere where the last security bug was found and fixed? Is there a major piece of software anywhere that has been, and continues to be, vulnerability-free?

Yet again and again we react with surprise when a system has a vulnerability. Last weekend at the hacker convention DefCon, I saw new attacks against supervisory control and data acquisition (SCADA) systems—those are embedded control systems found in infrastructure systems like fuel pipelines and power transmission facilities—electronic badge-entry systems, MySpace, and the high-security locks used in places like the White House. I will guarantee you that the manufacturers of these systems all claimed they were secure, and that their customers believed them.

Earlier this month, the government disclosed that the computer system of the US-Visit border control system is full of security holes. Weaknesses existed in all control areas and computing device types reviewed, the report said. How exactly is this different from any large government database? I'm not surprised that the system is so insecure; I'm surprised that anyone is surprised.

We've been assured again and again that RFID passports are secure. When researcher Lukas Grunwald successfully cloned one last year at DefCon, industry experts told us there was little risk. This year, Grunwald revealed that he could use a cloned passport chip to sabotage passport readers. Government officials are again downplaying the significance of this result, although Grunwald speculates that this or another similar vulnerability could be used to take over passport readers and force them to accept fraudulent passports. Anyone care to guess who's more likely to be right?

It's all backward. Insecurity is the norm. If any system—whether a voting machine, operating system, database, badge-entry system, RFID passport system, etc.—is ever built completely vulnerability-free, it'll be the first time in the history of mankind. It's not a good bet.

Once you stop thinking about security backward, you immediately understand why the current software security paradigm of patching doesn't make us any more secure. If vulnerabilities are so common, finding a few doesn't materially reduce the quantity remaining. A system with 100 patched vulnerabilities isn't more secure than a system with 10, nor is it less secure. A patched buffer overflow doesn't mean that there's one less way attackers can get into your system; it means that your design process was so lousy that it permitted buffer overflows, and there are probably thousands more lurking in your code.

Diebold Election Systems has patched a certain vulnerability in its voting-machine software twice, and each patch contained another vulnerability. Don't tell me it's my job to find another vulnerability in the third patch; it's Diebold's job to convince me it has finally learned how to patch vulnerabilities properly.

Several years ago, former National Security Agency technical director Brian Snow began talking about the concept of "assurance" in security. Snow, who spent 35 years at the NSA building systems at security levels far higher than anything the commercial world deals with, told audiences that the agency couldn't use modern commercial systems with their backward security thinking. Assurance was his antidote:

Assurances are confidence-building activities demonstrating that:

- The system's security policy is internally consistent and reflects the requirements of the organization,
- There are sufficient security functions to support the security policy,
- The system functions to meet a desired set of properties and *only* those properties,
- The functions are implemented correctly, and
- The assurances *hold up* through the manufacturing, delivery and life cycle of the system.

Basically, demonstrate that your system is secure, because I'm just not going to believe you otherwise.

Assurance is less about developing new security techniques than about using the ones we have. It's all the things described in books like *Building Secure Software*, *Software Security*, and *Writing Secure Code*. It's some of what Microsoft is trying to do with its Security Development Lifecycle (SDL). It's the Department of Homeland Security's Build Security In program. It's what every aircraft manufacturer goes through before it puts a piece of software in a critical role on an aircraft. It's what the NSA demands before it purchases a piece of security equipment. As an industry, we know how to provide security assurance in software and systems; we just tend not to bother.

And most of the time, we don't care. Commercial software, as insecure as it is, is good enough for most purposes. And while backward security is more expensive over the life cycle of the software, it's cheaper where it counts: at the beginning. Most software companies are short-term smart to ignore the cost of never-ending patching, even though it's long-term dumb.

Assurance is expensive, in terms of money and time for both the process and the documentation. But the NSA needs assurance for critical military systems; Boeing needs it for its avionics. And the government needs it more and more: for voting machines, for databases entrusted with our personal information, for electronic passports, for communications systems, for the computers and systems controlling our critical infrastructure. Assurance requirements should be common in IT contracts, not rare. It's time we stopped thinking backward and pretending that computers are secure until proven otherwise.

Combating Spam

Originally published in Crypto-Gram, *15 May 2005*

Spam is back in the news, and it has a new name. This time it's voice-over-IP spam, and it has the clever name of "spit" (spam over Internet telephony). Spit has the potential to completely ruin VoIP. No one is going to install the system if they're going to get dozens of calls a day from audio spammers. Or, at least, they're only going to accept phone calls from a white list of previously known callers.

VoIP spam joins the ranks of e-mail spam, Usenet newsgroup spam, instant message spam, cell phone text message spam, and blog comment spam. And, if you think broadly enough, these computer-network spam delivery mechanisms join the ranks of computer telemarketing (phone spam), junk mail (paper spam), billboards (visual space spam), and cars driving through town with megaphones (audio spam). It's all basically the same thing—unsolicited marketing messages—and only by understanding the problem at this level of generality can we discuss solutions.

In general, the goal of advertising is to influence people. Usually it's to influence people to purchase a product, but it could just as easily be to influence people to support a particular political candidate or position. Advertising does this by implanting a marketing message into the brain of the recipient. The mechanism of implantation is simply a tactic.

Tactics for unsolicited marketing messages rise and fall in popularity based on their cost and benefit. If the benefit is significant, people are willing to spend more. If the benefit is small, people will only do it if it is cheap. A 30-second prime-time television ad costs 1.8 cents per adult viewer, a full-page color magazine ad about 0.9 cents per reader. A highway billboard costs 0.21 cents per car. Direct mail is the most expensive, at over 50 cents per third-class letter mailed. (That's why targeted mailing lists are so valuable; they increase the per-piece benefit.)

Spam is such a common tactic not because it's particularly effective; the response rates for spam are very low. It's common because it's ridiculously cheap. Typically, spammers charge less than a hundredth of a cent per e-mail. (And that number is just what spamming houses charge their customers to deliver spam; if you're a clever hacker, you can build your own spam network for much less money.) If it is worth $10 for you to successfully influence one person—to buy your product, vote for your guy, whatever—then you only need a 1 in a 100,000 success rate. You can market really marginal products with spam.

So far, so good. But the cost/benefit calculation is missing a component: the "cost" of annoying people. Everyone who is not influenced by the marketing message is annoyed to some degree. The advertiser pays a partial cost for annoying people; they might boycott his product. But most of the time he does not, and the cost of the advertising is paid by the person: The beauty of the landscape is ruined by the billboard, dinner is disrupted by a telemarketer, spam costs money to ship around the Internet and time to wade through, etc. (Note that I am using "cost" very generally here, and not just monetarily. Time and happiness are both costs.)

This is why spam is so bad. For each e-mail, the spammer pays a cost and receives benefit. But there is an additional cost paid by the e-mail recipient. Because so much spam is unwanted, that additional cost is huge—and it's a cost that the spammer never sees. If spammers could be made to bear the total cost of spam, then its level would be more along the lines of what society would find acceptable.

This economic analysis is important, because it's the only way to understand how effective different solutions will be. This is an economic problem, and the solutions need to change the fundamental economics. (The analysis is largely the same for VoIP spam, Usenet newsgroup spam, blog comment spam, and so on.)

The best solutions raise the cost of spam. Spam filters raise the cost by increasing the amount of spam that someone needs to send before someone will read it. If 99% of all spam is filtered into trash, then sending spam becomes 100 times more expensive. This is also the idea behind white lists—lists of senders a user is willing to accept e-mail from—and blacklists: lists of senders a user is not willing to accept e-mail from.

Filtering doesn't just have to be at the recipient's e-mail. It can be implemented within the network to clean up spam, or at the sender. Several ISPs are already filtering outgoing e-mail for spam, and the trend will increase.

Anti-spam laws raise the cost of spam to an intolerable level; no one wants to go to jail for spamming. We've already seen some convictions in the U.S. Unfortunately, this only works when the spammer is within the reach of the law, and is less effective against criminals who are using spam as a mechanism to commit fraud.

Other proposed solutions try to impose direct costs on e-mail senders. I have seen proposals for e-mail "postage," either for every e-mail sent or for every e-mail above a reasonable threshold. I have seen proposals where the sender of an e-mail posts a small bond, which the receiver can cash if the e-mail is spam. There are other proposals that involve "computational puzzles": time-consuming tasks the sender's computer must perform, unnoticeable to someone who is sending e-mail normally, but too much for someone sending e-mail in bulk. These solutions generally involve re-engineering the Internet, something that is not done lightly, and hence are in the discussion stages only.

All of these solutions work to a degree, and we end up with an arms race. Anti-spam products block a certain type of spam. Spammers invent a tactic that gets around those products. Then the products block that spam. Then the spammers invent yet another type of spam. And so on.

Blacklisting spammer sites forced the spammers to disguise the origin of spam e-mail. People recognizing e-mail from people they knew, and other anti-spam measures, forced spammers to hack into innocent machines and use them as launching pads. Scanning millions of e-mails looking for identical bulk spam forced spammers to individualize each spam message. Semantic spam detection forced spammers to design even more clever spam. And so on.

Each defense is met with yet another attack, and each attack is met with yet another defense.

Remember that when you think about host identification, or postage, as an anti-spam measure. Spammers don't care about tactics; they want to send their e-mail. Techniques like this will simply force spammers to rely more on hacked innocent machines. As long as the underlying computers are insecure, we can't prevent spammers from sending.

This is the problem with another potential solution: re-engineering the Internet to prohibit the forging of e-mail headers. This would make it easier for spam detection software to detect spamming IP addresses, but spammers would just use hacked machines instead of their own computers.

Honestly, there's no end in sight for the spam arms race. Currently 80% to 90% of email is spam, and that percentage is rising. I am continually battling with comment spam in my blog. But even with all that, spam is one of computer security's success stories. The current crop of anti-spam products work pretty well, if people are willing to do the work to tune them. I get almost no spam, and very few legitimate e-mails end up in my spam trap. I wish they would work better—*Crypto-Gram* is occasionally classified as spam by one service or another, for example—but they're working pretty well. It'll be a long time before spam stops clogging up the Internet, but at least there are technologies to ensure that we don't have to look at it.

Sony's DRM Rootkit: The Real Story

Originally published in Wired, *17 November 2005*

It's a David and Goliath story of the tech blogs defeating a mega-corporation.

On October 31, Mark Russinovich broke the story in his blog: Sony BMG Music Entertainment distributed a copy-protection scheme with music CDs that secretly installed a rootkit on computers. This software tool is run without your knowledge or consent—if it's loaded on your computer with a CD, a hacker can gain and maintain access to your system and you wouldn't know it.

The Sony code modifies Windows so you can't tell it's there, a process called "cloaking" in the hacker world. It acts as spyware, surreptitiously sending information about you to Sony. And it can't be removed; trying to get rid of it damages Windows.

This story was picked up by other blogs (including mine), followed by the computer press. Finally, the mainstream media took it up.

The outcry was so great that on November 11, Sony announced it was temporarily halting production of that copy-protection scheme. That still wasn't enough—on November 14, the company announced it was pulling copy-protected CDs from store shelves and offered to replace customers' infected CDs for free.

But that's not the real story here.

It's a tale of extreme hubris. Sony rolled out this incredibly invasive copy-protection scheme without ever publicly discussing its details, confident that its profits were worth modifying its customers' computers. When its actions were first discovered, Sony offered a "fix" that didn't remove the rootkit, just the cloaking.

Sony claimed the rootkit didn't phone home when it did. On November 4, Thomas Hesse, Sony BMG's president of global digital business, demonstrated the company's disdain for its customers when he said, "Most people don't even know what a rootkit is, so why should they care about it?" in an NPR interview. Even Sony's apology only admits that its rootkit "includes a feature that may make a user's computer susceptible to a virus written specifically to target the software."

However, imperious corporate behavior is not the real story either.

This drama is also about incompetence. Sony's latest rootkit-removal tool actually leaves a gaping vulnerability. And Sony's rootkit—designed to stop copyright infringement—itself may have infringed on copyright. As amazing as it might seem, the code seems to include an open-source MP3 encoder in violation of that library's license agreement. But even that is not the real story.

It's an epic of class-action lawsuits in California and elsewhere, and the focus of criminal investigations. The rootkit has even been found on computers run by the Department of Defense, to the Department of Homeland Security's displeasure. While Sony could be prosecuted under U.S. cybercrime law, no one thinks it will be. And lawsuits are never the whole story.

This saga is full of weird twists. Some pointed out how this sort of software would degrade the reliability of Windows. Someone created malicious code that used the rootkit to hide itself. A hacker used the rootkit to avoid the spyware of a popular game. And there were even calls for a worldwide Sony boycott. After all, if you can't trust Sony not to infect your computer when you buy its music CDs, can you trust it to sell you an uninfected computer in the first place? That's a good question, but—again—not the real story.

It's yet another situation where Macintosh users can watch, amused (well, mostly) from the sidelines, wondering why anyone still uses Microsoft Windows. But certainly, even that is not the real story.

The story to pay attention to here is the collusion between big media companies who try to control what we do on our computers and computer-security companies who are supposed to be protecting us.

Initial estimates are that more than half a million computers worldwide are infected with this Sony rootkit. Those are amazing infection numbers, making this one of the most serious Internet epidemics of all time—on a par with worms like Blaster, Slammer, Code Red, and Nimda.

What do you think of your antivirus company, the one that didn't notice Sony's rootkit as it infected half a million computers? And this isn't one of those lightning-fast Internet worms; this one has been spreading since mid-2004. Because it spread through infected CDs, not through Internet connections, they didn't notice? This is exactly the kind of thing we're paying those companies to detect—especially because the rootkit was phoning home.

But much worse than not detecting it before Russinovich's discovery was the deafening silence that followed. When a new piece of malware is found, security companies fall over themselves to clean our computers and inoculate our networks. Not in this case.

McAfee didn't add detection code until November 9, and as of November 15 it doesn't remove the rootkit, only the cloaking device. The company admits on its web page that this is a lousy compromise. "McAfee detects, removes and prevents reinstallation of XCP." That's the cloaking code. "Please note that removal will not impair the copyright-protection mechanisms installed from the CD. There have been reports of system crashes possibly resulting from uninstalling XCP." Thanks for the warning.

Symantec's response to the rootkit has, to put it kindly, evolved. At first the company didn't consider XCP malware at all. It wasn't until November 11 that Symantec posted a tool to remove the cloaking. As of November 15, it is still wishy-washy about it, explaining that "this rootkit was designed to hide a legitimate application, but it can be used to hide other objects, including malicious software."

The only thing that makes this rootkit legitimate is that a multinational corporation put it on your computer, not a criminal organization.

You might expect Microsoft to be the first company to condemn this rootkit. After all, XCP corrupts Windows' internals in a pretty nasty way. It's the sort of behavior that could easily lead to system crashes—crashes that customers would blame on Microsoft. But it wasn't until November 13, when public pressure was just too great to ignore, that Microsoft announced it would update its security tools to detect and remove the cloaking portion of the rootkit.

Perhaps the only security company that deserves praise is F-Secure, the first and the loudest critic of Sony's actions. And Sysinternals, of course, which hosts Russinovich's blog and brought this to light.

Bad security happens. It always has and it always will. And companies do stupid things; always have and always will. But the reason we buy security products from Symantec, McAfee, and others is to protect us from bad security.

I truly believed that even in the biggest and most-corporate security company there are people with hackerish instincts, people who will do the right thing and blow the whistle. That all the big security companies, with over a year's lead time, would fail to notice or do anything about this Sony rootkit demonstrates incompetence at best, and lousy ethics at worst.

Microsoft I can understand. The company is a fan of invasive copy protection—it's being built into the next version of Windows. Microsoft is trying to work with media companies like Sony, hoping Windows becomes the media-distribution channel of choice. And Microsoft is known for watching out for its business interests at the expense of those of its customers.

What happens when the creators of malware collude with the very companies we hire to protect us from that malware?

We users lose, that's what happens. A dangerous and damaging rootkit gets introduced into the wild, and half a million computers get infected before anyone does anything.

Who are the security companies really working for? It's unlikely that this Sony rootkit is the only example of a media company using this technology. Which security company has engineers looking for the others who might be doing it? And what will they do if they find one? What will they do the next time some multinational company decides that owning your computers is a good idea?

These questions are the real story, and we all deserve answers.

The Storm Worm

Originally published in Wired, *20 September 2007*

The Storm worm first appeared at the beginning of the year, hiding in e-mail attachments with the subject line: "230 dead as storm batters Europe." Those who opened the attachment became infected, their computers joining an ever-growing botnet.

Although it's most commonly called a worm, Storm is really more: a worm, a Trojan horse, and a bot all rolled into one. It's also the most successful example we have of a new breed of worm, and I've seen estimates that between 1 million and 50 million computers have been infected worldwide.

Old-style worms—Sasser, Slammer, Nimda—were written by hackers looking for fame. They spread as quickly as possible (Slammer infected 75,000 computers in 10 minutes) and garnered a lot of notice in the process. The onslaught made it easier for security experts to detect the attack, but required a quick response by antivirus companies, sysadmins, and users hoping to contain it. Think of this type of worm as an infectious disease that shows immediate symptoms.

Worms like Storm are written by hackers looking for profit, and they're different. These worms spread more subtly, without making noise. Symptoms don't appear immediately, and an infected computer can sit dormant for a long time. If it were a disease, it would be more like syphilis, whose symptoms may be mild or disappear altogether, but which will eventually come back years later and eat your brain.

Storm represents the future of malware. Let's look at its behavior:

- Storm is patient. A worm that attacks all the time is much easier to detect; a worm that attacks and then shuts off for a while hides much more easily.
- Storm is designed like an ant colony, with separation of duties. Only a small fraction of infected hosts spread the worm. A much smaller fraction are C2: command-and-control servers. The rest stand by to receive orders. By only allowing a small number of hosts to propagate the virus and act as command-and-control servers, Storm is resilient against attack. Even if those hosts shut down, the network remains largely intact, and other hosts can take over those duties.
- Storm doesn't cause any damage, or noticeable performance impact, to the hosts. Like a parasite, it needs its host to be intact and healthy for its own survival. This makes it harder to detect, because users and network administrators won't notice any abnormal behavior most of the time.
- Rather than having all hosts communicate to a central server or set of servers, Storm uses a peer-to-peer network for C2. This makes the

Storm botnet much harder to disable. The most common way to disable a botnet is to shut down the centralized control point. Storm doesn't have a centralized control point, and thus can't be shut down that way.

This technique has other advantages, too. Companies that monitor net activity can detect traffic anomalies with a centralized C2 point, but distributed C2 doesn't show up as a spike. Communications are much harder to detect.

One standard method of tracking root C2 servers is to put an infected host through a memory debugger and figure out where its orders are coming from. This won't work with Storm: An infected host may only know about a small fraction of infected hosts—25 to 30 at a time—and those hosts are an unknown number of hops away from the primary C2 servers.

And even if a C2 node is taken down, the system doesn't suffer. Like a hydra with many heads, Storm's C2 structure is distributed.

- Not only are the C2 servers distributed, but they also hide behind a constantly changing DNS technique called "fast flux." So even if a compromised host is isolated and debugged, and a C2 server identified through the cloud, by that time it may no longer be active.

- Storm's payload—the code it uses to spread—morphs every 30 minutes or so, making typical AV (antivirus) and IDS techniques less effective.

- Storm's delivery mechanism also changes regularly. Storm started out as PDF spam, then its programmers started using e-cards and YouTube invites—anything to entice users to click on a phony link. Storm also started posting blog-comment spam, again trying to trick viewers into clicking infected links. While these sorts of things are pretty standard worm tactics, it does highlight how Storm is constantly shifting at all levels.

- The Storm e-mail also changes all the time, leveraging social engineering techniques. There are always new subject lines and new enticing text: "A killer at 11, he's free at 21 and ...," "football tracking program" on NFL opening weekend, and major storm and hurricane warnings. Storm's programmers are very good at preying on human nature.

- Last month, Storm began attacking anti-spam sites focused on identifying it—spamhaus.org, 419eater, and so on—and the personal website of Joe Stewart, who published an analysis of Storm. I am reminded of a basic theory of war: Take out your enemy's reconnaissance. Or a basic theory of urban gangs and some governments: Make sure others know not to mess with you.

Not that we really have any idea how to mess with Storm. Storm has been around for almost a year, and the antivirus companies are pretty much powerless to do anything about it. Inoculating infected machines individually is simply not going to work, and I can't imagine forcing ISPs to quarantine infected hosts. A quarantine wouldn't work in any case: Storm's creators could easily design another worm—and we know that users can't keep themselves from clicking on enticing attachments and links.

Redesigning the Microsoft Windows operating system would work, but that's ridiculous to even suggest. Creating a counterworm would make a great piece of fiction, but it's a really bad idea in real life. We simply don't know how to stop Storm, except to find the people controlling it and arrest them.

Unfortunately, we have no idea who controls Storm, although there's some speculation that they're Russian. The programmers are obviously very skilled, and they're continuing to work on their creation.

Oddly enough, Storm isn't doing much so far, except gathering strength. Aside from continuing to infect other Windows machines and attacking particular sites that are attacking it, Storm has only been implicated in some pump-and-dump stock scams. There are rumors that Storm is leased out to other criminal groups. Other than that, nothing.

Personally, I'm worried about what Storm's creators are planning for Phase II.

The Ethics of Vulnerability Research

Originally published in InfoSecurity Magazine, *May 2008*

The standard way to take control of someone else's computer is by exploiting a vulnerability in a software program on it. This was true in the 1960s when buffer overflows were first exploited to attack computers. It was true in 1988 when the Morris worm exploited a Unix vulnerability to attack computers on the Internet, and it's still how most modern malware works.

Vulnerabilities are software mistakes—mistakes in specification and design, but mostly mistakes in programming. Any large software package will have thousands of mistakes. These vulnerabilities lie dormant in our software systems, waiting to be discovered. Once discovered, they can be used to attack systems. This is the point of security patching: eliminating known vulnerabilities. But many systems don't get patched, so the Internet is filled with known, exploitable vulnerabilities.

New vulnerabilities are hot commodities. A hacker who discovers one can sell it on the black market, blackmail the vendor with disclosure, or simply publish it without regard to the consequences. Even if he does none of these, the mere fact the vulnerability is known by someone increases the risk to every user of that software. Given that, is it ethical to research new vulnerabilities?

Unequivocally, yes. Despite the risks, vulnerability research is enormously valuable. Security is a mindset, and looking for vulnerabilities nurtures that mindset. Deny practitioners this vital learning tool, and security suffers accordingly.

Security engineers see the world differently than other engineers. Instead of focusing on how systems work, they focus on how systems fail, how they can be made to fail, and how to prevent—or protect against—those failures. Most software vulnerabilities don't ever appear in normal operations, only when an attacker deliberately exploits them. So security engineers need to think like attackers.

People without the mindset sometimes think they can design security products, but they can't. And you see the results all over society—in snake-oil cryptography, software, Internet protocols, voting machines, and fare card and other payment systems. Many of these systems had someone in charge of "security" on their teams, but it wasn't someone who thought like an attacker.

This mindset is difficult to teach, and may be something you're born with or not. But in order to train people possessing the mindset, they need to search for and find security vulnerabilities—again and again and again. And this is true regardless of the domain. Good cryptographers discover vulnerabilities in others' algorithms and protocols. Good software security experts find vulnerabilities in others' code. Good airport security designers figure out new ways to subvert airport security. And so on.

This is so important that when someone shows me a security design by someone I don't know, my first question is, "What has the designer broken?" Anyone can design a security system that he cannot break. So when someone announces, "Here's my security system, and I can't break it," your first reaction should be, "Who are you?" If he's someone who has broken dozens of similar systems, his system is worth looking at. If he's never broken anything, the chance is zero that it will be any good.

Vulnerability research is vital because it trains our next generation of computer security experts. Yes, newly discovered vulnerabilities in software and airports put us at risk, but they also give us more realistic information about how good the security actually is. And yes, there are more and less responsible—and more and less legal—ways to handle a new vulnerability. But the bad guys are constantly searching for new vulnerabilities, and if we have any hope of securing our systems, we need the good guys to be at least as competent. To me, the question isn't whether it's ethical to do vulnerability research. If someone has the skill to analyze and provide better insights into the problem, the question is whether it is ethical for him not to do vulnerability research.

Is Penetration Testing Worth It?

Originally published in Information Security, *March 2007*

There are security experts who insist penetration testing is essential for network security, and you have no hope of being secure unless you do it regularly. And there are contrarian security experts who tell you penetration testing is a waste of time; you might as well throw your money away. Both of these views are wrong. The reality of penetration testing is more complicated and nuanced.

Penetration testing is a broad term. It might mean breaking into a network to demonstrate you can. It might mean trying to break into a network to document vulnerabilities. It might involve a remote attack, physical penetration of a data center, or social engineering attacks. It might use commercial or proprietary vulnerability scanning tools, or rely on skilled white-hat hackers. It might just evaluate software version numbers and patch levels, and make inferences about vulnerabilities.

It's going to be expensive, and you'll get a thick report when the testing is done.

And that's the real problem. You really don't want a thick report documenting all the ways your network is insecure. You don't have the budget to fix them all, so the document will sit around waiting to make someone look bad. Or, even worse, it'll be discovered in a breach lawsuit. Do you really want an opposing attorney to ask you to explain why you paid to document the security holes in your network, and then didn't fix them? Probably the safest thing you can do with the report, after you read it, is shred it.

Given enough time and money, a penetration test will find vulnerabilities; there's no point in proving it. And if you're not going to fix all the uncovered vulnerabilities, there's no point in uncovering them. But there is a way to do penetration testing usefully. For years I've been saying security consists of protection, detection, and response—and you need all three to have good security. Before you can do a good job with any of these, you have to assess your security. And done right, penetration testing is a key component of a security assessment.

I like to restrict penetration testing to the most commonly exploited critical vulnerabilities, like those found on the SANS Top 20 list. If you have any of those vulnerabilities, you really need to fix them.

If you think about it, penetration testing is an odd business. Is there an analogue to it anywhere else in security? Sure, militaries run these exercises all the time, but how about in business? Do we hire burglars to try to break into our warehouses? Do we attempt to commit fraud against ourselves? No, we don't.

Penetration testing has become big business because systems are so complicated and poorly understood. We know about burglars and kidnapping and fraud, but we don't know about computer criminals. We don't know what's dangerous today, and what will be dangerous tomorrow. So we hire penetration testers in the belief they can explain it.

There are two reasons why you might want to conduct a penetration test. One, you want to know whether a certain vulnerability is present because you're going to fix it if it is. And two, you need a big, scary report to persuade your boss to spend more money. If neither is true, I'm going to save you a lot of money by giving you this free penetration test: You're vulnerable.

Now, go do something useful about it.

Anonymity and the Tor Network

Originally published in Wired, *4 October 2007*

As the name implies, Alcoholics Anonymous meetings are anonymous. You don't have to sign anything, show ID, or even reveal your real name. But the meetings are not private. Anyone is free to attend. And anyone is free to recognize you: by your face, by your voice, by the stories you tell. Anonymity is not the same as privacy.

That's obvious and uninteresting, but many of us seem to forget it when we're on a computer. We think "it's secure," and forget that "secure" can mean many different things.

Tor is a free tool that allows people to use the Internet anonymously. Basically, by joining Tor, you join a network of computers around the world that pass Internet traffic randomly amongst each other before sending it out to wherever it is going. Imagine a tight huddle of people passing letters around. Once in a while a letter leaves the huddle, and is sent off to some destination. If you can't see what's going on inside the huddle, you can't tell who sent what letter based on watching letters leave the huddle.

I've left out a lot of details, but that's basically how Tor works. It's called "onion routing," and it was first developed at the Naval Research Laboratory. The communications between Tor nodes are encrypted in a layered protocol—hence the onion analogy—but the traffic that leaves the Tor network is in the clear. It has to be.

If you want your Tor traffic to be private, you need to encrypt it. If you want it to be authenticated, you need to sign it as well. The Tor website even says: "Yes, the guy running the exit node can read the bytes that come in and out there. Tor anonymizes the origin of your traffic, and it makes sure to encrypt everything inside the Tor network, but it does not magically encrypt all traffic throughout the Internet."

Tor anonymizes, nothing more.

Dan Egerstad is a Swedish security researcher; he ran five Tor nodes. Last month, he posted a list of 100 e-mail credentials—server IP addresses, e-mail accounts and the corresponding passwords—for embassies and government ministries around the globe, all obtained by sniffing exit traffic for usernames and passwords of e-mail servers.

The list contains mostly third-world embassies: Kazakhstan, Uzbekistan, Tajikistan, India, Iran, Mongolia—but there's a Japanese embassy on the list, as well as the U.K. Visa Application Center in Nepal, the Russian Embassy in Sweden, the Office of the Dalai Lama, and several Hong Kong human rights groups. And this is just the tip of the iceberg; Egerstad sniffed more than 1,000 corporate accounts this way, too. Scary stuff, indeed.

Presumably, most of these organizations are using Tor to hide their network traffic from their host countries' spies. But because anyone can join the Tor network, Tor users necessarily pass their traffic to organizations they might not trust: various intelligence agencies, hacker groups, criminal organizations, and so on.

It's simply inconceivable that Egerstad is the first person to do this sort of eavesdropping; Len Sassaman published a paper on this attack earlier this year. The price you pay for anonymity is exposing your traffic to shady people.

We don't really know whether the Tor users were the accounts' legitimate owners, or if they were hackers who had broken into the accounts by other means and were now using Tor to avoid being caught. But certainly most of these users didn't realize that anonymity doesn't mean privacy. The fact that most of the accounts listed by Egerstad were from small nations is no surprise; that's where you'd expect weaker security practices.

True anonymity is hard. Just as you could be recognized at an AA meeting, you can be recognized on the Internet as well. There's a lot of research on breaking anonymity in general—and Tor specifically—but sometimes it doesn't even take much. Last year, AOL made 20,000 anonymous search queries public as a research tool. It wasn't very hard to identify people from the data.

A research project called Dark Web, funded by the National Science Foundation, even tried to identify anonymous writers by their style: "One of the tools developed by Dark Web is a technique called Writeprint, which automatically extracts thousands of multilingual, structural, and semantic features to determine who is creating 'anonymous' content online. Writeprint can look at a posting on an online bulletin board, for example, and compare it with writings found elsewhere on the Internet. By analyzing these certain features, it can determine with more than 95% accuracy if the author has produced other content in the past."

And if your name or other identifying information is in just *one* of those writings, you can be identified.

Like all security tools, Tor is used by both good guys and bad guys. And perversely, the very fact that something is on the Tor network means that someone—for some reason—wants to hide the fact he's doing it.

As long as Tor is a magnet for "interesting" traffic, Tor will also be a magnet for those who want to eavesdrop on that traffic—especially because more than 90% of Tor users don't encrypt.

Kill Switches and Remote Control ━━━━━━━

Originally published in Wired, *26 June 2008*

It used to be that just the entertainment industries wanted to control your computers—and televisions and iPods and everything else—to ensure that you didn't violate any copyright rules. But now everyone else wants to get their hooks into your gear.

OnStar will soon include the ability for the police to shut off your engine remotely. Buses are getting the same capability, in case terrorists want to re-enact the movie Speed. The Pentagon wants a kill switch installed on airplanes, and is worried about potential enemies installing kill switches on their own equipment.

Microsoft is doing some of the most creative thinking along these lines, with something it's calling "Digital Manners Policies." According to its patent application, DMP-enabled devices would accept broadcast "orders" limiting capabilities. Cell phones could be remotely set to vibrate mode in restaurants and concert halls, and be turned off on airplanes and in hospitals. Cameras could be prohibited from taking pictures in locker rooms and museums, and recording equipment could be disabled in theaters. Professors finally could prevent students from texting one another during class.

The possibilities are endless, and very dangerous. Making this work involves building a nearly flawless hierarchical system of authority. That's a difficult security problem even in its simplest form. Distributing that system among a variety of different devices—computers, phones, PDAs, cameras, recorders—with different firmware and manufacturers, is even more difficult. Not to mention delegating different levels of authority to various agencies, enterprises, industries, and individuals, and then enforcing the necessary safeguards.

Once we go down this path—giving one device authority over other devices—the security problems start piling up. Who has the authority to limit functionality of my devices, and how do they get that authority? What prevents them from abusing that power? Do I get the ability to override their limitations? In what circumstances, and how? Can they override my override?

How do we prevent this from being abused? Can a burglar, for example, enforce a "no photography" rule and prevent security cameras from working? Can the police enforce the same rule to avoid another Rodney King incident?

Do the police get "superuser" devices that cannot be limited, and do they get "supercontroller" devices that can limit anything? How do we ensure that only they get them, and what do we do when the devices inevitably fall into the wrong hands?

It's comparatively easy to make this work in closed specialized systems— OnStar, airplane avionics, military hardware—but much more difficult in open-ended systems. If you think Microsoft's vision could possibly be securely designed, all you have to do is look at the dismal effectiveness of the various copy-protection and digital rights-management systems we've seen over the years. That's a similar capabilities-enforcement mechanism, albeit simpler than these more general systems.

And that's the key to understanding this system. Don't be fooled by the scare stories of wireless devices on airplanes and in hospitals, or visions of a world where no one is yammering loudly on their cell phones in posh restaurants. This is really about media companies wanting to exert their control further over your electronics. They not only want to prevent you from surreptitiously recording movies and concerts, they want your new television to enforce good "manners" on your computer, and not allow it to record any programs. They want your iPod to politely refuse to copy music to a computer other than your own. They want to enforce *their* legislated definition of manners: to control what you do and when you do it, and to charge you repeatedly for the privilege whenever possible.

"Digital Manners Policies" is a marketing term. Let's call this what it really is: Selective Device Jamming. It's not polite, it's dangerous. It won't make anyone more secure—or more polite.

References

What the Terrorists Want

Incidents:

http://www.dailymail.co.uk/pages/live/articles/news/news.html?in_article_id=401419&in_page_id=1770 or http://tinyurl.com/k5njg

http://news.bbc.co.uk/2/hi/uk_news/england/5267884.stm

http://www.cbsnews.com/stories/2006/08/17/national/main1906433.shtml

http://www.cbc.ca/story/canada/national/2006/08/18/doctor-winnipeg.html or http://tinyurl.com/emnox

http://www.heraldnet.com/stories/06/08/16/100wir_port1.cfm

http://www.miami.com/mld/miamiherald/news/local/states/florida/counties/broward_county/15321870.htm or http://tinyurl.com/s5oxe

http://www.usatoday.com/news/nation/2006-08-20-fbi-passenger_x.htm

http://www.theage.com.au/articles/2006/08/17/1155407916156.html

http://www.guardian.co.uk/uklatest/story/0,,-6024132,00.html

http://news.bbc.co.uk/2/hi/europe/5283476.stm

http://forums.worldofwarcraft.com/thread.html?topicId=11211166

There have been many more incidents since I wrote this—all false alarms. I've stopped keeping a list.

The chemical unreality of the plot:

http://www.theregister.co.uk/2006/08/17/flying_toilet_terror_labs/print.html or http://tinyurl.com/eeen2

http://www.interesting-people.org/archives/interesting-people/200608/msg00087.html or http://tinyurl.com/etrl8

http://www.boingboing.net/2006/08/14/tatp_about_that_pyro.html

http://www.timesonline.co.uk/article/0,,2-2306994,00.html

http://www.cnn.com/2006/US/08/10/us.security/index.html

http://www.wondermark.com/d/220.html

http://kfmonkey.blogspot.com/2006/08/wait-arent-you-scared.html

This essay also makes the same point that we're overreacting, as well as describing a 1995 terrorist plot that was remarkably similar in both materials and modus operandi—and didn't result in a complete ban on liquids:

http://www.salon.com/opinion/feature/2006/08/17/airport_futility/

My previous related writings:

http://www.schneier.com/essay-096.html

http://www.schneier.com/essay-038.html

http://www.schneier.com/blog/archives/2006/08/terrorism_secur.html

http://www.schneier.com/essay-087.html
http://www.schneier.com/essay-045.html

This essay originally appeared in *Wired*:

http://www.wired.com/news/columns/0,71642-0.html

Movie-Plot Threats

This essay was originally published in *Wired*:

http://www.wired.com/news/business/0,1367,68789,00.html

Fixing Intelligence Failures

My original articles:

http://www.counterpane.com/crypto-gram-0109a.html#4
http://www.counterpane.com/crypto-gram-0109a.html#8

Data Mining for Terrorists

This essay originally appeared on Wired.com:

http://www.wired.com/news/columns/0,70357-0.html

TIA:

http://www.epic.org/privacy/profiling/tia/
http://www.fas.org/sgp/congress/2003/tia.html

Its return:

http://nationaljournal.com/about/njweekly/stories/2006/0223nj1.htm

GAO report:

http://www.epic.org/privacy/profiling/gao_dm_rpt.pdf

MATRIX:

http://www.aclu.org/privacy/spying/15701res20050308.html

Base rate fallacy:

http://www.cia.gov/csi/books/19104/art15.html#ft145

The New York Times on the NSA eavesdropping program:

http://www.schneier.com/blog/archives/2006/01/post_1.html

The Architecture of Security

The New York Times article about the change:

http://www.nytimes.com/2006/10/07/nyregion/nyregionspecial3/
07bollard.html?_r=1&oref=slogin

This essay originally appeared on Wired.com.

```
http://www.wired.com/news/columns/0,71968-0.html
```

The War on the Unexpected

Ad campaigns:

```
http://www.mta.info/mta/security/index.html
http://www.manchestereveningnews.co.uk/news/s/1000/1000981_help_us_spot_
terrorists__police.html or http://tinyurl.com/27wuan
http://www.schneier.com/blog/archives/2007/04/citizencountert.html
```

Administration comments:

```
http://www.washingtonpost.com/wp-srv/nation/attacked/transcripts/
ashcroft_100801.htm
http://www.usatoday.com/news/washington/2005-07-07-dc-londonblasts_x.htm
or http://tinyurl.com/25vf3y
http://query.nytimes.com/gst/fullpage.html?res=
9C05E6DC1F3AF932A05752C0A9649C8B63 or http://tinyurl.com/2463aw
```

Incidents:

```
http://news.bbc.co.uk/1/hi/northern_ireland/6387857.stm
http://www.schneier.com/blog/archives/2007/09/woman_arrested.html
http://www.lineofduty.com/content/view/84004/128/
http://www.schneier.com/blog/archives/2007/05/uk_police_blow.html
http://www.startribune.com/462/story/826056.html
http://dir.salon.com/story/tech/col/smith/2004/07/21/
askthepilot95/index.html or http://tinyurl.com/2bn3qo
http://www.schneier.com/blog/archives/2006/10/this_is_what_vi.html
http://www.schneier.com/blog/archives/2007/10/latest_terroris.html
http://www.msnbc.msn.com/id/20441775/
http://www.thisisbournemouth.co.uk/display.var.1717690.0.seized_by_the_
police.php or http://tinyurl.com/36dgj8
http://alternet.org/rights/50939/
http://www.schneier.com/blog/archives/2007/04/english_profess.html
http://www.mercurynews.com/breakingnews/ci_7084101?nclick_check=1
http://www.boston.com/news/globe/city_region/breaking_news/2007/01/
bomb_squad_remo.html or http://tinyurl.com/ywumfl
http://www.postgazette.com/pg/06081/674773.stm
http://www.schneier.com/blog/archives/2007/04/another_boston.html
```

CYA:

```
http://www.schneier.com/blog/archives/2007/02/cya_security_1.html
```

Public campaigns:

```
http://www.schneier.com/blog/archives/2005/12/truckers_watchi.html
```

```
http://www.winnipegfirst.ca/article/2007/09/24/report_suspicious_
behaviour_u_of_m_tells_students or http://tinyurl.com/2c2t2a
http://www.underwatertimes.com/print.php?article_id=64810251370
http://en.wikipedia.org/wiki/Operation_TIPS
```

Law protecting tipsters:

```
http://www.post-gazette.com/pg/07245/813550-37.stm
```

Successful tips:

```
http://www.washingtonpost.com/wp-dyn/content/article/2007/05/08/
AR2007050800465.html or http://tinyurl.com/38t6vd
http://www.pe.com/localnews/publicsafety/stories/PE_News_Local_D_
honor06.3ee3472.html or http://tinyurl.com/2g26xv
```

This essay originally appeared on Wired.com:

```
http://www.wired.com/politics/security/commentary/securitymatters/2007/11/
securitymatters_1101 or http://tinyurl.com/yqvoy6
```

Some links didn't make it into the original article. There's this creepy "if you see a father holding his child's hands, call the cops" campaign:

```
http://www.bloggernews.net/18108
```

There's this story of an iPod found on an airplane:

```
http://forums.worldofwarcraft.com/thread.html?topicId=11211166&pageNo=1 or
http://tinyurl.com/ogpbv
```

There's this story of an "improvised electronics device" trying to get through airport security:

```
http://www.makezine.com/blog/archive/2007/09/microcontroller_
programme.html?CMP=OTC-0D6B48984890 or http://tinyurl.com/2ynbru
```

This is a good essay on the "war on electronics":

```
http://www.cnet.com/surveillance-state/8301-13739_1-9782861-46.html
```

Portrait of the Modern Terrorist as an Idiot

There are a zillion links associated with this essay. You can find them on the online version:

```
http://www.schneier.com/blog/archives/2007/06/portrait_of_the.html
```

This essay originally appeared on Wired.com:

```
http://www.wired.com/politics/security/commentary/securitymatters/2007/06/
securitymatters_0614 or http://tinyurl.com/29mxc5
```

Correspondent Inference Theory and Terrorism

```
http://www.mitpressjournals.org/doi/pdf/10.1162/isec.2006.31.2.42
http://en.wikipedia.org/wiki/Correspondent_inference_theory
```

Cognitive biases:

http://www.healthbolt.net/2007/02/14/26-reasons-what-you-think-is-right-is-wrong/ or http://tinyurl.com/2oo5nk

This essay originally appeared on Wired.com:

http://www.wired.com/politics/security/commentary/securitymatters/2007/07/securitymatters_0712 or http://tinyurl.com/3y322f

The Security Threat of Unchecked Presidential Power

This essay was published on December 21, 2005 as an op-ed in the *Minneapolis Star Tribune*:

http://www.startribune.com/562/story/138326.html

Here's the opening paragraph of the Yoo memo. Remember, think of this power in the hands of your least favorite politician when you read it:

> *"You have asked for our opinion as to the scope of the President's authority to take military action in response to the terrorist attacks on the United States on September 11, 2001. We conclude that the President has broad constitutional power to use military force. Congress has acknowledged this inherent executive power in both the War Powers Resolution, Pub. L. No. 93-148, 87 Stat. 555 (1973), codified at 50 U.S.C. §§ 1541-1548 (the "WPR"), and in the Joint Resolution passed by Congress on September 14, 2001, Pub. L. No. 107-40, 115 Stat. 224 (2001). Further, the President has the constitutional power not only to retaliate against any person, organization, or State suspected of involvement in terrorist attacks on the United States, but also against foreign States suspected of harboring or supporting such organizations. Finally, the President may deploy military force preemptively against terrorist organizations or the States that harbor or support them, whether or not they can be linked to the specific terrorist incidents of September 11."*

There's a similar reasoning in the Braybee memo, which was written in 2002 about torture:

Yoo memo:

http://www.usdoj.gov/olc/warpowers925.htm

Braybee memo:

http://www.washingtonpost.com/wp-srv/nation/documents/dojinterrogationmemo20020801.pdf

This story has taken on a life of its own. But there are about a zillion links and such listed here:

http://www.schneier.com/blog/archives/2005/12/the_security_th_1.html

I am especially amused by the bit about NSA shift supervisors making decisions legally reserved for the FISA court.

NSA and Bush's Illegal Eavesdropping

A version of this essay originally appeared in *Salon*:

http://www.salon.com/opinion/feature/2005/12/20/surveillance/

Text of FISA:

http://www.law.cornell.edu/uscode/html/uscode50/usc_sup_01_50_10_36_20_
I.html or http://tinyurl.com/d7ra4

Summary of annual FISA warrants:

http://www.epic.org/privacy/wiretap/stats/fisa_stats.html

Rockefeller's secret memo:

http://talkingpointsmemo.com/docs/rock-cheney1.html

Much more here:

http://www.schneier.com/blog/archives/2005/12/nsa_and_bushs_i.html

Private Police Forces

http://www.washingtonpost.com/wp-dyn/content/article/2007/01/01/
AR2007010100665.html or http://tinyurl.com/y26xgr

http://www.nlg-npap.org/html/research/LWprivatepolice.pdf

This op-ed originally appeared in the *Minneapolis Star-Tribune*:

http://www.startribune.com/562/story/1027072.html

Recognizing "Hinky" vs. Citizen Informants

Hinky:

http://www.schneier.com/blog/archives/2005/07/profiling.html

RIT story:

http://www.nj.com/news/ledger/morris/index.ssf?/base/news-2/
1177047289122820.xml&coll=1 or http://tinyurl.com/228zm8

Casino security and the "Just Doesn't Look Right (JDLR)" principle:

http://www.casinosurveillancenews.com/jdlr.htm

Commentary:

http://www.cato-at-liberty.org/2007/04/26/id-be-ok-with-hinky-given-post-
hoc-articulation/ or http://tinyurl.com/2b3bfz

The blog post has many more links to the specific things mentioned in the essay:

http://www.schneier.com/blog/archives/2007/04/recognizing_hin_1.html

When I posted this on my blog, I got a lot of negative comments from Libertarians who believe that somehow, the market makes private policemen more responsible to the public than government policemen. I'm sorry, but this is nonsense. Best Buy is going to be responsive to its customers; an apartment complex is going to be responsive to its renters. Petty criminals who prey on those businesses are an economic externality; they're not going to enter into the economic arguments. After all, people might be more likely to shop at Best Buy if their security guards save them money by keeping crime down—who cares if they crack a few non-customer heads while doing it.

None of this is meant to imply that public police forces are magically honorable and ethical; just that the economic forces are different. So people can consider carefully which is the lesser of two evils, here's Radley Balko's paper "Overkill: The Rise of Paramilitary Police Raids in America":

http://www.cato.org/pub_display.php?pub_id=6476

And an interactive map of public police raids gone bad:

http://www.cato.org/raidmap/

Dual-Use Technologies and the Equities Issue

Estonia's cyberwar:

http://www.wired.com/politics/security/magazine/15-09/ff_estonia
http://blog.wired.com/27bstroke6/2008/01/we-traced-the-c.html

Cyberwar, cyberterrorism, etc.:

http://www.schneier.com/blog/archives/2007/06/cyberwar.html

NSA and DHS cybersecurity initiatives:

http://www.schneier.com/blog/archives/2007/01/nsa_helps_micro_1.html
http://www.nsa.gov/selinux/
http://www.eweek.com/c/a/Security/DHS-Funds-OpenSource-Security-Project/
or http://tinyurl.com/3ggg5g
http://www.schneier.com/blog/archives/2007/01/us_government_t.html

This essay originally appeared on Wired.com:

http://www.wired.com/politics/security/commentary/securitymatters/2008/05/
blog_securitymatters_0501 or http://tinyurl.com/68zj7m

Identity-Theft Disclosure Laws

California's SB 1386:

http://info.sen.ca.gov/pub/01-02/bill/sen/sb_1351-1400/sb_1386_bill_
20020926_chaptered.html or http://tinyurl.com/dgh0

Existing state disclosure laws:

http://www.pirg.org/consumer/credit/statelaws.htm

http://www.cwalsh.org/cgi-bin/blosxom.cgi/2006/04/20#breachlaws

HR 4127 - Data Accountability and Trust Act:

http://thomas.loc.gov/cgi-bin/query/C?c109:./temp/~c109XvxF76

HR 3997:

http://thomas.loc.gov/cgi-bin/query/C?c109:./temp/~c109gnLQGA

ID Analytics study:

http://www.idanalytics.com/news_and_events/20051208.htm

My essay on identity theft:

http://www.schneier.com/blog/archives/2005/04/mitigating_iden.html

A version of this essay originally appeared on Wired.com:

http://www.wired.com/news/columns/0,70690-0.html

Academic Freedom and Security

This essay was originally published in the *San Jose Mercury News*:

http://www.mercurynews.com/mld/mercurynews/9710963.htm?1c

Sensitive Security Information (SSI)

Background on SSI:

http://www.cjog.net/background_ssi_sensitive_security_in.html

TSA's Regulation on the Protection of SSI:

http://www.fas.org/sgp/news/2004/05/fr051804.html

Controversies surrounding SSI:

http://www.fas.org/sgp/crs/RS21727.pdf

My essay explaining why secrecy is often bad for security:

http://www.schneier.com/crypto-gram-0205.html#1

The Director of the National Security Archive at George Washington University on the problems of too much secrecy:

http://www.gwu.edu/

Fingerprinting Foreigners

A version of this essay originally appeared in *Newsday*:

http://www.newsday.com/news/opinion/ny-vpsch143625202jan14,0,1880923.story

or http://tinyurl.com/2yy7t

Office of Homeland Security webpage for the program:

http://www.dhs.gov/dhspublic/interapp/editorial/editorial_0333.xml

News articles:

http://www.washtimes.com/national/20031201-115121-4339r.htm

http://www.washtimes.com/national/20031027-112510-5818r.htm

http://www.nytimes.com/reuters/news/news-security-usa-visas.html

http://gcn.com/vol1_no1/daily-updates/24536-1.html

http://www.sunspot.net/news/custom/attack/bal-airport0106,0,42711.story

http://www.cnn.com/2004/US/01/04/visit.program/

http://www.nytimes.com/2004/01/05/national/05CND-SECU.html

http://www.ilw.com/lawyers/immigdaily/doj_news/2004,0106-hutchinson.shtm

http://www.theage.com.au/articles/2004/01/06/1073268031785.html

http://www.thestar.co.za/index.php?fSectionId=132&fArticleId=318749

http://www.ilw.com/lawyers/articles/2003,1231-krikorian.shtm

Opinions:

http://news.mysanantonio.com/story.cfm?xla=saen&xlb=1020&xlc=1074396

http://www.rockymountainnews.com/drmn/opinion/article/0,1299,DRMN_38_
2475765,00.html or http://tinyurl.com/3bqze

http://www.shusterman.com/pdf/advocacy61703.pdf

http://www.washingtontechnology.com/ad_sup/homeland-coalition/2.html

Brazil fingerprints U.S. citizens in retaliation:

http://reprints.msnbc.com/id/3875747/

U.S. Medical Privacy Law Gutted

News article:

http://www.nytimes.com/2005/06/07/politics/07privacy.html

Swire's essay:

http://www.americanprogress.org/site/pp.asp?c=biJRJ8OVF&b=743281

Airport Passenger Screening

http://archives.cnn.com/2002/US/03/25/airport.security/

http://www.msnbc.msn.com/id/11863165/

http://www.msnbc.msn.com/id/11878391/

A version of this essay originally appeared on Wired.com:

http://www.wired.com/news/columns/0,70470-0.html

No-Fly List

Additional information:

http://www.aclu.org/SafeandFree/SafeandFree.cfm?ID=12740&c=206
http://www.wired.com/news/privacy/0,1848,58386,00.html
http://www.salon.com/tech/feature/2003/04/10/capps/index.html
http://www.commondreams.org/headlines02/0927-01.htm
http://www.truthout.org/cgi-bin/artman/exec/view.cgi/6/3520
http://www.belleville.com/mld/newsdemocrat/8371700.htm

Kennedy's story:

http://www.msnbc.msn.com/id/5765143
http://abcnews.go.com/wire/US/reuters20040820_78.html

Getting off the list by using your middle name:

http://www.contracostatimes.com/mld/cctimes/news/world/9466229.htm

This essay originally appeared in *Newsday*:

http://www.newsday.com/news/opinion/ny-vpsch253941385aug25,0,3252599.story
or http://makeashorterlink.com/?W29816849

Trusted Traveler Program

This essay originally appeared in *The Boston Globe*:

http://www.boston.com/news/globe/editorial_opinion/oped/articles/2004/0
8/24/an_easy_path_for_terrorists/ or http://makeashorterlink.com/?E2E224939

Screening People with Clearances

This essay originally appeared on Wired.com:

http://www.wired.com/news/columns/1,71906-0.html

Forge Your Own Boarding Pass

This is my 30th essay for Wired.com:

http://www.wired.com/news/columns/0,72045-0.html

News:

http://j0hn4d4m5.bravehost.com
http://slightparanoia.blogspot.com/2006/10/post-fbi-visit.html
http://slightparanoia.blogspot.com/2006/10/fbi-visit-2.html
http://blog.wired.com/27bstroke6/2006/10/congressman_ed_.html
http://markey.house.gov/index.php?option=content&task=view&id=
2336&Itemid=125 or http://tinyurl.com/ymjkxa
http://blog.wired.com/27bstroke6/2006/10/boarding_pass_g.html

Older mentions of the vulnerability:

http://www.csoonline.com/read/020106/caveat021706.html
http://www.slate.com/id/2113157/fr/rss/
http://www.senate.gov/~schumer/SchumerWebsite/pressroom/press_releases/
2005/PR4123.aviationsecurity021305.html or http://tinyurl.com/yzoon6
http://www.schneier.com/crypto-gram-0308.html#6

No-fly list:

http://www.schneier.com/blog/archives/2005/12/30000_people_mi.html
http://www.schneier.com/blog/archives/2005/09/secure_flight_n_1.html
http://www.schneier.com/blog/archives/2006/10/nofly_list.html
http://www.schneier.com/blog/archives/2005/08/infants_on_the.html

Our Data, Ourselves

This essay previously appeared on Wired.com:

http://www.wired.com/politics/security/commentary/securitymatters/2008/05/
securitymatters_0515

The Value of Privacy

A version of this essay originally appeared on Wired.com:

http://www.wired.com/news/columns/0,70886-0.html

Daniel Solove comments:

http://www.concurringopinions.com/archives/2006/05/is_there_a_good.html or
http://tinyurl.com/nmj3u

The Future of Privacy

This essay was originally published in the *Minneapolis Star-Tribune*:

http://www.startribune.com/562/story/284023.html

Privacy and Power

The inherent value of privacy:

http://www.schneier.com/essay-114.html

Erik Crespo story:

http://www.nytimes.com/2007/12/08/nyregion/08about.html
http://abcnews.go.com/TheLaw/wireStory?id=3968795

Cameras catch a policeman:

http://www.officer.com/web/online/Top-News-Stories/Cameras-Turn-Lens-on-
Police-Activities-/1$40169 or http://tinyurl.com/2ltqcy

Security and control:

http://www.schneier.com/essay-203.html

This essay originally appeared on Wired.com:

http://www.wired.com/politics/security/commentary/securitymatters/2008/03/
securitymatters_0306 or http://tinyurl.com/2xrcnn

Commentary/rebuttal by David Brin:

http://www.wired.com/politics/security/news/2008/03/brin_rebuttal

Security vs. Privacy

McConnell article from *New Yorker*:

http://www.newyorker.com/reporting/2008/01/21/080121fa_fact_wright
http://arstechnica.com/news.ars/post/20080117-us-intel-chief-wants-carte-
blanche-to-peep-all-net-traffic.html or http://tinyurl.com/2xkwvu
http://blog.wired.com/27bstroke6/2008/01/feds-must-exami.html

Trading off security and privacy:

http://www.huffingtonpost.com/ka-taipale/privacy-vs-security-se_b_71785
.html or http://tinyurl.com/2gdqbn
http://www.huffingtonpost.com/marc-rotenberg/privacy-vs-security-pr_b_
71806.html or http://tinyurl.com/2hozm8
http://findarticles.com/p/articles/mi_m0GER/is_2002_Winter/ai_97116472/
pg_1 or http://tinyurl.com/2yk23v
http://www.rasmussenreports.com/public_content/politics/current_events/
general_current_events/51_say_security_more_important_than_privacy or
http://tinyurl.com/ypcen8
http://www.scu.edu/ethics/publications/briefings/privacy.html
http://www.csmonitor.com/2002/1015/p11s02-coop.html

False dichotomy:

http://www.schneier.com/crypto-gram-0109a.html#8
http://www.wired.com/politics/law/commentary/circuitcourt/2006/05/70971

Donald Kerr's comments:

http://www.schneier.com/blog/archives/2007/11/redefining_priv.html

Related essays:

http://www.schneier.com/essay-008.html
http://www.schneier.com/essay-096.html
http://www.schneier.com/essay-036.html
http://www.schneier.com/essay-160.html
http://www.schneier.com/essay-100.html
http://www.schneier.com/essay-108.html
http://www.schneier.com/essay-163.html

http://arstechnica.com/news.ars/post/20080119-analysis-metcalfes-law-real-id-more-crime-less-safety.html or http://tinyurl.com/23h88d
http://www.schneier.com/blog/archives/2007/09/more_on_the_ger_1.html
http://www.schneier.com/blog/archives/2007/06/portrait_of_the_1.html
http://www.schneier.com/blog/archives/2006/05/the_value_of_pr.html"

This essay originally appeared on Wired.com:

http://www.wired.com/politics/security/commentary/securitymatters/2008/01/securitymatters_0124 or http://tinyurl.com/yr98nf

Is Big Brother a Big Deal?

This essay appeared in the May 2007 issue of *Information Security*, as the second half of a point/counterpoint with Marcus Ranum:

http://informationsecurity.techtarget.com/magItem/0,291266,sid42_gci1253144,00.html or http://tinyurl.com/2a8wpf

Marcus's half:

http://www.ranum.com/security/computer_security/editorials/point-counterpoint/bigbrother.html or http://tinyurl.com/2cfuwy

How to Fight

Privacy International's Stupid Security Awards:

http://www.privacyinternational.org/activities/stupidsecurity/

Stupid Security Blog:

http://www.stupidsecurity.com/

Companies Cry 'Security' to Get A Break From the Government:

http://online.wsj.com/article_email/0,,SB105415726210410 00,00.html

Gilmore's suit:

http://freetotravel.org/

Relevant Minnesota pharmacist rules:

http://www.revisor.leg.state.mn.us/arule/6800/3110.html

How you can help right now:
Tell Congress to Get Airline Security Plan Under Control!

http://actioncenter.ctsg.com/admin/adminaction.asp?id=2557

TIA Update: Ask Your Senators to Support the Data-Mining Moratorium Act of 2003!

http://actioncenter.ctsg.com/admin/adminaction.asp?id=2401

Congress Takes Aim at Your Privacy

http://actioncenter.ctsg.com/admin/adminaction.asp?id=1723

Total Information Awareness: Public Hearings Now!

http://actioncenter.ctsg.com/admin/adminaction.asp?id=2347

Don't Let the INS Violate Your Privacy

http://actioncenter.ctsg.com/admin/adminaction.asp?id=2436

Demand the NCIC Database Be Accurate

http://www.petitiononline.com/mod_perl/signed.cgi?ncic

Citizens' Guide to the FOIA

http://www.fas.org/sgp/foia/citizen.html

Toward Universal Surveillance

This essay originally appeared on CNet:

http://news.com.com/2010-1028-5150325.html

Kafka and the Digital Person

The book's website:

http://www.law.gwu.edu/facweb/dsolove/Solove-Digital-Person.htm

Order the book on Amazon:

http://www.amazon.com/exec/obidos/ASIN/0814798462/counterpane

CCTV Cameras

CCTV research:

http://electronics.howstuffworks.com/police-camera-crime1.htm

http://www.scotcrim.u-net.com/researchc2.htm

http://news.bbc.co.uk/1/hi/uk/2192911.stm

http://www.homeoffice.gov.uk/rds/pdfs05/hors292.pdf

http://www.sfgate.com/cgi-bin/article.cgi?f=/c/a/2007/08/14/MNIPRHRPE.DTL

http://www.temple.edu/cj/misc/PhilaCCTV.pdf

http://archives.cnn.com/2002/LAW/10/21/ctv.cameras/

http://www.guardian.co.uk/uk/2008/may/06/ukcrime1

London's cameras:

http://www.channel4.com/news/articles/society/factcheck+how+many+cctv+cameras/2291167

http://www.ico.gov.uk/upload/documents/library/data_protection/practical_application/surveillance_society_full_report_2006.pdf

CCTV abuses:

http://news.bbc.co.uk/2/hi/uk_news/england/merseyside/4609746.stm

http://www.timesonline.co.uk/tol/news/uk/article743391.ece

http://community.seattletimes.nwsource.com/archive/?date=19960324&
slug=2320709

http://news.bbc.co.uk/2/hi/europe/4849806.stm

Orwellian cameras:

http://wuntvor.mirror.waffleimages.com/files/44/
44cb4b91287cfcd8111d471867502a3cac861ab0.jpg

http://lifeandhealth.guardian.co.uk/family/story/0,,2280044,00.html

Privacy concerns:

http://epic.org/privacy/surveillance/

http://www.aclu.org/privacy/spying/14863res20020225.html

Surveillance in China:

http://www.rollingstone.com/politics/story/20797485/chinas_allseeing_eye

This essay was:

http://www.guardian.co.uk/technology/2008/jun/26/politics.ukcrime

Anonymity and Accountability

This essay originally appeared in *Wired*:

http://www.wired.com/news/columns/0,70000-0.html

Kelly's original essay:

http://www.edge.org/q2006/q06_4.html

Gary T. Marx on anonymity:

http://web.mit.edu/gtmarx/www/anon.html

Facebook and Data Control

This essay originally appeared on Wired.com:

http://www.wired.com/news/columns/0,71815-0.html

http://www.danah.org/papers/FacebookAndPrivacy.html

http://www.motherjones.com/interview/2006/09/facebook.html

http://www.nytimes.com/2006/09/10/fashion/10FACE.html?ei=5090&en=
ccb86e3d53ca671f&ex=1315540800&adxnnl=1&partner=rssuserland&emc=
rss&adxnnlx=1160759797-MRZvPT2RgJLviJOZ11NuRQ or http://tinyurl.com/ycwl6o

http://blog.facebook.com/blog.php?post=2208197130

http://blog.facebook.com/blog.php?post=2208562130

http://mashable.com/2006/08/25/facebook-profile

Facebook privacy policy:

http://www.facebook.com/policy.php

The Death of Ephemeral Conversation

This essay originally appeared on Forbes.com:

http://www.forbes.com/security/2006/10/18/nsa-im-foley-tech-security-cx_bs_1018security.html or http://tinyurl.com/ymmnee

Automated Targeting System

News articles:

http://news.yahoo.com/s/ap_travel/20061208/ap_tr_ge/travel_brief_traveler_screening or http://tinyurl.com/yygbda
http://www.washingtonpost.com/wp-dyn/content/article/2006/11/02/AR2006110201810.html or
http://tinyurl.com/yl92on
http://www.ledger-enquirer.com/mld/ledgerenquirer/news/local/16196947.htm
or http://tinyurl.com/y7lbnp

Federal Register posting:

http://edocket.access.gpo.gov/2006/06-9026.htm

Comments from civil liberties groups:

http://www.epic.org/privacy/pdf/ats_comments.pdf
http://www.eff.org/Privacy/ats/ats_comments.pdf
http://www.aclu.org/privacy/gen/27593leg20061201.html
http://www.epic.org/privacy/travel/ats/default.html
http://www.epic.org/privacy/surveillance/spotlight/1006/default.html

Automated terror profiling:

http://www.schneier.com/essay-108.html
http://www.schneier.com/essay-115.html
http://www.newyorker.com/fact/content/articles/060206fa_fact
http://www.cato.org/pub_display.php?pub_id=6784

No-fly list:

http://alternet.org/story/42646/
http://www.aclu.org/safefree/resources/17468res20040406.html

Secure Flight:

http://www.schneier.com/blog/archives/2005/07/secure_flight.html

Total Information Awareness:

http://www.epic.org/privacy/profiling/tia/

ATS may be illegal:

http://hasbrouck.org/IDP/IDP-ATS-comments.pdf

http://www.washingtonpost.com/wp dyn/content/article/2006/12/08/
AR2006120801833.html or http://tinyurl.com/u2j9s
http://www.wired.com/news/technology/0,72250-0.html
http://www.ledger-enquirer.com/mld/ledgerenquirer/news/local/16196947.htm
http://leahy.senate.gov/press/200612/120606.html

This essay, without the links, was published in *Forbes*:

http://www.forbes.com/forbes/2007/0108/032_print.html

They also published a rebuttal by William Baldwin, although it doesn't seem to rebut any of the actual points. "Here's an odd division of labor: a corporate data consultant argues for more openness, while a journalist favors more secrecy." It's only odd if you don't understand security.

http://www.forbes.com/forbes/2007/0108/014.html

Anonymity and the Netflix Dataset

http://www.cs.utexas.edu/~shmat/shmat_netflix-prelim.pdf
http://www.cs.utexas.edu/~shmat/netflix-faq.html
http://www.securityfocus.com/news/11497
http://arxivblog.com/?p=142

2001 IEEE paper:

http://people.cs.vt.edu/~naren/papers/ppp.pdf

De-anonymizing the AOL data:

http://query.nytimes.com/gst/fullpage.html?res=
9E0CE3DD1F3FF93AA3575BC0A9609C8B63 or http://tinyurl.com/2dhgot
http://www.securityfocus.com/brief/286

Census data de-anonymization:

http://privacy.cs.cmu.edu/dataprivacy/papers/LIDAP-WP4abstract.html
http://crypto.stanford.edu/~pgolle/papers/census.pdf

Anonymous cell phone data:

http://arxivblog.com/?p=88

Wholesale surveillance and data collection:

http://www.schneier.com/blog/archives/2006/03/the_future_of_p.html
http://www.schneier.com/blog/archives/2007/05/is_big_brother_1.html

This essay originally appeared on Wired.com:

http://www.wired.com/politics/security/commentary/securitymatters/2007/12/
securitymatters_1213 or http://tinyurl.com/2gk18a

Does Secrecy Help Protect Personal Information?

This essay appeared in the January 2007 issue of *Information Security*, as the second half of a point/counterpoint with Marcus Ranum:

http://informationsecurity.techtarget.com/magItem/0,291266,sid42_gci 1238789,00.html or http://tinyurl.com/2h5y5u

Marcus's half:

http://www.ranum.com/security/computer_security/editorials/point-counterpoint/personal_info.html or http://tinyurl.com/27e2gj

Risks of Data Reuse

Individual data and the Japanese internment:

http://www.sciam.com/article.cfm?articleID=A4F4DED6-E7F2-99DF-32E46B0AC1FDE0FE&sc=I100322 or http://tinyurl.com/33kcy3

http://www.usatoday.com/news/nation/2007-03-30-census-role_N.htm

http://www.homelandstupidity.us/2007/04/05/census-bureau-gave-up-wwii-internment-camp-evaders/ or http://tinyurl.com/2haky8

http://rawstory.com/news/afp/Census_identified_Japanese_American_03302007.html or http://tinyurl.com/2ctnl3

Marketing databases:

http://www.wholesalelists.net

http://www.usdatacorporation.com/pages/specialtylists.html

Secure Flight:

http://www.epic.org/privacy/airtravel/secureflight.html

Florida disenfranchisement in 2000:

http://www.thenation.com/doc/20010430/lantigua

This article originally appeared on Wired.com:

http://www.wired.com/politics/onlinerights/commentary/securitymatters/2007/06/securitymatters_0628 or http://tinyurl.com/34mr2g

National ID Cards

This essay originally appeared in the *Minneapolis Star Tribune*:

http://www.startribune.com/stories/1519/4698350.html

Kristof's essay in the *The New York Times*:

http://www.nytimes.com/2004/03/17/opinion/17KRIS.html?ex=1394946000&en=938b60e9bdb051f7&ei=5007&partner=USERLAND or http://tinyurl.com/26fg2

My earlier essay on National ID cards:

http://www.schneier.com/crypto-gram-0112.html#1

My essay on identification and security:

http://www.schneier.com/crypto-gram-0402.html#6

REAL-ID: Costs and Benefits

REAL-ID:

http://thomas.loc.gov/cgi-bin/bdquerytr/z?d109:HR01268:

The REAL-ID Act: National Impact Analysis:

http://www.nga.org/Files/pdf/0609REALID.pdf

There's REAL-ID news. Maine became the first state to reject REAL-ID. This means that a Maine state driver's license will not be recognized as valid for federal purposes, although I'm sure the Feds will back down over this. My guess is that Montana will become the second state to reject REAL-ID, and New Mexico will be the third.

http://www.northcountrygazette.org/articles/2007/012807RealID.html
http://www.usatoday.com/news/nation/2007-01-30-realID_x.htm

More info on REAL-ID:

http://www.realnightmare.org

RFID Passports

http://news.com.com/E-passports+to+put+new+face+on+old+documents/
2100-7337_3-5313650.html
http://www.theregister.co.uk/2004/05/20/us_passports/

The Security of RFID Passports

Government announcement:

http://edocket.access.gpo.gov/2005/05-21284.htm

RFID privacy problems:

http://www.epic.org/privacy/rfid/
http://rfidkills.com/

My previous writings on RFID passports:

http://www.schneier.com/essay-060.html
http://www.schneier.com/blog/archives/2005/04/rfid_passport_s.html
http://www.schneier.com/blog/archives/2005/08/rfid_passport_s_1.html

This essay previously appeared on Wired.com:

http://www.wired.com/news/privacy/0,1848,69453,00.html

Multi-Use ID Cards

This essay originally appeared on Wired.com:

http://www.wired.com/news/technology/0,70167-0.html

Giving Driver's Licenses to Illegal Immigrants

This op-ed originally appeared in the *Detroit Free Press*:

http://www.schneier.com/essay-205.html

Voting Technology and Security

This essay originally appeared on Forbes.com:

http://www.forbes.com/home/security/2006/11/10/voting-fraud-security-tech-security-cz_bs_1113security.html

http://www.schneier.com/essay-068.html

http://www.schneier.com/blog/archives/2004/11/the_problem_wit.html

http://www.votingintegrity.org/archive/news/e-voting.html

http://www.verifiedvoting.org/article.php?id=997

http://www.ecotalk.org/VotingMachineErrors.htm

http://evote-mass.org/pipermail/evote-discussion_evote-mass.org/2005-January/000080.html or http://tinyurl.com/yhvb2a

http://avirubin.com/vote/analysis/index.html

http://www.freedom-to-tinker.com/?p=1080

http://www.freedom-to-tinker.com/?p=1081

http://www.freedom-to-tinker.com/?p=1064

http://www.freedom-to-tinker.com/?p=1084

http://www.bbvforums.org/cgi-bin/forums/board-auth.cgi?file=/1954/15595.html or http://tinyurl.com/9ywcn

http://itpolicy.princeton.edu/voting

http://www.ss.ca.gov/elections/voting_systems/security_analysis_of_the_diebold_accubasic_interpreter.pdf or http://tinyurl.com/eqpbd

http://www.blackboxvoting.org

http://www.brennancenter.org/dynamic/subpages/download_file_38150.pdf

http://avirubin.com/judge2.html

http://avirubin.com/judge.html

http://www.usatoday.com/news/washington/2006-10-29-voting-systems-probe_x.htm or http://tinyurl.com/ylnba6

How to Steal an Election:

http://arstechnica.com/articles/culture/evoting.ars

Florida 13:

http://www.heraldtribune.com/apps/pbcs.dll/article?AID=/20061111/NEWS/611110643 or http://tinyurl.com/ygo731

http://www.heraldtribune.com/apps/pbcs.dll/article?Date=20061108&Category
=NEWS&ArtNo=611080506 or http://tinyurl.com/yahvve
http://www.heraldtribune.com/apps/pbcs.dll/article?AID=/20061109/NEWS/
611090343 or http://tinyurl.com/yhkwdt
http://www.nytimes.com/2006/11/10/us/politics/10florida.html
http://www.lipsio.com/SarasotaFloridaPrecinct22IncidentPhotos/

Value of stolen elections:

http://www.schneier.com/essay-046.html

Perception:

http://www.npr.org/templates/story/story.php?storyId=6449790

Voter suppression:

http://blackprof.com/stealingd.html

ID requirements:

http://www.lwvwi.org/cms/images/stories/PDFs/VR%20Photo%20ID.pdf
http://www.demos.org/page337.cfm

Foxtrot cartoon:

http://www.gocomics.com/foxtrot/2006/10/29

Avi Rubin wrote a good essay on voting for *Forbes* as well:

http://www.forbes.com/home/free_forbes/2006/0904/040.html

Computerized and Electronic Voting

CRS Report on Electronic Voting:

http://www.epic.org/privacy/voting/crsreport.pdf

Voting resource pages:

http://www.epic.org/privacy/voting/
http://www.eff.org/Activism/E-voting/
http://www.verifiedvoting.org/
http://electioncentral.blog-city.com/index.cfm

Bills in U.S. Congress to force auditable balloting:

http://graham.senate.gov/pr120903.html
http://holt.house.gov/issues2.cfm?id=5996

Virginia story:

http://www.washingtonpost.com/ac2/wp-dyn?pagename=article&node=
&contentId=A6291-2003Nov5 or http://tinyurl.com/z9uc

Indiana story:

http://www.indystar.com/articles/1/089939-1241-014.html

Nevada story:

http://www.lasvegassun.com/sunbin/stories/lv-gov/2003/dec/10/
515999082.html or http://tinyurl.com/z9ud

California Secretary of State's statement on e-voting paper trail requirement:

http://www.ss.ca.gov/executive/press_releases/2003/03_106.pdf

Maryland story:

http://www.gazette.net/200350/montgomerycty/state/191617-1.html

More opinions:

http://www.pbs.org/cringely/pulpit/pulpit20031204.html

http://www.securityfocus.com/columnists/198

http://www.sacbee.com/content/opinion/story/7837475p-8778055c.html

Voter Confidence and Increased Accessibility Act of 2003

http://www.wired.com/news/print/0,1294,61298,00.html

http://www.theorator.com/bills108/hr2239.html

My older essays on this topic:

http://www.schneier.com./crypto-gram-0012.html#1

http://www.schneier.com./crypto-gram-0102.html#10

Why Election Technology is Hard

This essay originally appeared in the *San Francisco Chronicle*:

http://www.sfgate.com/cgi-
bin/article.cgi?file=/chronicle/archive/2004/10/31/EDG229GREK1.DTL or
http://makeashorterlink.com/?J353212C9

Also read Avi Rubin's op-ed on the subject:

http://www.avirubin.com/vote/op-ed.html

Electronic Voting Machines

A version of this essay appeared on openDemocracy.com:

http://www.opendemocracy.com/debates/article-8-120-2213.jsp

http://avirubin.com/judge2.html

http://www.eff.org/deeplinks/archives/cat_evoting.php

http://votingintegrity.org/archive/news/e-voting.html

http://www.blackboxvoting.org/

http://www.verifiedvoting.org/

http://www.dailykos.com/story/2004/11/3/04741/7055

http://www.alternet.org/election04/20416/

http://www.newstarget.com/002076.html

http://ustogether.org/Florida_Election.htm

http://www.washingtondispatch.com/spectrum/archives/000715.html

http://www.michigancityin.com/articles/2004/11/04/news/news02.txt

http://edition.cnn.com/2004/ALLPOLITICS/11/05/voting.problems.ap/index.html or http://makeashorterlink.com/?B283122C9

http://www.palmbeachpost.com/politics/content/news/epaper/2004/11/05/a29a_BROWVOTE_1105.html or http://makeashorterlink.com/?X3A323CB9

http://www.ansiblegroup.org/furtherleft/index.php?option=content&task=view&id=51 or http://makeashorterlink.com/?C593122C9

http://www.truthout.org/docs_04/110504V.shtml

http://www.truthout.org/docs_04/110604Z.shtml

http://www.commondreams.org/views04/1106-30.htm

http://www.truthout.org/docs_04/110804A.shtml

Revoting

Florida 13th:

http://www.heraldtribune.com/apps/pbcs.dll/article?AID=/20061111/NEWS/611110643 or http://tinyurl.com/ygo73l

http://www.nytimes.com/2006/11/10/us/politics/10florida.html

http://www.newsbackup.com/about496345.html

This essay originally appeared on Wired.com:

http://www.wired.com/news/columns/0,72124-0.html

Hacking the Papal Election

Rules for a papal election:

http://www.vatican.va/holy_father/john_paul_ii/apost_constitutions/documents/hf_jp-ii_apc_22021996_universi-dominici-gregis_en.html or http://tinyurl.com/3ldzm

There's a picture of choir dress on this page:

http://dappledphotos.blogspot.com/2005/01/biretta-sightings.html

First Responders

This essay originally appeared on Wired.com:

http://www.wired.com/politics/security/commentary/securitymatters/2007/08/securitymatters_0823

In blog comments, people pointed out that training and lack of desire to communicate are bigger problems than technical issues. This is certainly true. Just giving first responders interoperable radios won't automatically solve the problem; they need to want to talk to other groups as well.

Minneapolis rescue workers:

http://www.cnn.com/2007/US/08/02/bridge.responders/
http://www.ecmpostreview.com/2007/August/8irprt.html
http://www.cnn.com/2007/US/08/02/bridge.collapse/index.html
http://michellemalkin.com/2007/08/01/minneapolis-bridge-collapse/
http://www.cnn.com/2007/US/08/02/bridge.collapse.schoolbus/index.html

Utah rescue-worker deaths:

http://www.boston.com/news/nation/articles/2007/08/17/rescue_worker_killed
_at_utah_mine/ or http://tinyurl.com/ywdg6q

1996 report:

http://ntiacsd.ntia.doc.gov/pubsafe/publications/PSWAC_AL.PDF

Dennis Smith:

http://www.amazon.com/Report-Ground-Zero-Dennis-Smith/dp/0452283957/
ref=pd_bbs_sr_3/104-8159320-0735926?ie=UTF8&s=books&qid=1187284193&sr=8-3
or http://tinyurl.com/223cwb
http://www.9-11commission.gov/hearings/hearing11/smith_statement.pdf

9/11 Commission Report:

http://www.gpoaccess.gov/911/index.html

Wasted security measures:

http://www.schneier.com/blog/archives/2006/03/80_cameras_for.html
http://blog.wired.com/defense/2007/08/armed-robots-so.html
http://www.cnsnews.com/ViewPolitics.asp?Page=/Politics/archive/200702/
POL20070223b.html or http://tinyurl.com/2qv5tb
http://sfgate.com/cgi-bin/article.cgi?f=/c/a/2006/02/19/INGDDH8E311.DTL or
http://tinyurl.com/yvpw5w

Minnesota and interoperable communications:

https://www.dps.state.mn.us/comm/press/newPRSystem/viewPR.asp?PR_Num=244
or http://tinyurl.com/2765hp

Stanek quote:

http://www.washingtonpost.com/wp-dyn/content/article/2007/08/02/
AR2007080202262.html or http://tinyurl.com/yuf6se

Katrina:

http://www.nationaldefensemagazine.org/issues/2006/jan/inter-agency.htm or
http://tinyurl.com/233778
http://katrina.house.gov/

Conference of Mayors report:

http://www.usmayors.org/72ndAnnualMeeting/interoperabilityreport_062804.pdf
or http://tinyurl.com/yv7ocj

Collective action problem:

http://en.wikipedia.org/wiki/The_Logic_of_Collective_Action

Jerry Brito paper:

http://www.jerrybrito.com/2007/01/30/sending-out-an-sos-public-safety-communications-interoperability-as-a-collective-action-problem/ or http://tinyurl.com/29oyqw

Me on overly specific terrorism defense:

http://www.schneier.com/essay-087.html

More research:

http://www.infospheres.caltech.edu/crisis_web/executive-summary.html

Security at the Olympics

News articles:

http://www.cnn.com/2004/TECH/08/10/olympics.security.ap/index.html

http://www.elecdesign.com/Articles/ArticleID/8484/8484.html

http://cryptome.org/nyt-athens.htm

http://www.smh.com.au/olympics/articles/2004/07/27/1090693966896.html

http://www.news24.com/News24/Olympics2004/OutsideTrack/0,,2-1652-1655_1574262,00.html or http://makeashorterlink.com/?V1E651849

A version of this essay originally appeared in the *Sydney Morning Herald*, during the Olympics:

http://smh.com.au/articles/2004/08/25/1093246605489.html

Blaster and the August 14th Blackout

A preliminary version of this essay appeared on news.com:

http://news.com.com/2010-7343-5117862.html

Interim Report: Causes of the August 14th Blackout in the United States and Canada:

https://reports.energy.gov/814BlackoutReport.pdf

The relevant data is on pages 28-29 of the report.
FirstEnergy was hit by Slammer:

http://www.securityfocus.com/news/6868

http://www.computerworld.com/securitytopics/security/recovery/story/0,10801,84203,00.html or http://tinyurl.com/z9to

How worms can infect internal networks:

http://www.networm.org/faq/#enterprise

Blackout not caused by worm:

```
http://news.com.com/2100-7355_3-5111816.html
```
News article on the report:
```
http://www.iht.com/articles/118457.html
```
Geoff Shively talked about possible Blaster/blackout links just a few days after the blackout:
```
http://seclists.org/lists/bugtraq/2003/Sep/0053.html
```

Avian Flu and Disaster Planning

```
http://www.computerworld.com/action/article.do?command=viewArticleBasic&
taxonomyName=security&articleId=275619 or http://tinyurl.com/ymlmz4
http://www.computerworld.com/action/article.do?command=viewArticleBasic&
articleId=9026179 or http://tinyurl.com/2crd9n
http://www.computerworld.com/action/article.do?command=viewArticleBasic&
articleId=298413&pageNumber=1 or http://tinyurl.com/2xtgdq
http://www.computerworld.com/blogs/node/5854
```
Family disaster planning:
```
http://nielsenhayden.com/makinglight/archives/005763.html
http://nielsenhayden.com/makinglight/archives/006539.html
http://www.sff.net/people/doylemacdonald/emerg_kit.htm
```
Disaster Recovery Journal:
```
http://www.drj.com
```
Bird flu:
```
http://www.cdc.gov/flu/avian/
http://infectiousdiseases.about.com/od/faqs/f/whynot1918.htm
http://www.msnbc.msn.com/id/6861065/
http://news.bbc.co.uk/2/hi/health/4295649.stm
http://www.cnn.com/2004/HEALTH/11/25/birdflu.warning/index.html
```
Blogger comments:
```
http://www.computerworld.com/blogs/node/5854
```
Man-eating badgers:
```
http://news.bbc.co.uk/1/hi/world/middle_east/6295138.stm
```
A good rebuttal to this essay:
```
http://www.computerweekly.com/blogs/david_lacey/2007/07/no-disaster-is-
too-large-to-pl.html or http://tinyurl.com/288ybo
```
This essay originally appeared on Wired.com:
```
http://www.wired.com/print/politics/security/commentary/securitymatters/
2007/07/securitymatters_0726 or http://tinyurl.com/2mb8bg
```

Economics and Information Security

Links to all the WEIS papers are available here:

http://weis2006.econinfosec.org

Ross Anderson's, "Why Information Security Is Hard—An Economic Perspective":

http://www.cl.cam.ac.uk/ftp/users/rja14/econ.pdf

Aligning Interest with Capability

This essay originally appeared on Wired.com:

http://www.wired.com/news/columns/0,71032-0.html

National Security Consumers

This essay originally appeared, in a shorter form, on News.com:

http://news.com.com/2010-7348-5204924.html

Liabilities and Software Vulnerabilities

Schmidt's comments:

http://news.zdnet.co.uk/software/developer/0,39020387,39228663,00.htm

SlashDot thread on Schmidt's concerns:

http://developers.slashdot.org/article.pl?sid=05/10/12/1335215&tid=172
&tid=8 or http://tinyurl.com/dvpd7

Dan Farber has a good commentary on my essay:

http://blogs.zdnet.com/BTL/?p=2046

This essay originally appeared on Wired.com:

http://www.wired.com/news/privacy/0,1848,69247,00.html

There has been some confusion about this in the comments—both in *Wired* and on my blog—that somehow this means that software vendors will be expected to achieve perfection and that they will be 100% liable for anything short of that. Clearly that's ridiculous, and that's not the way liabilities work. But equally ridiculous is the notion that software vendors should be 0% liable for defects. Somewhere in the middle there is a reasonable amount of liability, and that's what I want the courts to figure out.

Howard Schmidt writes: "It is unfortunate that my comments were reported inaccurately; at least Dan Farber has been trying to correct the inaccurate reports with his blog I do not support PERSONAL LIABILITY for the developers NOR do I support liability against vendors. Vendors are nothing more than people (employees included) and anything against them hurts the very people who need to be given better tools, training and support."

Howard wrote this essay on the topic, to explain what he really thinks. He is against software liabilities.

http://news.com.com/Give+developers+secure-coding+ammo/2010-1002_3-5929364
.html or http://tinyurl.com/dmlgh

But the first sentence of his last paragraph nicely sums up what's wrong with this argument: "In the end, what security requires is the same attention any business goal needs." If security is to be a business goal, then it needs to make business sense. Right now, it makes more business sense not to produce secure software products than it does to produce secure software products. Any solution needs to address that fundamental market failure, instead of simply wishing it were true.

Lock-In

Apple and the iPhone:

http://www.nytimes.com/2007/09/29/technology/29iphone.html
http://www.bloomberg.com/apps/news?pid=20601087&sid=aWmgiO8ZjbpM
http://www.engadget.com/2007/10/17/apple-planning-iphone-sdk-for-february/
or http://tinyurl.com/yvx5hr
http://www.engadget.com/2008/01/28/iphone-sdk-key-leaked/

Shapiro and Varian's book:

http://www.amazon.com/Information-Rules-Strategic-Network-
Economy/dp/087584863X/ref=sr_1_1?ie=UTF8&s=books&qid=1202236504&sr=1-1 or
http://tinyurl.com/2eo23e

Microsoft and Trusted Computing:

http://schneier.com/crypto-gram-0208.html#1
http://www.cl.cam.ac.uk/~rja14/Papers/tcpa.pdf
http://www.microsoft.com/technet/archive/security/news/ngscb.mspx
http://www.schneier.com/blog/archives/2005/08/trusted_computi.html

Commentary:

http://yro.slashdot.org/yro/08/02/07/2138201.shtml
http://stumble.kapowaz.net/post/25792347
http://www.kryogenix.org/days/2008/02/08/there-can-be-no-fud
http://girtby.net/archives/2008/2/8/vendor-lock-in

This essay previously appeared on Wired.com:

http://www.wired.com/politics/security/commentary/securitymatters/2008/02/
securitymatters_0207 or http://tinyurl.com/2mf82q

Third Parties Controlling Information

Internet Archive:

http://www.archive.org/

Greatest Journal:

http://dropbeatsnotbombs.vox.com/library/post/farewell-gj-youll-kind-of-be-missed.html or http://tinyurl.com/2t2yg5

http://barry095.vox.com/library/post/greatest-journal-death.html

Other hacks:

http://www.schneier.com/blog/archives/2005/02/tmobile_hack_1.html

http://www.wired.com/politics/security/news/2008/01/myspace_torrent

This essay originally appeared on Wired.com:

http://www.wired.com/politics/security/commentary/securitymatters/2008/02/securitymatters_0221 or http://tinyurl.com/2a4go3

Who Owns Your Computer?

This essay originally appeared on Wired.com:

http://www.wired.com/news/columns/1,70802-0.html

Trusted computing:

http://www.schneier.com/crypto-gram-0208.html#1

A Security Market for Lemons

Risks of data in small packages:

http://www.wired.com/politics/security/commentary/securitymatters/2006/01/70044 or http://tinyurl.com/ypqntk

Secustick and review:

http://www.secustick.nl/engels/index.html

http://tweakers.net/reviews/683

Snake oil:

http://www.schneier.com/crypto-gram-9902.html#snakeoil

http://www.schneier.com/crypto-gram-9810.html#cipherdesign

"A Market for Lemons":

http://en.wikipedia.org/wiki/The_Market_for_Lemons

http://www.students.yorku.ca/~siccardi/The%20market%20for%20lemons.pdf

Kingston USB drive:

http://www.kingston.com/flash/dt_secure.asp

Slashdot thread:

http://it.slashdot.org/article.pl?sid=07/04/19/140245

This essay originally appeared in *Wired*:

http://www.wired.com/politics/security/commentary/securitymatters/2007/04/
securitymatters_0419 or http://tinyurl.com/2fh325

Websites, Passwords, and Consumers

Phishing:

http://www.msnbc.msn.com/id/5184077/
http://www.internetweek.com/e-business/showArticle.jhtml?articleID=22100149

The Trojan:

http://news.com.com/Pop-up+program+reads+keystrokes%2C+steals+
passwords/2100-7349_3-5251981.html
http://www.pcworld.com/news/article/0%2Caid%2C116761%2C00.asp

A shorter version of this essay originally appeared in *IEEE Security and Privacy*:

http://csdl.computer.org/comp/mags/sp/2004/04/j4088abs.htm

The Feeling and Reality of Security

Getting security trade-offs wrong:

http://www.schneier.com/essay-162.html

Cognitive biases that affect security:

http://www.schneier.com/essay-155.html

"In Praise of Security Theater":

http://www.schneier.com/essay-154.html

The security lemon's market:

http://www.schneier.com/essay-165.html

Airline security and agenda:

http://www.schneier.com/blog/archives/2005/08/airline_securit_2.html

This essay originally appeared on Wired.com:

http://www.wired.com/politics/security/commentary/securitymatters/2008/04/
securitymatters_0403 or http://tinyurl.com/2xu2zb

Behavioral Assessment Profiling

This article originally appeared in *The Boston Globe*:

http://www.boston.com/news/globe/editorial_opinion/oped/articles/2004/
11/24/profile_hinky/ or http://makeashorterlink.com/?X2071260A
http://news.airwise.com/stories/2004/11/1100157618.html
http://www.usatoday.com/travel/news/2004-01-27-logan-security_x.htm

In Praise of Security Theater

This essay appeared on Wired.com, and is dedicated to my new godson, Nicholas Quillen Perry:

http://www.wired.com/news/columns/0,72561-0.html

Infant abduction:

http://www.saione.com/ispletter.htm

Blog entry URL:

http://www.schneier.com/blog/archives/2007/01/in_praise_of_se.html

CYA Security

http://www.schneier.com/blog/archives/2007/02/nonterrorist_em.html

Airplane security:

http://www.schneier.com/blog/archives/2006/08/terrorism_secur.html

Searching bags in subways:

http://www.schneier.com/blog/archives/2005/07/searching_bags.html

No-fly list:

http://www.schneier.com/essay-052.html

More CYA security:

http://entertainment.iafrica.com/news/929710.htm

http://www.news24.com/News24/Entertainment/Oscars/0,,2-1225-1569_
1665860,00.html or http://tinyurl.com/24uuuo

http://www.schneier.com/blog/archives/2005/09/major_security.html

http://www.schneier.com/blog/archives/2006/03/80_cameras_for.html

http://www.schneier.com/blog/archives/2007/01/realid_costs_an.html

http://www.slate.com/id/2143104/

Commentary:

http://www.networkworld.com/community/?q=node/11746

http://yro.slashdot.org/yro/07/02/22/214246.shtml

This essay originally appeared on Wired.com:

http://www.wired.com/news/columns/0,72774-0.html

Copycats

http://www.philly.com/mld/inquirer/news/local/16824777.htm

http://kyw1060.com/pages/254744.php?contentType=4&contentId=340063

http://www.delawareonline.com/apps/pbcs.dll/article?AID=/20070222/NEWS/
702220360/1006/NEWS or http://tinyurl.com/2f3gyj

http://www.nbc10.com/news/11155984/detail.html?subid=10101521

Dan Cooper and the Cooper Vane:

http://www.crimelibrary.com/criminal_mind/scams/DB_Cooper/index.html
http://en.wikipedia.org/wiki/Cooper_Vane

Green-card lawyers:

http://www.wired.com/news/politics/0,1283,19098,00.html

This essay originally appeared on Wired.com:

http://www.wired.com/news/columns/0,72887-0.html

Blog entry URL:

http://www.schneier.com/blog/archives/2007/03/post.html

Rare Risk and Overreactions

Irrational reactions:

http://arstechnica.com/news.ars/post/20070502-student-creates-counter-strike-map-gets-kicked-out-of-school.html or http://tinyurl.com/2dbl67
http://www.boingboing.net/2007/05/03/webcomic_artist_fire.html
http://www.yaledailynews.com/articles/view/20843
http://yaledailynews.com/articles/view/20913
http://www.msnbc.msn.com/id/18645623/

Risks of school shootings from 2000:

http://www.cdc.gov/HealthyYouth/injury/pdf/violenceactivities.pdf

Crime statistics—strangers vs. acquaintances:

http://www.fbi.gov/ucr/05cius/offenses/expanded_information/data/shrtable_09.html or http://tinyurl.com/2qbtae

Me on the psychology of risk and security:

http://www.schneier.com/essay-155.html

Risk of shark attacks:

http://www.oceanconservancy.org/site/DocServer/fsSharks.pdf

Ashcroft speech:

http://www.highbeam.com/doc/1G1-107985887.html

Me on security theater:

http://www.schneier.com/essay-154.html

Baseball beer ban:

http://blogs.csoonline.com/baseballs_big_beer_ban

Nicholas Taub essay:

http://www.fooledbyrandomness.com/nyt2.htm
http://www.telegraph.co.uk/opinion/main.jhtml?xml=/opinion/2007/04/22/do2201.xml or http://tinyurl.com/3bewfy

VA Tech and gun control:

http://abcnews.go.com/International/wireStory?id=3050071&CMP=OTC-RSSFeeds
0312 or http://tinyurl.com/25js4o

http://www.cnn.com/2007/US/04/19/commentary.nugent/index.html

VA Tech hindsight:

http://news.independent.co.uk/world/americas/article2465962.ece

http://www.mercurynews.com/charliemccollum/ci_5701552

John Stewart video:

http://www.comedycentral.com/motherload/player.jhtml?ml_video=85992

Me on movie-plot threats:

http://www.schneier.com/essay-087.html

Another opinion:

http://www.socialaffairsunit.org.uk/blog/archives/000512.php

This essay originally appeared on Wired.com, my 42nd essay on that site:

http://www.wired.com/politics/security/commentary/securitymatters/2007/05/
securitymatters_0517 or http://tinyurl.com/26cxcs

French translation:

http://archiloque.net/spip.php?rubriques2&periode=2007-06#

Tactics, Targets, and Objectives

Safari security advice:

http://www.cybertracker.co.za/DangerousAnimals.html

School shooter security advice:

http://www.ucpd.ucla.edu/ucpd/zippdf/2007/Active%20Shooter%20Safety%20Tips
.pdf or http://tinyurl.com/2qvgyg

Burglar security advice:

http://www.pfadvice.com/2007/02/05/the-best-place-to-hide-money-
conversation-with-a-burglar/ or http://tinyurl.com/ywdoy9

http://www.pfadvice.com/2007/03/06/dont-hide-money-in-the-toilet-more-
conversation-with-a-burglar/ or http://tinyurl.com/236wbs

Me on terrorism:

http://www.schneier.com/essay-096.html

http://www.schneier.com/blog/archives/2006/08/terrorism_secur.html

http://www.schneier.com/blog/archives/2005/09/katrina_and_sec.html

http://www.schneier.com/blog/archives/2006/08/what_the_terror.html

Learning behavior in tigers:

http://www.cptigers.org/animals/species.asp?speciesID=9

This essay originally appeared on Wired.com:

`http://www.wired.com/print/politics/security/commentary/securitymatters/`
`2007/05/securitymatters_0531` or `http://tinyurl.com/2zdghw`

The Security Mindset

SmartWater:

`http://www.smartwater.com/products/securitySolutions.html`
`http://www.schneier.com/blog/archives/2005/02/smart_water.html`

CSE484:

`http://www.cs.washington.edu/education/courses/484/08wi/`
`http://cubist.cs.washington.edu/Security/2007/11/22/why-a-computer-`
`security-course-blog/` or `http://tinyurl.com/3m94ag`

CSE484 blog:

`http://cubist.cs.washington.edu/Security/`
`http://cubist.cs.washington.edu/Security/category/security-reviews/`
`http://cubist.cs.washington.edu/Security/2008/03/14/security-review-`
`michaels-toyota-service-center/` or `http://tinyurl.com/456b5y`

Britney Spears's medical records:

`http://www.msnbc.msn.com/id/23640143`

This essay originally appeared on Wired.com:

`http://www.wired.com/politics/security/commentary/securitymatters/2008/03/`
`securitymatters_0320` or `http://tinyurl.com/2lkg5f`

Comments:

`http://www.freedom-to-tinker.com/?p=1268`
`http://blog.ungullible.com/2008/03/hacking-yourself-to-ungullibility-`
`part.html` or `http://tinyurl.com/3fl9np`
`http://www.daemonology.net/blog/2008-03-21-security-is-mathematics.html` or
`http://tinyurl.com/34y2en`

My Open Wireless Network

RIAA data:

`http://www.sptimes.com/2007/10/02/Business/Minn_woman_takes_on_r.shtml`
`http://www.npd.com/press/releases/press_0703141.html`
`http://www.guardian.co.uk/technology/2007/mar/22/musicnews.newmedia`

Rulings on "stealing" bandwidth:

`http://www.ibls.com/internet_law_news_portal_view_prn.aspx?s=latestnews`
`&id=1686` or `http://tinyurl.com/35ww16`
`http://arstechnica.com/news.ars/post/20080103-the-ethics-of-stealing-a-`
`wifi-connection.html` or `http://tinyurl.com/yseb8v`

Amusing story of someone playing with a bandwidth stealer:

http://www.ex-parrot.com/~pete/upside-down-ternet.html

ISPs:

http://w2.eff.org/Infrastructure/Wireless_cellular_radio/wireless_
friendly_isp_list.html or http://tinyurl.com/216pmn

http://www.nytimes.com/2007/04/14/technology/14online.html?_r=1&ex=1181188
800&en=06978ee1a8aa9cde&ei=5070&oref=slogin or http://tinyurl.com/2t5cjw

Fon:

http://www.iht.com/articles/2006/01/30/business/wireless31.php

http://www.fon.com/en/

This essay originally appeared on Wired.com:

http://www.wired.com/politics/security/commentary/securitymatters/2008/01/
securitymatters_0110 or http://tinyurl.com/22s3wx

It has since generated a lot of controversy:

http://hardware.slashdot.org/article.pl?sid=08/01/10/1449228

Opposing essays:

http://wifinetnews.com/archives/008126.html

http://www.dslreports.com/shownews/Bruce-Schneier-Wants-You-To-Steal-His-
WiFi-90869 or http://tinyurl.com/2nqg4s

http://www.networkworld.com/community/node/23714

And here are supporting essays:

http://www.boingboing.net/2008/01/10/why-its-good-to-leav.html

http://techdirt.com/articles/20080110/100007.shtml

http://blogs.computerworld.com/open_wireless_oh_my

Presumably there will be a lot of back and forth in the blog comments section
here as well:

http://www.schneier.com/blog/archives/2008/01/my_open_wireles.html#comments

Debating Full Disclosure

This essay originally appeared on CSOOnline:

http://www2.csoonline.com/exclusives/column.html?CID=28073

It was part of a series of essays on the topic. Marcus Ranum wrote against the
practice of disclosing vulnerabilities:

http://www2.csoonline.com/exclusives/column.html?CID=28072

Mark Miller of Microsoft wrote in favor of responsible disclosure:

http://www2.csoonline.com/exclusives/column.html?CID=28071

These are sidebars to a very interesting article in *CSO Magazine*, "The Chilling Effect," about the confluence of forces that are making it harder to research and disclose vulnerabilities in web-based software:

http://www.csoonline.com/read/010107/fea_vuln.html

All the links are worth reading in full.
A Simplified Chinese translation by Xin Li:

http://blog.delphij.net/archives/001694.html

Doping in Professional Sports

http://www.msnbc.msn.com/id/14059185/

Armstrong's case:

http://www.schneier.com/blog/archives/2005/09/lance_armstrong.html

Baseball and HGH:

http://sports.yahoo.com/mlb/news?slug=jp-hgh061206&prov=yhoo&type=lgns
http://sports.yahoo.com/mlb/news?slug=jp-hgh060706&prov=yhoo&type=lgns

This essay originally appeared on Wired.com:

http://www.wired.com/news/columns/0,71566-0.html

Do We Really Need a Security Industry?

http://software.silicon.com/security/0,39024655,39166892,00.htm
http://www.techworld.com/security/blogs/index.cfm?blogid=1&entryid=467
http://techdigest.tv/2007/04/security_guru_q.html
http://www.itbusinessedge.com/blogs/top/?p=114

Complexity and security:

http://www.schneier.com/crypto-gram-0003.html#8

Commentary on essay:

http://www.networkworld.com/community/?q=node/14813
http://it.slashdot.org/it/07/05/03/1936237.shtml
http://matt-that.com/?p=5

This essay originally appeared in *Wired*:

http://www.wired.com/politics/security/commentary/securitymatters/2007/05/
securitymatters_0503 or http://tinyurl.com/23b3av

Basketball Referees and Single Points of Failure
This is my 50th essay for Wired.com:

http://www.wired.com/politics/security/commentary/securitymatters/2007/09/
securitymatters_0906 or http://tinyurl.com/2kl98z
http://sports.espn.go.com/espn/page2/story?page=simmons/070722

http://sports.espn.go.com/nba/columns/story?columnist=munson_lester&id
=2976241 or http://tinyurl.com/24mvha
http://sports.espn.go.com/nba/columns/story?columnist=stein_marc&id=2947543
or http://tinyurl.com/yq9h9x
http://sports.espn.go.com/nba/columns/story?columnist=sheridan_chris
&id=2948746 or http://tinyurl.com/2ahge3
http://msn.foxsports.com/nba/story/7047984
http://sports.espn.go.com/espn/blog/index?entryID=2979711&name=sheridan_
chris or http://tinyurl.com/2aa6nb
http://www.eog.com/news/industry.aspx?id=28416
http://sports.espn.go.com/nba/news/story?page=expertexplainsNBAbets

Chemical Plant Security and Externalities

Risks:

http://www.usatoday.com/news/washington/2007-04-23-chlorine-truck-bomb_N
.htm or http://tinyurl.com/2zk2a5
http://www.chemsafety.gov/index.cfm?folder=news_releases&page=news&NEWS_
ID=379 or http://tinyurl.com/23bokt
http://www.bt.cdc.gov/agent/phosgene/basics/facts.asp
http://www.opencrs.com/document/M20050627/2005-06-27%2000:00:00
http://digital.library.unt.edu/govdocs/crs/permalink/meta-crs-9917
http://www.washingtonmonthly.com/features/2007/0703.levine1.html

Regulations:

http://www.boston.com/news/nation/washington/articles/2007/04/03/chemical_
plants_at_risk_us_agency_says/ or http://tinyurl.com/2babz5
http://www.usatoday.com/printedition/news/20070427/a_chemplant27.art.htm
or http://tinyurl.com/22xwab

This essay previously appeared on Wired.com:

http://www.wired.com/politics/security/commentary/securitymatters/2007/10/
securitymatters_1018 or http://tinyurl.com/yr2cd2

Mitigating Identity Theft

This essay was previously published on CNet:

http://www.news.com/Mitigating-identity-theft/2010-1071_3-5669408.html

LifeLock and Identity Theft

LifeLock:

http://www.lifelock.com

FACTA:

http://www.ftc.gov/opa/2004/06/factaidt.shtm

http://www.treasury.gov/offices/domestic-finance/financial-institution/cip/pdf/fact-act.pdf

Fraud alerts:

http://www.consumersunion.org/creditmatters/creditmattersfactsheets/001626.html

The New York Times article:

http://www.nytimes.com/2008/05/24/business/yourmoney/24money.html?8dpc

Lawsuits:

http://www.networkworld.com/news/2008/022108-credit-reporting-firm-sues-lifelock.html

http://www.insidetech.com/news/2148-id-protection-ads-come-back-to-bite-lifelock-pitchman

Identity theft:

http://www.schneier.com/crypto-gram-0504.html#2

http://www.ftc.gov/opa/2007/11/idtheft.shtm

http://www.consumer.gov/sentinel/pubs/top10fraud2007.pdf

http://www.privacyrights.org/ar/idtheftsurveys.htm#Jav2007

Free credit reports:

http://www.annualcreditreport.com/

http://blog.washingtonpost.com/securityfix/2005/09/beware_free_credit_report_scam_1.html

http://www.msnbc.msn.com/id/7803368/

http://ezinearticles.com/?The-Free-Credit-Report-Scam&id=321877

Defending yourself:

http://www.nytimes.com/2008/05/24/business/yourmoney/24moneyside.html
http://www.savingadvice.com/blog/2008/06/04/102143_never-pay-someone-to-protect-your-identity.html

This essay originally appeared in *Wired*:

http://www.wired.com/politics/security/commentary/securitymatters/2008/06/securitymatters_0612

Phishing

California law:

http://www.msnbc.msn.com/id/9547692/

Definitions:

http://en.wikipedia.org/wiki/Phishing

http://en.wikipedia.org/wiki/Pharming
http://www-03.ibm.com/industries/financialservices/doc/content/news/magazine/1348544103.html or http://tinyurl.com/b32dh
http://www-03.ibm.com/industries/financialservices/doc/content/news/pressrelease/1368585103.html or http://tinyurl.com/9rkas

Who pays for identity theft:

http://www.informationweek.com/showArticle.jhtml?articleID=166402700

Me on semantic attacks:

http://www.schneier.com/crypto-gram-0010.html#1

Me on economics and security:

http://www.schneier.com/book-sand1-intro2.html

Me on identity theft:

http://www.schneier.com/blog/archives/2005/04/mitigating_iden.html

Discussion of my essay:

http://it.slashdot.org/article.pl?sid=05/10/06/199257&tid=172&tid=98

This essay originally appeared in *Wired*:

http://www.wired.com/news/politics/0,1283,69076,00.html

Bot Networks

This essay originally appeared on Wired.com:

http://www.wired.com/news/columns/0,71471-0.html

Distributed.net:

http://www.distributed.net

SETI@home:

http://setiathome.berkeley.edu

MafiaBoy:

http://www.infoworld.com/articles/hn/xml/01/01/18/010118hnmafiaboy.html

1.5-million-node bot network:

http://www.techweb.com/wire/security/172303160

Cyber-Attack

http://www.fcw.com/article98016-03-22-07-Web

Allowing the entertainment industry to hack:

http://www.politechbot.com/docs/berman.coble.p2p.final.072502.pdf
http://www.freedom-to-tinker.com/?cat=6

Clarke's comments:

http://www.usatoday.com/tech/news/2002/02/14/cyberterrorism.htm

This essay originally appeared in *Wired*:

http://www.wired.com/politics/security/commentary/securitymatters/2007/04/securitymatter_0405 or http://tinyurl.com/2dkpcc

Counterattack

Automated law enforcement:

http://www.foxnews.com/story/0,2933,64688,00.html

Mullen's essay:

http://www.hammerofgod.com/strikeback.txt

Berman legislation:

http://www.counterpane.com/crypto-gram-0208.html#5

Cyberwar

My previous essay on cyberterrorism:

http://www.schneier.com/crypto-gram-0306.html#1

Militaries and Cyberwar

My interview in the Iranian newspaper (to be honest, I have no idea what it says):

http://www.jamejamdaily.net/shownews2.asp?n=26454&t=com

The Truth About Chinese Hackers

Article originally published in *Discovery Tech*:

http://dsc.discovery.com/technology/my-take/computer-hackers-china.html

Safe Personal Computing

Others have disagreed with these recommendations:

http://www.getluky.net/archives/000145.html

http://www.berylliumsphere.com/security_mentor/2004/12/heres-another-really-good-twelve.html or http://makeashorterlink.com/?Z3772560A

My original essay on the topic:

http://www.schneier.com/crypto-gram-0105.html#8

This essay previously appeared on CNet:

http://news.com.com/Who+says+safe+computing+must+remain+a+pipe+dream/2010-1071_3-5482340.html or http://makeashorterlink.com/?V6872560A

How to Secure Your Computer, Disks, and Portable Drives

This essay previously appeared on Wired.com:

```
http://www.wired.com/politics/security/commentary/securitymatters/2007/11/
securitymatters_1129
```

Why was the U.K. event such a big deal? Certainly the scope: 40% of the British population. Also the data: bank account details; plus information about children. There's already a larger debate on the issue of a database on kids that this feeds into. And it's a demonstration of government incompetence (think Hurricane Katrina). In any case, this issue isn't going away anytime soon. Prime Minister Gordon Brown has apologized. The head of the Revenue and Customs office has resigned. More fallout is probably coming. U.K.'s privacy Chernobyl:

```
http://www.timesonline.co.uk/tol/news/uk/article2910705.ece
http://news.bbc.co.uk/1/hi/uk_politics/7104945.stm
http://politics.guardian.co.uk/economics/story/0,,2214566,00.html
http://www.timesonline.co.uk/tol/news/uk/article2910635.ece
http://www.theregister.co.uk/2007/11/21/response_data_breach/
```

U.S. VA privacy breach:

```
http://www.wired.com/techbiz/media/news/2006/05/70961
```

PGP Disk:

```
http://www.pgp.com/products/wholediskencryption/
```

Choosing a secure password:

```
http://www.schneier.com/blog/archives/2007/01/choosing_secure.html
http://www.iusmentis.com/security/passphrasefaq/
```

Risks of losing small memory devices:

```
http://www.schneier.com/blog/archives/2005/07/risks_of_losing.html
```

Laptop snatching:

```
http://www.sfgate.com/cgi-bin/article.cgi?file=/chronicle/archive/2006/04/
08/MNGE9I686K1.DTL or http://tinyurl.com/fszeh
```

Microsoft BitLocker:

```
http://www.schneier.com/blog/archives/2006/05/bitlocker.html
```

TrueCrypt:

```
http://www.truecrypt.org/
```

Crossing Borders with Laptops and PDAs

My advice on choosing secure passwords:

```
http://www.schneier.com/essay-148.html
```

This essay originally appeared in *The Guardian*:

`http://www.guardian.co.uk/technology/2008/may/15/computing.security`

Choosing Secure Passwords

Analyzing 24,000 MySpace passwords:

`http://www.wired.com/news/columns/0,72300-0.html`

Choosing passwords:

`http://psychology.wichita.edu/surl/usabilitynews/81/Passwords.htm`
`http://www.microsoft.com/windows/IE/community/columns/passwords.mspx`
`http://www.brunching.com/passwordguide.html`

AccessData:

`http://www.accessdata.com`

Password Safe:

`http://www.schneier.com/passsafe.html`

This essay originally appeared on Wired.com:

`http://www.wired.com/news/columns/1,72458-0.html`

Secrecy, Security, and Obscurity

Kerckhoffs' Paper (in French):

`http://www.cl.cam.ac.uk/~fapp2/kerckhoffs/la_cryptographie_militaire_i.htm`

Another essay along similar lines:

`http://online.securityfocus.com/columnists/80`

More on Two-Factor Authentication

This essay previously appeared in *Network World* as a "Face Off":

`http://www.nwfusion.com/columnists/2005/040405faceoff-counterpane.html` or
`http://tinyurl.com/5nuod`

Joe Uniejewski of RSA Security wrote an opposing position:

`http://www.nwfusion.com/columnists/2005/040405faceoff-rsa.html`

Another rebuttal:

`http://www.eweek.com/article2/0,1759,1782435,00.asp`

My original essay:

`http://www.schneier.com/essay-083.html`

Home Users: A Public Health Problem?

This essay is the first half of a point/counterpoint with Marcus Ranum in the September 2007 issue of *Information Security*. You can read his reply here:

http://www.ranum.com/security/computer_security/editorials/point-counterpoint/homeusers.htm.

Security Products: Suites vs. Best-of-Breed

This essay originally appeared as the second half of a point/counterpoint with Marcus Ranum in *Information Security*:

http://searchsecurity.techtarget.com/magazineFeature/0,296894,sid14_gci130 3850_idx2,00.html

Marcus's half:

http://searchsecurity.techtarget.com/magazineFeature/0,296894,sid14_gci130 3850,00.html or http://tinyurl.com/36zhml

Separating Data Ownership and Device Ownership

New timing attack on RSA:

http://www.newscientisttech.com/article/dn10609
http://eprint.iacr.org/2006/351.pdf

My essay on side-channel attacks:

http://www.schneier.com/crypto-gram-9806.html#side

My paper on data/device separation:

http://www.schneier.com/paper-smart-card-threats.html

Street-performer protocol: an alternative to DRM:

http://www.schneier.com/paper-street-performer.html

Ontario lottery fraud:

http://www.cbc.ca/canada/toronto/story/2006/10/26/ombudsman-probe.html

This essay originally appeared on Wired.com:

http://www.wired.com/news/columns/0,72196-0.html

Assurance

California reports:

http://www.sos.ca.gov/elections/elections_vsr.htm

Commentary and blog posts:

http://www.freedom-to-tinker.com/?p=1181
http://blog.wired.com/27bstroke6/2007/07/ca-releases-res.html
http://www.schneier.com/blog/archives/2007/07/california_voti.html
http://www.freedom-to-tinker.com/?p=1184
http://blog.wired.com/27bstroke6/2007/08/ca-releases-sou.html
http://avi-rubin.blogspot.com/2007/08/california-source-code-study-results
.html or http://tinyurl.com/2bz7ks
http://www.crypto.com/blog/ca_voting_report/
http://twistedphysics.typepad.com/cocktail_party_physics/2007/08/caveat-
voter.html or http://tinyurl.com/2737c7
http://www.schneier.com/blog/archives/2007/08/more_on_the_cal.html

California's recertification requirements:

http://arstechnica.com/news.ars/post/20070806-california-to-recertify-
insecure-voting-machines.html or http://tinyurl.com/ytesbj

DefCon reports:

http://www.defcon.org/
http://www.physorg.com/news105533409.html
http://blog.wired.com/27bstroke6/2007/08/open-sesame-acc.html
http://www.newsfactor.com/news/Social-Networking-Sites-Are-
Vulnerable/story.xhtml?story_id=012000EW8420 or http://tinyurl.com/22uoza
http://blog.wired.com/27bstroke6/2007/08/jennalynn-a-12-.html

US-VISIT database vulnerabilities:

http://www.washingtonpost.com/wp-
dyn/content/article/2007/08/02/AR2007080202260.html or
http://tinyurl.com/33cglf

RFID passport hacking:

http://www.engadget.com/2006/08/03/german-hackers-clone-rfid-e-passports/
or http://tinyurl.com/sy439
http://www.rfidjournal.com/article/articleview/2559/2/1/
http://www.wired.com/politics/security/news/2007/08/epassport
http://money.cnn.com/2007/08/03/news/rfid/?postversion=2007080314

How common are bugs:

http://www.rtfm.com/bugrate.pdf

Diebold patch:

http://www.schneier.com/blog/archives/2007/08/florida_evoting.html

Brian Snow on assurance:

http://www.acsac.org/2005/papers/Snow.pdf

Books on secure software development:

http://www.amazon.com/Building-Secure-Software-Security-Problems/
dp/020172152X/ref=counterpane/ or http://tinyurl.com/28p4hu
http://www.amazon.com/Software-Security-Building-Addison-Wesley/
dp/0321356705/ref=counterpane/ or http://tinyurl.com/ypkkwk
http://www.amazon.com/Writing-Secure-Second-Michael-Howard/
dp/0735617228/ref=counterpane/ or http://tinyurl.com/2f5mdt

Microsoft's SDL:

http://www.microsoft.com/MSPress/books/8753.asp

DHS's Build Security In program:

https://buildsecurityin.us-cert.gov/daisy/bsi/home.html

This essay originally appeared on Wired.com:

http://www.wired.com/politics/security/commentary/securitymatters/2007/08/
securitymatters_0809 or http://tinyurl.com/2nyo8c

Sony's DRM Rootkit: The Real Story

This essay originally appeared in *Wired*:

http://www.wired.com/news/privacy/0,1848,69601,00.html

There are a lot of links in this essay. You can see them on *Wired*'s page. Or here:

http://www.schneier.com/essay-094.html

These are my other blog posts on this:

http://www.schneier.com/blog/archives/2005/11/sony_secretly_i_1.html
http://www.schneier.com/blog/archives/2005/11/more_on_sonys_d.html
http://www.schneier.com/blog/archives/2005/11/still_more_on_s_1.html
http://www.schneier.com/blog/archives/2005/11/the_sony_rootki.html

There are lots of other links in these posts.

The Storm Worm

This essay originally appeared on Wired.com:

http://www.wired.com/politics/security/commentary/securitymatters/2007/10/
securitymatters_1004 or http://tinyurl.com/2xevsm
http://www.informationweek.com/news/showArticle.jhtml?articleID=201804528
or http://tinyurl.com/3ae6gt
http://www.informationweek.com/showArticle.jhtml;jsessionid=
SNSXKAZRQO4MMQSNDLRSKHSCJUNN2JVN?articleID=201803920 or
http://tinyurl.com/21q3xt

http://www.informationweek.com/showArticle.jhtml;jsessionid=
SNSXKAZRQO4MMQSNDLRSKHSCJUNN2JVN?articleID=201805274 or
http://tinyurl.com/3bb4f5
http://www.scmagazineus.com/Storm-Worm-uses-e-cards-to-push-spam-near-all-
time-high/article/35321/ or http://tinyurl.com/33chht
http://www.usatoday.com/tech/news/computersecurity/wormsviruses/2007-08-
02-storm-spam_N.htm or http://tinyurl.com/2c6te7

Fast flux:

http://ddanchev.blogspot.com/2007/09/storm-worms-fast-flux-networks.html
or http://tinyurl.com/2xwgln

Storm's attacks:

http://www.spamnation.info/blog/archives/2007/09/419eater_ddosd.html
http://ddanchev.blogspot.com/2007/09/storm-worms-ddos-attitude.html
http://www.disog.org/2007/09/opps-guess-i-pissed-off-storm.html

Stewart's analysis:

http://www.secureworks.com/research/threats/storm-worm/

Counterworms:

http://www.schneier.com/crypto-gram-0309.html#8

The Ethics of Vulnerability Research

This was originally published in *InfoSecurity Magazine*, as part of a point-counterpoint with Marcus Ranum. You can read Marcus's half here:

http://searchsecurity.techtarget.com/magazineFeature/0,296894,sid14_
gci1313268,00.html

Is Penetration Testing Worth It?

This essay appeared in the March 2007 issue of *Information Security*, as the first half of a point/counterpoint with Marcus Ranum:

http://informationsecurity.techtarget.com/magItem/0,291266,sid42_
gci1245619,00.html or http://tinyurl.com/yrjwol

Marcus's half:

http://www.ranum.com/security/computer_security/editorials/point-
counterpoint/pentesting.html or http://tinyurl.com/23ephv

Anonymity and the Tor Network

This essay previously appeared on Wired.com:

http://www.wired.com/politics/security/commentary/securitymatters/2007/09/
security_matters_0920 or http://tinyurl.com/2ux6ae

Tor:

https://tor.eff.org/

http://tor.eff.org/overview.html.en

http://wiki.noreply.org/noreply/TheOnionRouter/TorFAQ#ExitEavesdroppers or

http://tinyurl.com/2ozo2b

Onion routing:

http://www.onion-router.net/

Egerstad's work:

http://www.derangedsecurity.com/deranged-gives-you-100-passwords-to-governments-embassies/ or http://tinyurl.com/?8ya7?

http://www.heise-security.co.uk/news/95778

http://www.securityfocus.com/news/11486

http://www.derangedsecurity.com/time-to-reveal%e2%80%a6/

http://www.wired.com/politics/security/news/2007/09/embassy_hacks

Sassaman's paper:

http://www.cosic.esat.kuleuven.be/publications/article-896.pdf

Anonymity research:

http://www.cs.utexas.edu/~shmat/abstracts.html#netflix

http://www.nd.edu/~netsci/TALKS/Kleinberg.pdf

http://citeseer.ist.psu.edu/novak04antialiasing.html

http://www.cl.cam.ac.uk/~sjm217/papers/oakland05torta.pdf

http://www.nytimes.com/2006/08/09/technology/09aol.html

Dark Web:

http://www.nsf.gov/news/news_summ.jsp?cntn_id=110040

Tor users:

http://advocacy.globalvoicesonline.org/wp-content/plugins/wp-downloadMonitor/user_uploads/Anonymous_Blogging.pdf or

http://tinyurl.com/2szyxw

http://blog.wired.com/27bstroke6/2007/07/cyber-jihadists.html

Tor server operator shuts down after police raid:

http://www.heise.de/english/newsticker/news/96107

Tools for identifying the source of Tor data:

http://www.securityfocus.com/news/11447

Kill Switches and Remote Control

Kill switches:

http://www.informationweek.com/news/mobility/showArticle.jhtml?articleID=202400922

http://www.nypost.com/seven/06082008/news/regionalnews/busting_terror_
114567.htm

http://blog.wired.com/defense/2008/06/the-pentagons-n.html

http://spectrum.ieee.org/may08/6171

Digital Manners Policies:

http://arstechnica.com/news.ars/post/20080611-microsoft-patent-brings-
miss-manners-into-the-digital-age.html

http://appft1.uspto.gov/netacgi/nph-
Parser?Sect1=PTO1&Sect2=HITOFF&d=PG01&p=1&u=%2Fnetahtml%2FPTO%2Fsrchnum
.html&r=1&f=G&l=50&s1=%2220080125102%22.PGNR.&OS=DN/20080125102&RS=DN/
20080125102

This essay originally appeared on Wired.com:

http://www.wired.com/politics/security/commentary/securitymatters/2008/06/
securitymatters_0626

Index

A

Abrahms, Max, 20–21
academic freedom
  references, 274
  U.S. immigration and visa
    laws and, 40–41
AccessData, 234–237
accidents. *See also* large-scale
  incidents
    (disasters/accidents)
  dangers of chemical plants,
    201
  differences in preparing for
    attacks vs. accidents,
    134–135
  preparing for, 133–134
accountability
  anonymity and, 82–84
  improvements in computer
    security resulting from,
    151
ACLU (American Civil
  Liberties Union), 173
advertising, spam and, 250–251
adware, 162
aerial photography,
  surveillance techniques,
  65
agendas, using fear/threats to
  further, 171
airline travel, 49–60
  fake boarding passes, 56–59
  No-Fly List, 51–53
  passenger screening, 49–51
  references, 275, 296
  screening people with
    clearances, 55–56
  security policies, 69–70
  "Trusted Traveler" program,
    53–54

Akerlof, George, 164
aligning interest with
  capability
  ATM fraud example, 148
  cash register example,
    147–148
  computer security and,
    148–149
  Italian tax fraud example,
    149
  references, 293
Al-Qaeda, 184
American Civil Liberties Union
  (ACLU), 173
Anderson, Ross, 145
anonymity
  accountability and, 82–84
  NetFlix dataset and, 90–92
  privacy and, 70
  references, 281, 283,
    312–313
  Tor network and, 262–264
  voting machines and, 121
anti-terror approach, 3
antivirus software
  Sony's DRM rootkit and, 255
  who owns your computer,
    162
Apple, lock-in policies,
  156–158
applications, computer
  security recommendations,
    228
  who owns your computer,
    162
architecture
  Internet, 13
  references related to
    architecture of security,
    268–269
  security, 12–13

Ashcroft, John (Attorney
  General)
  erosion of freedoms and, 6, 8
  ruling on retention and
    dissemination of
    gathered information, 28
  on success of anti-terrorist
    policies, 180
assurance concept
  references, 309–311
  in security, 249
asymmetrical information
  theory (Akerlof), 164
athletes, doping in professional
  sports, 193–195
ATM fraud, aligning interest
  with capability and,
    147–148
attacks, computer. *See also*
  counterattacks
  active style, 240
  August 14th Blackout,
    138–140, 291–292
  cyber-attacks, 215–216,
    305–306
  denial-of-service, 35–36,
    213–214, 220–221, 224
  password-guessing, 166–167,
    234–237
  phishing, 210–213, 239, 296,
    304–305
  on RSA cryptosystem, 246
  side-channel, 246–247
attacks, physical
  on chemical plants, 201
  preparing for attacks vs.
    accidents, 134–135
auditing
  computerized voting and,
    118, 122

trusted insiders and,
200–201
voting machines and,
115–116
August 14th Blackout
Blaster and, 138–140
references, 291–292
authentication
centralized system for, 107
expiration issues, 238–239
identity theft and, 206–207
two-factor authentication,
239–242
Automated Targeting System
governmental surveillance
programs, 88–90
questioning legality of, 90
references, 282–283
automatic updates, who owns
your computer, 162
avian flu pandemic
disaster preparedness,
140–143
references, 292

B

backups, security
recommendations, 227
bandwidth theft
dangers of, 190–191
references, 300–301
banks, liability for fraudulent
transactions, 206
base rate fallacy, in data
mining, 11
basketball referees
references, 302–303
single points of failure,
199–201
behavioral assessment profiling
expertise as basis of
effectiveness, 34–35
overview of, 171–173
references, 296
best-of-breed
references, 309
suites vs., 244–245
"Big Brother", 70–72, 279
Bin Laden, 21–22
biometrics
identity theft solutions,
206–207
as universal ID system, 108

U.S. fingerprint program,
43–45
BitLocker, encryption program,
232
Blaster, August 14th Blackout,
138–140
Bloomberg, Mayor Michael, 16
boarding passes
forging, 56–59
references, 276–277
Boden, Vitek, 23
borders, international
crossing borders with laptops
and PDAs, 232–234
police authority to require
access to computer
data, 232
bot networks, 213–215
defined, 213
denial-of-service attacks by,
213–214
references, 305
Storm worm, 256–259
branding issues, multi-use ID
cards and, 108–109
"Bricked", 156
Brito, Jerry, 133
browsing, security
recommendations, 228
brute force attacks, 166
bugs, cyberterrorism risks
and, 22
Bush, President George W.
appeals to patriotism in war
on terror, 6
authorization of illegal
eavesdropping, 29–31
defense of spying on
Americans, 25–26

C

CAPPS-II
applying cost-benefit analysis
to, 150–151
behavioral assessment
profiling compared
with, 172
consumers of national
security and, 149
passenger screening, 76
Cartwright, Gen. James, 215
cash registers, as security
device, 147–148

castles, architecture of security
and, 12
CCTV cameras
pros/cons of, 80–82
references, 280–281
Census Bureau, role in locating
Japanese Americans, 94
checks and balances, in U.S.
Constitution, 31
chemical plants
externalities and, 201–203
references, 303
Chertoff, Michael, 17
Chinese hackers
not government backed,
225–226
references, 306
ChoicePoint, 83
identity theft and, 206
lack of incentive to protect
personal data, 93
market-driven nature of "Big
Brother", 71
pseudo-anonymity and, 83
RFID chips and, 105
sale of personal information
to criminals, 38
CIA, 151
eavesdropping and, 29
FBI as domestic version of,
7–8
pre-9/11 leads and, 17
citizen informants, 33–35
civil rights, private vs.
government police and,
32
civil service, protection of laws
and rights by, II;31
classified information
levels of, 41
new level: SSI (sensitive
security information),
42–43
click fraud, 214
*Code and Other Laws of
Cyberspace* (Lessig), 13
cognitive biases
correspondent inference
theory and, 20
references, 296
collective action problem,
in disaster response,
132–133
commons (community
interest)

Internet security as, 154
software as, 155
communications
cyberwar and, 221
first responders and, 131–
133
community, Web socialization
and, 159–160
commuter terrorism, movie-
plot threats, 4
computer control issues
overview of, 161–163
references, 295
computer security
aligning interest with
capability and, 148–149
collusion between big media
and computer-security
companies, 255–256
crossing borders with laptops
and PDAs, 232–234
cyberterrorism and
cybercrime, 24
eavesdropping and, 64–65
economics of, 145–146, 156
home users and, 243–244
Internet and, 167
lemons and, 164–165
liability as mechanism
for improvement in,
151–154
references, 307
securing computers,
227–230
securing disks, and portable
drives, 230–232
security arms race, 167
separating data ownership
from device ownership,
245–247
computerized voting
audit trails for, 115–116, 122
error rates, 119–121
fallibility/reliability issues,
114, 118
fraud issues, 114–115
hacking threat to, 121
software issues, 122
Congress
checks on presidential
powers, 25–26
identity-theft disclosure laws
and, 37
Constitution, U.S.
abuses of, 8

regulation of police abuse in,
32
separation of powers in, 31
consumers
password security and,
166–167
product evaluation and, 165
security cost benefit trade-
offs, 149–151
control. *See also* remote
control
computer companies
controlling products
they sell, 156–157
data reuse and, 95
kill switches and remote
control, 265–266
liberty vs., 70
lock-in and, 158
power imbalances and,
67–68
privacy and, 78–80, 84–86
third parties controlling
information on Web,
159–160
who owns your computer,
161–163
conversation
everyday conversation no
longer ephemeral,
86–88
references, 282
Cooper, Dan, 178
copycats
criminal, 178
references, 297–298
terrorist, 179
copyrights issues
entertainment industry
advocating
counterattacks on
violators, 215–217
information security and
economics and, 146
lawsuits and, 190
Sony's DRM rootkit, 252–253
corporations, surveillance by,
64–65
correspondent inference
theory, 19–22
as cognitive bias, 19–20
ineffectiveness of terrorism
and, 20–22
references, 270–271

counterattacks, 216–218
appeals and dangers of,
215–216
references, 306
vigilantism, 216–218
countermeasures
adaptability of human tactics
and, 183–184
cost-benefit analysis in,
150–151
CYA attitudes and, 175–177
cyberwar/cyberterrorism/
cybercrime/
cybervandalism, 223
tactics and, 182–183
Counterpane Internet Security,
198
counterterrorism
best uses of money in, 184
fear of what is different and,
13–14
need for flexibility in, 179
Cox, Mike, 109
credit bureaus
attacks on LifeLock
company, 208–209
market-driven nature of "Big
Brother", 38
credit card companies
fraud and, 93
identity theft and, 205
liability for fraudulent
transactions, 206
credit cards
authentication, 242
data mining and fraud and,
10
fraud alerts and, 208
credit reports
FACTA and, 208–211
obtaining fraudulent credit
cards and, 206
references, 304
crime. *See also* cybercrime
balancing freedom with
opportunity for, 45
effectiveness of security
cameras and, 81
following money, 166
tactics, 178
cryptography. *See* encryption
customs agents, ability to
access data on seized
computers, 232–233

CYA (cover your ass) security
countermeasure effectiveness
undermined by,
175–177
counterterrorism and, 13–14
references, 297
cyber-attacks
as the best defense, 215–216
references, 305–306
cybercrime
bot networks and, 213–215
cyberwar/cyberterrorism/cyb
ervandalism compared
with, 223
defined, 219
dual-use technologies and,
35–36
identity theft, 37, 205–208
LifeLock company and,
208–210
more a threat than
cyberterrorism, 23–24
phishing attacks, 210–213
cyberterrorism
defined, 219
dual-use technologies and,
35–36
risks of, 22–24
cybervandalism, 219
cyberwar
attack on Estonia, 35–36
attacks as the best defense,
215–216
Chinese hackers and,
225–226
counterattacks, 216–218
defined, 219
military and, 224–225
overview of, 218–220
properties of, 221–223
references, 306
waging, 220–221

D

Dark Web, 264
data. *See also* personal
information
analysis vs. collection as key
to intelligence, 6–7
correlation, 7
data ownership vs. device
ownership, 245–247,
309
information age and, 61, 66

proper use and disposal by
police, 28–29
protecting sensitive data
while crossing borders,
233–234
security of university
networks, 195–197
DATA (Data Accountability
and Trust Act), 38–39
data control
Facebook, 84–86
references, 281
data mining, 9–12
Echelon and, 30
freedom vs. security, 10
limitations of, 10–12
privacy vs. security, 9
references, 268
Data Protection Act, 207
data protection laws
EU vs. US, 78
need for comprehensive, 62
data reuse
personal information, 94–96
references, 284
databases
state driver's licenses, 109
vulnerability of database of
national IDs, 98, 101
Davis, Keith, 19
Dean, Diana, 171
decision making
cost-benefit analysis in, 150
security, 7
Declaration of the Rights of
Man and of the Citizen,
216, 218
Defreitas, Russell, 16
denial-of-service attacks
cyberwar and, 220–221, 224
Estonia example, 35–36
Department of Homeland
Security. *See* Homeland
Security, Department of
Department of Motor Vehicles
(DMV), immigration
status of licensees and,
109–110
devices
hierarchy of authority and
control issues, 265
separating data ownership
from device ownership,
244–245

dictatorial powers, Bush's
claim regarding wartime
powers, 26
dictionary attacks, 166
Digital Manners Policies
(DMP), 265–266, 314
digital person, 79–80, 280
*The Digital Person: Technology
and Privacy in the
Information Age* (Solove),
79–80
digital rights management. *See*
DRM (digital rights
management)
Direct Record Electronic
(DRE) voting machines,
120–122
disasters. *See also* large scale
incidents
(disasters/accidents)
avian flu pandemic and,
140–141
benefits of preparedness,
133, 143
planning for, 132
references, 292
scale and scope of incidents
and ability to plan for,
142
disclosure laws, security
breaches and, 38
DMP (Digital Manners
Policies), 265–266, 314
DMV (Department of Motor
Vehicles), immigration
status of licensees and,
109–110
DOJ. *See* Justice Department
Donaghy, Tim, 199
doping, in professional sports
references, 302
as security issue, 193–195
DRE (Direct Record
Electronic) voting
machines, 120–122
driver's licenses
issuing to illegal immigrants,
109–110
references, 286
terrorists having fraudulent,
98, 100
DRM (digital rights
management)
information security and
economics and, 146

lock-in and, 158
separating data ownership
from device ownership
and, 246–247
Sony system, 161–162
DRM rootkit
overview of, 253–256
references, 311
drug testing, as security issue.
See doping, in
professional sports
dual-use technologies
overview of, 35–37
references, 273

E

eavesdropping. *See also*
surveillance
Bush's authorization of
illegal, 29–31
cyberwar and, 221, 225
references, 272
Tor network example,
263–264
wholesale nature of, 64–65
eBay, accountability and, 82
Echelon, 30
economics of security, 145–167
aligning interest with
capability, 147–149
chemical plant example, 202
computer control issues,
161–163
consumers and password
security, 166–167
consumers of national
security, 149–151
cost vs. effectiveness trade-
offs, 56, 150
doping, 195
eavesdropping, 11
information security, 145–
147
lemons, 163–166
liability and, 151–154, 207
lock-in (control issues),
156–158
phishing attacks, 211, 212
security trade-offs, 169–170
software vulnerabilities,
154–156
spam, 251–252
third parties controlling
information, 159–160
US-VISIT program, 44

Egerstad, Dan, 263
election security
computerized and electronic
voting, 114–116
difficulties in applying
technologies to voting,
116–119
electronic voting machines,
118–123
papal election process, 125–
129
recounts, 123–125
references, 286–288
voting technologies, 111–114
electronic voting
assurances, 247–250
audit trails for, 115–116, 122
error rates, 119–121
fallibility/reliability issues,
114
fraud issues, 114–115
hacking threat to, 121
references, 287–289
software issues, 122
threat to fairness and
accuracy of elections,
111–114
e-mail
scams, 211
security recommendations,
228
Storm worm and, 256–259
emergency response
benefits of investing in, 137
first responders, 131–133
emotions. *See* feeling of
security
EMTs, as first responders to
disasters, 131
encryption
attacks on RSA cryptosystem,
246
benefits of, 230–232
economics of security and,
146
protecting hard drives, 233
RFID chips and, 105–106
science of cryptography, 40
securing USB memory sticks,
163
security recommendations,
229
U.S. government-sponsored
competition, 37
wireless networks and, 189

entertainment software, who
owns your computer,
161–162
"equities issue"
cyberattack vs. cyberdefense
and, 221
dual-use technologies and,
36
references, 273
U.S. military and, 225
espionage, cyberwar, 222
executive branch, separation of
powers in U.S.
Constitution, 31. *See also*
presidential powers
Experian
attacks on LifeLock
company, 208–209
market driven nature of "Big
Brother", 71
expiration issues,
authentication, 238–239
externalities
chemical plant security and,
201–203
identity theft and, 212
private vs. public police
forces and, 273

F

Facebook
data control issues, 84–86
references, 281
FACTA (Fair and Accurate
Credit Transaction Act)
credit card fraud and,
208–211
references, 304
fail-safe mechanisms, chemical
plants, 201–202
Fake Boarding Pass Generator
website, 56
false alarms, terrorism, 1–2
false negatives/false positives
No-Fly List and, 52
weaknesses of data mining,
10
FBI
intelligence gathering not
mission of, 7–8
laws expanding government
powers, 76
pre-9/11 leads and, 17

reasons for transferring
eavesdropping to NSA,
30–31
tools for information
gathering, 27–28
fear
as a campaign tactic, 2
personal/corporate agendas
for manipulating, 171
of what is different, 13–15
feeling of security
vs. reality, 169–171
references, 296–297
security theater and, 180
trade-offs and, 175
field work, in intelligence
gathering, 7–8
financial institutions
liability for fraudulent
transactions, 206–207
phishing attacks and,
212–213
fingerprint program
applied to visitors to U.S.,
43–45
moving toward universal
surveillance, 76
references, 274–275
firemen, as first responders to
disasters, 131
firewalls
audits result in demand for,
152
economics of security and,
146
IT security industry and, 197
security recommendations,
229
first responders
communication issues and,
131–133
references, 289–291
FISA (Foreign Intelligence
Surveillance Act) of 1978
regulatory purpose of, 29
tools for information
gathering, 27–28
FISC (Foreign Intelligence
Surveillance Court), 30
flash worms, 214
Florida election debacle
(2000), 116
Foley, Rep. Mark, 86–88
Fon wireless access points,
191, 301

Foreign Intelligence
Surveillance Act (FISA)
of 1978
regulatory purpose of, 29
tools for information
gathering, 27–28
Foreign Intelligence
Surveillance Court
(FISC), 30
foreigners. *See also*
immigration
fingerprint program, 43–45
profiling, 33
forgery
boarding passes, 276
national ID cards, 98, 102
state driver's licenses, 109
Fort Dix plot, 15–16, 18
Fourth Amendment
Bush overriding, 27
illegal search and, 25
fraud
bot networks and, 214
credit card companies and,
93
credit cards, 209–210
elections, 112
identity theft, 37, 167,
205–208
national ID cards and, 98
open systems and, 129
references, 304
two-factor authentication
and, 239, 241
freedom. *See also* liberty
balancing with security, 45
erosion of due to terrorist
backlash, 6
legislation as means of
protecting, 86
No-Fly List and, 53
full disclosure
references, 301–302
of security vulnerabilities,
191–193

G

Gmail, 66
Google
anonymity issues, 91
anti-fraud systems, 214
governmental power. *See also*
"Big Brother"; police
states

fingerprint program and, 45
laws expanding, 76
MATRIX program, 9
USA Patriot Act, 27–28
Grunwald, Lukas, 248
guerrilla warfare, 223

H

hackers
ability to affect elections, 112
adeptness at finding
vulnerabilities, 192
bot networks and, 213–214
Chinese hackers, 225–226
as hooligans not terrorists,
23–24
who owns your computer,
161
hard disks
references, 307
securing, 230–232
healthcare industry, opposition
to HIPPA regulations, 46
Help America Vote Act, 116
"hinky" behavior
behavioral assessment
profiling and, 171–172
expertise required in
assessing, 33–35
references, 272–273
HIPPA regulations, 45–47
home users
computer security, 243–244
references, 309
Homeland Security,
Department of
airline security rules, 4
assurance concept and, 249
bureaucratic inefficiencies,
8–9
move-plot threats and, 3
regulation of chemical
plants, 203
US-VISIT program, 44
human rights, privacy as, 63

I

ID cards
boarding airlines and, 58
driver's licenses for illegal
immigrants, 109–110
multi-use, 107–109
national, 97–99

Real ID, 99–102
references, 284–286
RFID passports, 103–104
security of RFID passports,
104–107
identity theft
bot networks and, 214
disclosure laws, 37–40
frequency of, 79
Internet trends, 211–212
LifeLock company offering
protection against,
208–210
mitigating, 205–208
references, 273–274,
303–304
scope of, 167
two-factor authentication
and, 239
illegal search, Fourth
Amendment and, 25
immigration
academic freedom and
immigration laws, 40–
41
issuing driver's licenses to
illegal immigrants,
109–110
references, 286
impersonation. See also
identity theft
fraud and, 205
liability for, 207
two-factor authentication
and, 241
informants
citizen informants, 33–35
computers vs., 71
information age
amount of data in, 61
creating infrastructure for
universal surveillance,
72
data pollution, 66
information security
economics of, 145–147
references, 293, 295
third parties controlling
information on Web,
159–160
infrastructure
cyberattacks targeting, 222
outsourcing, 245

intelligence
benefits of investing in, 137
cyberwar exploits and, 224
failures and terrorism, 5–9,
268
vs. law enforcement, 7
Internet
architecture of, 13
as commons (community
interest), 154
cyberwar and, 220–221, 224
McConnell plan to monitor
all communications on,
69
who owns your computer,
162
Internet Service Providers. See
ISPs (Internet Service
Providers)
Interstate 35W bridge
(Minneapolis), collapse
of, 131
Iraq invasion, cost vs. security
trade-off, 150
ISPs (Internet Service
Providers)
open wireless networks and,
191
references, 301
responsibility to be IT
department for home
users, 244
IT department, in universities,
196–197
IT technologies
"equities issue", 36–37
security products and
directions in, 197–199

J

JFK Airport incident, 16–18
Jones, Edward, 19
Judicial branch
checks on illegal search, 25
separation of powers in U.S.
Constitution, 31
Justice Department
laws expanding government
powers, 76
police state mentality and,
77–78
policy regarding saving
communications, 87–88

K

Kafka, Franz, 79, 280
Katrina disaster, 132
Kelly, Kevin, 82–83
Kerr, Donald, 70
keyboard sniffers, 167
kill switches
references, 313–314
remote control and, 265–266
Kohno, Tadayoshi, 185
Kristof, Nicholas, 97

L

laptop computers
crossing borders with,
232–234
references, 307–308
security recommendations,
227
large scale incidents
(disasters/accidents)
avian flu, 140–143
Blaster and August 14th
Blackout, 138–140
first responders, 131
Olympic games security,
136–137
security incidents and,
133–135
Las Vegas (Dec. 2003),
surveillance example, 27
law enforcement
dangers of private police,
32–33
intelligence vs., 7
spam, 252
state driver's licenses and,
109–110
tip assessment, 15
lawsuits
chemical plant liability and,
202
copyrights issues and, 190
credit bureau attacks on
LifeLock company,
208–209
DRM rootkit and, 254
identity theft mitigation, 304
security theater and, 174
legislation
California phishing law,
210–211
DATA (Data Accountability
and Trust Act), 38–39

FACTA (Fair and Accurate
   Credit Transaction Act),
   208–211, 304
FISA (Foreign Intelligence
   Surveillance Act),
   27–28, 29
Help America Vote Act, 116
product liability laws, 153
protecting data privacy, 96
protecting freedoms, 86
protecting personal
   information, 94
Real ID Act, 100–102, 285
USA Patriot Act, 27–28, 45,
   76, 181
legislative branch, separation
   of powers in
   Constitution, 31
lemons market
   economics of, 163–164
   references, 295–296
   signals for quality products
      and, 165–166
Lessig, Lawrence, 13
LexisNexis incident, 38
liability
   for fraudulent transactions,
      206
   holding software
      manufacturers
      accountable for
      security, 154–156
   improvements in computer
      security resulting from,
      151–154
   references, 293–294
liberty. *See also* freedom
   control vs., 70
   erosion of due to terrorist
      backlash, 6
   legislation as means of
      protecting, 86
   lock-in policies and, 158
LifeLock company
   protection against identity
      theft, 208–210
   references, 303–304
link rot, 159
lock-in
   Apple example, 156–157
   defined, 157
   references, 294
   security mechanisms
      supporting, 158

M

man-in-the-middle attacks,
   240
MATRIX, government uses of
   data mining, 9
Mauskopf, Roslynn R., 16
McAfee, DRM rootkit and, 255
McConnell, Michael, 69
McVeigh, Timothy, 54
medical privacy
   employers and, 62
   HIPPA regulations and,
      45–47
   references, 275
Miami 7, 17
Microsoft
   Blaster infecting operating
      systems, 139
   DMP (Digital Manners
      Policies), 265–266, 314
   liability laws and, 154
   lock-in policies, 157–158
   PR issues regarding software
      vulnerabilities, 192
   reaction to DRM rootkit,
      255–256
   SDL (Security Development
      Lifecycle), 249
   security recommendations,
      228
military
   classification systems for
      military secrets, 41–43
   cyberwar and, 224–225
   planning for cyberwar, 220
minimization (no fishing
      expeditions), principles
      guiding use of personal
      information by police, 28
monitoring
   phone calls (NSA), 87
   trusted insiders, 200–201.
      See also auditing
Mossberg, Walter S., 244
motivations, correspondent
   inference theory and,
   19–20
Moussaoui, Zacarias, 30
movie plots
   references, 268
   terrorist threats in, 3–5
multi-use ID cards, 107–109
   arguments for, 107
   branding issues, 108–109

references, 286
security and reliability issues,
   108

N

Narayanan, Arvind, 90, 92
National Guard, 174
national ID cards
   as multi-use ID cards, 107
   Real ID Act, 99–102
   references, 284–285
   weaknesses of, 97–99
national security, 25–47
   academic freedom and,
      40–41
   Bush's authorization of illegal
      eavesdropping, 29–31
   checks on presidential
      powers and, 25–27
   consumers of, 149–151
   dual-use technologies and,
      35–37
   expertise required in
      assessing "hinky"
      behavior, 33–35
   foreigners and, 43–45
   identity-theft disclosure laws,
      37–40
   medical privacy, 45–47
   principles guiding use of
      personal information by
      police, 28–29
   private police forces and,
      31–33
   references, 293
   SSI (sensitive security
      information), 41–43
   surveillance examples and
      issues, 27–28
national security letters, 27–28
Navy Cyber Defense Operations
   Command, 36
NetFlix dataset
   anonymity issues, 90–92
   references, 90–92
network security
   economics of security and,
      152–153
   penetration testing and,
      261–262
   university networks,
      195–197
   wireless networks, 189–191

No-Fly List
  CYA attitudes preventing
      removal from, 177
  profiling and, 102
  references, 276
  weaknesses and
      inconsistencies in,
      51–53
NSA
  assurance concept, 250
  Bush's authorization of illegal
      eavesdropping, 29–31
  costs and ineffectiveness of
      eavesdropping
      program, 11
  eavesdropping programs, 9
  "equities issue", 36–37,
      221–222, 225
  references, 272
  wholesale nature of
      eavesdropping, 64–65

O

objectives
  psychology of security and,
      182–184
  references, 299
Olympic games
  references, 291
  security at, 136–137
one-on-one negotiations,
      protecting personal
      information, 74
onion routing
  references, 313
  Tor network and, 263
online voting, 115
OnStar, 265
openness
  governments and lay persons
      and, 68
  secrecy of government
      operations vs., 43
  voting fraud and, 129
  wireless networks, 189–191
operating systems. See OSs
      (operating systems)
Orwell, George, 70
OSs (operating systems)
  Blaster infecting Microsoft
      OSs, 228
  security recommendations,
      228

outsourcing, suites vs. best-of-
      breed and, 245
overreactions, 179–182
  blame and, 182
  examples of, 179–180
  references, 298–299
  risk analysis and, 180–181
oversight
  FISA programs and, 31
  importance of balancing
      intelligence efforts, 8
  principles guiding use of
      personal information by
      police, 28

P

papal elections
  election security and,
      125–129
  references, 289
paper ballots. See also election
      security
  benefits of, 111, 113
  papal elections and, 126
passenger screening
  behavioral assessment
      profiling compared
      with, 172
  CAPPS-II, 76
  forged boarding passes and,
      56–59
  No-Fly List, 51–53
  overview of, 49–51
  references, 276
  security clearances and,
      55–56
  "Trusted Traveler" program,
      53–54
passports, RFID
  references, 285
  safety and privacy issues,
      103–104
  security of, 104–107, 248
passwords
  choosing, 234–238
  cracking, 166, 234–237
  ease of password guessing,
      242
  encryption password, 233
  losing control of, 240
  references, 308
  secure alternatives to, 167
  security recommendations,
      228

two-factor authentication,
      242
  vulnerabilities of, 166–167
  wireless networks and, 189
patches, vulnerabilities and,
      248–249
PCs (personal computers). See
      personal computing
PDAs
  crossing borders with,
      232–234
  references, 307–308
  security recommendations,
      227
penetration testing
  references, 312
  value of, 261–262
performance enhancing drugs.
      See doping, in
      professional sports
personal computing
  references, 306
  safety of, 227–230
  security recommendations,
      227
personal information
  availability and value of,
      211–212
  bot networks collecting, 214
  companies selling, 95
  control issues in Facebook
      example, 84–85
  control over, 79
  DATA (Data Accountability
      and Trust Act), 38–39
  data privacy laws, 62
  data reuse risks, 94–96
  data shadow and, 61–62
  identity theft, 205–206
  identity-theft disclosure
      laws, 37
  LexisNexis incident, 38
  ownership by collector, 66
  principles guiding use by
      police, 28–29
  protecting, 72–76, 92–93
  references, 277, 279–280,
      284
PGP Disk
  encryption protection, 231,
      233
  password-guessing attacks
      and, 235
pharming attacks, 211. See also
      phishing attacks

phishing attacks
  bot networks and, 214
  defined, 210–211
  financial institution
    responsibility and,
    212–213
  on passwords, 166–167
  references, 296, 304–305
  two-factor authentication,
    239
phone calls, NSA monitoring,
    87
PKI (public key
  infrastructure), 107
Plous, Scott, 181
police
  as first responders to
    disasters, 131
  principles guiding use of
    personal information,
    28–29
  remote control issues,
    265–266
  surveillance by, 64–65
police states
  comparing Orwell vision
    with current reality, 71
  dangers of, 8
  erosion of citizen and non-
    citizen rights in U.S.,
    76
  Justice Department and,
    77–78
  privacy vs. security, 69–70
politics
  CYA attitudes and, 177
  dangers of centralization of
    power, 31
  fear as a campaign tactic, 2
  No-Fly List as political
    harassment, 52
  protecting personal
    information via
    political activism, 75
  security motivations, 5–6
  war on terrorism and, 4, 19
Poole, Robert, 55
portable drives
  references, 307
  securing, 230–232
power
  ability to protect privacy and,
    73–74
  anonymity as protection, 84

governmental. See
    governmental power
  organizing to increase, 74–75
  presidential. See presidential
    powers
  privacy and, 67–68
  separation of powers in U.S.
    Constitution, 31
power failure, August 14th
    Blackout, 138–140
PR issues, corporate, 192
presidential powers
  checks on, 25–27
  references, 271–272
  separation of powers in U.S.
    Constitution, 31
press, terrorist tactics and, 2
Prisoner's Dilemma, 194
privacy
  anonymity and
    accountability and, 82–
    84
  anonymity issues in NetFlix
    dataset, 90–92
  Automated Targeting System
    and, 88–90
  "Big Brother" and, 70–72
  control of, 78–80
  data privacy laws, 62
  data reuse risks, 94–96
  of everyday conversation,
    86–88
  everyone's data shadow and,
    61–62
  Facebook and data control
    issues, 84–86
  future of, 64–66
  identity theft and, 205–206
  medical, 45–47
  national ID cards and, 98
  power and, 67–68
  protecting, 72–76
  protecting personal
    information, 92–93
  references, 277–280
  RFID chips and, 103, 105
  security cameras and, 80–82
  security vs., 9, 69–70
  universal surveillance and,
    76–78
  value of, 62–64
Privacy Commissioners,
    Canada, 78
private police forces
  dangers of, 31–33

references, 272
product reviews, lemons and,
    165
profiling
  abuses by citizen informants,
    33
  behavioral assessment,
    171–173
  difficulty of profiling
    terrorists, 54
  No-Fly List and, 102
  public awareness impacting,
    75
"Project Shamrock", 29, 31
prosecution, of terrorists,
    17–18
PRTK, password-guessing
    attacks, 234–237
pseudo-anonymity (Kelly), 83
psychology of security
  behavioral assessment
    profiling, 171–173
  copycats, 178–179
  CYA attitudes, 175–177
  feeling vs. reality of security,
    169–171
  rare risks and overreactions,
    179–182
  security mindset, 185–187
  security theater, 173–175
  tactics, targets, and
    objectives, 182–184
public awareness, protecting
    personal information
    and, 75
public health
  references, 309
  security of home users as,
    243–244
public key infrastructure
    (PKI), 107
public scrutiny, benefits of full
    disclosure, 192–193

R

random errors, election results
    and, 123
random screening, vs.
    profiling, 54
Ranum, Marcus, 279
Real ID Act
  national ID cards and,
    100–102
  references, 285

Recording Industry Association of America. *See* RIAA (Recording Industry Association of America)

recounts, 123–125
  references, 289
  types of voting errors and, 123–124
  weaknesses of electronic voting and, 112

referees, sports
  references, 302–303
  single points of failure, 199–201

Reid, Richard, 4

reliability issues, multi-use ID cards, 108

remote control
  of computers. *See* bot networks
  kill switches and, 265–266
  OnStar, 265
  references, 313

remote voting, potentials for abuse, 115

Ressam, Ahmed, 171

retaliation. *See* counterattacks

revotes, 124–125. *See also* recounts

RFID bracelets, as security theater, 174

RFID chips, separating data ownership from device ownership and, 246

RFID passports
  references, 285
  safety and privacy issues, 103–104
  security of, 104–107, 248

RIAA (Recording Industry Association of America)
  copyrights issues and, 190
  counterattack mentality of, 217
  references, 300

Richelieu, Cardinal, 63

Ridge, Tom, 44

risks
  anecdotal nature of risk analysis, 180–181
  cyberterrorism, 22–24, 223
  cyberwar, 223
  data reuse, 94–96
  economics of reducing, 154

rare risks and overreactions, 179–182
references, 298–299
systems most at risk, 199–201

Rockefeller, Sen. Jay, 31

rootkits, Sony's DRM rootkit, 252–254

Rotterdam (Sept. 2005), surveillance incident, 28

RSA cryptosystem, attacks on, 246

S

sabotage, chemical plant, 201

safety
  attacks vs. accidents and, 134
  personal computing, 227–230
  RFID chips and, 103

scams, e-mail, 211

scapegoats, overreactions and, 182

Schmidt, Howard, 154

screening. *See* passenger screening

script kiddies, 220, 225

SDL (Security Development Lifecycle), 249

secrecy
  full disclosure vs., 191, 193
  vs. openness in government operations, 43
  privacy and, 84–85
  protecting personal information, 92–93
  references, 284, 308

secret ballots, 116

Secrets and Lies (Schneier), 166

Secure Flight profiling program, 172

security architecture, 12–13

security arms race
  Apple example, 158
  authentication and, 242
  complexity of, 243
  computer security, 167
  copycats and, 179
  countermeasures, 184
  doping example, 193–194
  spam example, 252–253

security cameras, 80–82

security clearances, passenger screening and, 55–56

security decision making, 7

Security Development Lifecycle (SDL), 249

security incidents
  difficulty of preventing lone operators, 137
  disasters and, 133–135

security industry
  need for, 197–199
  references, 302

security mindset, 185–187
  course in, 185–186
  designing security products and, 260
  effectiveness of security and, 186
  references, 300
  world view based on, 185

security products
  references, 309
  suites vs. best-of-breed, 244–245

security theater, 173–175
  examples of, 173–174
  feeling of security and, 175, 180
  lawsuits and, 175
  references, 296

Selective Device Jamming, 266

Sensenbrenner, Rep. F. James, 99

sensitive data, protecting while crossing borders, 233–234

sensitive security information (SSI)
  classification systems for military secrets, 41–43
  references, 274

Shapiro, Carl, 157

Shmatikov, Vitaly, 90, 92

side-channel attacks, 246–247

simplicity, principles for voting technologies, 117

single points of failure
  references, 302–303
  system risks and (basketball example), 199–201

sky marshals, 70

Slammer virus, 140

smart cards
  attacks on, 247
  RFID chips, 103

SmartWater, 185

Smith, Dennis, 131

Snow, Brian, 249
social networking, 84
software
    companies not disclosing
        vulnerabilities, 192
    computerized voting and,
        122
    economics of software
        security, 152
    holding software
        manufacturers
        accountable for security
        of code, 154–156
    vulnerabilities, 154–156
Soghoian, Christopher, 56
Solove, Daniel, 79–80
Sony
    DRM rootkit, 253–256, 311
    who owns your computer,
        161–162
spam
    bot networks and, 214
    combating, 250–253
    security recommendations,
        229
spam filters, 252
spam over Internet telephony
    (spit), 250
spear phishing, 212
Specter, Sen. Arlen, 16
spit (spam over Internet
    telephony), 250
sports
    basketball referees as
        illustration of single
        points of failure,
        199–201
    drug testing as security issue,
        193–195
spying, Fourth Amendment
    and, 25. See also
    eavesdropping
spyware
    Sony's DRM rootkit, 253
    who owns your computer,
        162
SQL Slammer worm, 23
SSI (sensitive security
    information)
    classification systems for
        military secrets, 41–43
    references, 274
standardization
    computer security and, 154
    lemons and, 165

university networks and, 196
    voting systems and, 117
Staniford, Stuart, 139
statistics, of data mining, 11
Storm worm
    combining bot network with
        Trojan, 256–259
    references, 311–312
storytelling, risk analysis and,
    180–181
strike back. See counterattacks
suites vs. best-of-breed
    references, 309
    security products, 244–245
surveillance. See also
    eavesdropping
    computer role in, 71
    data analysis vs data
        collection as key to
        intelligence, 6–7
    examples and issues, 27–28
    future of privacy and, 64–66
    information age creating
        infrastructure for, 72
    Olympic security and, 136
    of phone calls (NSA), 87
    of police, 68
    president ignoring laws
        regulating, 26
    privacy vs. security, 69–70
    references, 280
    RFID chips and, 103–105
    security cameras and, 80–82
    universal, 76–78
    value of privacy and, 62–64
Symantec, DRM rootkit and,
    255
sysadmins
    computer maintenance and,
        243
    counterattack mentality and,
        215–216, 218
    role in containing worms,
        257
systematic errors, election
    results and, 123–124

T

tactics
    adaptability of humans and,
        183–184
    countermeasures and,
        182–183
    crimes, 178

cyber, 219
    psychology of security and,
        182–184
    references, 299
    spam, 251
    terrorist, 2
Taleb, Nicholas, 181
tamper-resistant packaging,
    174
targets
    psychology of security and,
        182–184
    references, 299
technology, dual-use
    national security and, 35–36
    references, 273
technology, IT
    "equities issue", 36–37
    security products and
        directions in, 197–199
technology, voting
    difficulties of, 116–118
    overview of, 111–114
terrorism
    alarmism and incompetence
        and, 15–19
    copycats, 179
    correspondent inference
        theory, 19–22
    cyberterrorism risks, 22–24
    data mining for terrorists, 9–
        12
    fear of what is different,
        13–15
    ineffectiveness of terrorists,
        20–22
    intelligence failures and, 5–9
    movie plot threats, 3–5
    objective of terrorists, 1–3
    profiling and, 172
    references, 267–268, 270
    SSI rules and, 43
    war on, 13–15
Terrorist Information and
    Prevention System
    (TIPS), 34
Thompson, Eric, 235
threats
    assessing, 14
    personal/corporate agendas
        for manipulating, 171
TIA (Total Information
    Awareness)
    governmental surveillance
        programs, 89

laws expanding government
powers, 76
privacy vs. security, 9
public opinion impacting, 75
TIPS (Terrorist Information
and Prevention System),
34
Tor network
anonymity issues, 262–264
references, 312–313
Total Information Awareness.
See TIA (Total
Information Awareness)
totalitarian states, 70–72. See
also police states
touch screen voting, 121–122
toxins, dangers of terrorists
attacks on chemical
plants, 201
trade-offs, security
cost vs. effectiveness, 150
economics of security, 56,
169–170
feeling of security vs. real
security, 175
freedoms vs., 10
references, 296
transparency
principles for use of personal
information by police,
28
principles for voting
technologies, 117
Transportation Security
Administration (TSA),
183
The Trial (Kafka), 79
Trojan horse attacks
active style attacks, 240
cyberwar and, 220
password attacks, 167
references, 296
Storm worm and, 256–259
TrueCrypt, 232–233
Trusted Computing, 162
trusted insiders, 199–201
"Trusted Traveler" program
passenger screening, 53–54
references, 276
Truth in Lending Law, 93
TSA (Transportation Security
Administration), 183
two-factor authentication
benefits of, 241–242
failure of, 239–241

identity theft solutions,
206–207
references, 308

U

uniformity, principles for
voting technologies, 117
universal surveillance, 76–78.
See also surveillance
university networks, 195–197
U.S. Constitution. See
Constitution, U.S.
U.S. immigration laws, 40–41
USA PATRIOT Act
governmental power and, 45
information gathering
powers of law
enforcement agencies
and, 27–28
as overreaction, 181
surveillance and, 76
USB disks, encrypting, 231
US-VISIT program
consumers of national
security, 149
fingerprint program, 43–45

V

Varian, Hal, 157
verifiability, principles for
voting technologies, 117
vigilantism. See counterattacks
Virginia Tech massacre, 179–
180
viruses. See worms/viruses
visa regulations, 40
voice over IP (VoIP), 250
VoIP (voice over IP), 250
voting
computerized and electronic,
114–116
difficulty applying
technology to, 116–118
electronic voting machines,
118–123
error rates, 119–121
recounts, 123
references, 286–287
requirements of voting
systems, 118–119
revotes, 124–125
technologies for, 111–114

vulnerabilities
bot networks taking
advantage of, 214
Chinese hackers hoarding,
226
commonness of, 248–249
cyberwar and, 220
electronic voting machines,
247–248
"equities issue", 221–222,
225
ethics of vulnerability
research, 259–261
full disclosure of, 191–193
password, 166–167
penetration testing and, 261–
262
references, 293, 312
single points of failure, 200

W

war, cyber. See cyberwar
war on the unexpected
fear of what is different,
13–15
references, 269–270
warranties, lemons and, 165
warrants, oversight principle
and, 28
wartime powers, of President,
26
watch lists
behavioral assessment
profiling compared
with, 172
No-Fly List, 51–53
websites, security
recommendations, 228
WEIS (Workshop on
Information Security)
information security and
economics and,
145–147
references, 293
Wikipedia, 82–83
wireless networks
open, 189–191
references, 300
wiretapping
history of illegal, 29
president ignoring laws
regulating, 26

Workshop on Information
  Security (WEIS)
information security and
    economics and,
    145–147
references, 293
worms/viruses
  antivirus software, 162, 255
  August 14th Blackout and,
    138–140

cyberterrorism and, 23
cyberwar and, 220
flash worms, 214
incidents caused by, 140
IT security industry and, 197
security recommendations,
    229
Storm worm, 256–259
WPA, wireless security
    protocol, 189

Writeprint, Dark Web, 264

X

X-ray machines, for passenger
    screening, 50

Y

Yoo, John, 25–26